THE MAKING OF THE
Jameel Gallery of Islamic Art
AT THE VICTORIA AND ALBERT MUSEUM

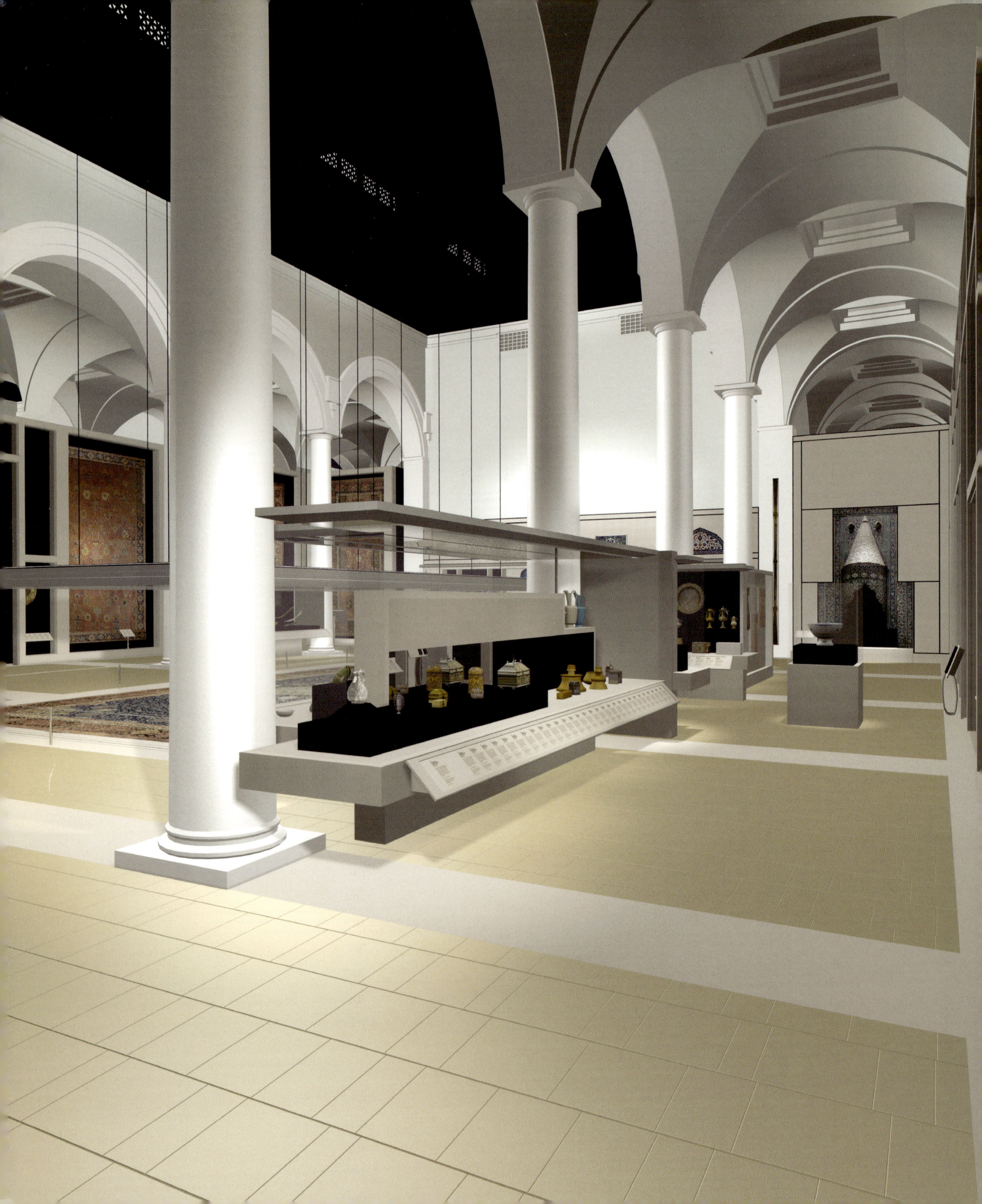

THE MAKING OF THE
Jameel Gallery of Islamic Art
AT THE VICTORIA AND ALBERT MUSEUM

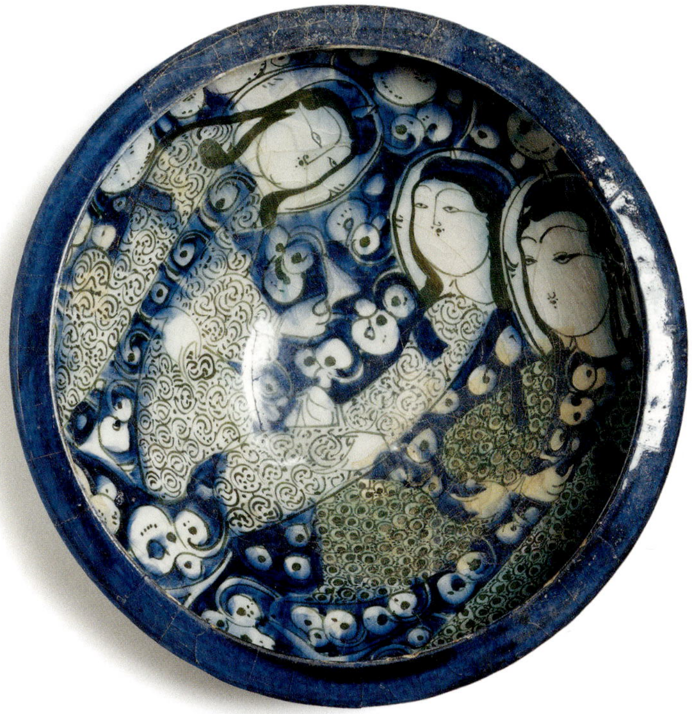

EDITED BY
Rosemary Crill and Tim Stanley

V&A Publications

First published by V&A Publications, 2006
V&A Publications
Victoria and Albert Museum
South Kensington
London SW7 2RL

Distributed in North America by Harry N. Abrams, Inc., New York

ISBN-10 1 85177 485 8
ISBN-13 978 1 85177 485 2

Library of Congress Control Number 2006928681

10 9 8 7 6 5 4 3 2 1

2010 2009 2008 2007 2006

A catalogue record for this book is available from the British Library.

Designed by Janet James
Project management by Geoff Barlow
New V&A photography by Maja Kardum, Peter Kelleher and Mike Kitcatt, V&A Photographic Studio
Map by Technical Art Services

Front jacket: Computer-generated view of the Jameel Gallery, looking south
Back jacket: Annotated working layout of the Turkish ceramics display
Frontispiece: Computer-generated view of the Jameel Gallery, from the south-east entrance
Title page: Fritware bowl, Iran, probably Kashan, *circa* 1200. V&A: C.125–1931
Contents page: Tilework pillar, Bukhara, *circa* 1360. V&A: 567–1900 and 586–1899

Printed in Italy

V&A Publications
Victoria and Albert Museum
South Kensington, London SW7 2RL
www.vam.ac.uk

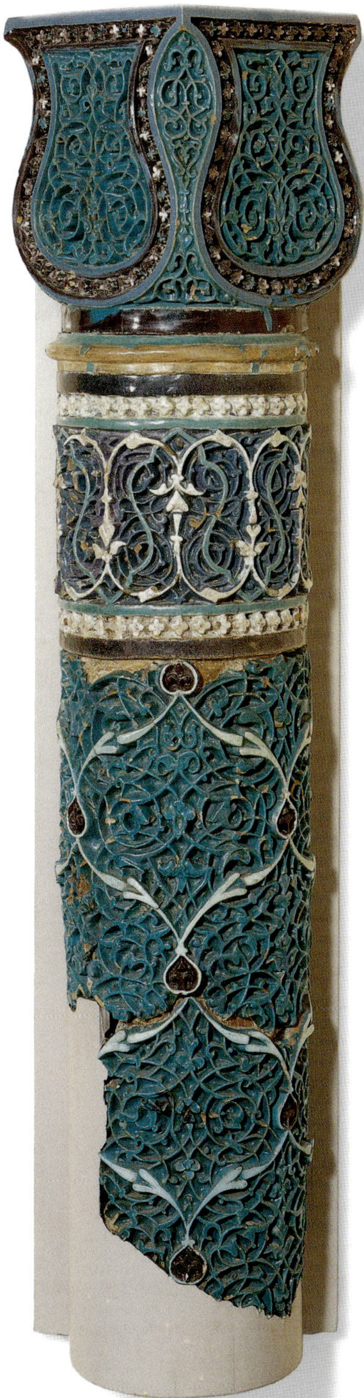

Contents

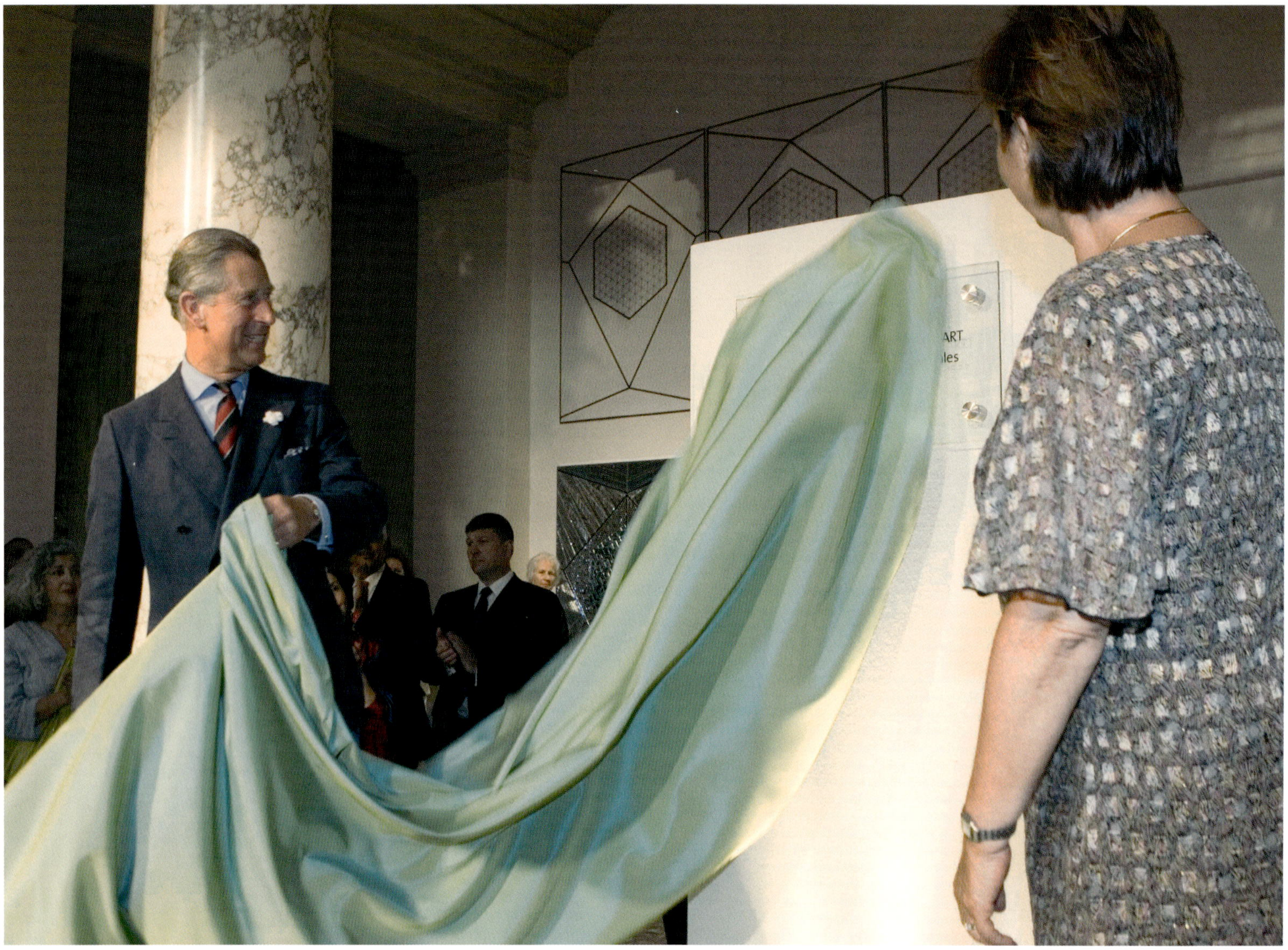

HRH The Prince of Wales opening the Jameel Gallery, watched by Paula Ridley, Chairman of the Trustees of the Victoria and Albert Museum

CLARENCE HOUSE

The Jameel Gallery is a splendid new setting for the Victoria and Albert Museum's collection from the Islamic Middle East which demonstrates so well the evolution of Islamic art over the thousand years, and more, since the great era of the Caliphate in the eighth and ninth centuries.

Ever since its foundation by Prince Albert, my Great-Great-Great Grandfather, in 1852, the Victoria and Albert Museum has recognized the importance of Islamic art and design. Over the last one hundred and fifty years, it has assembled one of the world's finest collections in this field; a collection which has helped to demonstrate the universal values that underlie the arts of the great traditions and faiths of the world, the links between the Islamic world and its neighbours in Asia and Europe and the ways in which they have influenced each other. The Museum's visionary approach has, moreover, inspired designers and craftsmen and has thus helped shape and inform British design. The Jameel Gallery will, I hope, not only reinforce these messages, but will also introduce the wonders of Islamic art and design to future generations and enhance the Victoria and Albert Museum's ability to inspire and influence the designers and craftsmen of tomorrow.

We are all indebted to Mr. Mohammed Abdul Latif Jameel for his great generosity and I would like to take this opportunity to record my heartfelt thanks for his support for this project, which will do so much to enrich the Victoria and Albert Museum.

Charles

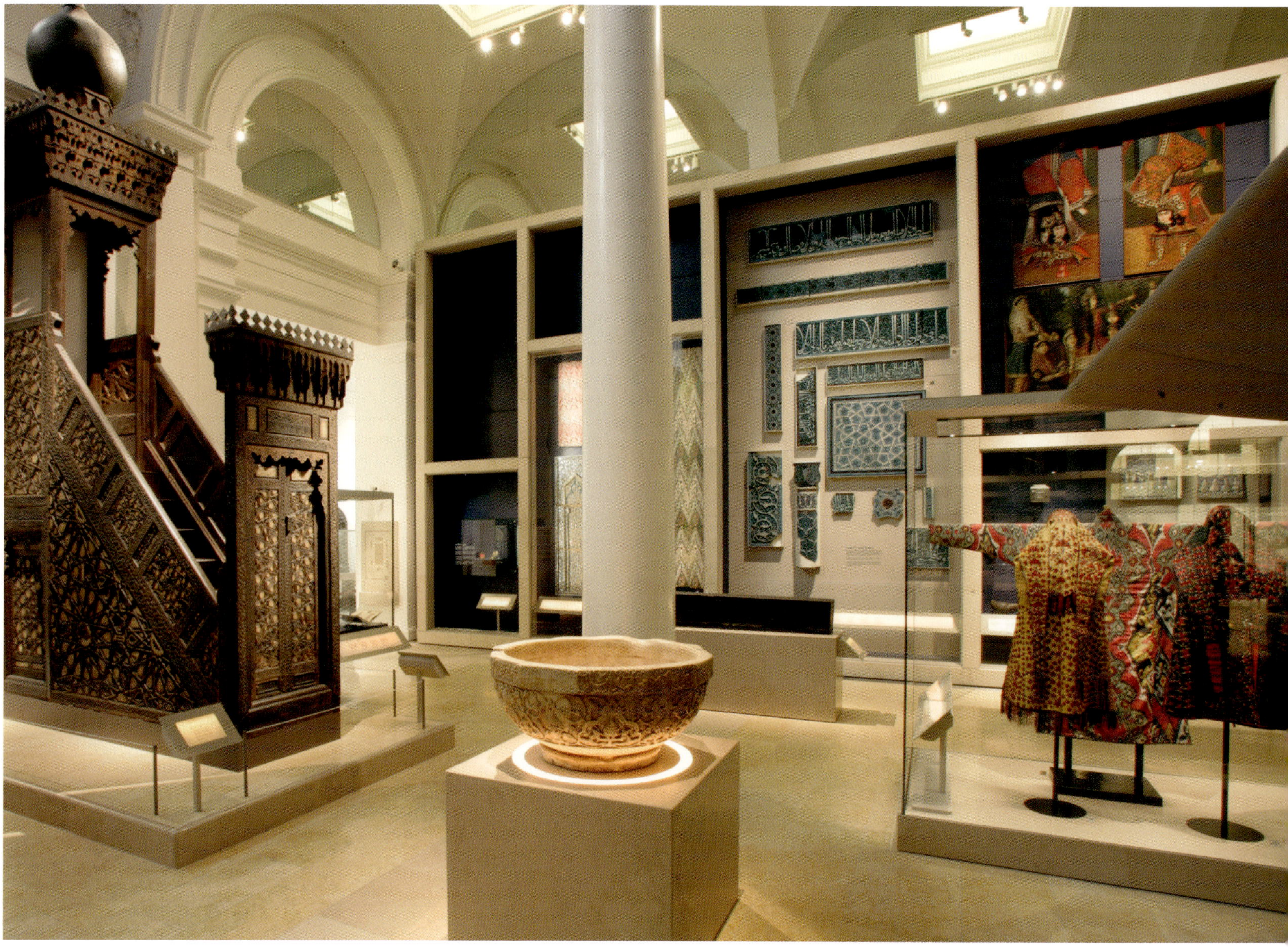

A view of part of the Jameel Gallery

Foreword *by* Mohammed Abdul Latif Jameel

I am delighted to be able to support the new Jameel Gallery of Islamic Art at the V&A. Our family has a keen interest in world cultures and in promoting understanding among them, and a commitment to increasing the understanding of the Islamic world in particular.

When I was first introduced to the Gallery in late 2002, it was in dire need of a complete overhaul. The objects in this fine collection had been painstakingly collected over time and were chosen for their outstanding quality, historical importance and visual impact, but they were not being presented in a fitting way. At this time, events had conspired to create an overwhelmingly negative image of Muslims and their faith in the world's media, and I felt it was important for people to gain a more positive understanding of Islam and what it has contributed to the world. The time was therefore right to make a significant donation to highlight the artistic culture of one of the world's great civilizations.

The idea that the objects destined for the new Gallery should go on a world tour came later. It seemed only fitting that as many people as possible should be given the opportunity to see these amazing artefacts, some of which have not left the Museum since they were acquired in the nineteenth century. I am pleased that, through our efforts, more than a quarter of a million visitors were able to see the *Palace and Mosque* exhibition during its tour to four venues in the United States, Japan and Great Britain.

It gives us great pleasure to be able to help the V&A, as it is the world's pre-eminent museum of applied and decorative art. I can think of no better home for the new Jameel Gallery of Islamic Art, which is dedicated to the memory of Abdul Latif Jameel, my late father and the founder of the Abdul Latif Jameel Group, and to my mother, Nafisa.

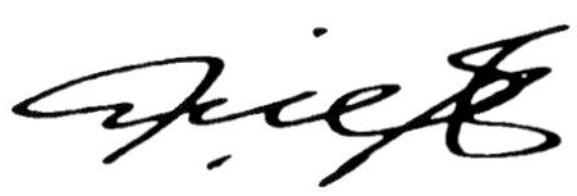

Map of the area covered by the Jameel Gallery

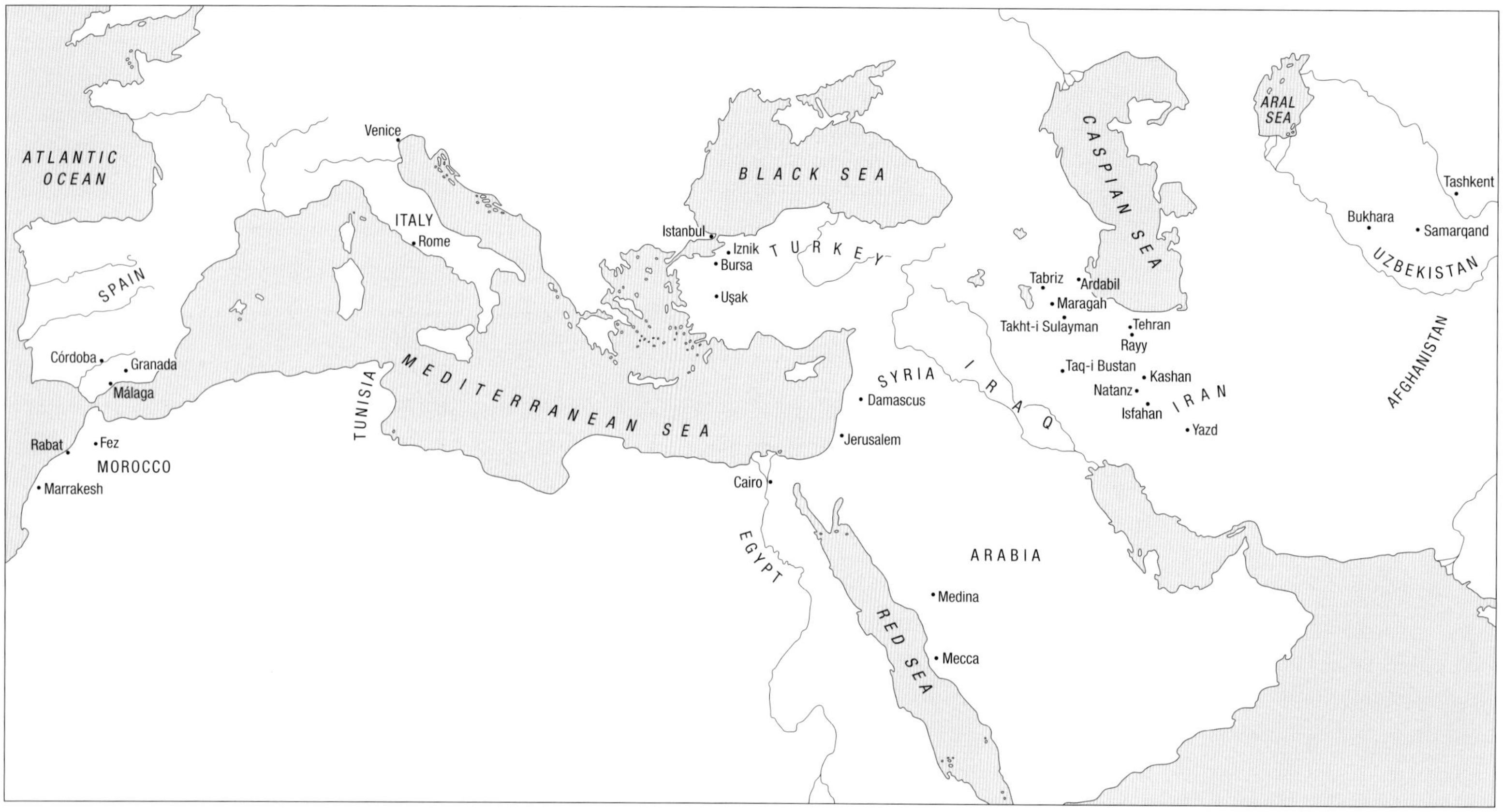

Foreword *by* Mark Jones

Director, Victoria and Albert Museum

The Victoria and Albert Museum is the world's greatest museum of applied and decorative arts, and it contains one of the world's most significant collections of Islamic art. Works from the Islamic Middle East were acquired for the Museum from its inception, as Islamic art was seen as a key source for improving design in Great Britain in the mid-nineteenth century. More recently, it has been seen as a way of illustrating Islamic culture in the broadest sense and of bringing a new understanding of this culture to a wider audience. The arts of the Islamic world have always been displayed in the V&A, and since the 1950s there has been a primary gallery devoted to the Islamic Middle East. The Jameel family has made a substantial donation to transform this gallery into a fitting home for our collection of Islamic art. This book tells the story of how the Jameel Gallery was created, with curators, designers, conservators and educators working together to present Islamic art in a fresh, contemporary setting that we hope will inspire a new generation of visitors to the V&A.

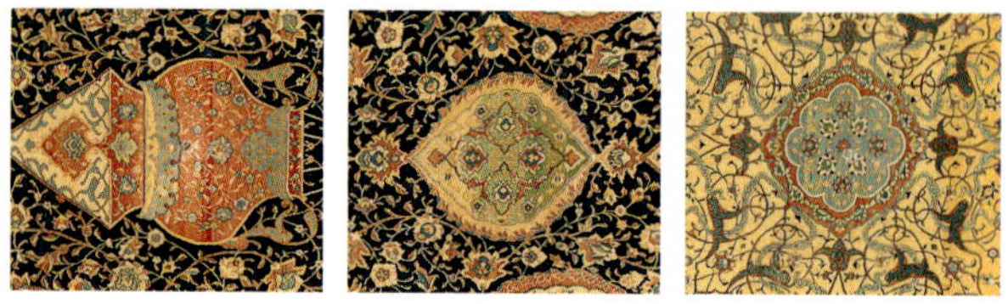

1 Islamic Art at the V&A

Tim Stanley

In Britain in the eighteenth and nineteenth centuries public museums were established for a variety of purposes, all of them linked to disseminating knowledge. The British Museum was founded in 1753 to promote the ideas of the Enlightenment, which taught that the study of things was a means of understanding the natural world and the history of human societies. When, a century later, the British government set up what is now the Victoria and Albert Museum, it had a more precisely practical objective, connected to the improvement of industrial design. The Museum's collections, created from nothing by purchases made with government funds, were to include examples of good design, which would provide models for those involved in manufacturing and would help to educate the taste of their customers. The concept was new, and its implementation created a new type of museum devoted to applied art. It also led to the accumulation of one of the world's most significant collections of Islamic art from the Middle East, now numbering more than 10,000 objects (see Chapter 3).

The British government's objective was achieved remarkably swiftly, at least according to foreign observers, who noted the rapid improvement in British industrial design. As a result, numerous museums of applied arts were founded in cities around the world. In the meantime, however, the nature of the prototype in London had begun to change. The Museum started to collect items of antiquarian interest, including those from the Middle East, soon after it was founded in 1852,

1.1 Rock-crystal ewer, Cairo, *circa* 1000–50. V&A: 7904–1862

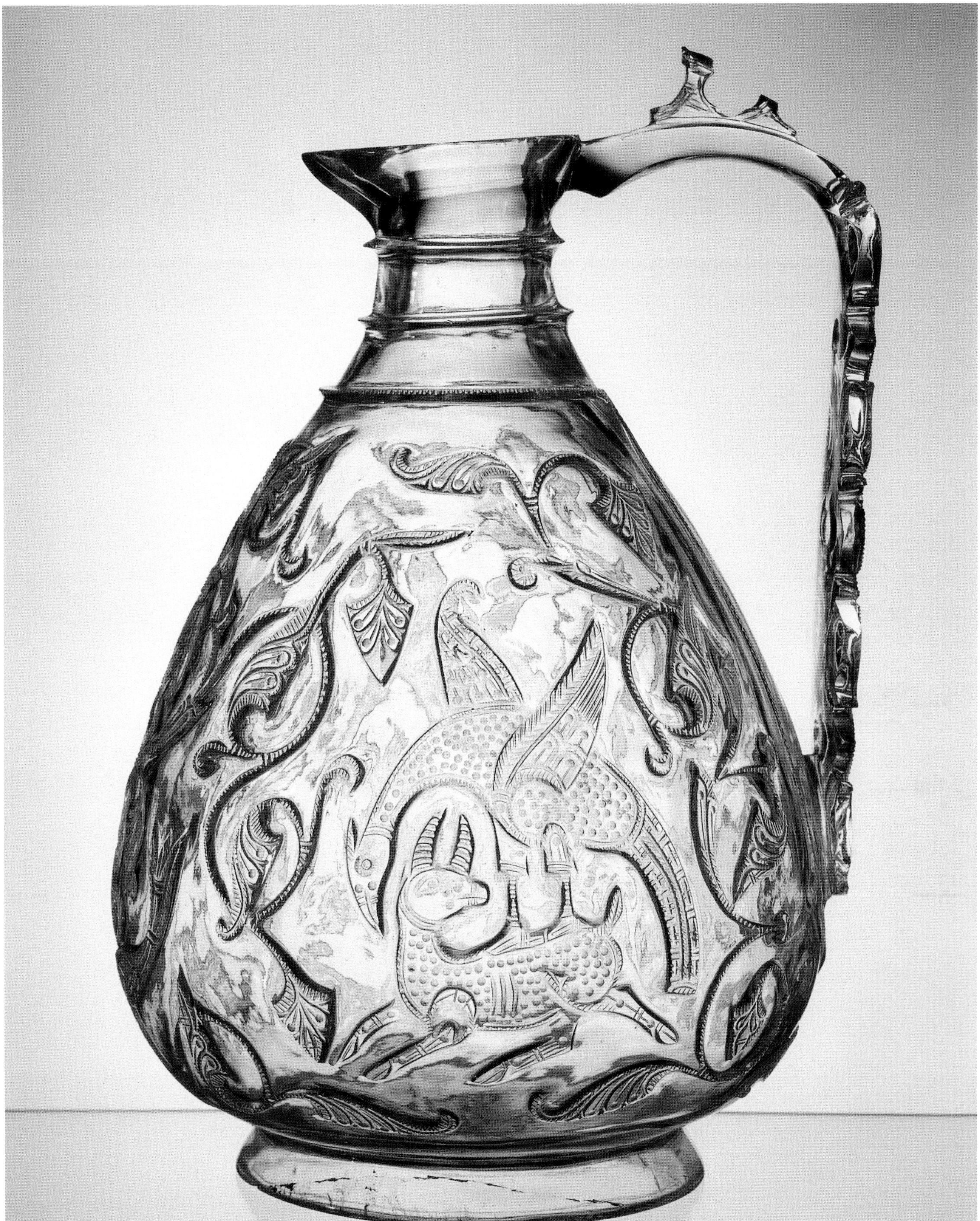

and it was not long before the sheer scale of its acquisitions of historical objects began to overwhelm its primary social purpose. By the early twentieth century it had become a treasure-house tended by connoisseurs and scholars, many of them widely respected in their field. Intermittently, the Museum has played an important role in the study of Islamic art of the Middle East, through the work of Arthur Lane and Oliver Watson, both leading specialists in Islamic ceramics, and B.W. Robinson, who is celebrated, among other things, for his systematic study of Persian manuscript illustration. Yet this area of expertise never gained an official place in the V&A's structure, and, despite the outstanding quality of its collection, the Museum's efforts to communicate with its visitors on this subject were limited.

In the later twentieth century the V&A regained some of its original verve and extroversion. It ceased being a government institution in 1983, and now relies on fundraising from private and public sources to achieve growth and renewal. Its recent success in doing so has made possible the first stages in a coordinated redevelopment of all the Museum's public spaces. The series of new gallery displays created as part of this work have been designed to be both attractive and informative, and they are combined with activities related to the displays that offer entertainment and education. The success of this programme can be judged by the award to the V&A's new British Galleries of the title of European Museum of the Year for 2003.

Early in 2002 the Museum was reorganized, and a new Asian Department was created by combining the Indian and South East Asian Department with the Far Eastern Department. At the same time a long-standing gap was filled by the creation of a third section specializing in the Islamic Middle East. This bureaucratic procedure was followed very rapidly by a revolution in the section's prospects. The Museum received an approach from a potential benefactor, Mohammed Abdul Latif Jameel, with a view to funding the redisplay of Islamic art in the Museum. By early 2003 Mr Jameel had undertaken to give the Museum a substantial sum to redevelop the main Islamic Middle East gallery, which lay close to the Museum's principal entrance. The donation also covered the expenses of an international touring exhibition, which was circulated while the gallery was closed (see Chapter 2).

Thanks to Mr Jameel's donation, the best of the V&A's collection of Islamic art from the Middle East can now be presented in a setting that matches its beauty and importance. In the Jameel Gallery of Islamic Art visitors can see more than 400 carefully selected objects in a display that is sympathetic to their outstanding, and varied, visual qualities. If they wish to, visitors can also use the texts and interactive devices in the Jameel Gallery to gain an understanding of how Islamic art came into being and how it developed. For the first time in the history of the Museum, a visit to the V&A's collections of Islamic art of the Middle East can be both a rewarding aesthetic experience and an opportunity to travel the first stage towards understanding the societies that produced it. At this juncture, it seems appropriate to examine how and why so many objects from the Islamic Middle East came to be in the Museum – and what happened to them once they were there.

The origins of the V&A

In the eighteenth century Britain was the first country to experience the Industrial Revolution, and the new production processes it developed were designed to outstrip the only competition, which came from goods produced by craftsmen using traditional methods. By the 1830s, however, production on an industrial scale had spread to other countries in Western Europe, most notably France. The design of French industrial goods was far more adventurous and sophisticated than that of their British equivalents, and their superiority in this respect began to have an effect. Although British goods were considered to be well made, they were losing out in the international market because of their poor design.

Concern about this issue began to be expressed in the British parliament, in which industrial towns such as Manchester and Birmingham had only begun to be represented as a result of the Reform Act of 1832. A select committee of the House of Commons was set up in 1835 to consider the 'Arts and their Connexion with Manufactures', as its report of August 1836 phrased it. The committee, chaired by the Radical MP William Ewart, concluded that Britain's poor performance in the field of industrial design was due to 'the want of instruction in design among our industrious population' and to 'the absence of public and freely open galleries containing approved specimens of art'. In this second phrase lie the origins of the V&A, although it would take more than a decade before the proposal was formally realized.

In July 1836, before the select committee had reported, the government approved the setting up of a School of Design in London, to be funded by the Treasury. A year later the School opened in Somerset House, in rooms then recently vacated by the Royal Academy of Arts and now part of the Courtauld Institute of Art. Soon the School's governing council began to send its agents on European tours, and one of their duties was to acquire 'specimens of art' that would provide models of good design for the students to absorb. This practice continued during the 1840s, and the collection grew accordingly, but in the School's cramped premises there was nowhere to display it. Indeed, this was only one respect in which the School of Design was regarded as less than a success.

In 1852 the School and its collections were moved to Marlborough House, a vacant royal residence close to Buckingham Palace. There, under the direction of Henry Cole, the 'specimens' assembled over the previous decade and more were arranged in galleries on the first floor, which were opened to visitors. They had become part of a regular public museum, separate from but developing in parallel with the School of Design, which eventually, in 1896, became the Royal College of Art. While it was at Marlborough House, from 1852 to 1857, this new institution was mostly known as the Museum of Ornamental Art. In 1857, after another move, it became the South Kensington Museum, and in 1899 it was renamed the Victoria and Albert Museum in honour of Queen Victoria and her husband, Prince Albert. The Prince died in 1861, but before that he had played a significant part in the history of the Museum that was to bear his name.

While the origins of the V&A's collections lie in the lacklustre School of Design set up in 1836, the impetus that led to the formation of the Museum as an independent institution, and to its subsequent move to South Kensington, came from a far more prosperous venture. This was the Great Exhibition of the Works of Industry of All Nations held in Hyde Park in London in 1851. The Great Exhibition comprised more than 100,000 objects and was housed in a vast ironwork and glass structure that soon became known as the Crystal Palace. Over a period of five and a half months it received more than 6,000,000 visitors, and this ensured its financial success, allowing it to produce a profit of £186,000.

Prince Albert had supported the Exhibition from the start, and he and the organizers – the most energetic of whom was Henry Cole – were determined to carry on the work they had begun in encouraging public interest in manufactures and their improvement through the application of art and science. Cole's appointment to and reinvigoration of the School of Design, its move to Marlborough House and the creation of the Museum of Ornamental Art were all part of their plan. The Museum was augmented by the purchase of 244 items from the Exhibition and, after it closed, the Prince and his advisers used the profit from it to purchase a large tract of land south of Hyde Park and renamed it South Kensington. It was to part of this site that the Museum moved in 1857.

Alhambresque and Saracenic

For the reasons mentioned above, France was the source of many of the 'approved specimens of art' acquired for the School of Design in the 1840s. One such piece was a vase bought from its maker, E.-D. Honoré, shortly after it was shown at the Public Exhibition of the Products of French Industry, held in Paris in 1844 (illus. 1.2). In shape the piece is a modified and scaled-down version of the huge 'Alhambra vases', made in Málaga in the south of Spain in the fourteenth century. These virtuoso ceramics are so called because they were thought to have been made for the Alhambra, the palace complex of Spain's last Islamic rulers in Granada. The decoration of the Honoré vase does not, though, follow that of the 'Alhambra vases'. The patterns that dominate it were inspired by the 'Moorish' decoration of the Alhambra itself.

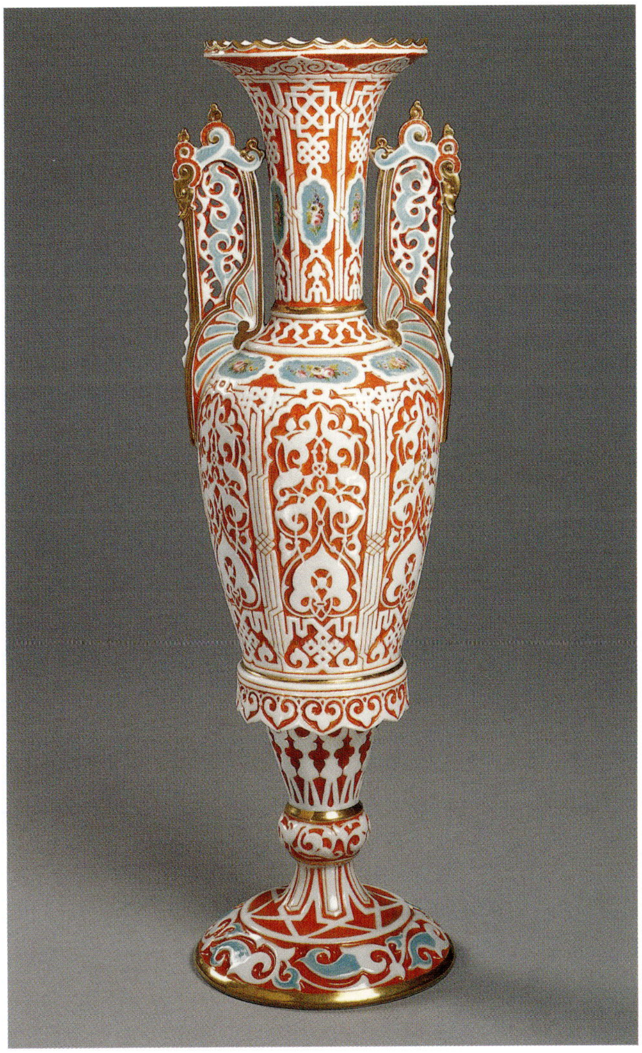

1.2 Vase in the 'Alhambresque' style, made by Honoré of Paris, *circa* 1840.
V&A: 3101–1846

The Honoré vase clearly found favour with the new Museum's official aestheticians, as it was prominently displayed at Marlborough House in the 1850s. Indeed, the ornament on the vase follows the principles they laid down for the improvement of applied art. They abhorred the faults they saw in contemporary British products, exemplified by the illusionistic motifs copied directly on to manufactured objects with no thought for the object's form or the medium in which it was made. By contrast, the arabesque designs filling the panels on the side of the vase were derived from tendril and leaf forms in nature, but had already undergone a complete transformation into a formalized, essentially two-dimensional pattern by the time they were used on the walls of the Alhambra. On the vase, this motif had been adapted to a new form, and to the material employed – porcelain rather than carved stucco.

The vogue enjoyed by the Alhambra and the 'Alhambresque' in the 1840s was a by-product of a passion for all things Spanish that had preceded it. In Britain, its foremost protagonist was the architect and designer Owen Jones (illus. 1.3). Jones's extended version of the Grand Tour, undertaken in the early 1830s, took him to Greece, where he met the young French architect Jules Goury. Both men were interested in the use of colour in architecture, and to widen their knowledge of its history they visited Egypt, Turkey and Spain, where Goury died in 1834. In 1836 Jones began to publish the studies they made of the Alhambra, using chromolithography for the first time in Britain. Jones became a master of this new printing technique, which he later used in his most famous work, *The Grammar of Ornament* (1856).

Jones's and Goury's work on the Alhambra eventually appeared in full in a two-volume work published in 1842 and 1845 (illus. 1.4), by which time Jones had begun to practise as an architect. He was responsible for the interior decoration of the Crystal Palace in 1851, and the following year he lectured at Marlborough House 'On the True and the False in the Decorative Arts'. In this way, Britain's only serious student of Islamic architectural decoration assisted in developing the theories that underlay the Museum's collections. In the event, Jones declined to take up a permanent post under Henry Cole, continuing instead in private practice, and the main theorist behind the School's and the Museum's doctrines on ornament was the painter Richard Redgrave, who had also been involved with the Great Exhibition.

1.3 Owen Jones at the Alhambra. RIBA collection, V&A

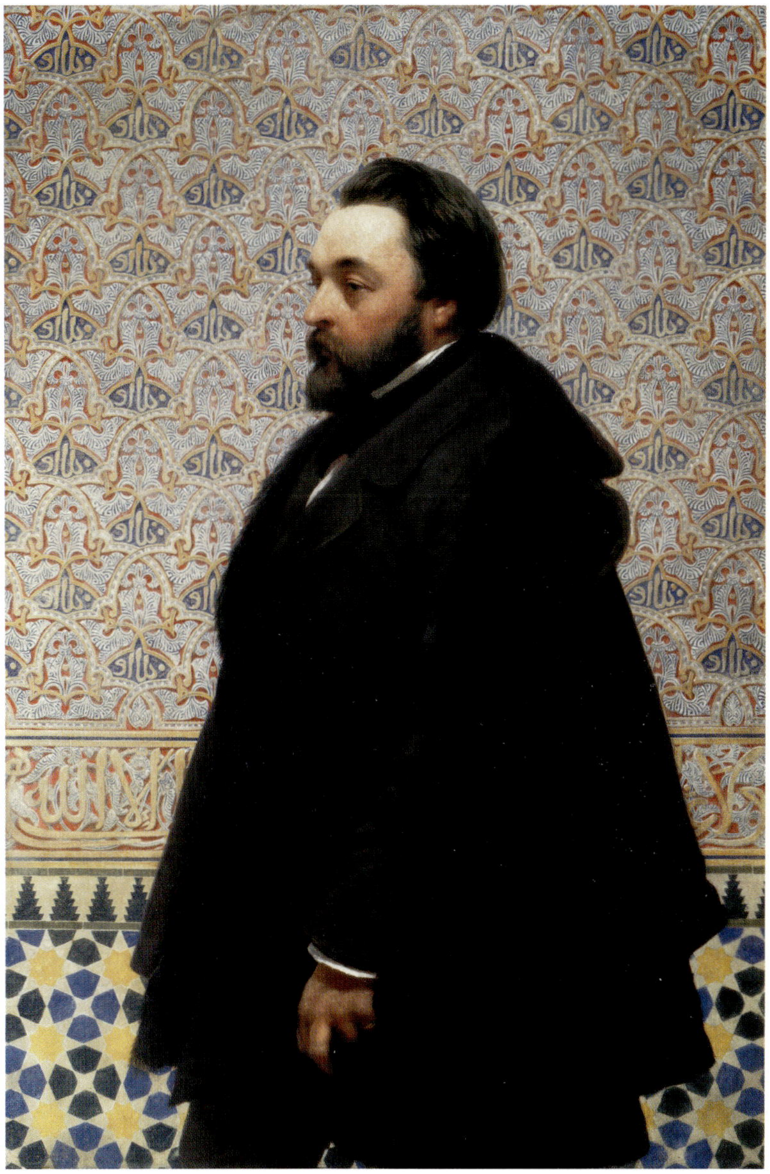

1.4 A plate from Owen Jones's and Jules Goury's *Plans, elevations, sections and details of the Alhambra*, 1842–5

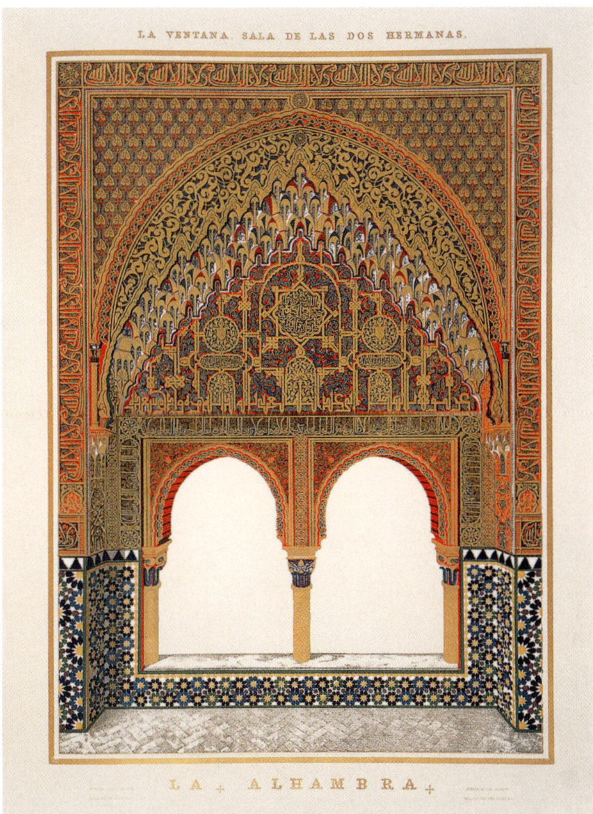

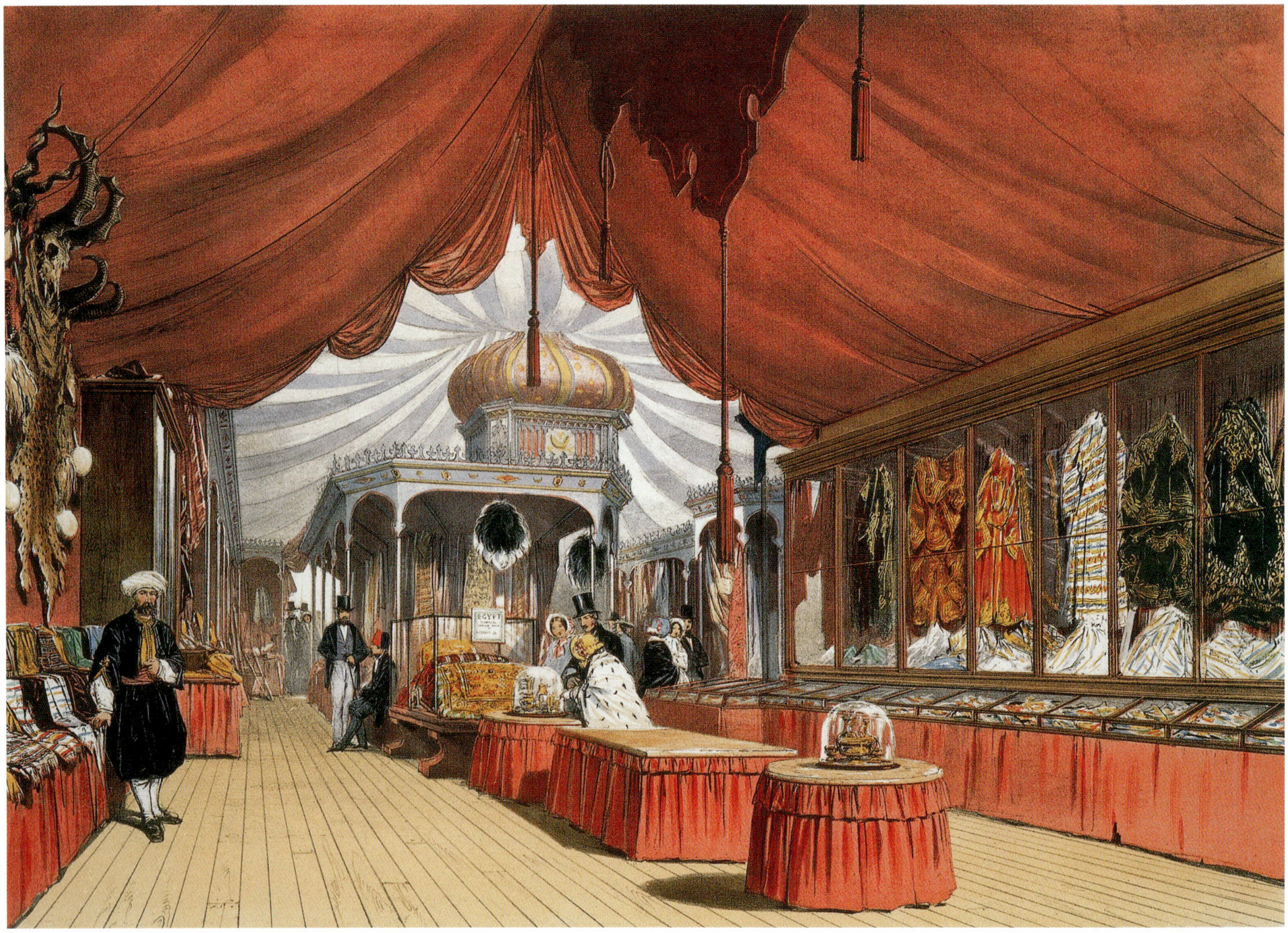

For Cole, Redgrave and others without Jones's opportunity for travel, the Exhibition was a chance to extend their experience of manufactures beyond Britain's immediate neighbours. The imperial net, cast very wide, brought in products from Tunisia and Turkey (illus. 1.5), and items from these countries figure among the 244 items bought from the Exhibition, which included more non-European than European pieces. An interest in Middle Eastern wares was demonstrated again when, after 1852, the Museum began to collect historical as well as contemporary items. Among the earliest antiquarian purchases, made in 1854, is a magnificent brass tray made in Egypt, probably in the 1360s (illus. 1.6).

1.5 The Turkish display at the Great Exhibition, 1851. From Dickinson's *Comprehensive Pictures of the Great Exhibition of 1851*, London, 1852

The tray's circular surface is neatly divided by concentric circles into four registers of different widths. At the very centre of the design is an inscription containing blessings on the ruling sultan, arranged to form a pattern suggestive of solar rays. It is surrounded by a pattern of interlace formed by repeating the same arc of a circle 24 times and using it to link 12 points on the inner circle with 12 points close to an outer circle. This device is surrounded by a narrow band divided into six sections by six small circular motifs. Then in the dominant register is an inscription with huge letters, which is divided into three parts by three circles that are divided into three concentric registers. The progression from 12 to six to three is not obvious to the eye, but it helps to create variety in a design that matches the overall shape of the object and respects the flatness of its surface. Such examples of Islamic art, then called by names such as 'Saracenic', matched Jones's and Redgrave's ideals in their harmony of ornament and form and their decoration with flat, non-illusionistic patterns.

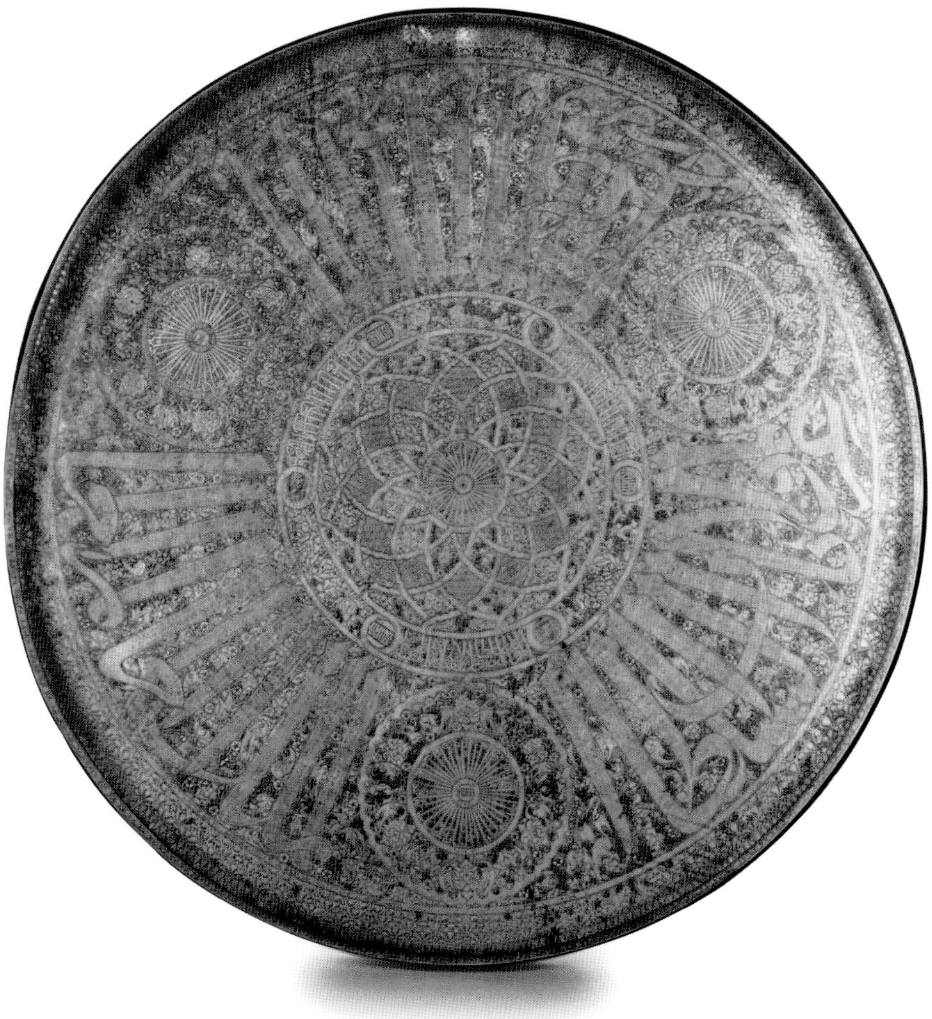

1.6 Mamluk brass tray, Egypt or Syria, *circa* 1341–63. V&A: 420–1854

Collecting treasures

While Redgrave devoted himself mostly to art education, another colleague of Cole's, J.C. Robinson, played a key role in forming the Museum. He was made curator of art collections in 1852 and kept the post for a decade, remaining as a paid adviser, or 'art referee', from 1862 to 1867. Robinson was a connoisseur of medieval art, and after his appointment the Museum's collecting policy underwent a fundamental change, from the acquisition solely of contemporary work to the accumulation of works of historical interest. One feature of medieval European culture was the high esteem in which the luxury products of the Middle East were held, and in Robinson's time the Museum acquired several outstanding Islamic items that had survived in European treasuries.

In 1862 a thin-walled, finely shaped and richly decorated rock-crystal ewer (illus. 1.1) was bought for the very reasonable sum of £450, equivalent to about £26,000 in today's prices. This hardly seems to reflect the exquisite quality of the ewer, which is reckoned one of the two finest rock crystals to have survived from medieval Egypt; nor its rarity, for it is one of only six examples of this form. Two of the other ewers are still in the Treasury of St Mark's; one still belongs to the cathedral treasury at Fermo in Italy; the ewer from the Medici collection is still in one of their palaces in Florence; and the example once owned by the abbey of Saint-Denis near Paris was transferred to the Musée du Louvre after the French Revolution. The V&A ewer is, then, the only example to have changed location in the last two centuries, showing how fortunate the Museum is to have acquired it.

The supply of Islamic items available to Robinson and his successors as they travelled in Western Europe was soon increased due to the success of the Great Exhibition. A series of similar events was held in South Kensington between 1862 and 1874, and *expositions universelles* were held at sites in Paris from 1855 onwards. These exhibitions, too, began to include historical objects as well as contemporary products. So it was that a collection of Islamic antiquities, including star items from the Mamluk period (1250–1517), appeared at the Paris exhibition of 1867. The Museum subsequently bought the collection, acquiring some of its most impressive Islamic objects. One of them was the enormous gilt leather binding and 20 vast leaves from one of the largest Qur'an manuscripts produced in Egypt in the Mamluk period (illus. 5.15). Another was the minbar of Sultan Qa'itbay (ruled 1468–96), which stands more than seven metres high (illus. 1.15, 2.6). The wooden minbar, many of its surfaces encrusted with carved ivory elements, was used as a pulpit during the prayer at midday on Friday.

Home and abroad

Henry Cole retired as director of the South Kensington Museum in 1873, and the years that followed are not considered as brilliant as those spent under his guidance. Nevertheless, the Islamic Middle East collections continued to be enhanced through the activities of the Museum's supporters. The greatest of these figures was Robert Murdoch Smith, an officer in the Royal Engineers, who revolutionized the Museum's holdings of art from Iran while resident there as director of the Indo-European Telegraph. In 1873 he undertook to render the Museum authorities 'any service in my power, in the way of purchasing artistic and ornamental objects', and by 1876 he had worked so rapidly that the Museum was able to mount a display of almost 2,000 objects from Iran. These he described in an accompanying catalogue, and he provided an introduction to the subject in a handbook called *Persian Art*, also published in 1876 (illus. 1.7). So well did Murdoch Smith do, in fact, that upon his return to Scotland in 1885 he was appointed director of Edinburgh's equivalent of the V&A, the Museum of Science and Art, later the Royal Scottish Museum and now part of the National Museums of Scotland.

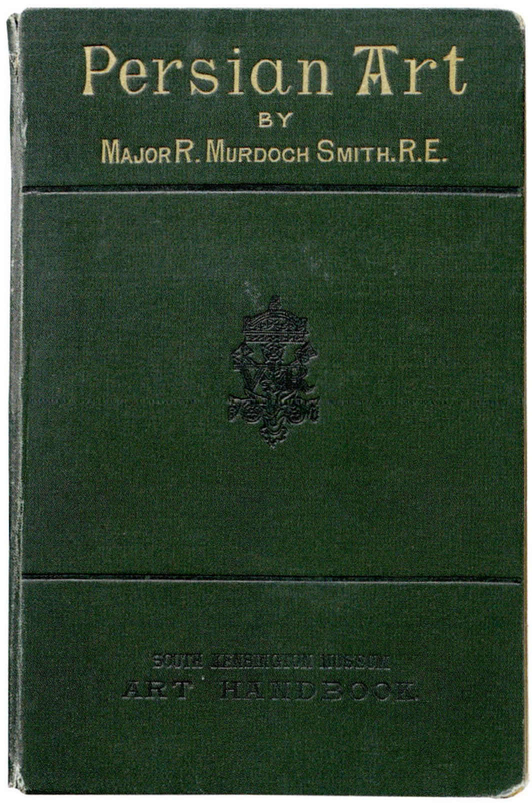

1.7 The front cover of Robert Murdoch Smith's *Persian Art*, 1876

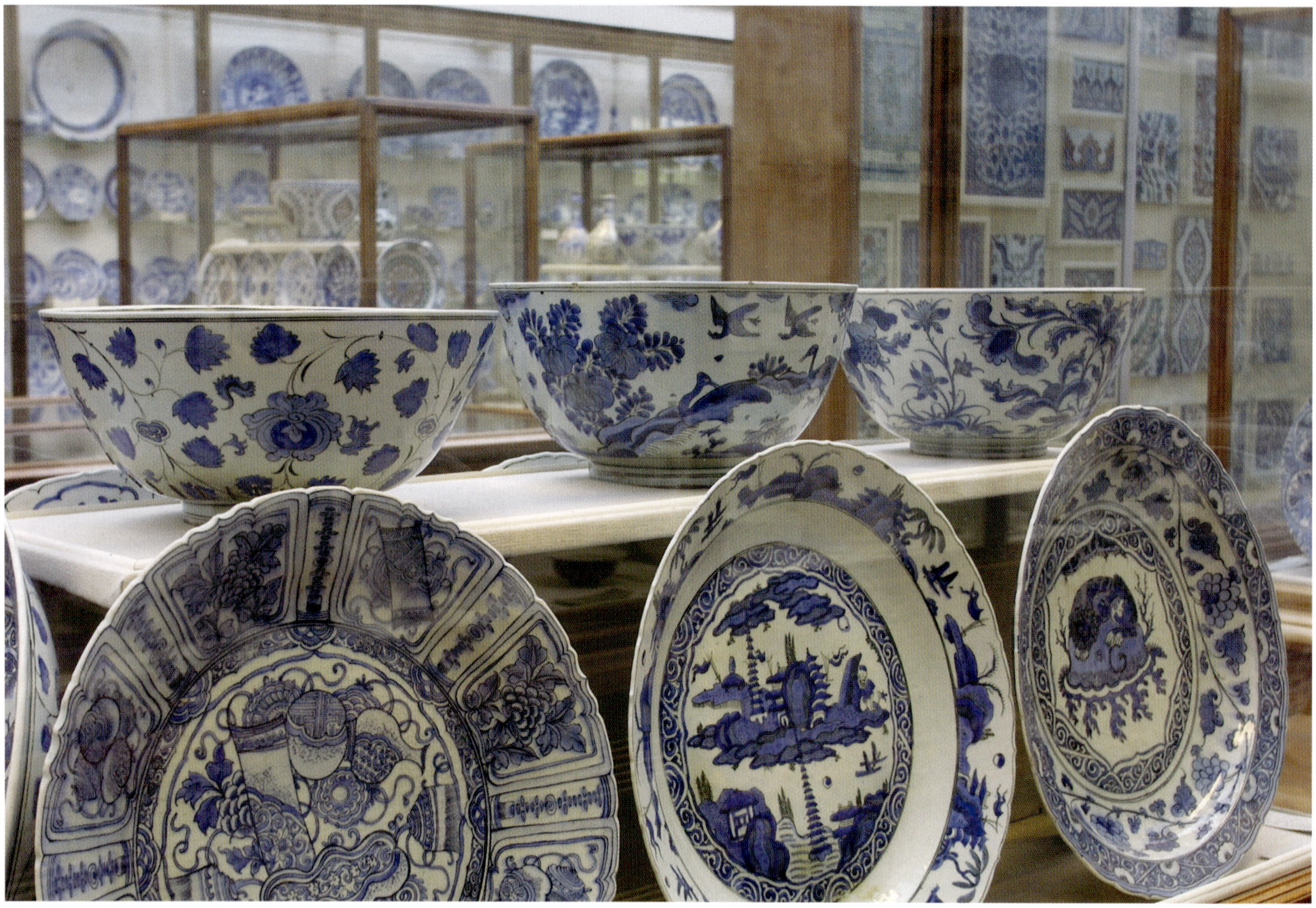

1.8 Iranian blue-and-white ceramics of the 17th century in Room 133, the V&A's ceramic study collection

Murdoch Smith's collecting occurred at a time when blue-and-white porcelain was in particular demand in Britain. The Middle East had been the original market for Chinese wares of this type when they were first produced in the fourteenth century, and in Iran Murdoch Smith was able to buy many outstanding specimens from this and later periods. From the fifteenth century, however, Iran had produced blue-and-white ceramics of its own, with production reaching a peak in the seventeenth century. These, too, Murdoch Smith bought in great numbers, and the V&A now has the largest collection in the world, exceeding 500 examples (illus. 1.8).

After Murdoch Smith's departure from Iran, the Museum continued to acquire historical items from the country, which were brought to London by commercial concerns. The greatest of these by far was the enormous Ardabil carpet, which forms the centrepiece of the Jameel Gallery (illus. 1.9). The carpet is one of a pair made for the shrine of Shaykh Safi al-Din in Ardabil in north-west Iran and was completed, according to the inscription at one end, in 1539–40. The pair were still in the shrine three centuries later, but by the mid-1880s they had been sold to the local agent of a Manchester-based importer. The V&A's Ardabil had sustained much damage over time, especially to one end, and when it arrived in Britain it was restored using material cut from its pair. The now 'complete' carpet was exhibited for sale in London in 1892, while the much-reduced pair was eventually given to the Los Angeles County Museum of Art.

A carpet collector, J.E. Taylor, approached the South Kensington Museum and offered to raise £500 towards the asking price of £2,000 if they would buy the Ardabil, of which he thought very highly. His estimation was shared by the great British designer William Morris, who advised the Museum on purchases. His opinion on the carpet was clear-cut: 'It would be a crime to let it go.' Morris offered £20 towards Taylor's £500, but in the end only £250 was raised, and the Museum had to pay £1,750.

According to Morris, the design of the Ardabil was 'of singular perfection; defensible on all points, logically and consistently beautiful, with no oddities or grotesqueries which might need an apology, and therefore most especially valuable for a Museum, the special aim of which is the education of the public in Art'. We can understand what he meant by comparing the Ardabil with the so-called Chelsea carpet, the other great Iranian carpet of the sixteenth century in the Museum's collection (illus. 1.10, 2.19). Although very beautiful, the design of the Chelsea carpet was created in an apparently *ad hoc* manner from disparate motifs.

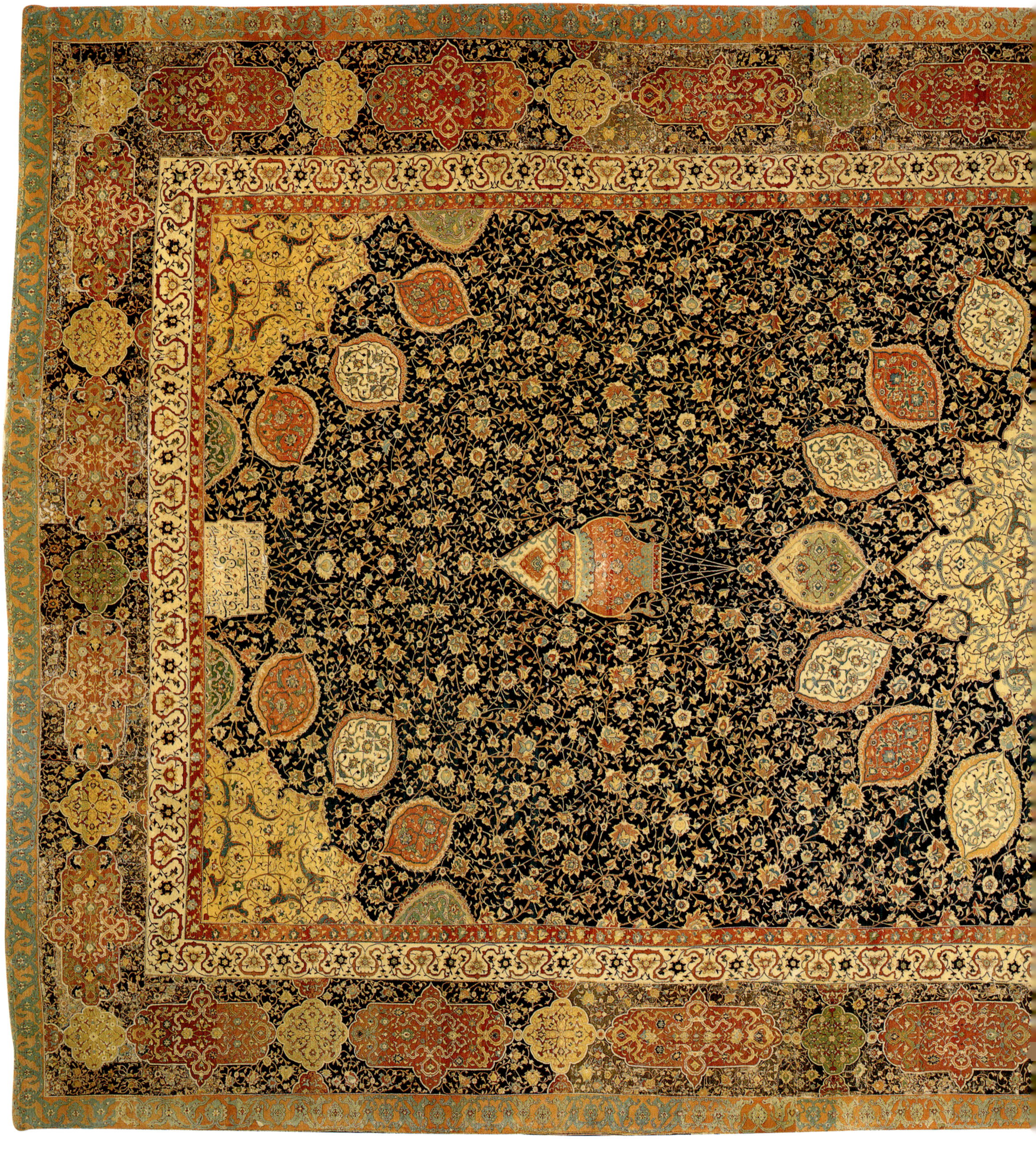

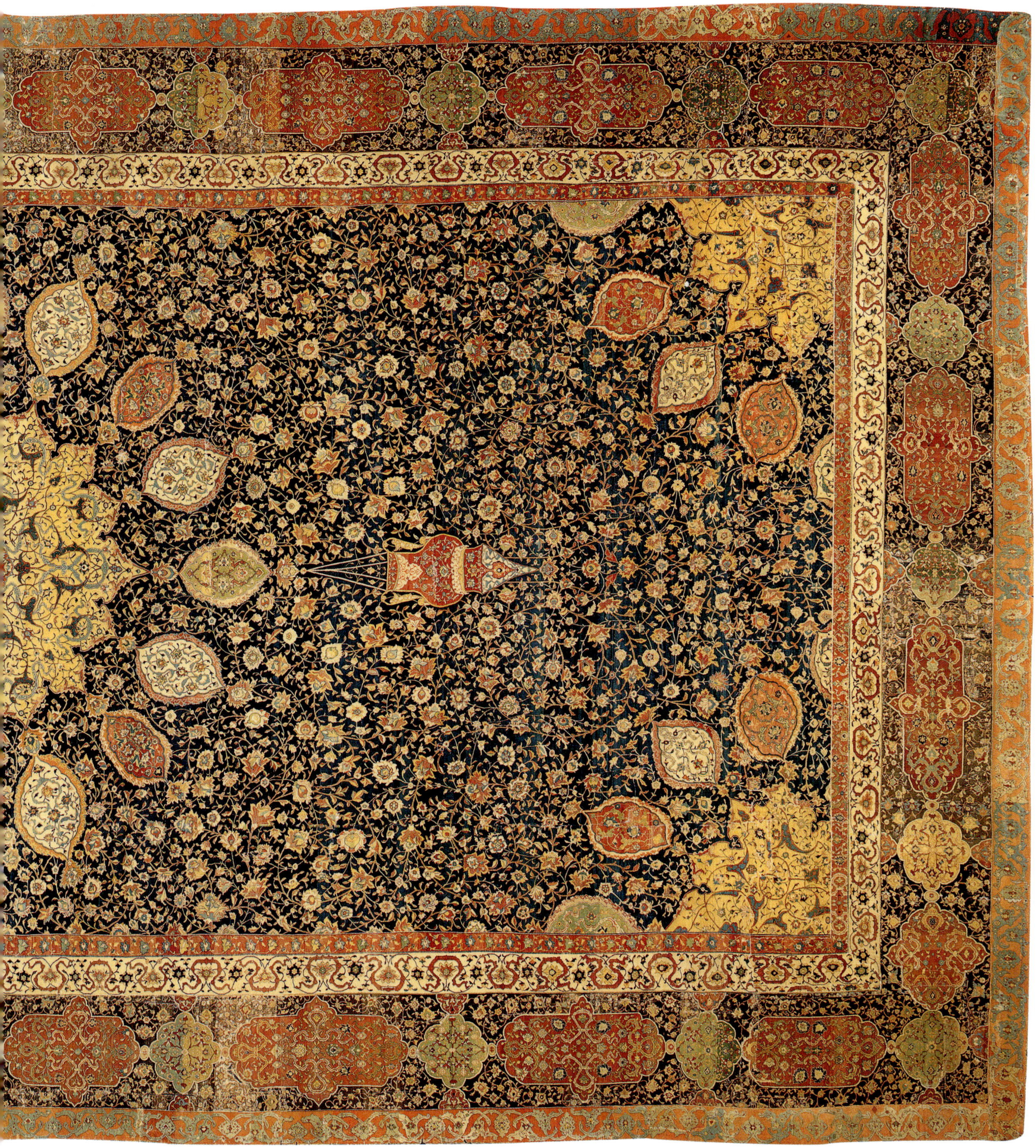

1.9 The Ardabil carpet, Iran, dated 1539–40. V&A: 272–1893

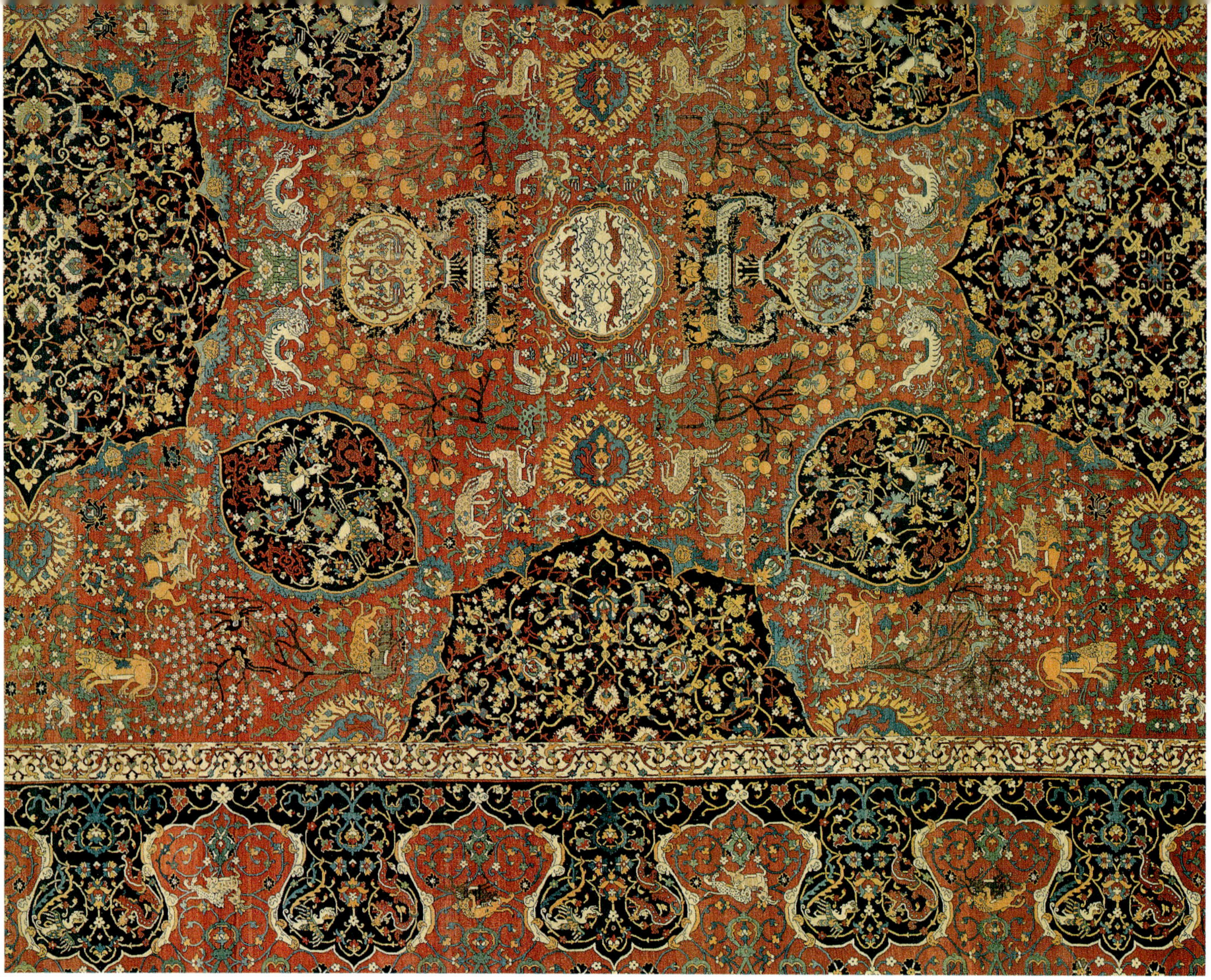

1.10 Detail of the Chelsea carpet, Iran, early 16th century. V&A: 589–1890

By contrast, the surface of the Ardabil, which is three times as large, is covered by a single unified design, and the ornament used is coordinated with great mastery.

From the beginning, the Museum displayed collections on loan as well as its own acquisitions, and as an interest in Islamic art developed among amateurs of decorative art, the loans came to include material from the Middle East. One of the most important loan collections was assembled by George Salting, who was born in Australia in 1836 and inherited a huge fortune based on sugar estates and sheep farms. In his thirties Salting moved to London, where he took up collecting as a way of life. From 1874 much of what he bought was displayed in South Kensington, and when he died in 1910, he bequeathed the V&A some 2,500 objects, almost universally of the highest quality. They included a number of outstanding objects from the Islamic Middle East, such as a footed basin of spectacular size made in Iznik in north-west Turkey in the early sixteenth century (illus. 1.11, 1.12). The Salting Bequest added lustre to the Museum's collection in this area, which, by the time of his death, had acquired exceptional significance.

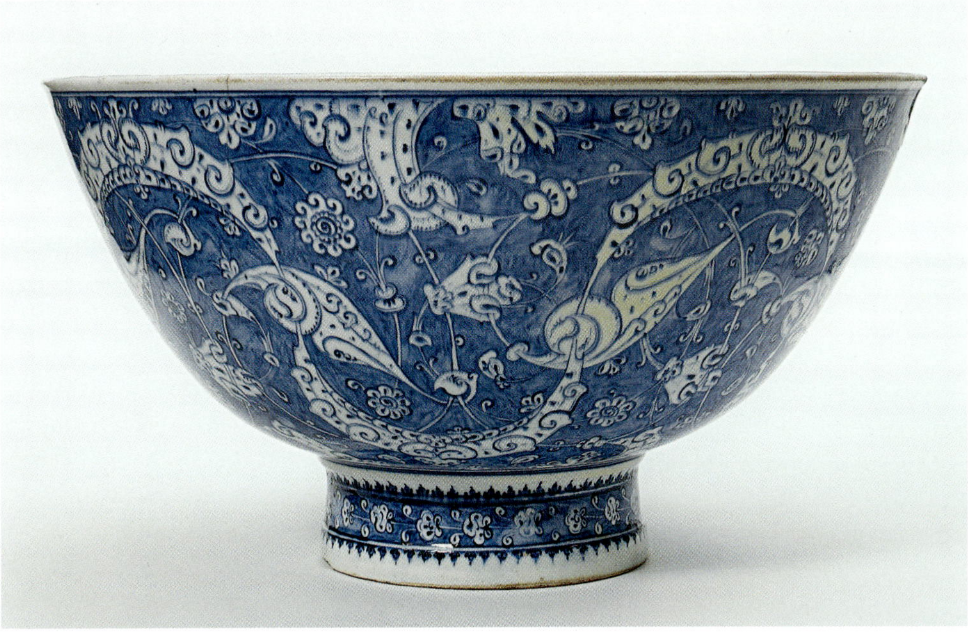

1.11 Footed bowl, Iznik, Turkey, early 16th century. V&A: C.1981–1910 (Salting Bequest)

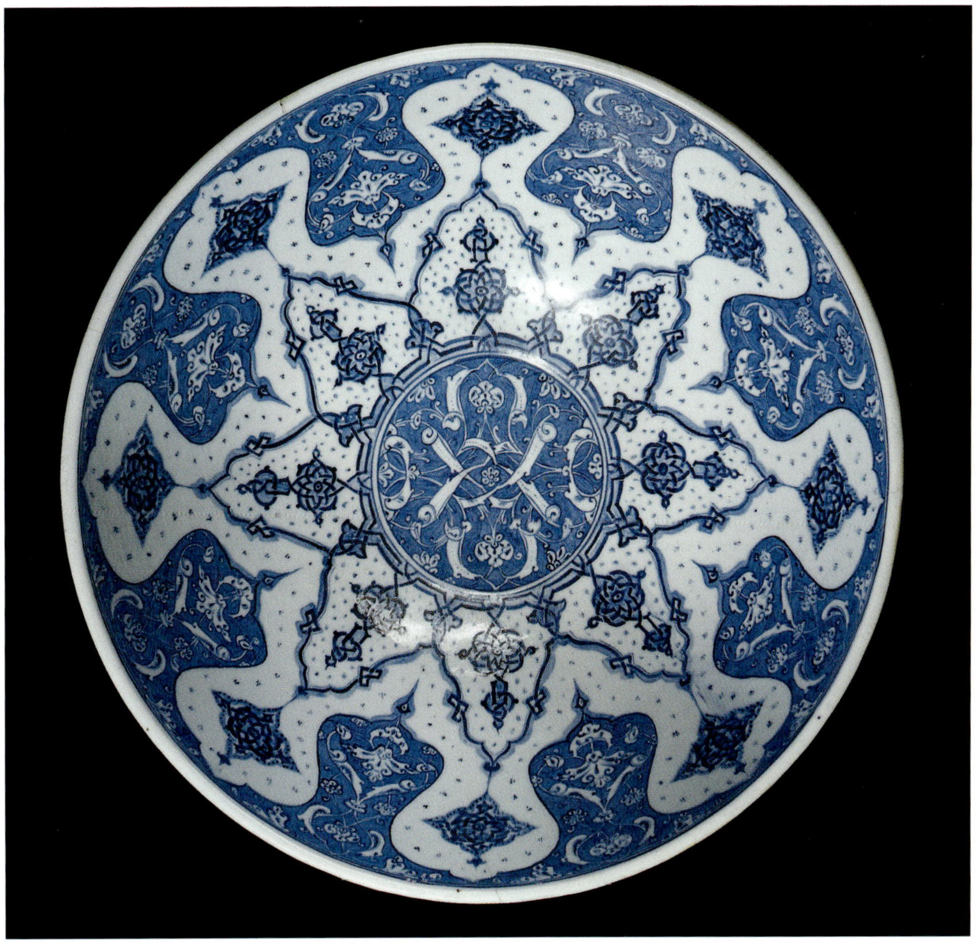

1.12 Footed bowl from above V&A: C.1981–1910 (Salting Bequest)

Displaying the collection

Prince Albert's ideal for the Museum at South Kensington was that its exhibits should follow the Great Exhibition in covering four categories, namely, raw materials, machinery, manufactures and art. This policy was never fully realized. Minerals and plants, for example, were omitted, since they were already represented in other museums in London, and South Kensington specialized in animal products. At the same time, collections of other types were added, including an Educational Museum, a Patent Museum, an Architectural Museum, a Food Museum, and many more. In addition, parts of the site were occupied by the School of Art and by the offices of the government's Department of Science and Art, which, under the secretaryship of Henry Cole, oversaw all the South Kensington institutions and many others. Yet the British government was very reluctant to spend money on new buildings at South Kensington, and progress was slow. This meant that for the first 50 years of its history, the Museum galleries were very crowded, and they failed to grow in line with the rapid increase in the size of the collections.

During this period different ideas about the display of art works from beyond the borders of Europe were at work. A large part of the world was all but ignored at South Kensington, because its products were classified as ethnographic material rather than art. What remained was 'the Orient', and by the mid-1860s examples of art from this vast region were being shown together. So it is that in the Museum guidebook published in 1871, we are told that 'The cloisters to the east of the South Court form the Oriental Courts decorated by Mr Owen Jones. Here are shown examples of the Art workmanship of the East Indies, China, Japan, Persia, &c.' Another approach required that objects made in the same material should be shown together, as their materials were seen as determining their character. So it was, too, that in 1871 the 'Keramic Gallery' on the first floor of the Museum included cases containing 'Persian, Arabic and Rhodian Glazed Pottery. Some pieces are remarkable for their beauty of form and colour, particularly for the happy combination of tints of blue.'

Rearrangements must have been frequent, as more and more pieces were added, and between 1894 and 1909 the main display of 'Japanese, Chinese, Persian and Saracenic Works of Art' disappeared from the main site altogether. It was moved across Exhibition Road, to the Cross Gallery of the old Imperial Institute. This period of exile coincided with a change in government policy, which led to funds being provided for a major building programme at the Museum. After an

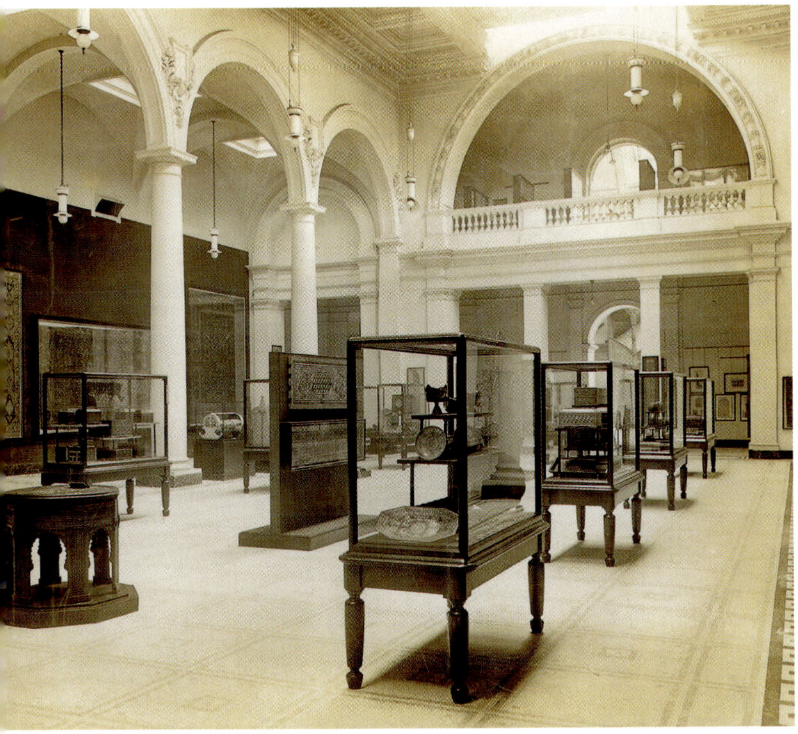

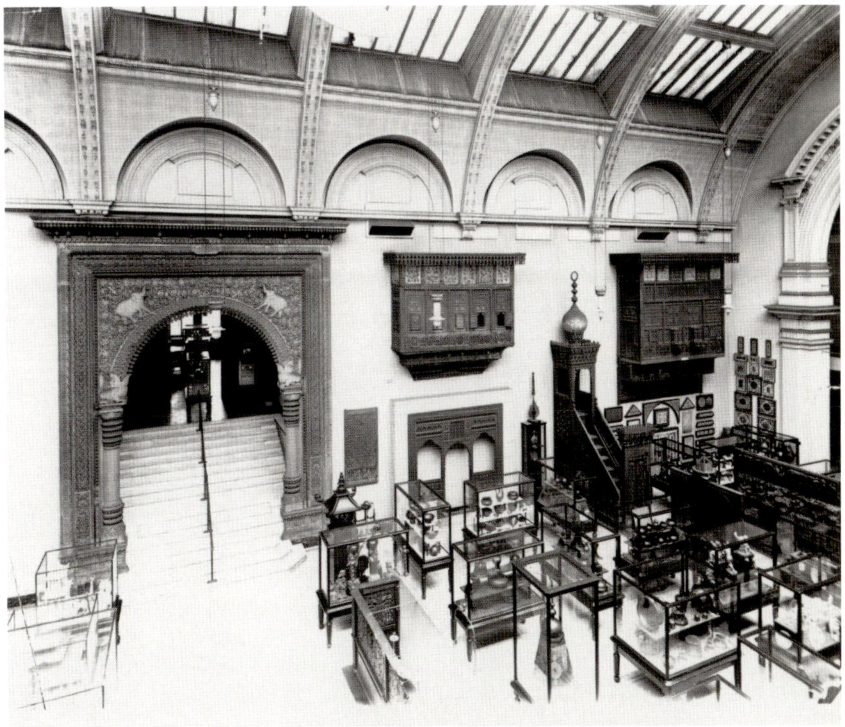

1.13 (*above*) Room 42 as it was in 1910

1.14 (*above right*) Room 48 as it was *circa* 1920

architectural competition won by Aston Webb, the large ranges of galleries that now form the main façades were erected, and when the extension opened in 1909 it provided a huge increase in the gallery space available. By this time, too, the extraneous collections and the administrative functions of the site had been eliminated, and it was solely devoted to the Royal School of Art and the newly named Victoria and Albert Museum.

The expansion of the galleries meant that a new arrangement had to be devised. By this time, it was becoming obvious that galleries filled with objects made from one material were of limited interest to the general public, and in other museums of decorative arts the displays were beginning to be arranged by period and style. At the V&A, however, the decision was passed to a committee convened in 1908, which opted for a materials-based arrangement. As a result, the Islamic Middle East collections were spread across the Museum in groups determined by the materials from which they were made. Room 42, now the Jameel Gallery of Islamic Art, was one of the new galleries designed by Webb, and it was initially devoted to a display of woodwork, combined with a selection of 'Persian' carpets hung on the walls (illus. 1.13). The minbar of Sultan Qa'itbay, however, was displayed in Room 48, the West Court, together with other Middle Eastern items (illus. 1.14).

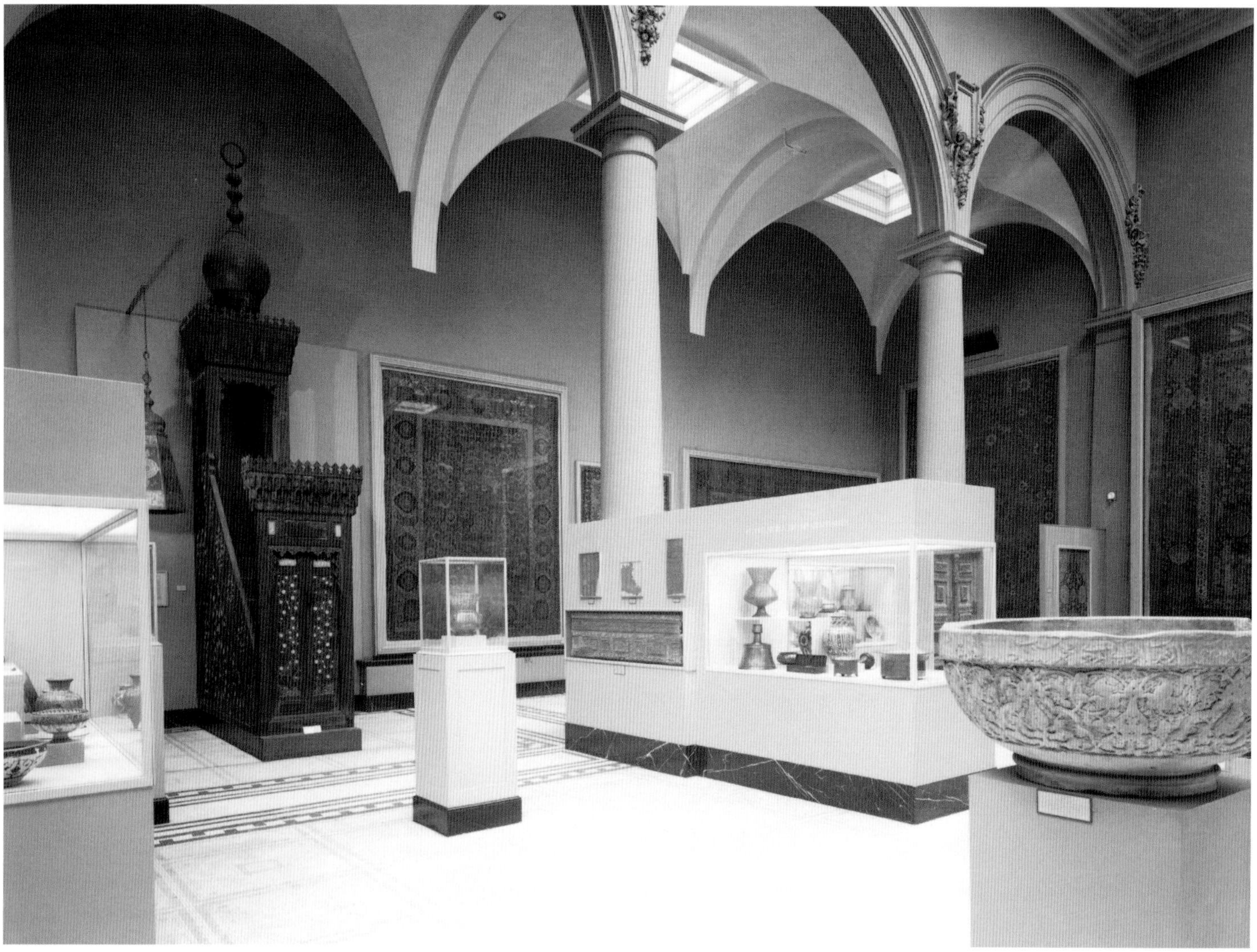

1.15 Room 42 in 1950

These displays were dismantled after the outbreak of the Second World War in 1939, and so when Leigh Ashton became director in 1945, he had the opportunity to reverse the decision of the committee of 1908. He recommended that the Museum's galleries should be divided into two categories so that the main part of the Museum, 'when rearranged, will consist of the finest things in the collections, arranged in a chronological and historical series in the main galleries in the front of the Museum'. This policy was officially announced in 1948, and Rooms 42 and 47c were opened under the title of 'Islamic Art' in January 1950 (illus. 1.15). Nevertheless, the huge majority of the Islamic Middle East collections, like those from other areas, continued to be displayed in the materials galleries on the upper floors, where they served visitors with more specialist interests (illus. 1.8).

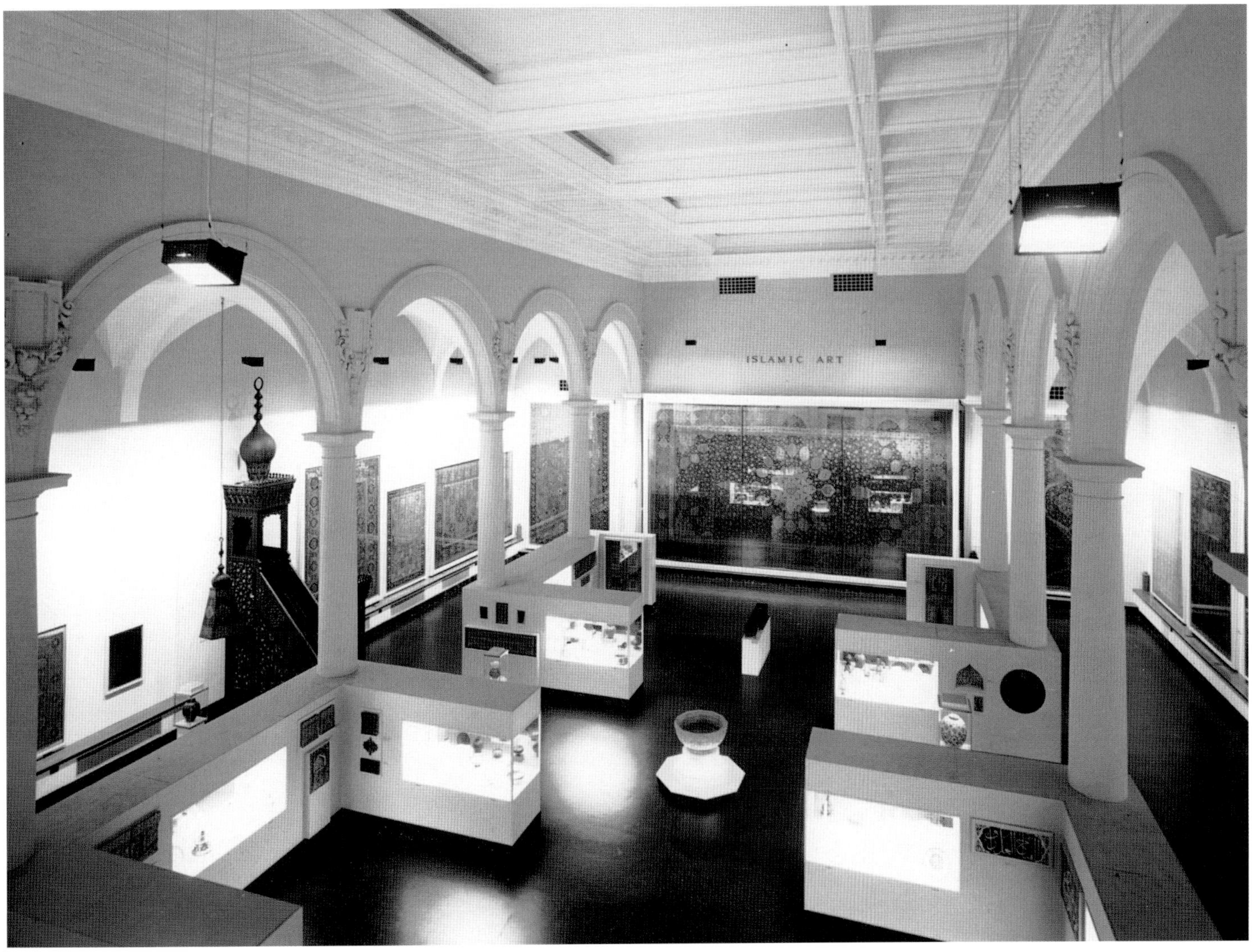

1.16 Room 42 in 1972

Since 1950

For the next five decades the Islamic Art gallery was administered by the Ceramics and Glass Department, and the basic elements in Ashton's scheme remained unchanged. In the 1960s black linoleum was laid over the mosaic floor as part of a general updating of the Museum's appearance, and the light level was reduced by blocking out the glass roofs, for conservation reasons. In 1971, the gallery was smartened up for a modest relaunch, designed to coincide with the celebrations for the 2,500th anniversary of the founding of the Persian monarchy (illus. 1.16). A major change in the early 1980s was the unblocking of the three central arches on the south side of the gallery, now occupied by three double-sided vitrines. The large tilework chimney-piece (illus. 2.7–2.13), which had been the main object on the gallery side of the partition, was relocated to the adjoining Room 47c, together with other outstanding examples of Ottoman ceramic production (illus. 1.17). The early Islamic items that had been shown in the wall cases on the outside of the same partition were accommodated in high-security cases from the V&A's great Fabergé exhibition, held in 1977, which were placed at the south end of Room 42.

The new displays in these cases were the work of Dr Oliver Watson, who joined the Museum's Ceramics and Glass Department in 1979 and eventually became its head. Before Watson's time important acquisitions had been made for the Islamic Middle East collections, but on a piecemeal basis. Some had been funded by the National Art Collections Fund and other similar sources, usually rescue operations for important items such as the Luck of Edenhall (illus. 1.18). Others had been private donations, the last important example being the gift of early thirteenth-century Iranian ceramics made in 1977 by Clement Ades in memory of his wife, Andrée. Watson, though, was a proactive collector, filling in many gaps in the Museum's holdings and, on occasion, acquiring new masterpieces.

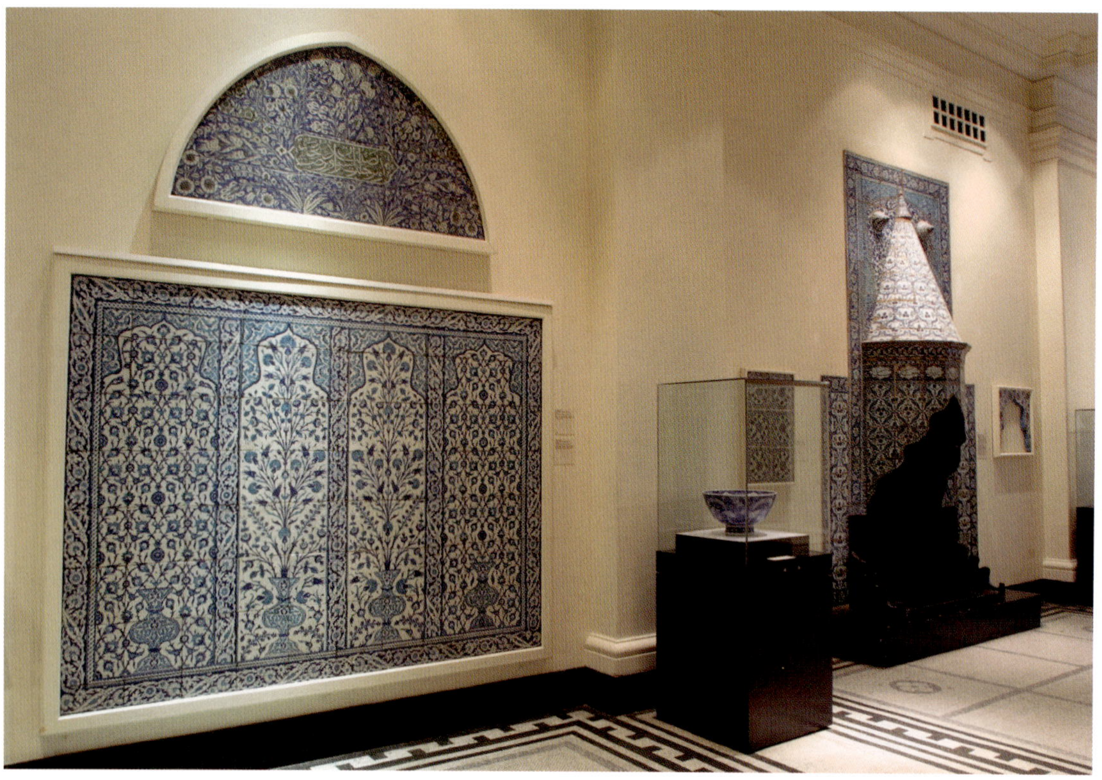

1.17 Room 47c in 2004

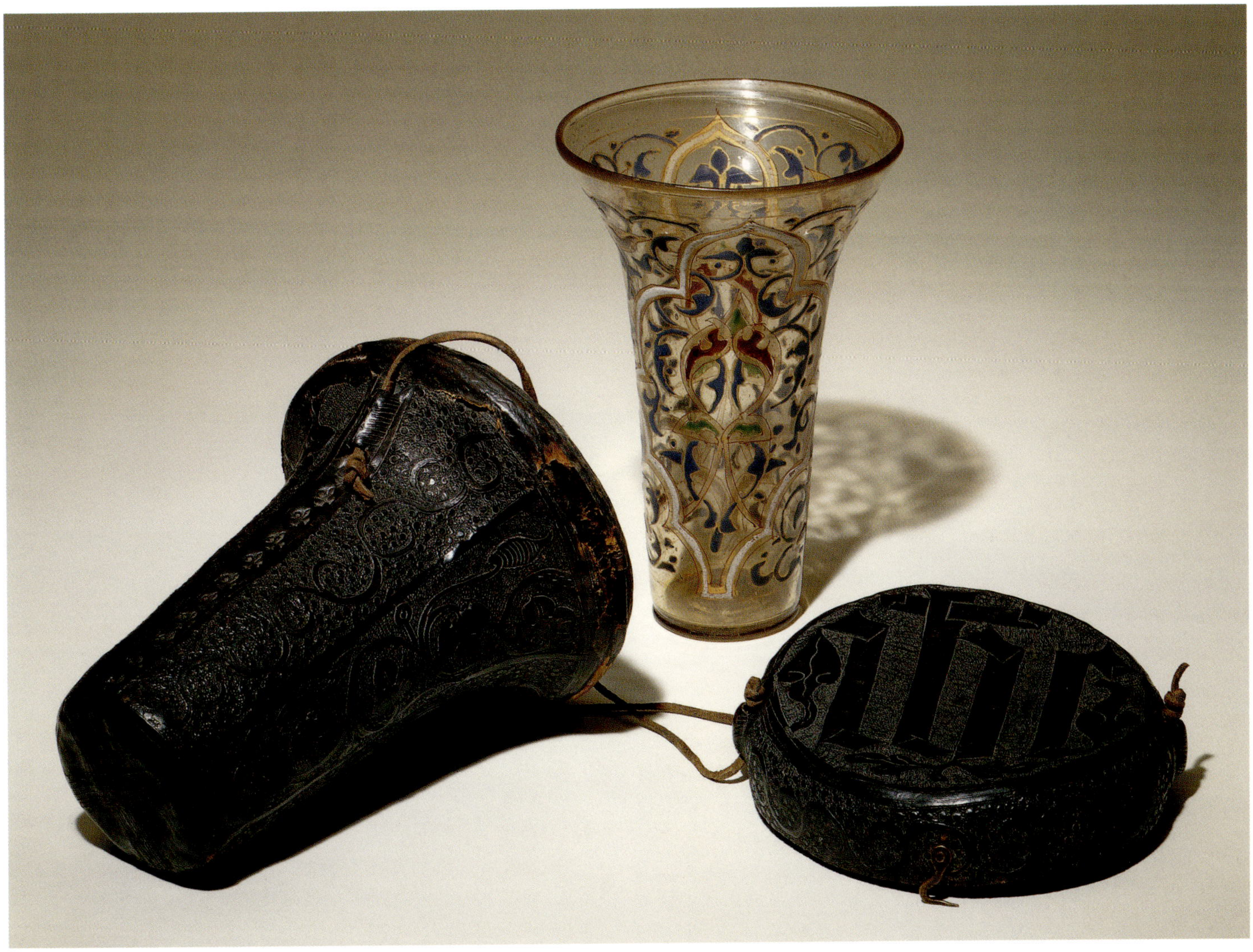

1.18 The 'Luck of Edenhall', Egypt or Syria, 13th century. V&A: C.1–1959 (Purchased with the assistance of the National Art Collections Fund, the Goldsmiths' Company, the Salters' Company, the Drapers' Company and the Merchant Taylors' Company)

In 1987, for example, he bought an outstanding tile-top table from the 1560s (illus. 1.20). This is a rare example of Ottoman court furniture outside the palace collections in Istanbul.

When it opened in 1950, the Islamic gallery in Room 42 was well received, and justifiably so. Ashton gave the Islamic Middle East a prominent place in the Museum, close to the main entrance, and the display methods employed were the best then available to a government institution of relatively modest means. By the time it closed in November 2003, however, the gallery was very dated, both in terms of display and interpretation. Much of it was also plunged in gloom, thanks to a progressive reduction in light levels, while other parts were lit more brightly, but inconsistently, thanks to the natural light spilling over from adjoining galleries and the neon-lit vitrines within the gallery showing pieces that were not light-sensitive (illus. 1.19). The objects on show had received their due share of attention from conservators, but the scruffiness of the display and the numerous dark corners created an overall air of neglect. Many of the framed items in the gallery, including the Ardabil carpet, were barely visible. This kept the carpet safe from fading, but it also defied the purpose of placing it on public view – that it should be seen and admired.

The touring exhibition *Palace and Mosque*, circulated in 2004–6, and the new Jameel Gallery have changed all that. We can now see the V&A's Islamic Middle East collections in all their glory. Light has been shone on these superb objects – at appropriate levels – and the V&A's main gallery of Islamic art is no longer a place just for cognoscenti with flashlights. It is for everyone.

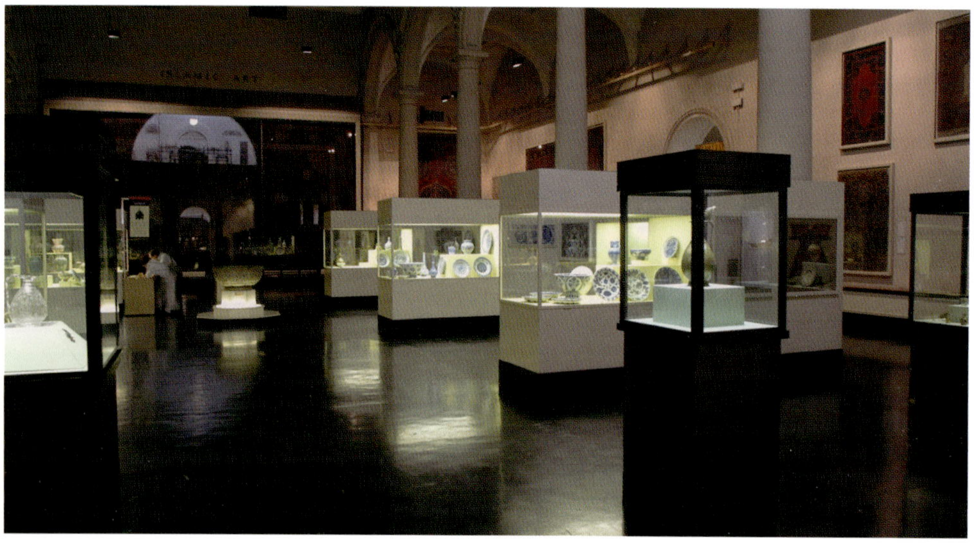

1.19 Room 42 *circa* 2000

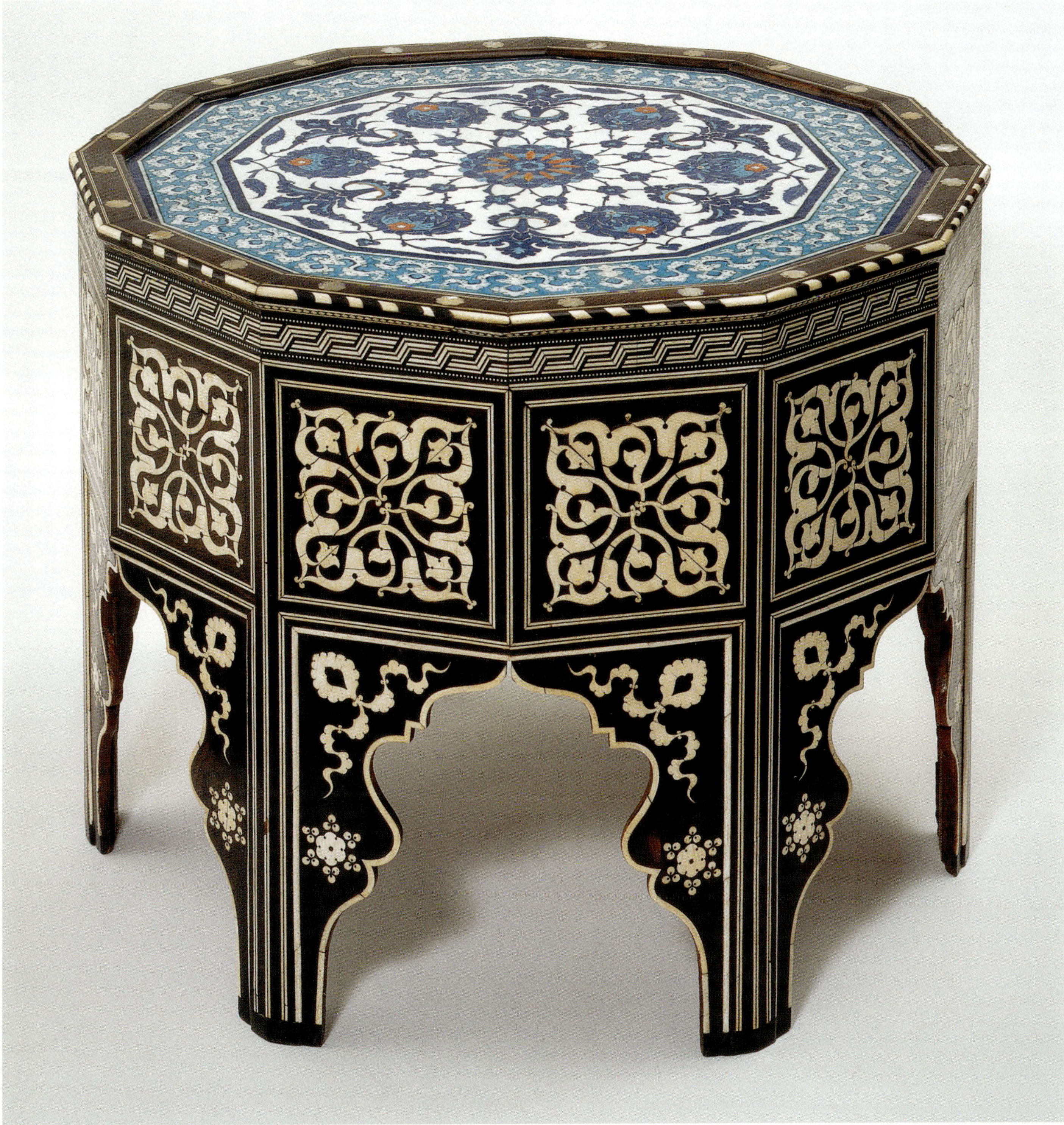

1.20 Ottoman table with tile top, Turkey, *circa* 1560. V&A: C.19–1987

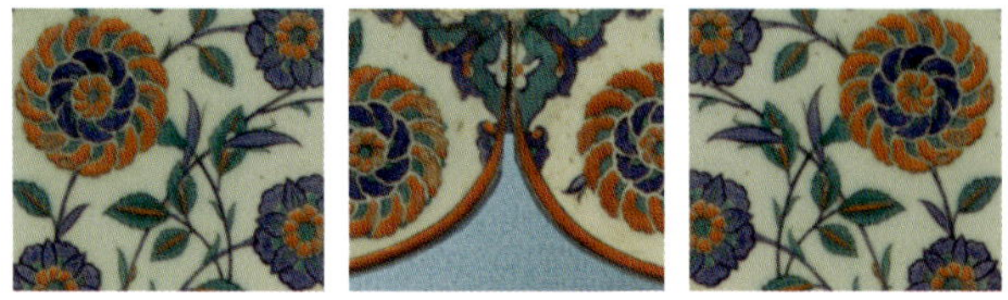

2 *PALACE AND MOSQUE:* THE EXHIBITION

Tim Stanley

The redevelopment of the main Islamic Middle East gallery at the V&A meant that the gallery's contents – the best of the Museum's holdings in this area – were scheduled to disappear from public view for two and a half years, from November 2003 to July 2006. Instead, thanks to the generosity of the gallery's benefactors, the closure provided an opportunity to send an exhibition containing more than a hundred of the best pieces on an international tour. Entitled *Palace and Mosque: Islamic Art from the Victoria and Albert Museum,* the exhibition was designed to introduce the Islamic art of the Middle East, and the wider culture that produced it, to new audiences around the world, and it has now been seen by more than 280,000 visitors in three continents.

The venues

The exhibition was first mooted during discussions with Mohammed Abdul Latif Jameel in the autumn of 2002. By December it was a firm proposal, and early in 2003 work began on creating an exhibition concept and selecting an object list. This work was substantially completed by July 2003. Over the same period, the Museum conducted a search for venues. In the time available – from late summer 2004 to spring 2006 – it was possible to take the exhibition to four different cities. We were

2.1 The 'Mosque, Shrine and Church' section of the exhibition at the Kimbell Art Museum, Fort Worth

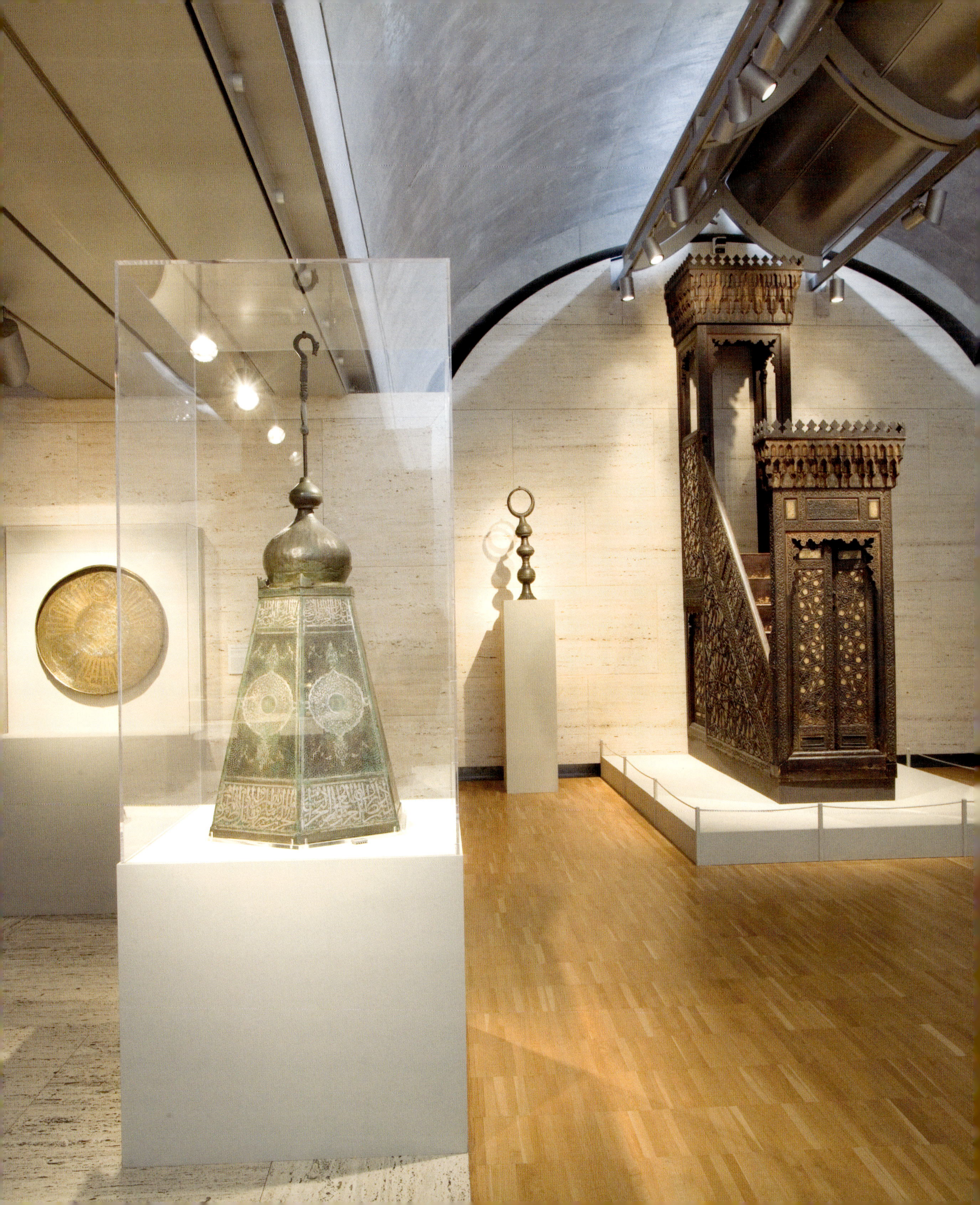

therefore seeking four museums with an exhibition space available during one of four time slots, and it was agreed with the sponsor that these would be distributed between two venues in North America and one venue each in Japan and Europe. Major museums and art galleries generally fix their exhibition schedules several years in advance, but with the prospect of a topical and well-funded exhibition, it was possible to secure an agreement with four venues that fitted the bill.

By mid-2003 we had a firm understanding with the National Gallery of Art in Washington, DC, that it would be the first venue. The NGA's East Building, designed by I.M. Pei and opened in 1978, stands in one of the most prominent sites in the world, at the foot of Capitol Hill, and is Washington's premier venue for art exhibitions. The Gallery is celebrated for its outstanding collection of western painting and sculpture, but it has consistently used its exhibition programme to bring aspects of non-western art to a general audience. A second venue was found in Texas, a state with no public collections of Islamic art to speak of, but with a growing museum culture. The Kimbell Art Museum in Fort Worth, built by another famous architect, Louis Kahn, and opened in 1972, has a small but very impressive collection of art, principally from Europe and Asia, but no Islamic pieces.

The importance of the United States as a venue for exhibitions on Islamic themes is self-evident, given the intensity of the country's involvement in the Middle East, and the negative image that Islam has acquired, especially since the attacks on New York and Washington on 11 September 2001. The Jameel family's long-standing business and personal connections with Japan meant that they were equally aware of the lack of familiarity with Islamic culture there. At the same time, the V&A has a long tradition of sending touring exhibitions to that country, often in collaboration with the Tokyo-based newspaper *Yomiuri Shimbun*. On this occasion the newspaper secured a venue at the Setagaya Art Museum in its home city. The museum, which opened in 1986, had received two exhibitions of the ancient art of the Middle East in recent years. *Palace and Mosque* extended this informal programme into the Islamic period. It was also the first exhibition on Islamic art held in Japan that covered such a wide timespan, geographical extent and range of materials.

The choice of the final venue, the Millennium Galleries in Sheffield, arose out of the partnership that the V&A has had with its parent body, the Sheffield Galleries and Museums Trust, since 1999. The V&A assisted in the development of the Millennium Galleries, which opened in April 2001, and in the temporary exhibition programme subsequently organized there. In Sheffield, too, *Palace and*

Mosque was the first general exhibition of Islamic art, and the first exhibition of any sort on an Islamic theme for 30 years.

At the Millennium Galleries, *Palace and Mosque* came home in a spectacular manner. It was opened by David Lammy, MP, the British Minister for Culture. The following week it was visited by HRH The Prince of Wales. It also formed the centrepiece of a Yorkshire-wide festival devoted to Muslim culture, called *Pillars of Light*. As a result of these and other events, the show received four times the press coverage that had been given to any other exhibition at the Galleries. Visitor numbers surged to almost double the projected figures, and there were a huge number of group visits by schools and community organizations. This provided a fitting prelude to the opening of the Jameel Gallery itself.

PALACE AND MOSQUE:
ISLAMIC ART FROM THE VICTORIA AND ALBERT MUSEUM

The National Gallery of Art, Washington, DC	18 July 2004 – 6 February 2005
The Kimbell Art Museum, Fort Worth, Texas	3 April – 4 September 2005
The Setagaya Art Museum, Setagaya-ku, Tokyo	1 October – 4 December 2005
The Millennium Galleries, Sheffield, Yorkshire	14 January – 16 April 2006

Palace and Mosque at the National Gallery of Art

The creation of the exhibition occurred in two main stages. First, the basic themes and the object list were drafted at the V&A. Then these were adapted to the needs of the first venue at the National Gallery of Art. Although further adaptations were required as the exhibition moved from venue to venue, it was in this shift from curatorial concept to practical design, accomplished through the collaboration of the curator at the V&A and the exhibition staff at the NGA, that the exhibition crystallized into its constituent parts. The original scheme survives unamended in the book *Palace and Mosque: Islamic Art from the Middle East*, which was published to coincide with the opening of the exhibition in July 2004. The book was not designed as the standard type of exhibition catalogue, as it had a wider purpose. In 2004–6 it provided a supplement to an exhibition visit by offering an introduction to the subject of Islamic art. After the exhibition closed, however, it became the V&A's 'gallery book' on Islamic art, to be available as further reading on the collections shown in the Jameel Gallery.

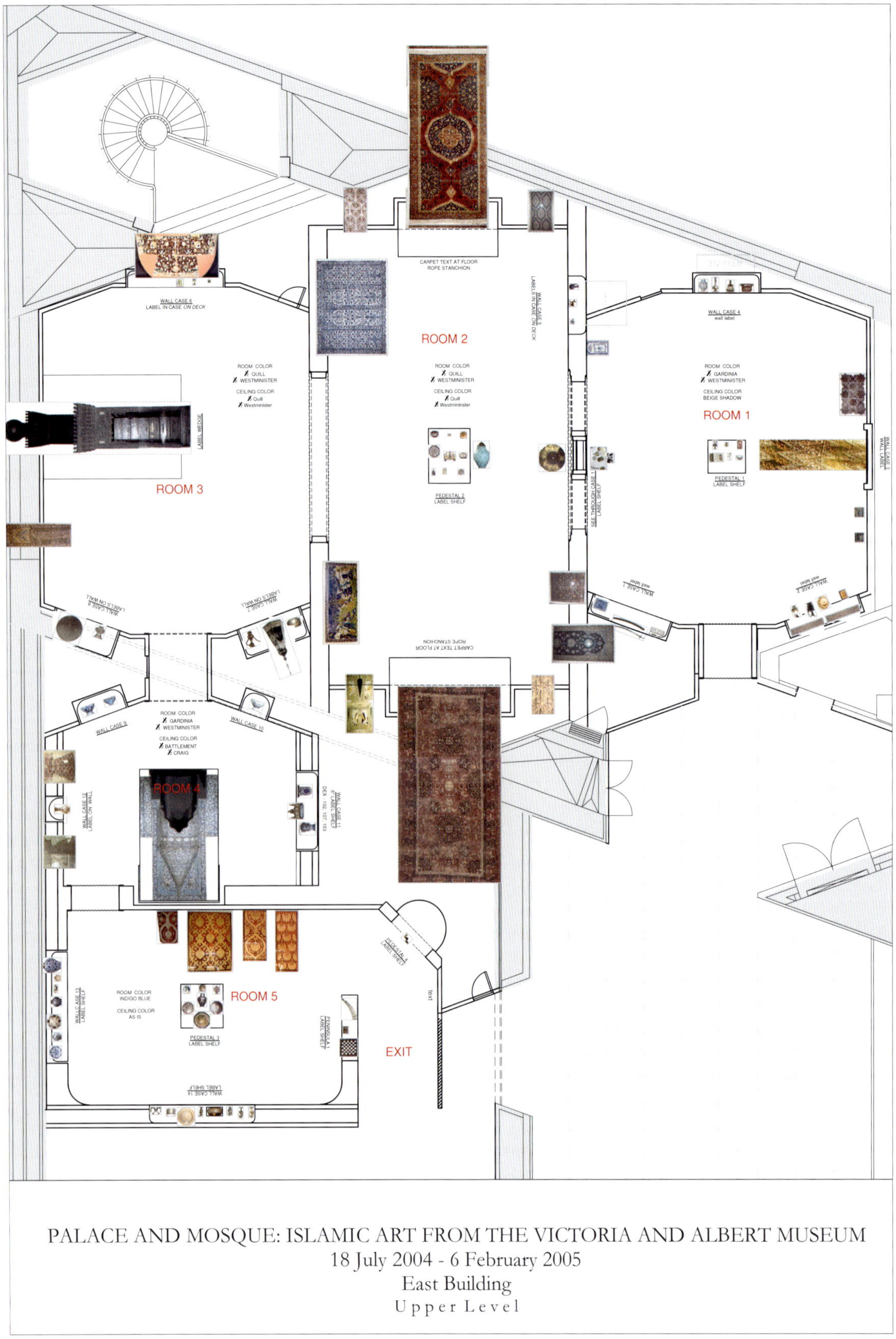

2.2 Plan of *Palace and Mosque* at the National Gallery of Art, Washington, DC

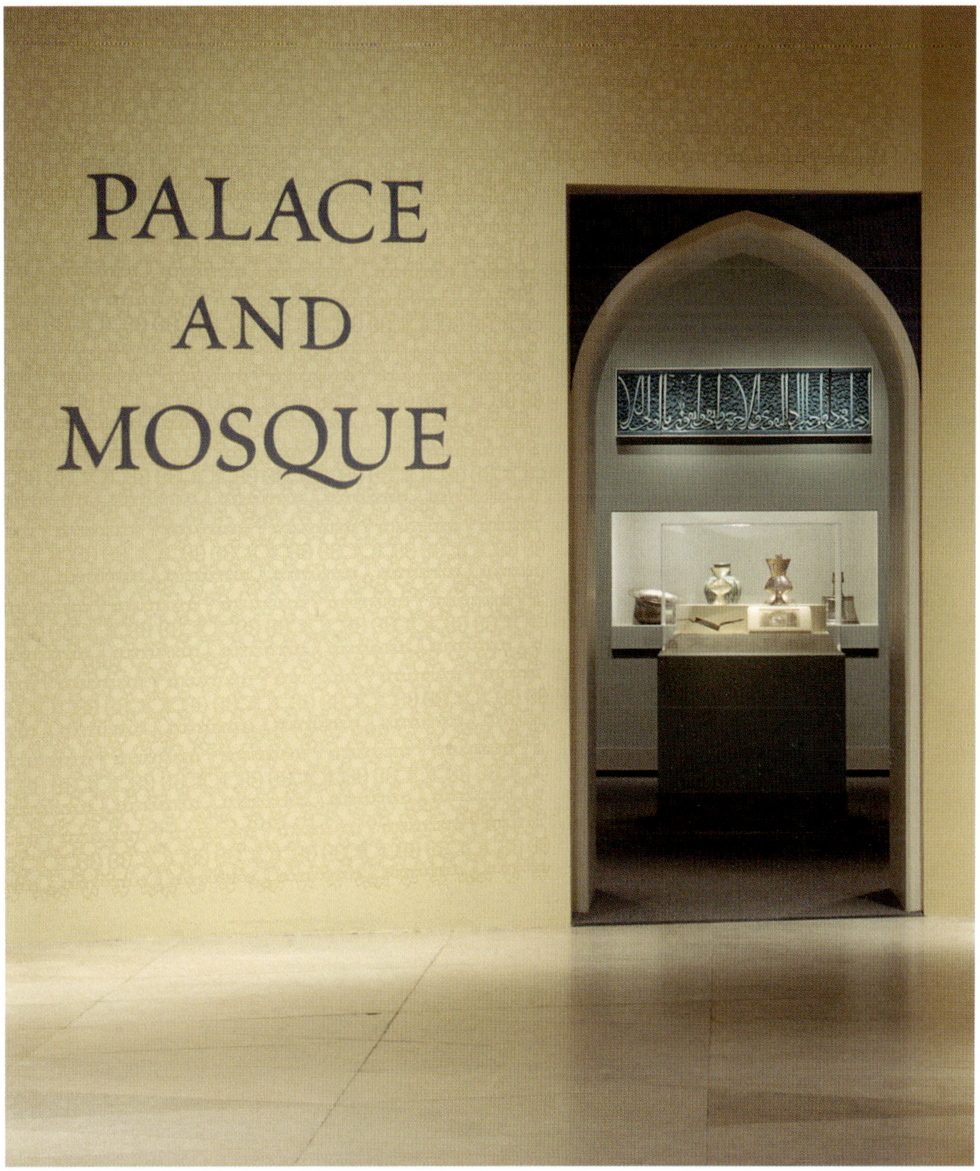

2.3 The entrance to *Palace and Mosque* at the National Gallery of Art

At the NGA, the exhibition was divided between five rooms (illus. 2.2). These were constructed especially for *Palace and Mosque*, because I.M. Pei's building provides an empty but very flexible shell around the exhibition spaces. It was therefore possible to accommodate the largest piece in the show, the minbar of Sultan Qa'itbay, at full height and in a setting spacious enough for it to assume the same relationship to its surroundings as it would have had in the building for which it was originally made (illus. 2.6). The approach to it was opened up by arches suggestive of those in a Mamluk building, allowing it to form the focal point of the first half of the exhibition, intended to draw visitors into the show (illus. 2.4, 2.5).

Much the same was done for the monumental tilework chimney-piece from eighteenth-century Istanbul, which was displayed in the next room (illus. 2.7). On the other hand, the other two oversized pieces, the Chelsea and Ushak carpets, were shown face to face, as they were there to demonstrate the contrast between Safavid and Ottoman dynastic styles in the sixteenth and seventeenth centuries (illus. 2.5). The V&A's Islamic collection is unusually rich in such large items, as well as in small but exquisite objects, such as carved ivory caskets. This allowed for variety in the presentation, as the visitor passed from the dense displays of small items at the beginning, through rooms dominated by large objects, back into the denser displays at the end.

2.4 View from Room 1 through to Room 3 at the National Gallery of Art

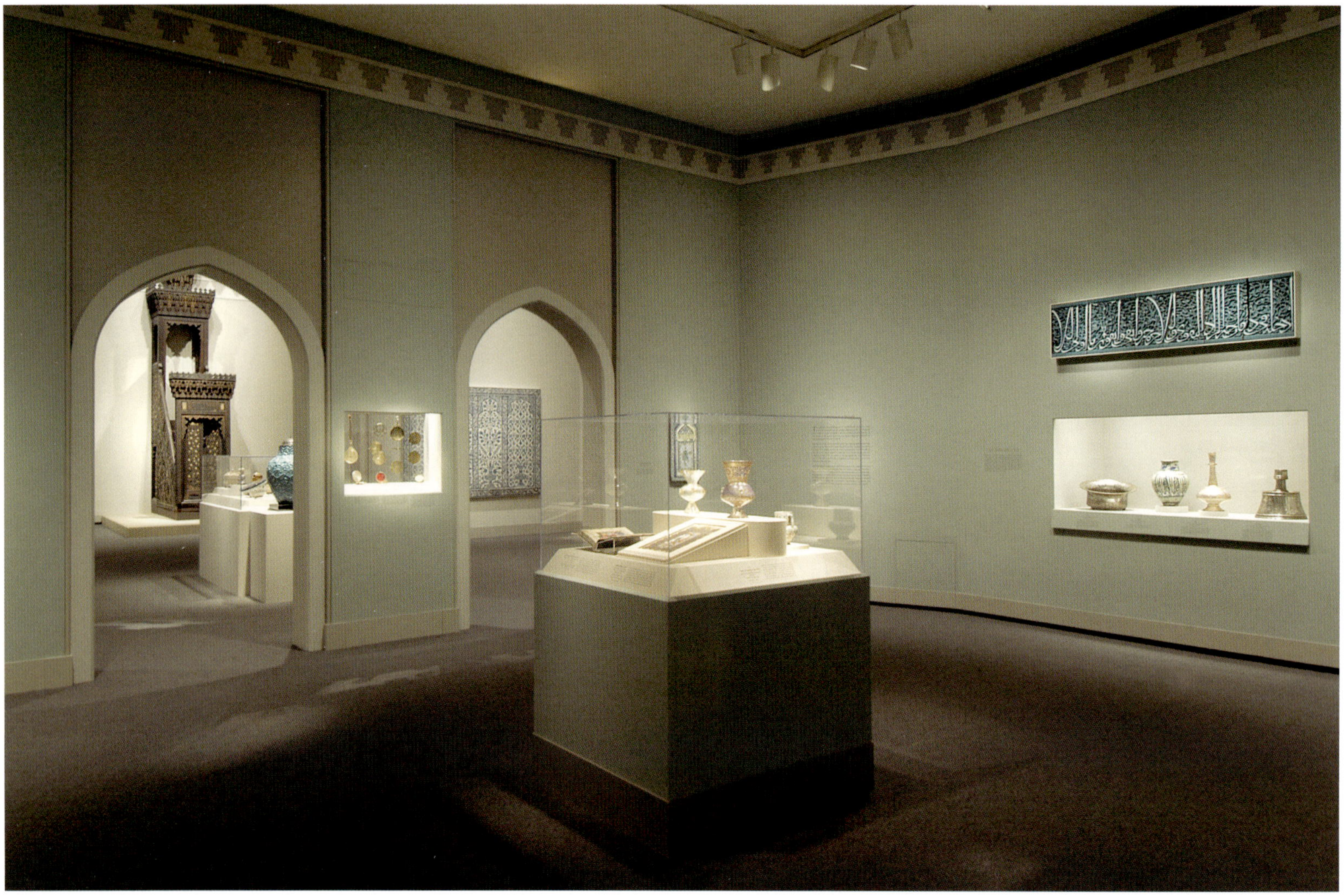

Words and pictures

The first room (illus. 2.4), which served as an introduction to the show, dealt with three separate but interconnected themes under the titles 'The Written Word', 'The Human Figure' and 'The Ka'bah'. 'The Written Word' was concerned with the use of Arabic calligraphy as a form of ornament. This is one of several features that distinguish Islamic art from its predecessors and its contemporaries, and it is the easiest to comprehend visually. The display included Qur'an manuscripts of the twelfth to seventeenth centuries and two architectural friezes from religious buildings, which have inscriptions composed of quotations from the Qur'an. Not all inscriptions in Arabic are quotations from such religious texts, however, and secular objects were shown that were also decorated with predominantly calligraphic ornament. The most important of these was a group of four large Mamluk pieces in different media – ceramics, glass and metalwork – in which large secular inscriptions in fine calligraphy can be seen as part of a dynastic style.

The display in Room 1 also challenged one of the great misconceptions about Islamic art, namely, that it does not permit the use of the human figure. Two paintings from a manuscript from seventeenth-century Isfahan were shown in the central case, providing a dramatic visual contrast with the sober copies of the Qur'an in the cases opposite; and the same contrast was illustrated by pairs of objects from secular and religious contexts, with figurative and non-figurative decoration, as appropriate.

The third theme dealt with in Room 1 concerned geography and science and how they relate to Islam as a religion. The sacred geography of Islam was illustrated by a seventeenth-century Ottoman tile painted with a diagram of the Noble Sanctuary in Mecca, and by three compasses from nineteenth-century Iran that were specially adapted to show the direction of prayer (towards the Ka'bah in Mecca) from different cities. The more sophisticated types of scientific instrument used by Muslims to establish the direction of the Ka'bah and to set the time of the daily prayers was represented by two planispheric astrolabes, which were mounted on a perspex screen, with one dismantled and the other set up for use.

'Courts and Courtiers'

In the second room (illus. 2.5), the theme of figurative art was dealt with in three ways. First, examples of small figures in the round were shown, all functional objects such as flower vases and water pipes. Second, it was also demonstrated that the use of human figures in decoration reflected the subject matter of Arabic and

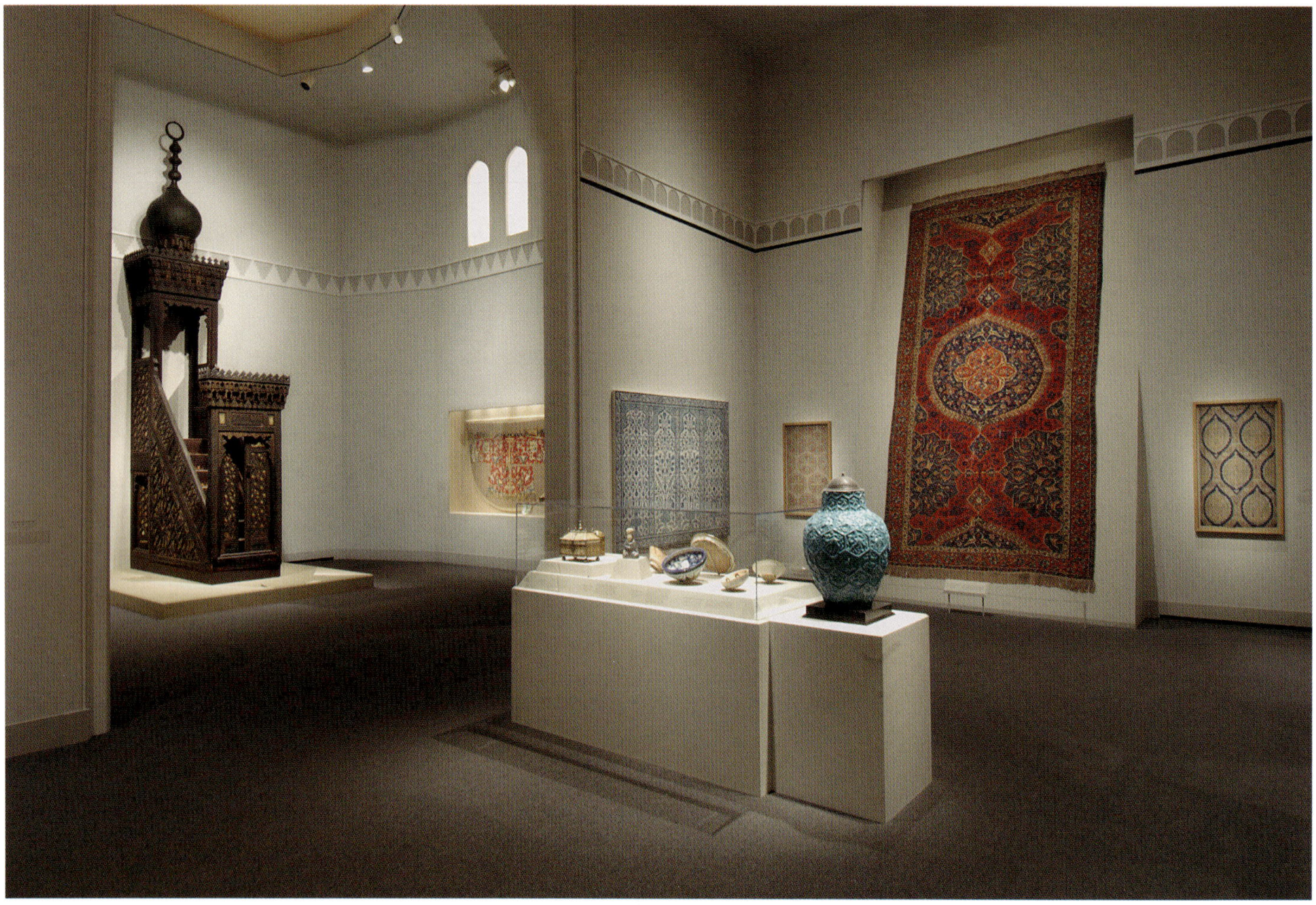

2.5 Room 2 at the National Gallery of Art

Persian poetry, especially that written at court. Examples were provided by the figurative designs on some of the V&A's collection of precious ivory caskets from tenth- and eleventh-century Spain. The verse current at a more popular level was represented by the quatrains on mystic love that appear on ceramics made in Kashan in Iran in the late twelfth and early thirteenth centuries.

The room was dominated, however, by two enormous carpets, the 'medallion Ushak' from Ottoman Turkey and the so-called Chelsea carpet from Safavid Iran. They were accompanied by tile panels and silk textiles produced in these two great empires in the sixteenth and seventeenth centuries. Many of the Safavid pieces were decorated with figurative designs, but these were completely absent from the Ottoman examples. This showed that in different times and at different places the attitude among Muslims towards the use of images varied a great deal.

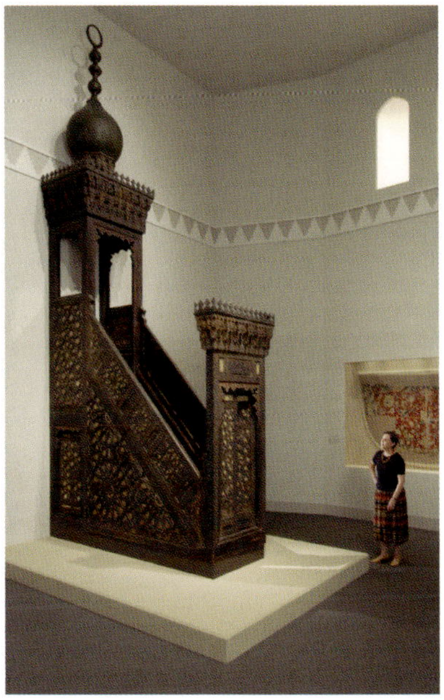

2.6 Room 3 at the National Gallery of Art

'Mosque, Shrine and Church'

The third room (illus. 2.6) was designed to accommodate the minbar that Sultan Qa'itbay had made for an important mosque somewhere in his empire. Other examples of purely religious art, such as a tilework tomb cover made of three enormous tiles from a shrine in Iran, were shown beside it, as were several examples of Islamic art made for Christian churches. These included the Isfahan cope, a spectacular if fragmentary semicircular vestment made for an Armenian church in that city. The population of the Middle East in the Islamic period was never entirely Muslim, and the Christian, Jewish and Zoroastrian subjects of Islamic rulers often played an important role in the design and production of what we call Islamic art. Indeed, in many cases the art made for these groups, even for their places of worship, cannot be distinguished in stylistic terms from the art made for Muslims.

The minbar was also the centrepiece of another theme in this room, namely, the role of individual patrons in shaping the development of Islamic art. The sultan who commissioned the minbar, Qa'itbay (ruled 1468–96), was the third and last great patron of the Mamluk period in Egypt and Syria (1250–1517), and the V&A also owns a group of three spectacular inlaid metalwork items made for Qa'itbay and his wife, which were displayed together (illus. 2.7).

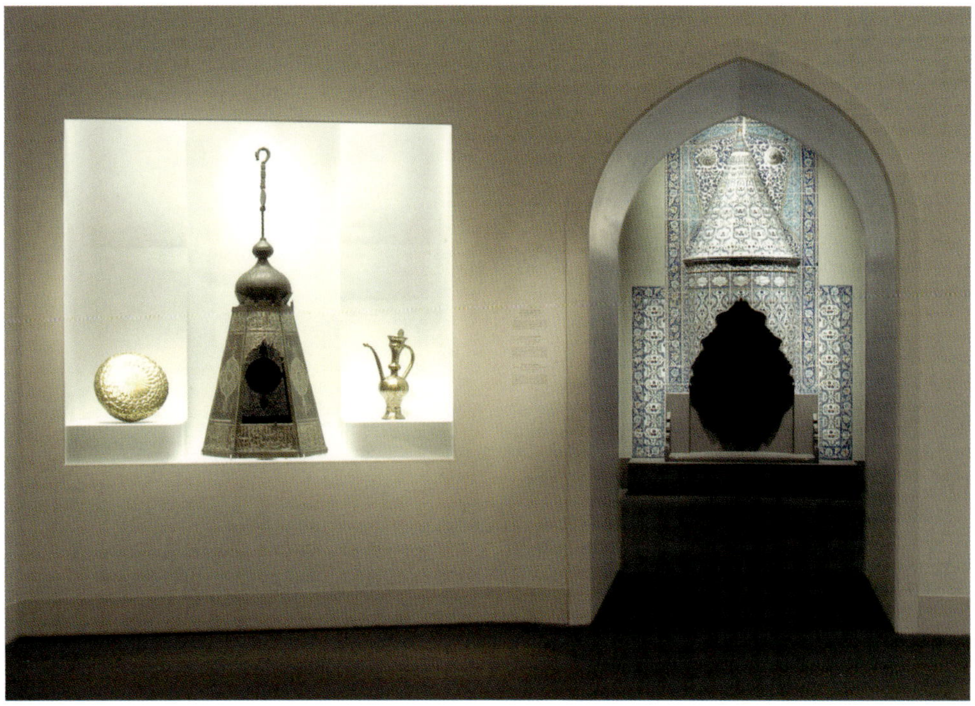

2.7 View from Room 3 into Room 4 at the National Gallery of Art

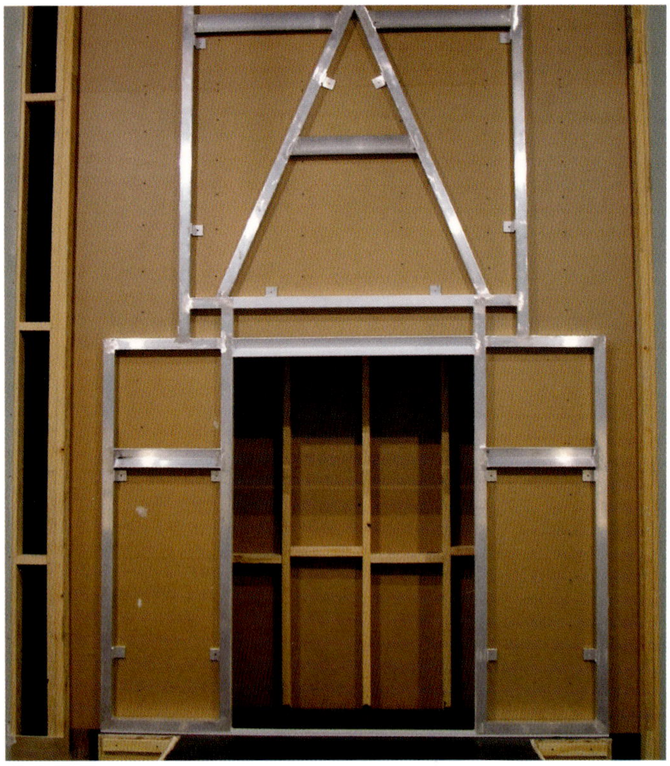

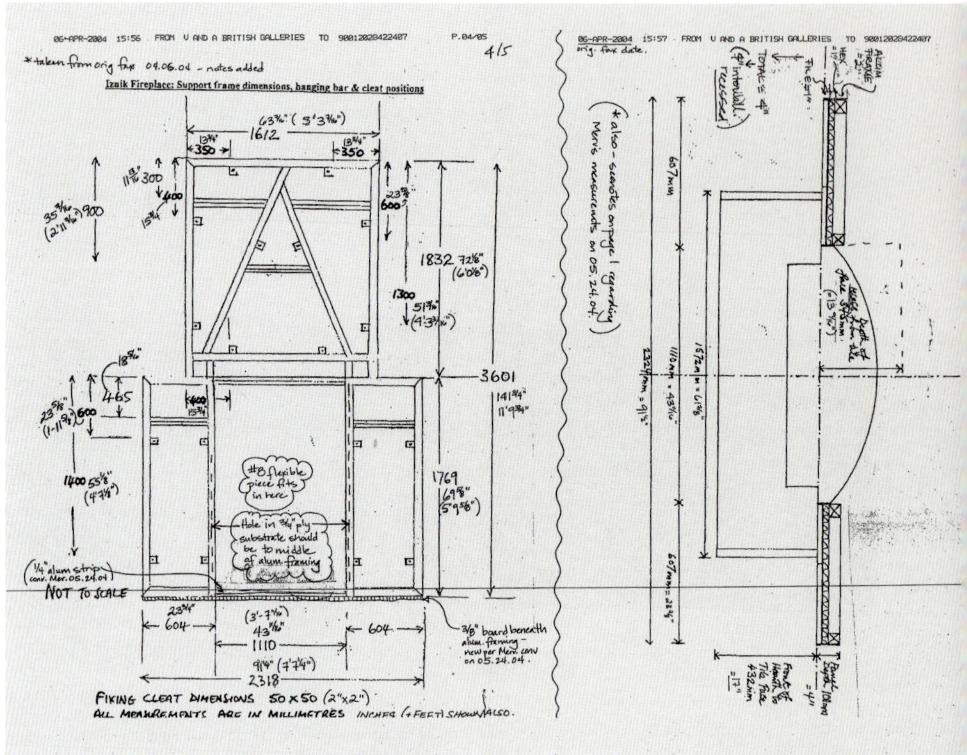

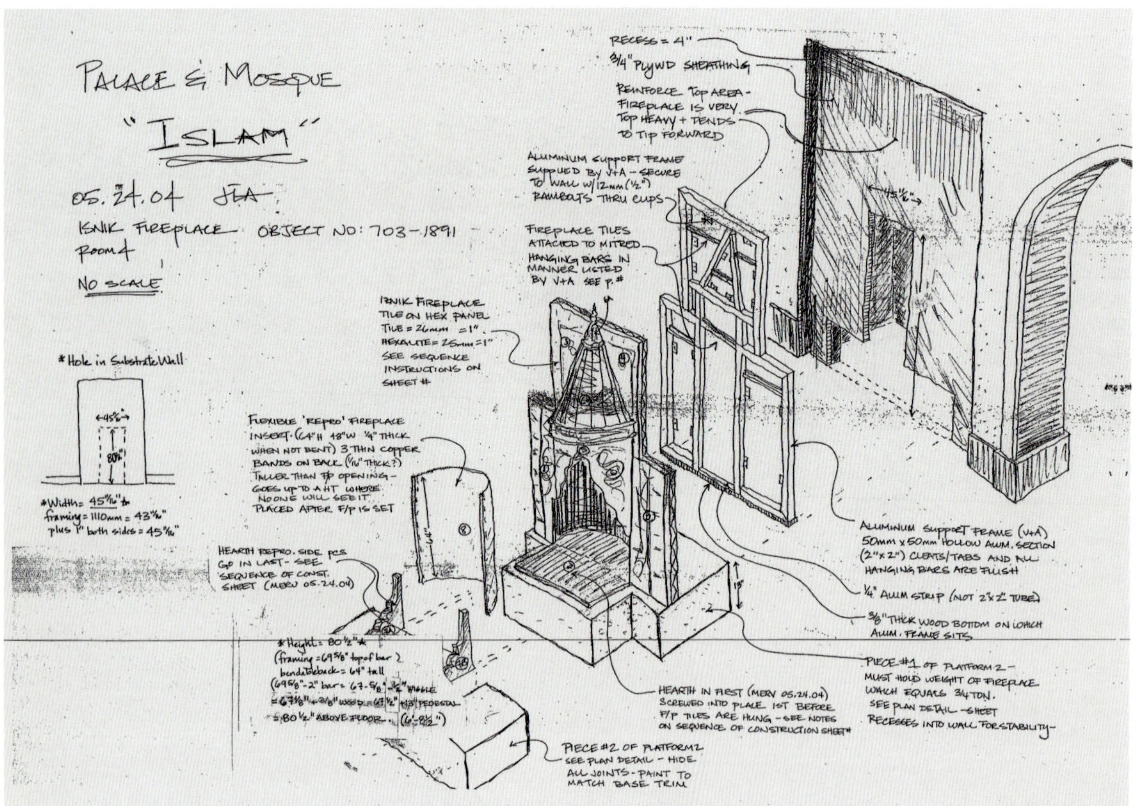

2.8 (*above left*) The framework for the Ottoman chimney-piece at the National Gallery of Art. V&A: 703–1891

2.9/2.10 (*above and left*) Sketches for the installation of the Ottoman chimney-piece at the National Gallery of Art

2.11 (*above right*) Unpacking the hood of the chimney-piece at the Kimbell Art Museum

2.12 (*right*) Installation of the chimney-piece at the Kimbell Art Museum

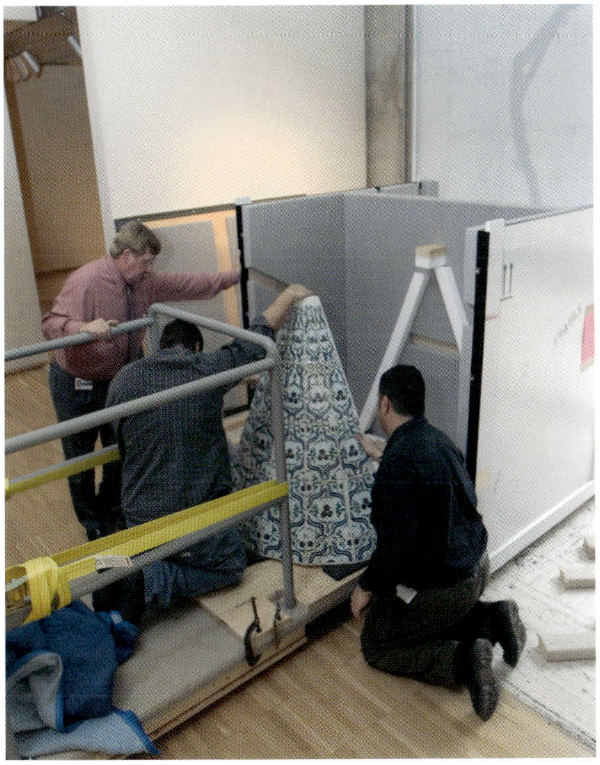

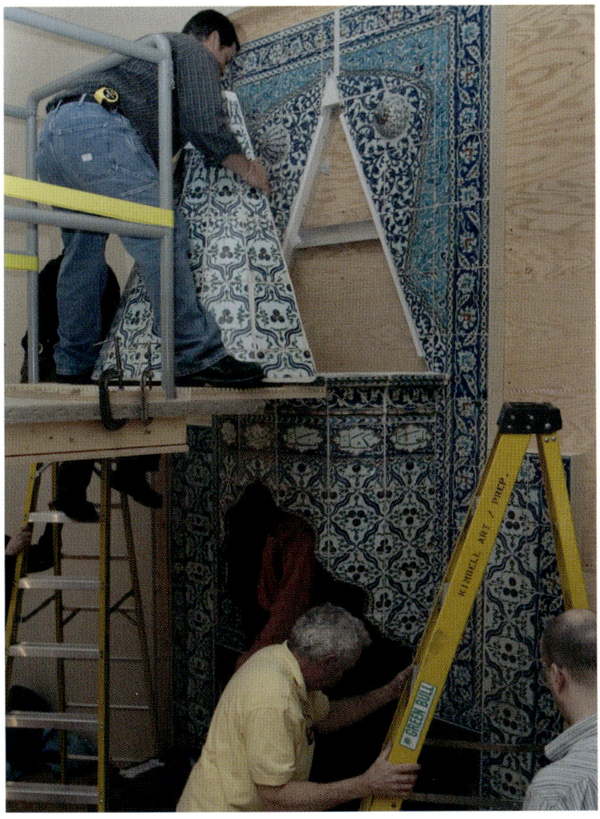

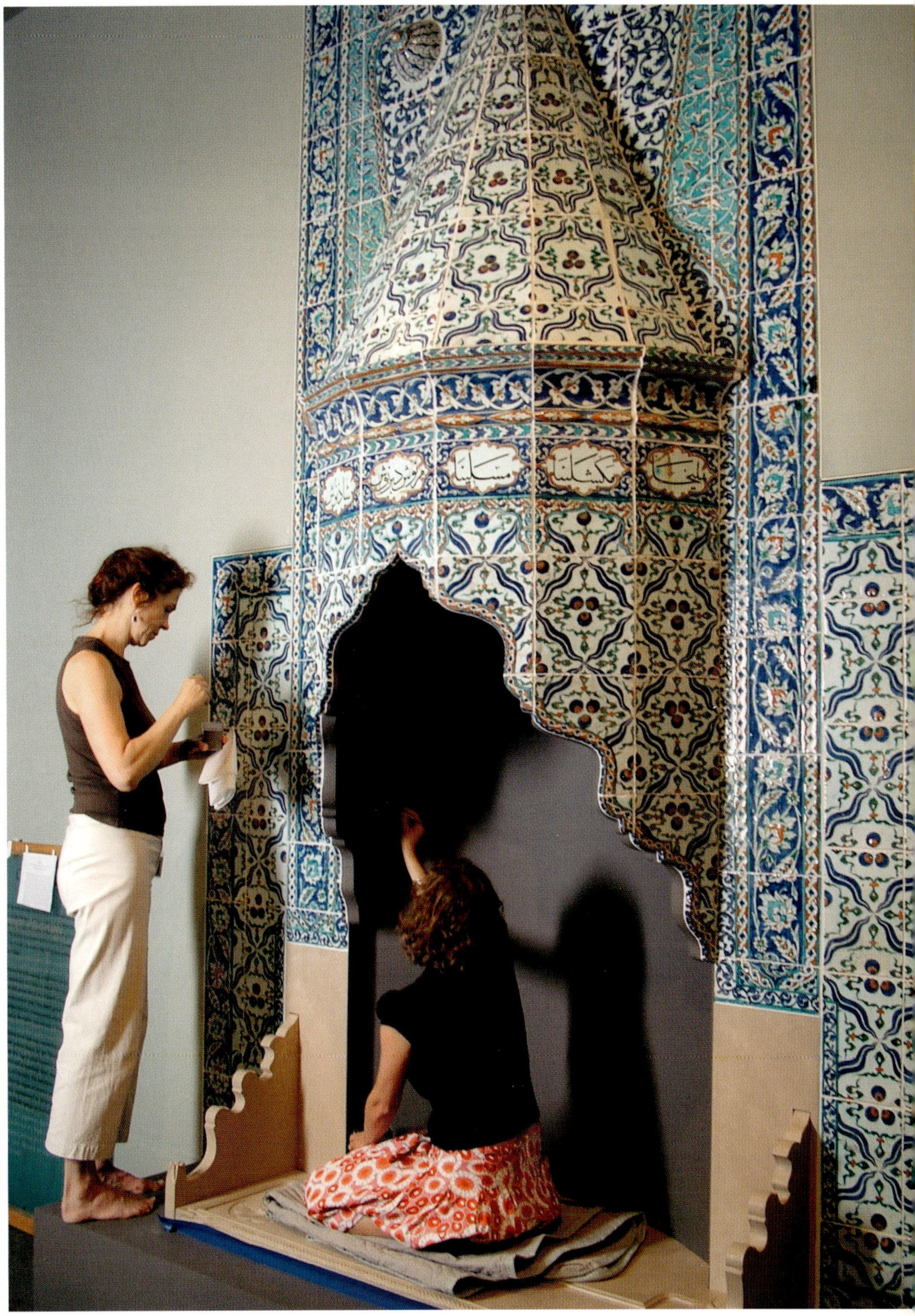

2.13 Putting finishing touches to the chimney-piece at the National Gallery of Art

'Ottoman Patronage'

The high point in the development of Islamic ceramics were the pottery and tiles produced at kilns in the small town of Iznik and at other sites in Turkey from the later fifteenth century. This is also the only ceramic ware for which imperial patronage is documented, and the V&A's magnificent collection of these pieces allowed us to show the impact of court patronage on this art form. Only one vessel of normal size was shown, and this object (a vase) is of outstanding quality, especially in terms of the adaptation of the theme of spring flowers in full bloom to its rounded form (illus. 2.14). The remainder were large pieces, such as three huge footed bowls, two of which were bequeathed to the Museum by George Salting (illus. 1.11, 1.12) and the tile-top table bought in 1987 (illus. 1.20). The largest item of all in this room, and the visual focus of this section of the exhibition, was the V&A's tilework chimney-piece, which was made in Istanbul in 1731 and was reportedly rescued from the palace of Fuat Pasha in the same city some time in the nineteenth century (illus. 2.13).

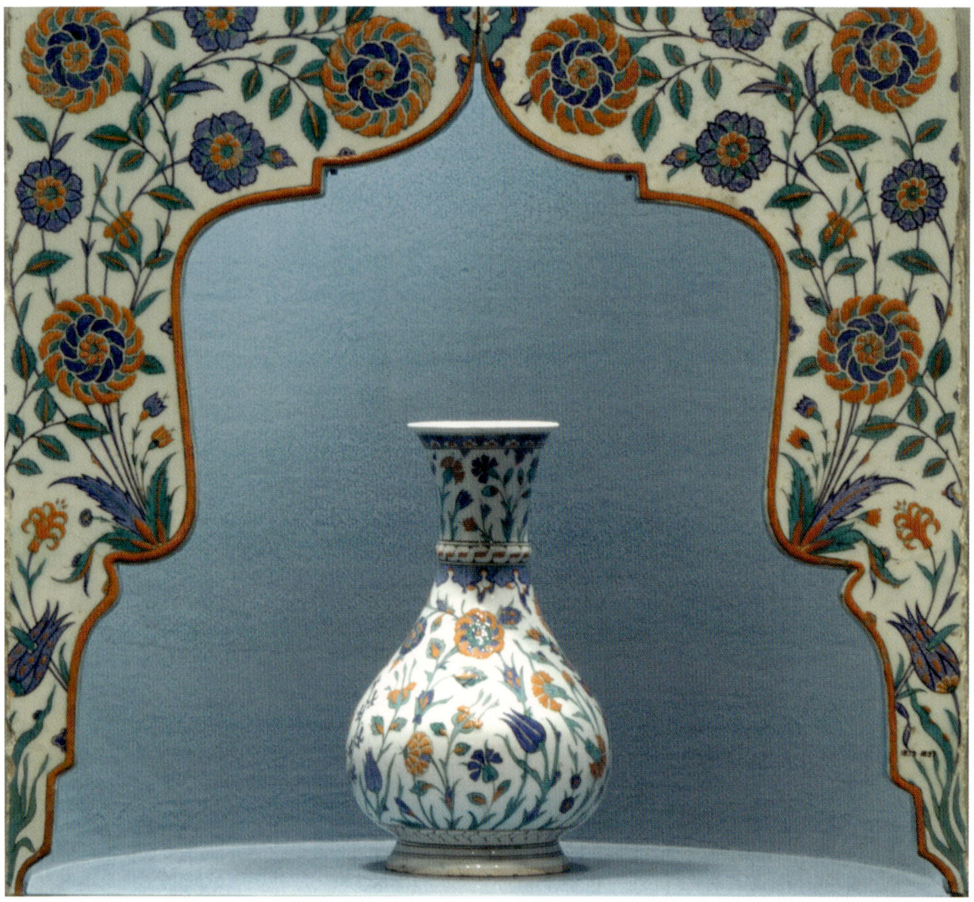

2.14 Ottoman vase and niche tiles in Room 4 at the National Gallery of Art. V&A: 232–1876, 1879–1897

'Interaction'

The final room of the exhibition (illus. 2.15) was dedicated to the interchange in artistic ideas between the Islamic Middle East and other regions that were not under Muslim rule. Relations with China were represented by the story of blue-and-white ceramics. Blue-and-white decoration was a Middle Eastern idea, and examples were produced there as early as the ninth century AD. The breakthrough came in fourteenth-century China, however, when the makers of porcelain mastered underglaze painting in cobalt. Imitations of blue-and-white then became an important part of Middle Eastern ceramic production, right down to the seventeenth century.

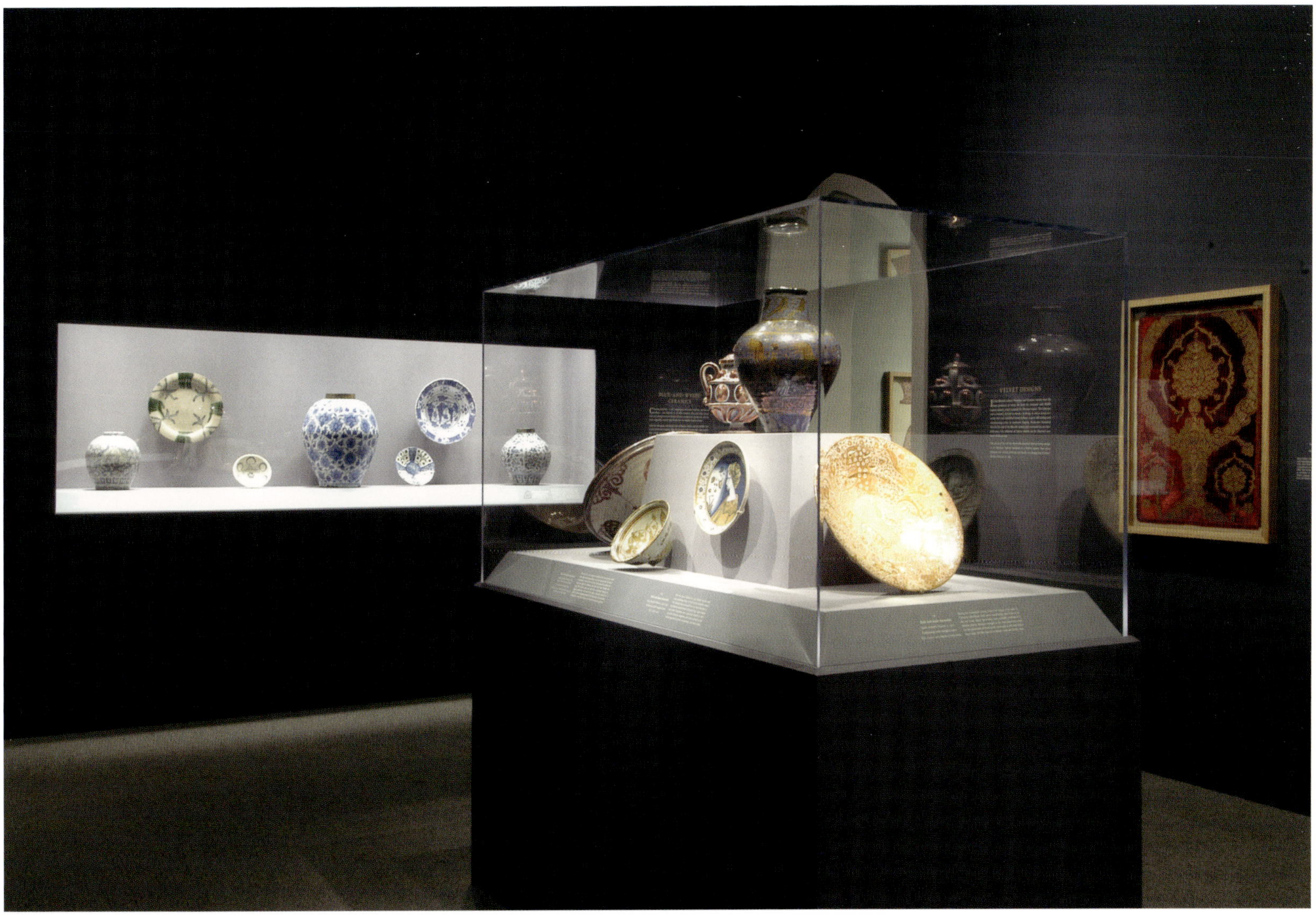

2.15 Room 5 at the National Gallery of Art

Interaction between Muslim-ruled territories around the Mediterranean and their European neighbours was also an important part of the history of art in the Middle East, and several examples from the fifteenth and sixteenth centuries were chosen for illustration. One thread was the development of the lustre technique, by which a thin layer of reflective metal was applied over glazed vessels, as was its transmission from the Middle East, where it was invented, to Islamic Spain and then to Italy, where it became a feature of ceramic production in the Renaissance. The reverse process happened in the case of velvets. Italian velvet designs were copied by weavers in Bursa in Turkey in the fifteenth and sixteenth centuries, and a sequence of four large examples with gold designs on a red ground showed how the Italian designs were first imitated literally and then adapted to Turkish taste. Objects in metal, ivory and wood showed interaction in both directions, across the boundary between Muslim- and Christian-ruled Spain, from Northern Europe to Ottoman Turkey, and from Egypt or Syria to Italy.

This rich combination of Middle Eastern, European and Chinese pieces culminated in the Luck of Edenhall, a thirteenth-century glass beaker from Egypt or Syria (illus. 1.18), which came to England at an early date and was provided with a leather case decorated with Christian symbols. The beaker was preserved by the Musgrave family of Edenhall in Cumberland, in the north of England, and eventually a very romantic legend about its origins grew up. It was, we are told, abandoned by fairies who were disturbed while picnicking at a fountain. As they fled, they cried, 'If this cup should break or fall, farewell the luck of Edenhall!'

Adapting the concept

The overall themes of the exhibition, and even individual groups of objects, were maintained as the show passed from venue to venue. Nevertheless, as has already been noted, it was necessary to adapt the scheme for each new museum. While the exhibition space in Washington was infinitely malleable, that in Fort Worth was not. Temporary walls and cases could be constructed, but the overall dimensions of the rooms were fixed, the most significant being the ceiling height, at 6.09 metres. On the other hand, the Kimbell Art Museum's walls of travertine marble provided

2.16 The 'Ottoman Patronage' section of the exhibition at the Kimbell Art Museum

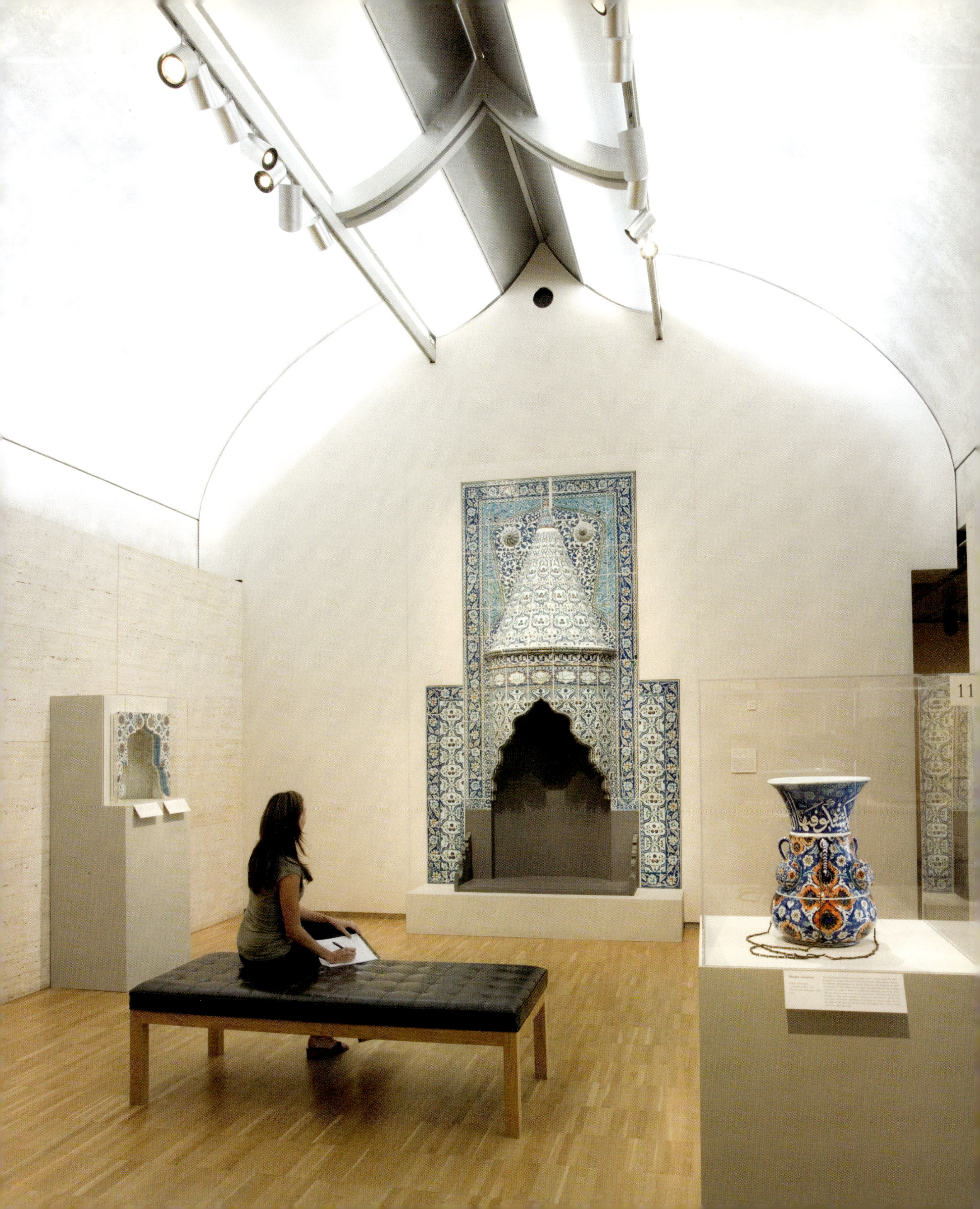
11

a superb backdrop to the show, as their rich but restrained tones of brown flattered the V&A's pieces (illus. 2.1, 2.16, 2.17, 2.19). A decision was made to take many of the pieces out of their groups and treat them as individual masterpieces, which gave this realization of the show a different and often very striking character. The Kimbell and the remaining two venues also accepted a number of pieces excluded from the NGA. Some were small, such as a group of shoes and shoe-like objects, but they also included four of the V&A's large oil paintings from nineteenth-century Iran (illus. 2.20). These, too, added to the richness of the display.

2.18 Plan of *Palace and Mosque* at the Kimbell Art Museum

2.17 The 'Interaction' section of the exhibition at the Kimbell Art Museum

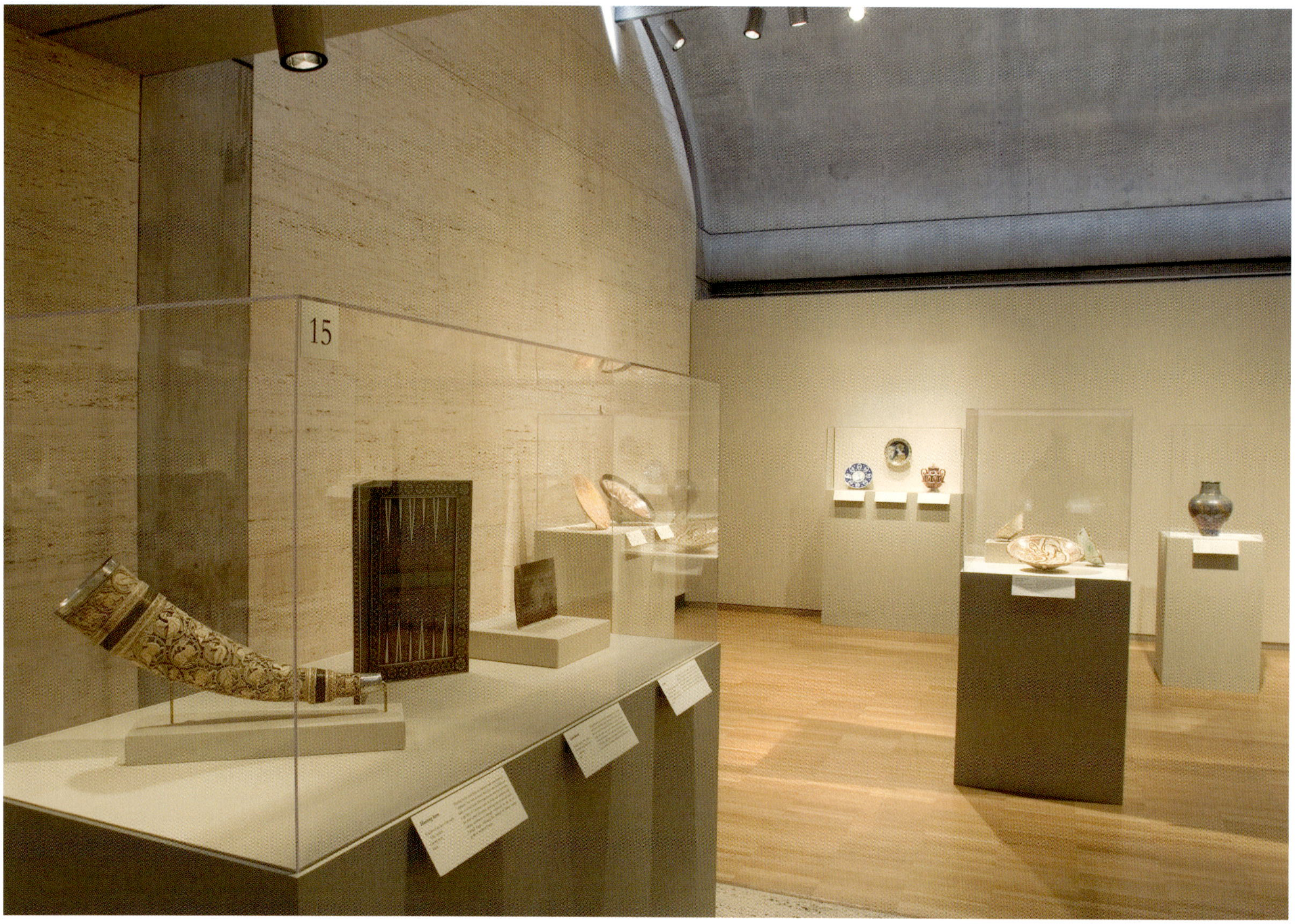

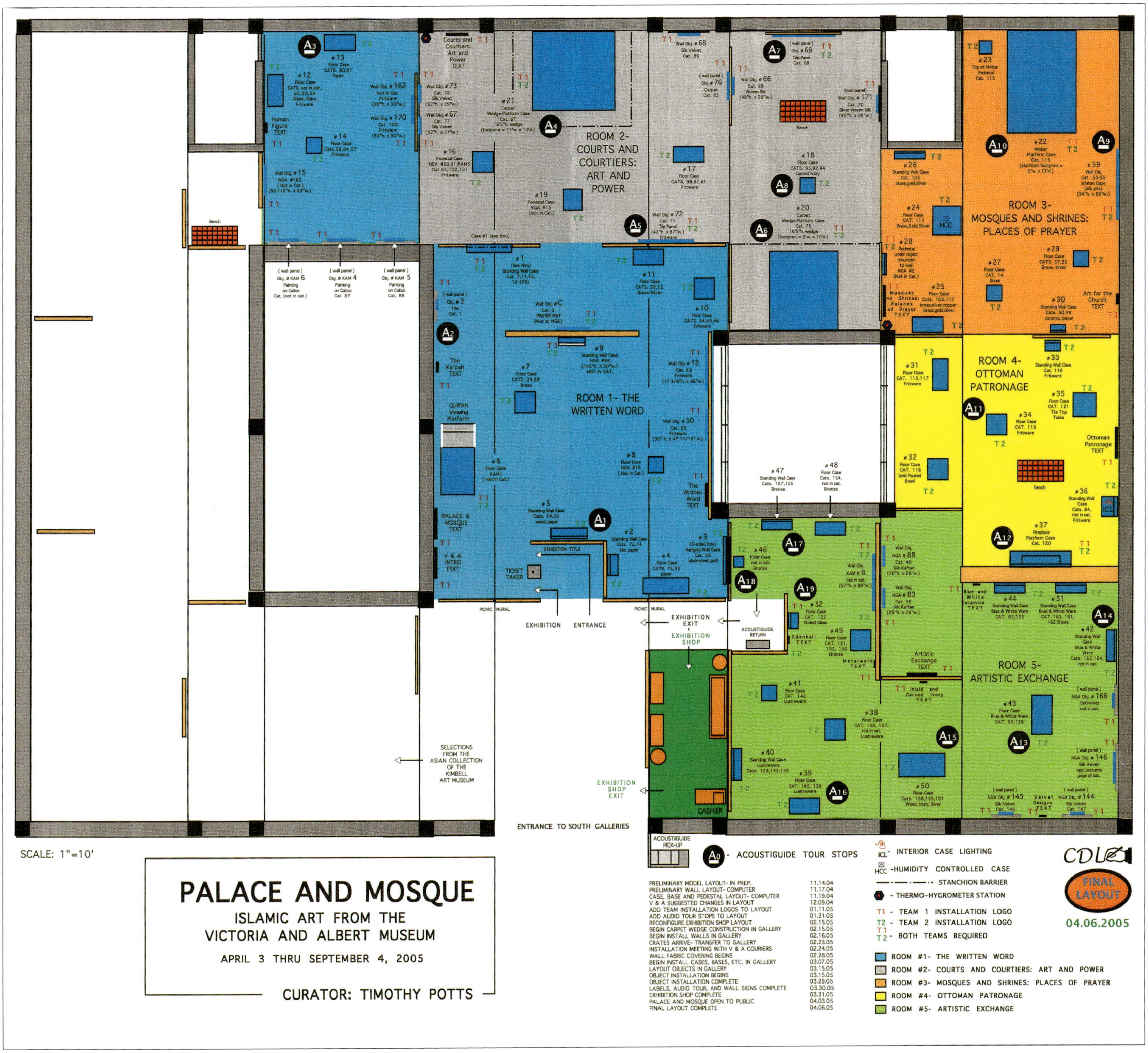
ROOM 1- THE WRITTEN WORD
ROOM 2- COURTS AND COURTIERS: ART AND POWER
ROOM 3- MOSQUES AND SHRINES: PLACES OF PRAYER
ROOM 4- OTTOMAN PATRONAGE
ROOM 5- ARTISTIC EXCHANGE
EXHIBITION
ENTRANCE
EXHIBITION EXIT
EXHIBITION SHOP
EXHIBITION SHOP EXIT
CASHIER
ENTRANCE TO SOUTH GALLERIES
SELECTIONS FROM THE ASIAN COLLECTION OF THE KIMBELL ART MUSEUM
SCALE: 1"=10'
PALACE AND MOSQUE
ISLAMIC ART FROM THE VICTORIA AND ALBERT MUSEUM
APRIL 3 THRU SEPTEMBER 4, 2005
CURATOR: TIMOTHY POTTS
ACOUSTIGUIDE PICK-UP
A0 - ACOUSTIGUIDE TOUR STOPS
PRELIMINARY MODEL LAYOUT- IN PREP. 11.14.04
PRELIMINARY WALL LAYOUT- COMPUTER 11.17.04
CASE, BASE AND PEDESTAL LAYOUT- COMPUTER 11.19.04
V & A SUGGESTED CHANGES IN LAYOUT 12.09.04
ADD TEAM INSTALLATION LOGOS TO LAYOUT 01.11.05
ADD AUDIO TOUR STOPS TO LAYOUT 01.31.05
RECONFIGURE EXHIBITION SHOP LAYOUT 02.15.05
BEGIN CARPET WEDGE CONSTRUCTION IN GALLERY 02.15.05
BEGIN INSTALL WALLS IN GALLERY 02.16.05
CRATES ARRIVE- TRANSFER TO GALLERY 02.23.05
INSTALLATION MEETING WITH V & A COURIERS 02.24.05
WALL FABRIC COVERING BEGINS 02.28.05
BEGIN INSTALL CASES, BASES, ETC. IN GALLERY 03.07.05
LAYOUT OBJECTS IN GALLERY 03.15.05
OBJECT INSTALLATION BEGINS 03.15.05
OBJECT INSTALLATION COMPLETE 03.29.05
LABELS, AUDIO TOUR, AND WALL SIGNS COMPLETE 03.30.05
EXHIBITION SHOP COMPLETE 03.31.05
PALACE AND MOSQUE OPEN TO PUBLIC 04.03.05
FINAL LAYOUT COMPLETE 04.06.05
ICL - INTERIOR CASE LIGHTING
HCC -HUMIDITY CONTROLLED CASE
STANCHION BARRIER
- THERMO-HYGROMETER STATION
T1 - TEAM 1 INSTALLATION LOGO
T2 - TEAM 2 INSTALLATION LOGO
T1 T2 - BOTH TEAMS REQUIRED
ROOM #1- THE WRITTEN WORD
ROOM #2- COURTS AND COURTIERS: ART AND POWER
ROOM #3- MOSQUES AND SHRINES: PLACES OF PRAYER
ROOM #4- OTTOMAN PATRONAGE
ROOM #5- ARTISTIC EXCHANGE
CDL
FINAL LAYOUT
04.06.2005

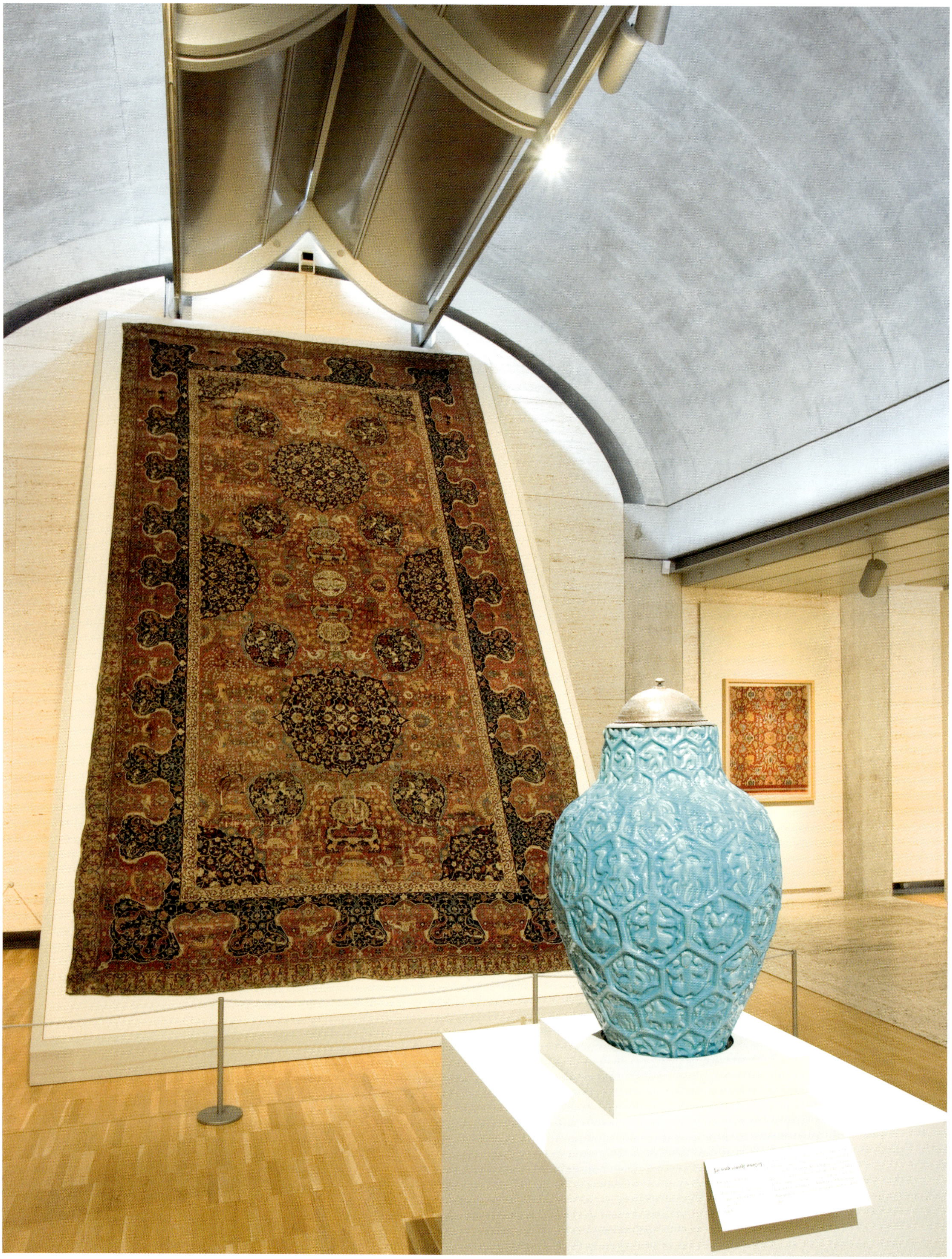

2.19 The 'Courts and Courtiers' section of the exhibition at the Kimbell Art Museum

2.20 Three of the Qajar oil paintings shown at the Kimbell Art Museum. V&A: 707–1876, 719–1876, 720–1876

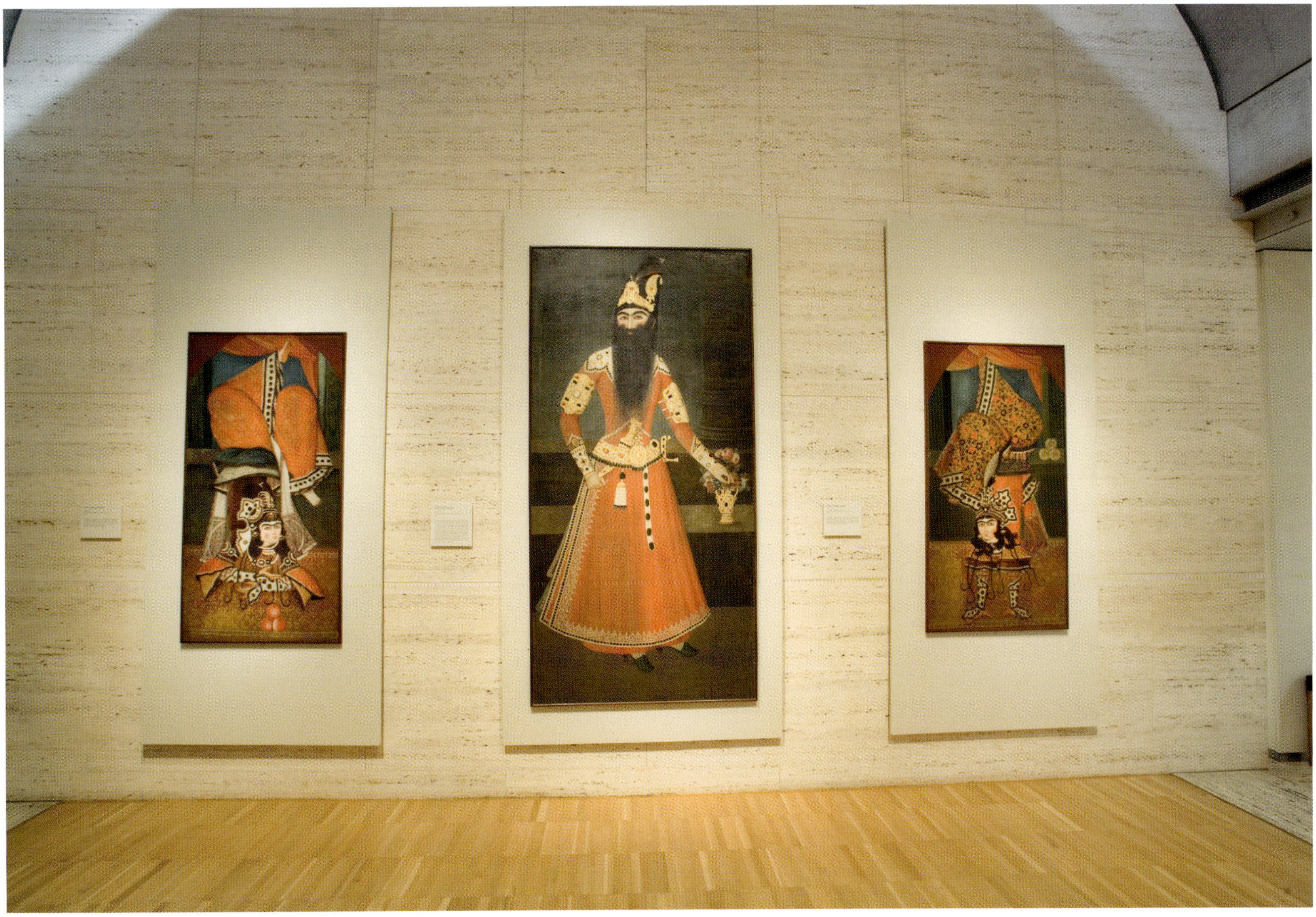

At the Setagaya Art Museum (illus. 2.21) the exhibition rooms were of different heights, and only one (the first) was high enough to accommodate the minbar of Sultan Qa'itbay. Thus the minbar became the centre of a display on religious art that absorbed both the geographical and scientific section from the NGA's Room 1 and 'Mosque, Shrine and Church' from Room 3, with the exception of the secular pieces made for Sultan Qa'itbay and his wife. These were moved to the second room, where the focus was shifted from their patronage to their decoration with inscriptions. Four rooms were made in the remainder of the space, and the grouping of objects created in Washington was more or less maintained. With the exception of three of the nineteenth-century oil paintings, which had been shown as part of 'Courts and Courtiers' in Fort Worth and were now moved to 'Interaction', changes occurred only within the rooms assigned to each theme.

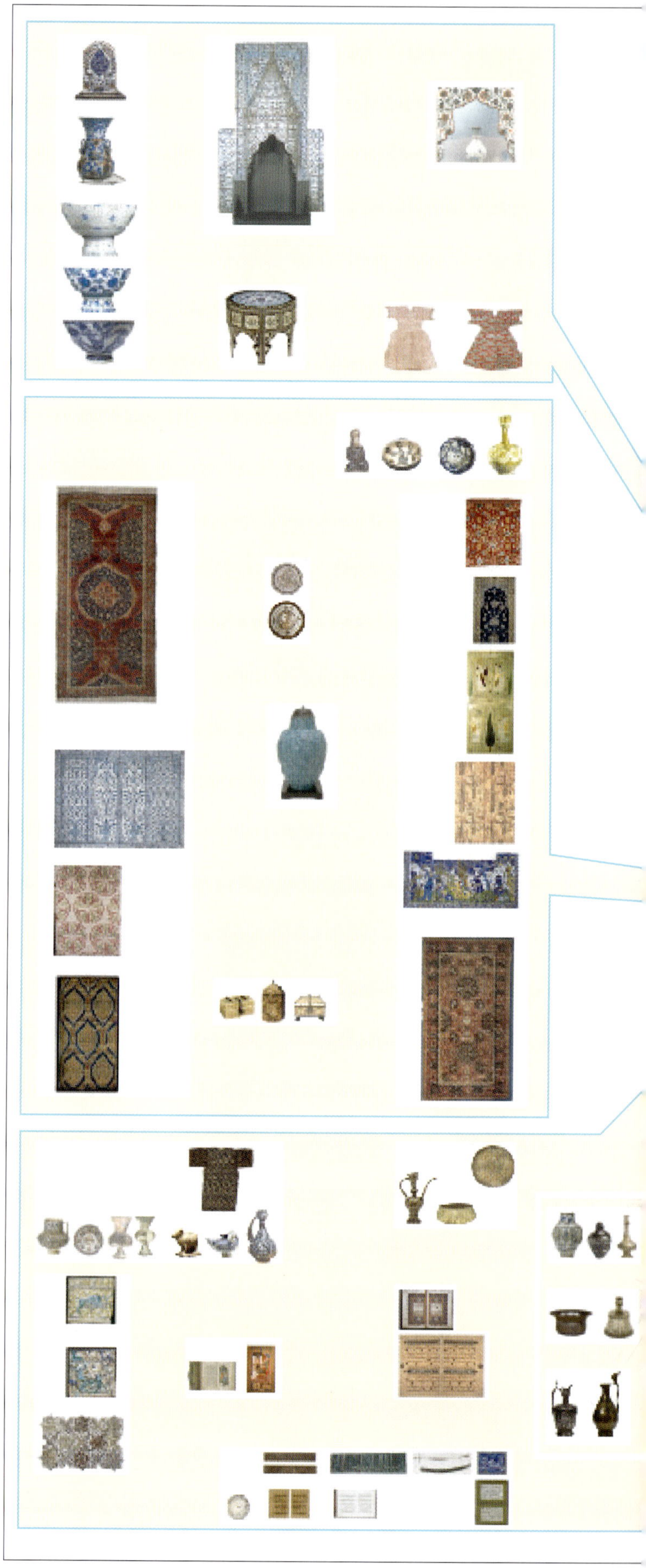

2.21 (*right*) Plan of *Palace and Mosque* at the Setagaya Art Museum, Tokyo

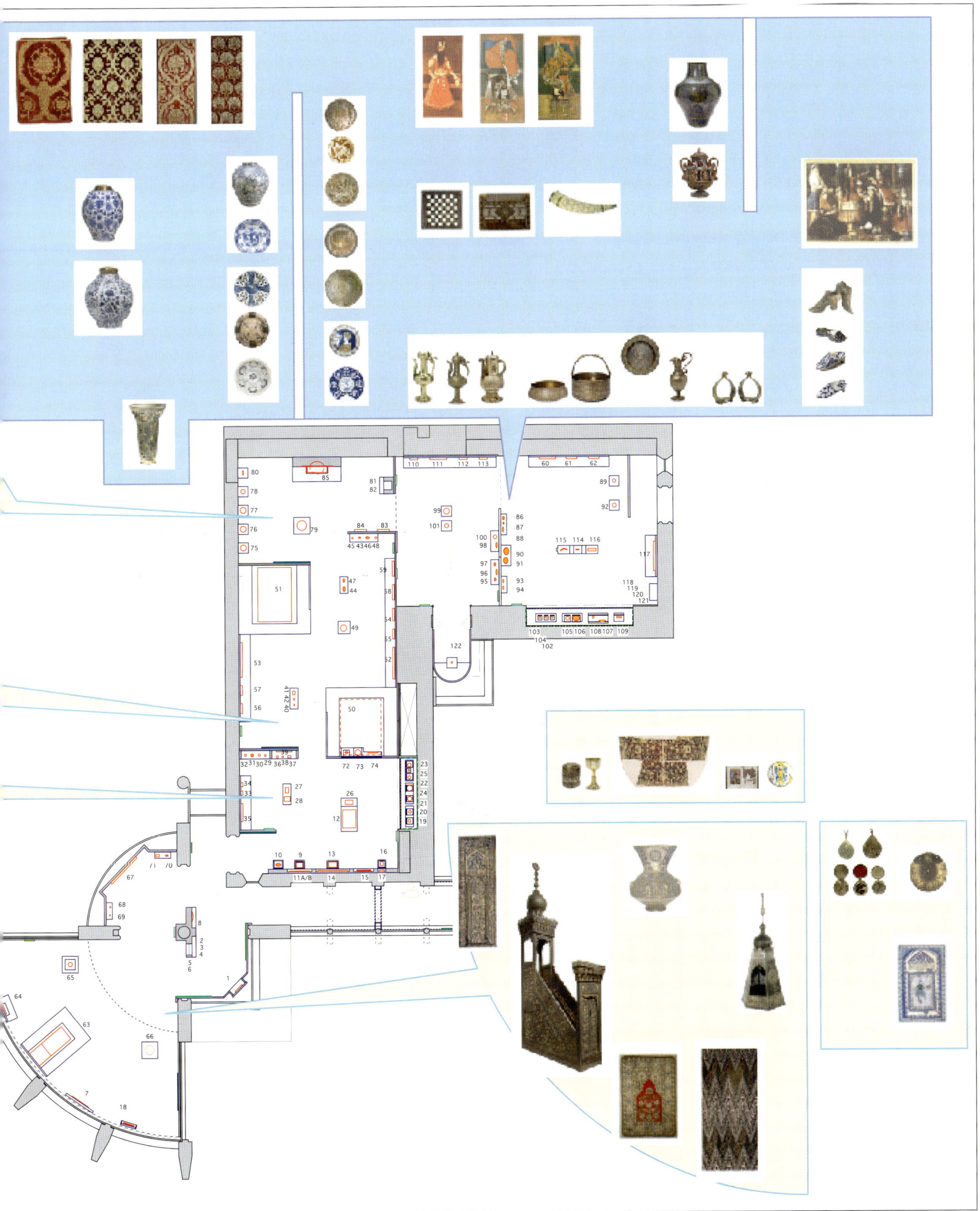

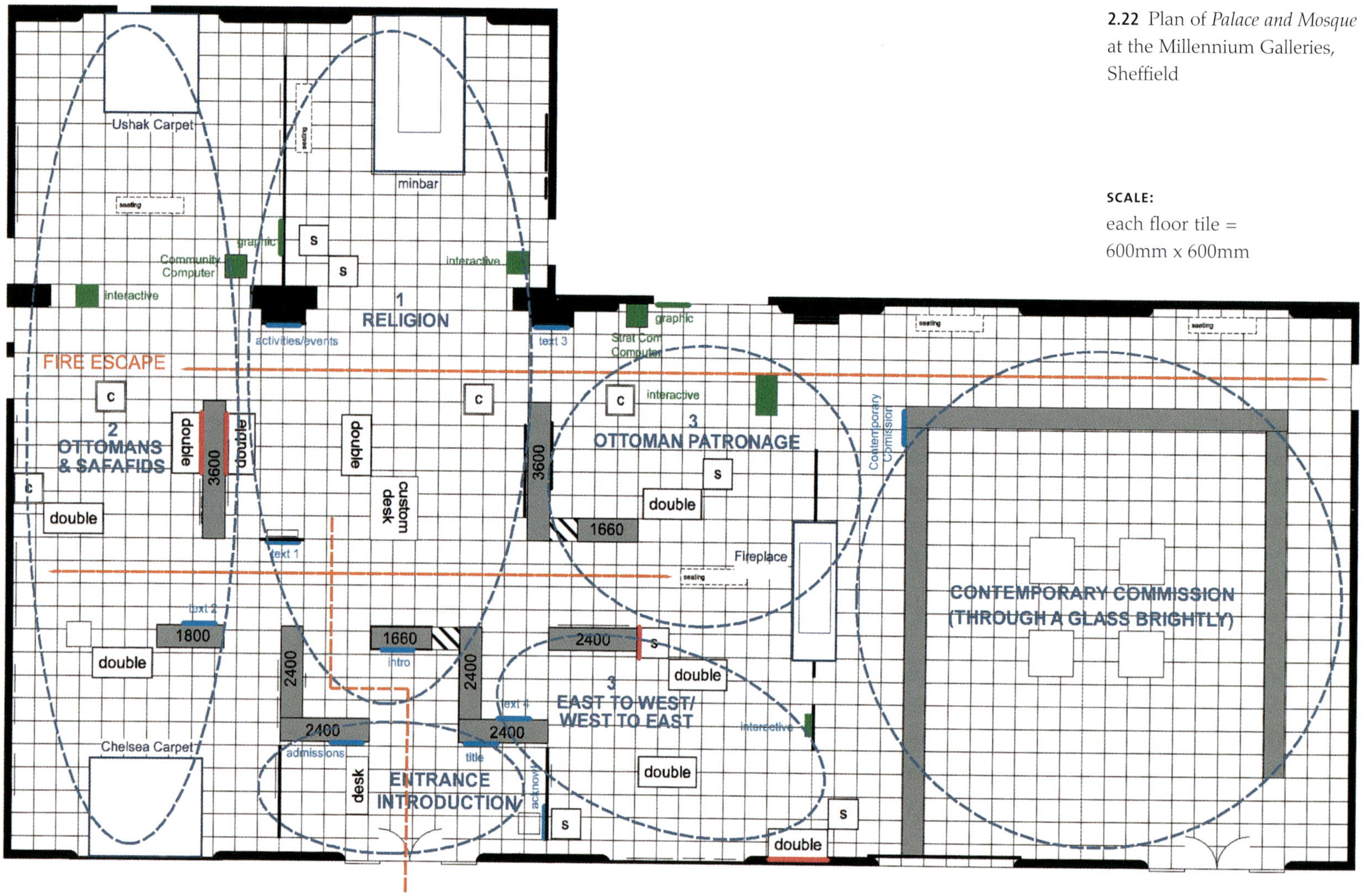

2.22 Plan of *Palace and Mosque* at the Millennium Galleries, Sheffield

SCALE:
each floor tile = 600mm x 600mm

In Sheffield (illus. 2.22) the display also had to be adapted to the layout and volume of the exhibition space, but there the more important change was in the interpretation. In the previous venues, the expectation was that visitors would be happy to apply themselves to a traditional combination of wall panels of 150–200 words and individual labels of 50–100 words. The Millennium Galleries wanted to attract an audience who would not necessarily have visited an art exhibition before, and it was therefore decided to use different types of labelling to create a more varied and attractive rhythm. Eight objects were selected for more detailed treatment in an accessible style, with the intention that a visitor who read only these eight longer labels would be able to grasp the main themes of the exhibition.

The tour of *Palace and Mosque* was successful in its own terms, as it enabled large numbers of people to see fine examples of Islamic art, and we can hope that they left the exhibition with a more positive impression of the Middle East and its culture over the last millennium and a half. The tour also performed a useful function in giving the staff of the V&A an opportunity for what in many respects was a dry run for the Jameel Gallery of Islamic Art, which opened after the exhibition returned to the Museum in April 2006.

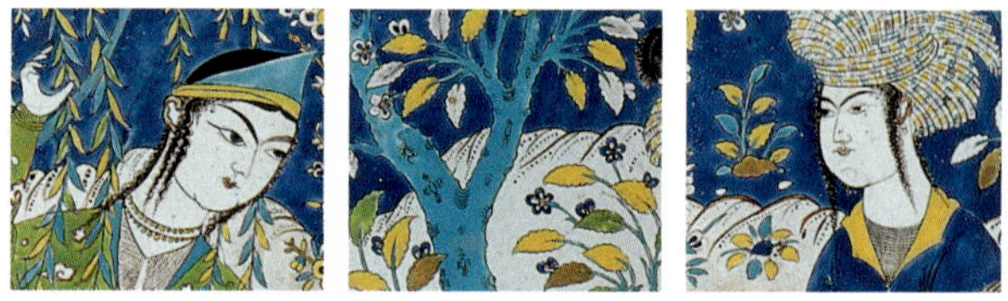

3 THE CONCEPT OF THE JAMEEL GALLERY

Tim Stanley

When the work of developing the new Jameel Gallery of Islamic Art began in 2003, the curatorial team was faced with a particular challenge. As we have seen in Chapter 1, the V&A has a very significant collection of Islamic art from the Middle East, but until 2002 this had not had a separate identity within the Museum. Instead, it was divided medium by medium between the materials-based departments set up at the end of the nineteenth century. The curators of the Jameel Gallery were therefore new to the V&A, or, in one case, new to the Middle East collections, care of which had not yet been transferred to the recently established Asian Department. Fortunately, a previous attempt at reforming the Museum's departmental structure had produced an outline description of the Middle East collections of the V&A, which was to prove very useful.

The Museum's South Asian collections were never dispersed among the materials-based departments. At the time of the organization of the departmental structure in 1896, a strong lobby group, including several former viceroys of India, ensured that they continued to be administered as a single unit. The Indian section remained the only regionally based curatorial division of the Museum until 1970, when a new department was created to look after the Museum's Far Eastern collections. In 1984 the same process was begun for the Middle East collections,

3.1 Málaga Ship bowl, Spain, *circa* 1425–50. V&A: 486–1864

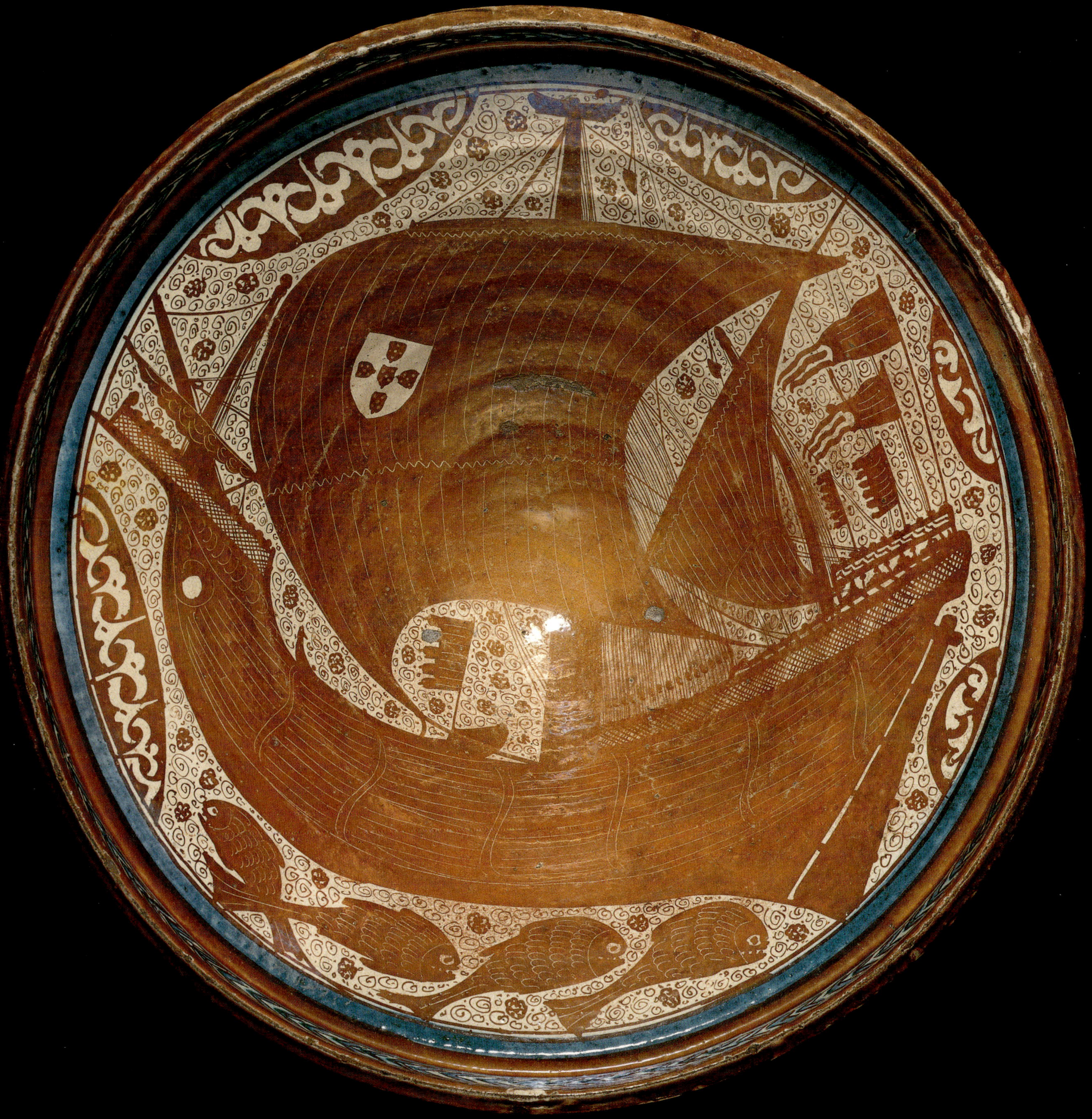

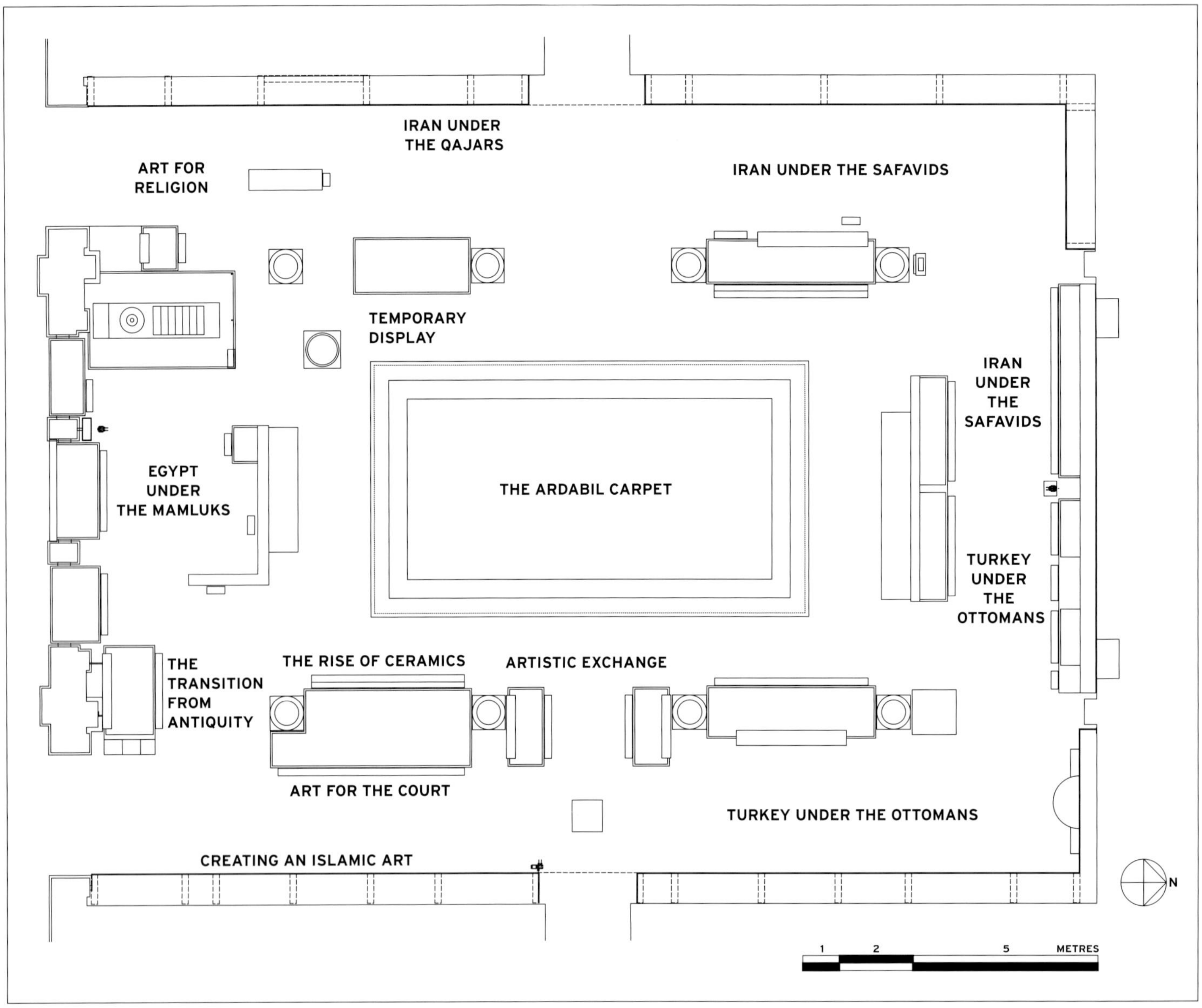

3.2 Plan of the themes of the Jameel Gallery at the V&A

but it soon came to naught. Nevertheless, it was the feasibility study carried out at this time that produced the very useful survey of the Museum's holdings of the Islamic art of the Middle East. This showed that the V&A owned in excess of 10,000 objects in this category, as well as a study collection of more than 8,500 ceramic sherds.

The largest proportions of these holdings were textiles (3,633 pieces), which constitute the British national collection in this field. The range is enormous, from the huge and exceptionally fine Ardabil carpet, produced in 1539–40 (illus. 1.9), to such medieval treasures as the silk with paired 'harpies' recovered from a grave in Rayy, near Tehran (illus. 3.3). The V&A's long-standing specialization in textile

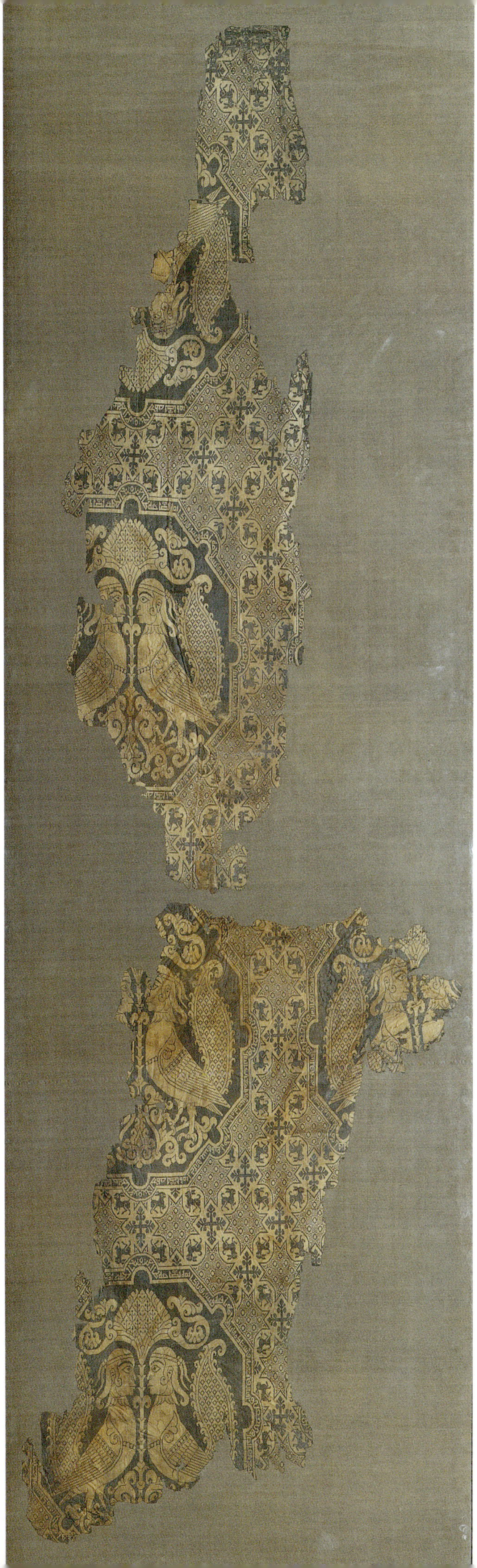

3.3 Silk textile, Iran, 10th–12th century. V&A: 1314–1888

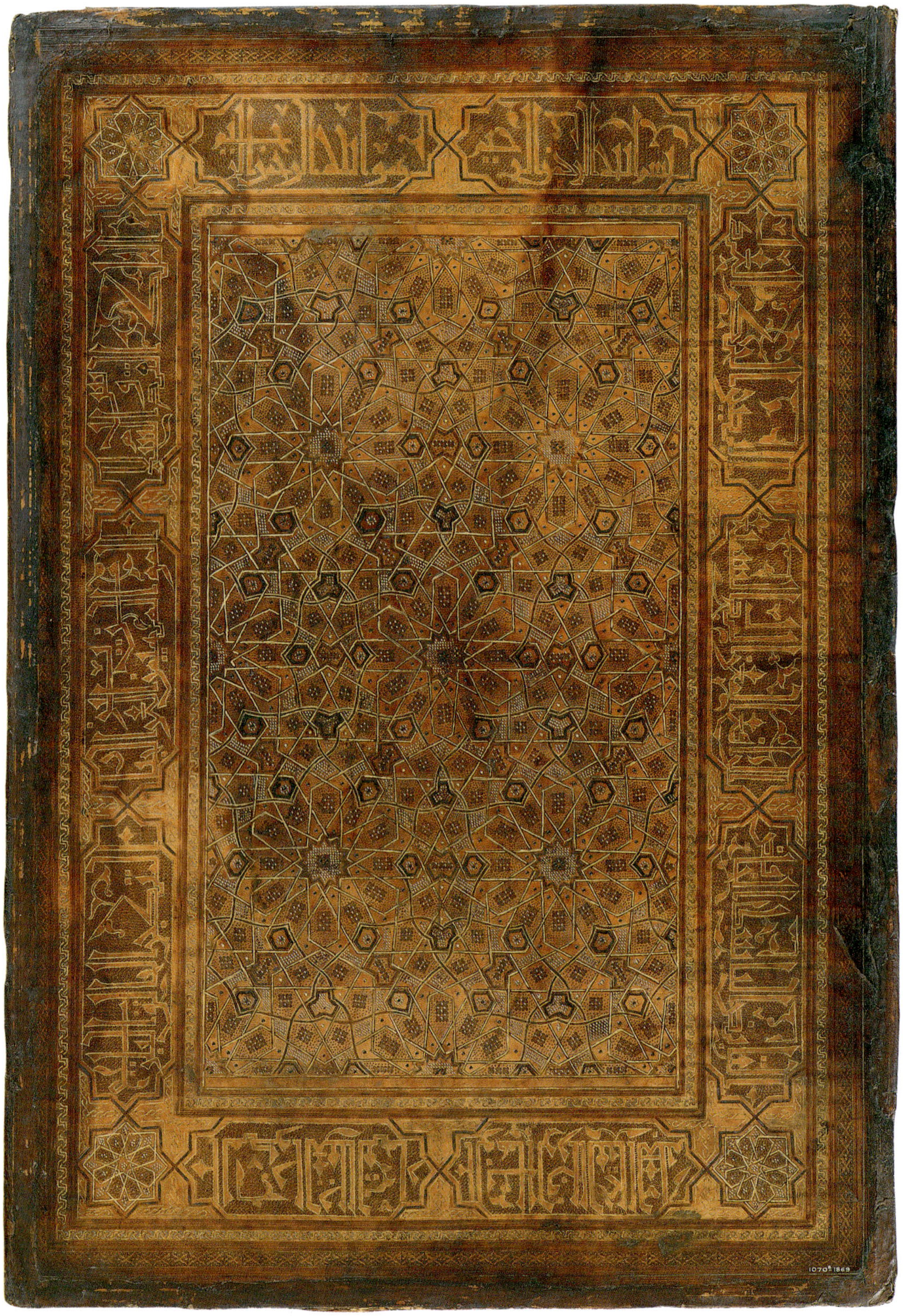

3.4 Mamluk leather binding, Cairo, 15th century. V&A: 1070b–1869

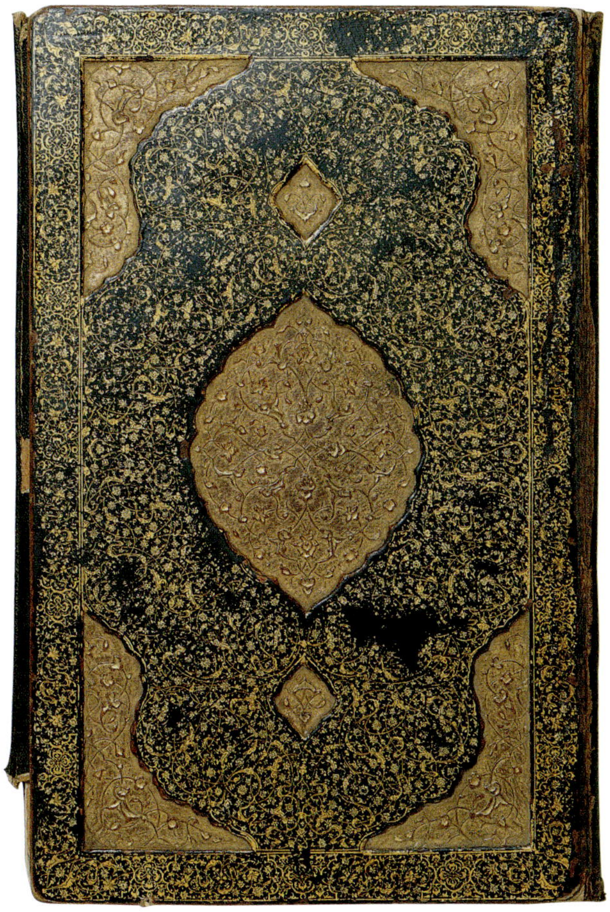

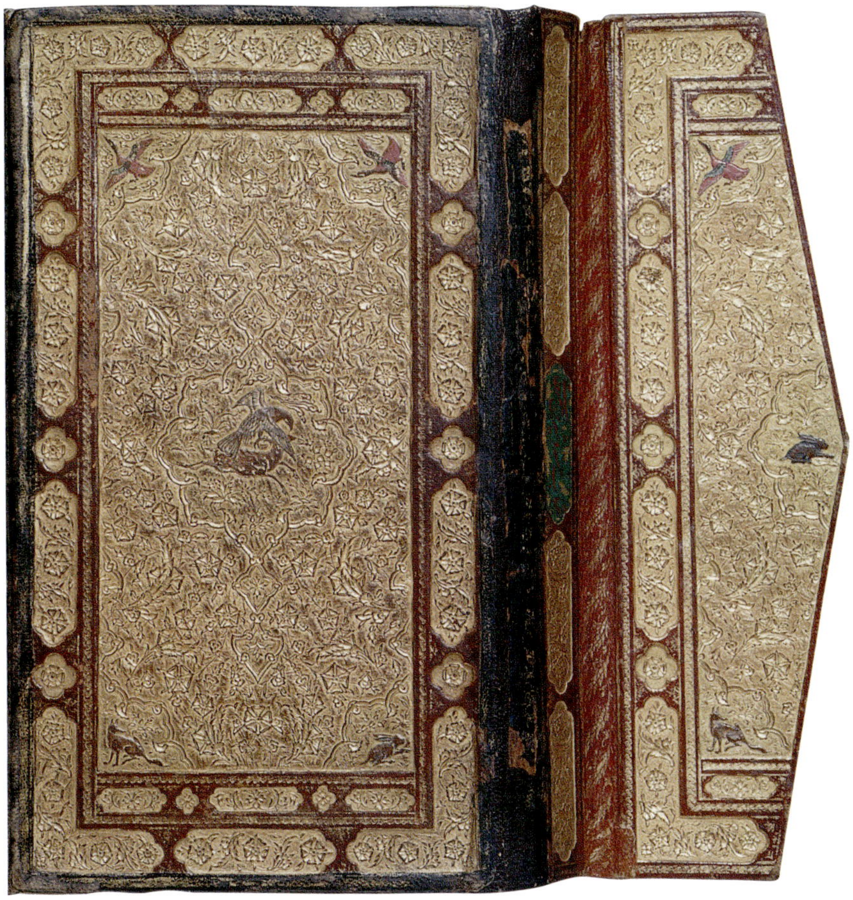

3.5 (*above*) Safavid lacquer binding, Iran, *circa* 1558. V&A: 618–1886

3.6 (*above right*) Safavid leather binding, Iran, *circa* 1632. V&A: 364–1885

collecting was matched by the British Museum's (now the British Library's) responsibility for collecting manuscript material. As a consequence, the collection of library items at the V&A is relatively small (950 pieces). Bookbindings form a large proportion of these objects (illus. 3.4), and, indeed, many of the V&A's Islamic manuscripts were acquired as good examples of the bookbinder's craft rather than for their texts, their calligraphy or their illumination (illus. 3.5, 3.6). Ceramics and glass (3,414 pieces) form the second-largest collection, which is considered the world's most comprehensive in this area, in terms of both vessels and tiles. The third-largest collection is metalwork (1,773 pieces), and there are important holdings of woodwork (233 pieces) and sculpture (267 pieces). In addition, about 250 items of Middle Eastern origin were held by the former Indian and South East Asian Department.

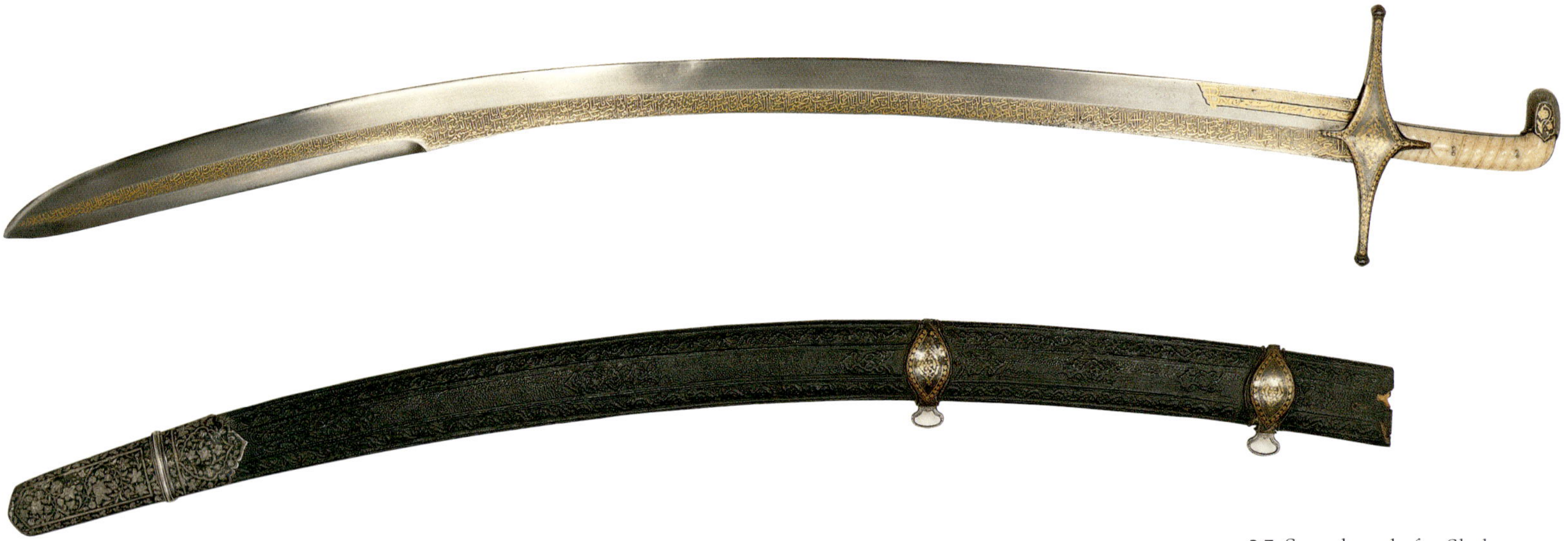

3.7 Sword made for Shah Tahmasp, Iran, 1524–76. V&A: 3378 IS

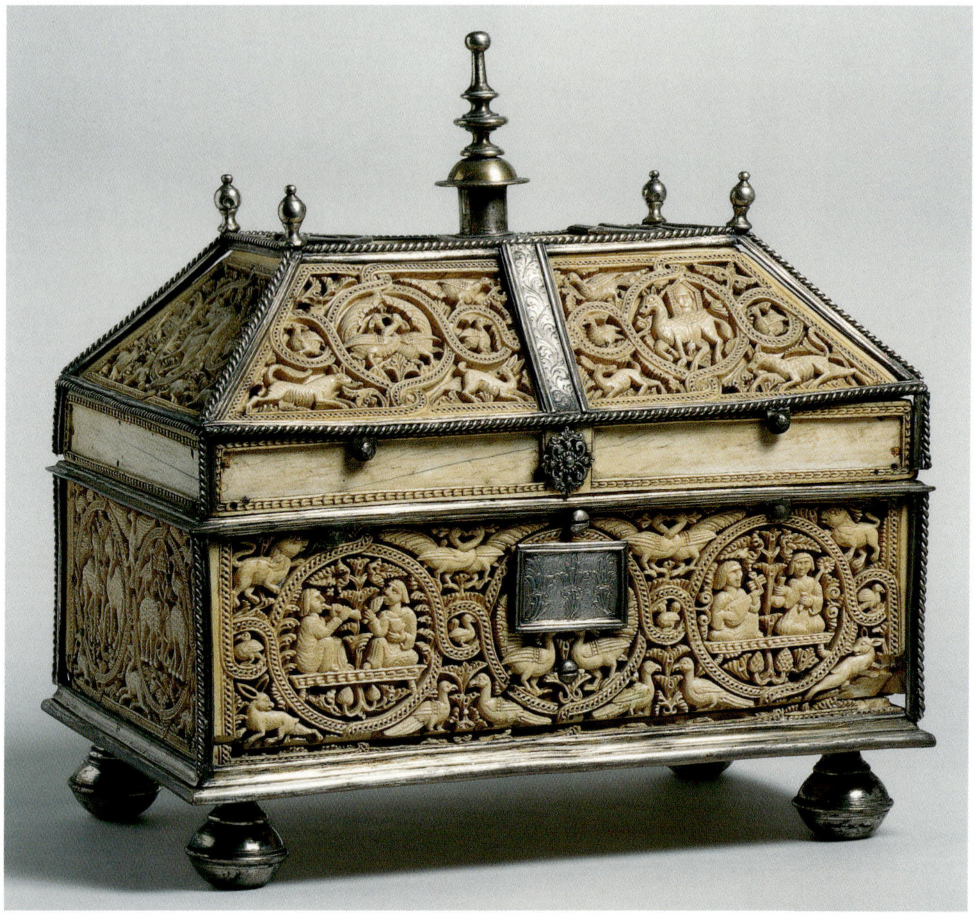

3.8 Ivory casket, Spain, early 11th century. V&A: 10–1866

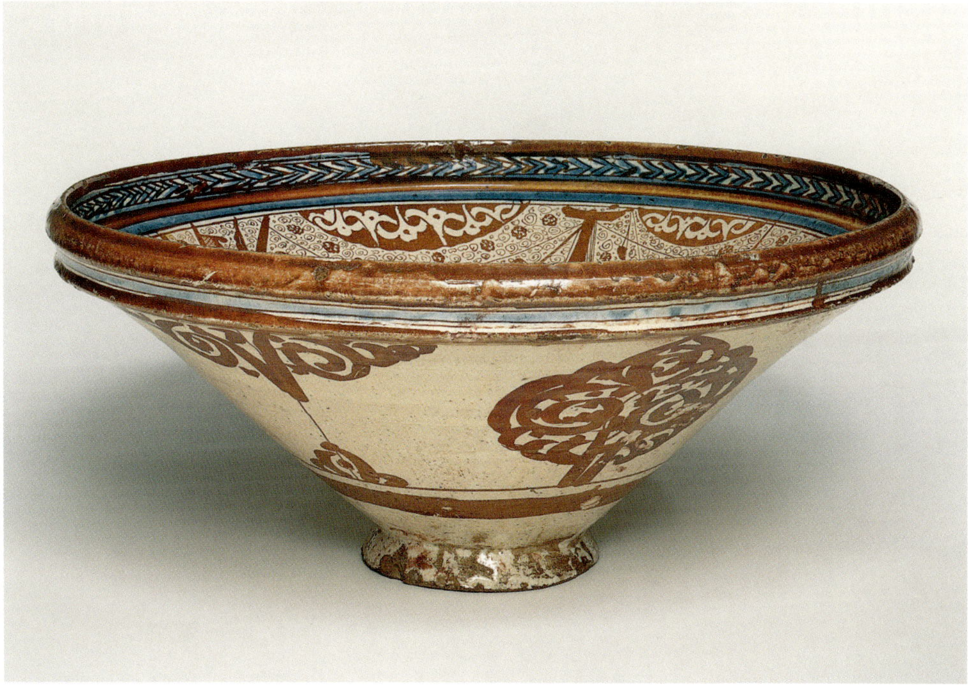

3.9 Profile of the Málaga Ship bowl (see illus. 3.1). V&A: 480–1864

All of these categories contain iconic items. The Indian Department owned the sword of Shah Tahmasp, for example (illus. 3.7) – as well as that of Simón Bolívar! The sculpture included a number of relatively small but precious items, such as the Fatimid rock-crystal ewer (illus. 1.1) and a collection of ivory caskets from tenth- and eleventh-century Islamic Spain (illus. 3.8). The same region was the source of the Ship bowl, made in Málaga in the first quarter of the fifteenth century (illus. 3.1, 3.9). Other ceramic masterpieces are the ceramic 'lamp' from the Süleymaniye mosque in Istanbul (illus. 3.10) and the Ottoman tilework chimney-piece, which is 3.65 metres high (illus. 2.7–2.13). The metalwork includes a superb incense-burner from thirteenth-century Syria (illus. 3.11). This has inlaid decoration in precious metal, which is also found on a much larger lamp-holder of brass with gold and silver inlay, of which only the walls survive (illus. 5.20). The patron of the lamp-holder was Sultan Qa'itbay, who also commissioned the Museum's celebrated minbar.

The minbar, at more than seven metres in height, had been one of the most impressive items in the old Islamic Middle East gallery, but even it was outclassed by the Ardabil carpet, which is almost 11 metres long and more than five metres wide (illus. 1.9). The Ardabil carpet, the Chelsea carpet (illus. 1.10), the Armenian 'cope' made in Isfahan (illus. 5.24) and the other iconic items were to be the *sine qua non* elements in the new Jameel Gallery, but they had to be knitted together by an overall scheme in which they would form the high points.

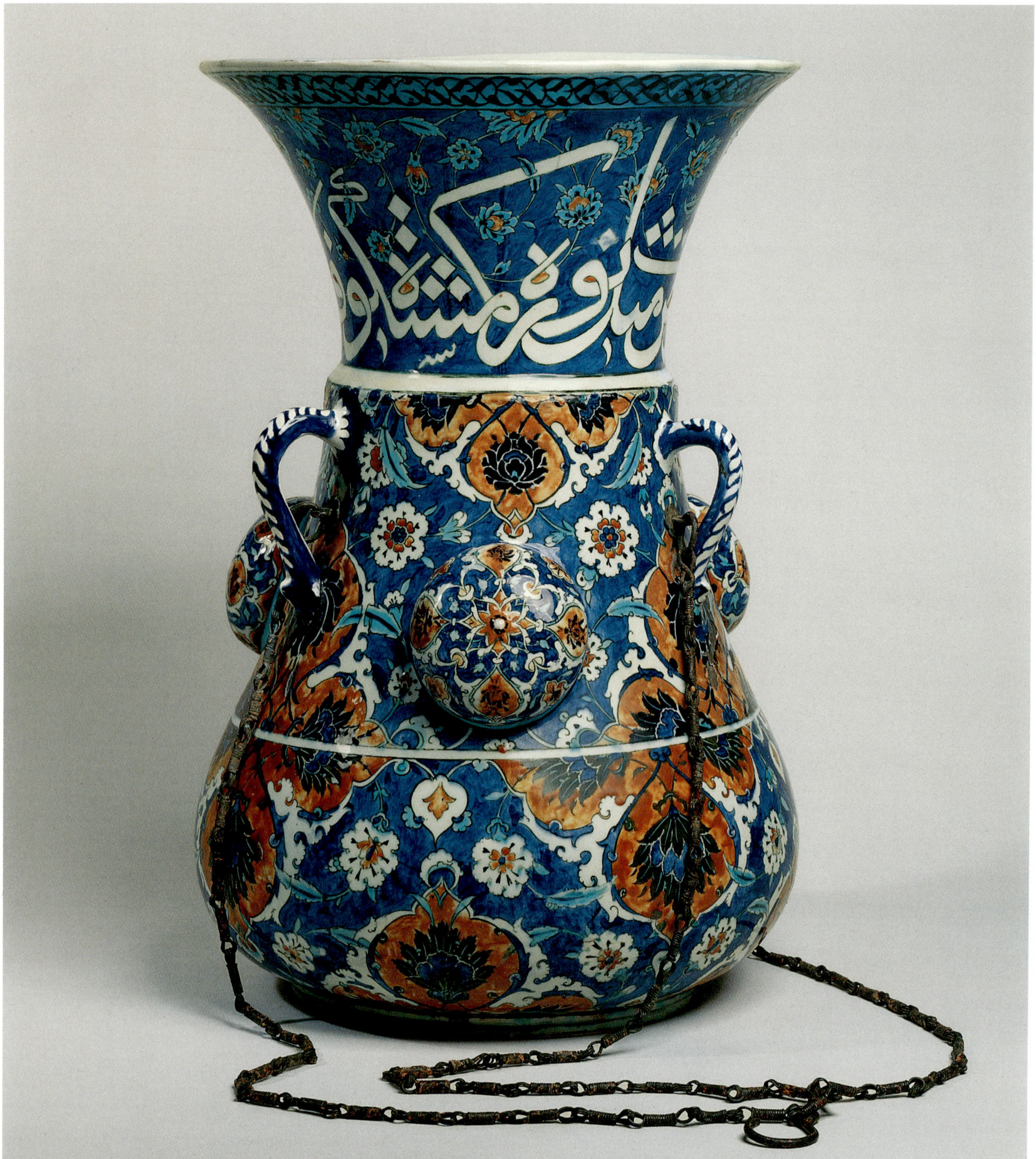

What, where, when?

In the context of the Jameel Gallery, the term 'Islamic art' is used as a cultural rather than a religious term. This is because Islam differed from Christianity and many other religions in an important respect. Islam crystallized as a separate religion in AD 622, when the Prophet Muhammad moved with his followers from Mecca to Medina, in an act known as the *Hijrah*, or Migration. At the same time, however, Muhammad established a separate political entity. Islam as a state was born at the same time as Islam as a religion, and from the beginning Islam developed as the ideology of a state as well as a framework for faith. Because of this, the definition of Islamic art used for the Gallery is not 'the art of Islam as a religion', but 'the art of a culture in which Islam played a dominant role'. The term Islamic art does indeed encompass the religious art of Islam, but it also includes the sophisticated secular art of the Islamic period, and even the art produced by and for the non-Muslim subjects of Islamic states, in both a secular and religious context (see the Safavid cope, illus. 5.24, for example, and p.35).

The use of the term 'Middle East' in the Jameel Gallery is also linked to the growth of the first Islamic state in the seventh and eighth centuries. By AD 750, this empire ruled most of what we generally understand to be the Middle East – that is, south-west Asia and Egypt. The one exception was Turkey, which did not become part of the Islamic world until after 1071, when Islamic art began to be produced there. On the other hand, the Islamic empire also extended as far as Spain and Morocco in the west and, in the east, to what are now Afghanistan and the republics of western Central Asia. All these lands are judged to have produced Islamic art in an authentic tradition so long as they maintained an Islamic form of government.

In 1492 Granada was conquered by Ferdinand of Aragon and Isabella of Castille, putting an end to the last Islamic state on the Iberian peninsula, and the art produced in Spain after this date is not counted as Islamic art. In most of the rest of the 'Middle East', however, Islamic rule was not seriously challenged until the nineteenth century, and in the Turkish heartlands of the Ottoman empire and Iran, the two most important states in terms of art production, it did not disappear until after the First World War (1914–18). In the context of the Jameel Gallery, then, the Islamic period began in AD 622 and ended in 1924–5, when the Ottoman caliphate was abolished in Turkey and the Qajar dynasty lost power in Iran.

3.10 Lamp-shaped ceramic vessel, Turkey, *circa* 1557. V&A: 131–1885

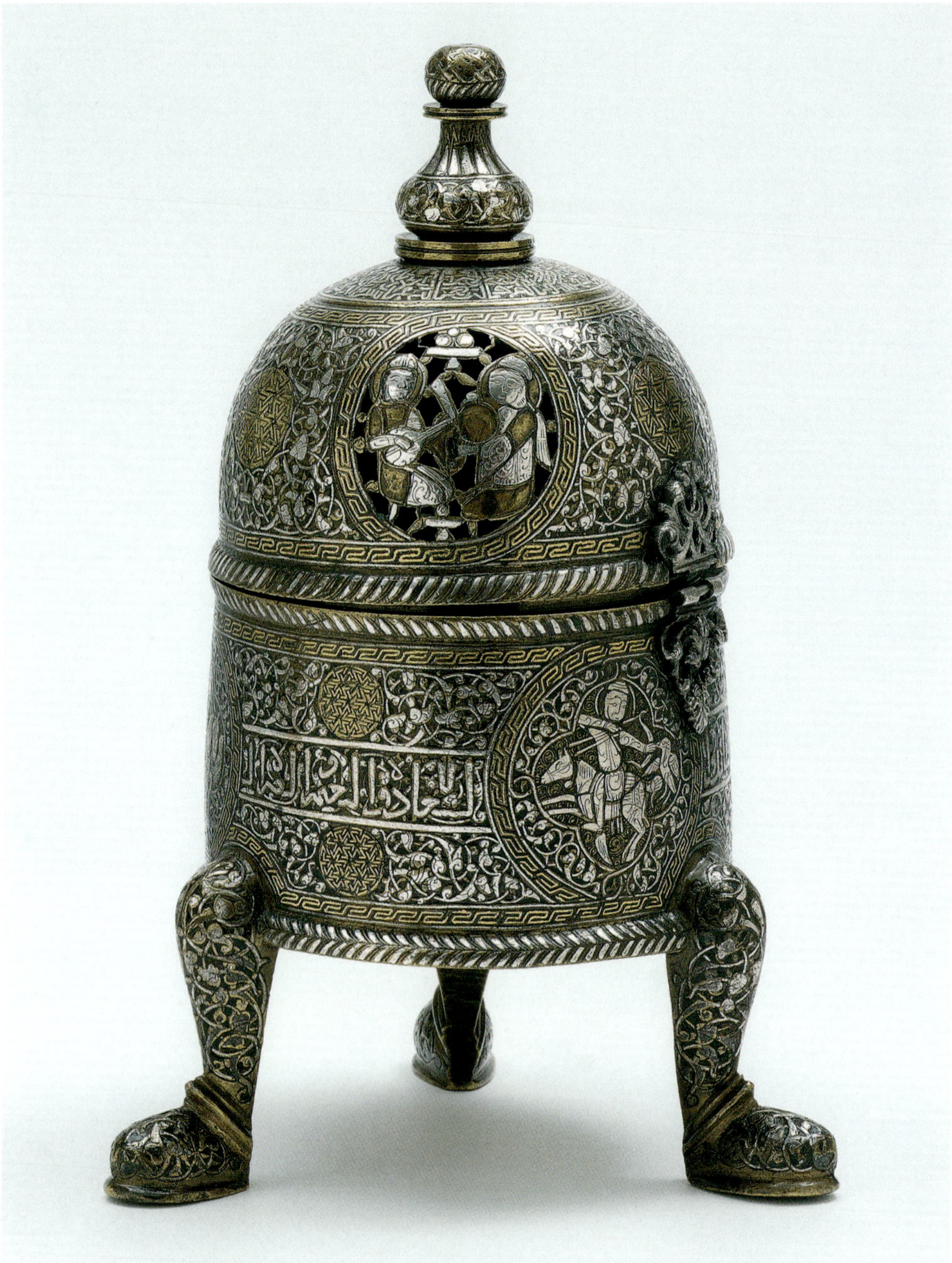

3.11 Incense-burner,
Syria, *circa* 1250–1300.
V&A: M.709–1910
(Salting Bequest)

A cæsura

With these temporal and geographical limits in mind, we first took account of a basic characteristic of the V&A's collection. This is the different nature of the material from the periods before and after 1500. Archaeologically recovered material is important before 1500, but not after that date. At the same time, the coverage for Islamic art produced before 1500 is uneven, while the coverage from 1500 onwards is consistent, and often comprehensive. A comparison of the Museum's Mamluk and Timurid collections shows the uneven nature of the earlier material. The patronage of the Mamluk sultans, who ruled Egypt and Syria from 1250 to 1517, is well represented at the V&A (illus. 3.4, 5.20, for example), while that of the Timurid dynasty, who ruled in Iran, Afghanistan and western Central Asia in the fifteenth century, is not. Overall, the survival rate of Timurid artefacts (as opposed to Timurid manuscripts) seems to have been relatively low, and Timurid art is generally sparsely represented in museum collections in Western Europe, even though it was of immense importance, both because of its fine quality and because of its influence on the Timurids' contemporaries and successors.

It therefore makes sense in terms of the collection to treat the periods before and after 1500 in different ways, and this division does not clash with the historical realities of the same period, since a number of major political changes occurred around the same time. In 1492, as we have seen, Granada was conquered, and the last Islamic state in Spain came to an end. In 1501 the Safavids took power in Iran, soon reuniting the country under their rule and converting it into the predominately Shi'ite country that it is today. And by 1517 the Ottoman sultan Selim I had conquered the entire Mamluk empire, turning his empire into one of the most powerful states in the world.

The initial proposal drawn up by the project's architects, Softroom, placed the Ardabil carpet at floor level in the centre of the Gallery, and this fact had to be accommodated in our planning. It was also clear that most visitors would enter the Gallery from the south, which would therefore be the preferred location for displays devoted to the earlier phases of Islamic history. As a consequence, we decided to group the pre-1500 material at the south end of the Gallery and to use it to convey themes that relate to Islamic art as a whole. The themes chosen generally have a time-bound element, but there is flexibility about their sequence.

By contrast, the post-1500 material would be presented in two geographical and chronological blocks at the north end of the Gallery. Ottoman art from Turkey would be displayed on the east side, and Safavid and Qajar art from Iran on the west side, adjacent to the Ardabil carpet, which is also a Safavid object from Iran. This location would allow the visitor to move directly from the Safavid display into the display of Islamic art made under the Mughals, their contemporaries to the east. This is displayed in the adjacent South Asian gallery, to which the Jameel Gallery is connected by an arch in the west wall. This link also allows the thematic display of Islamic art before 1500 at the south end of the Jameel Gallery to function as an introduction to the subject for both the Middle East and South Asia. To allow this physical link between the galleries to work, however, it was necessary to displace the Qajar display to the left of the arch, into the southern half of the room. The boundary between the northern and southern halves of the Gallery is in any case not expressed physically, and it is porous enough to have allowed a few post-1500 items to be used in the thematic displays.

Challenging misconceptions

In planning the content of the Jameel Gallery, we were aware from our own experience and from research done by the Museum's Learning and Interpretation division that many visitors would come to the Gallery with a number of misconceptions. We therefore decided that the Jameel Gallery would provide positive information that silently contradicts these ideas, and we also intended that visitors would leave with the impression that Islamic art is beautiful, varied and interesting.

We knew that the subtleties of our argument that Islamic art is a cultural and not a religious term would not have reached the huge majority of visitors before they came to the Gallery. They would therefore tend to presume that Islamic art is the art of Islam as a religion. Experience also showed that people who know a little about Islamic culture believe that there are no images of people in Islamic art. We therefore had to demonstrate that the reality was somewhat different. Our main point would be that Islam was an important factor in the formation of Islamic art, but that the sophisticated secular culture of the Islamic courts also played a crucial role in this process. Moreover, in many places and periods this court culture was not affected by distaste for images of humans and animals, and these are frequently used in the art produced for the courts.

Another point we wished to address was the emphasis that recent news coverage of the Islamic world had placed on strife with and polemic against non-Muslim societies, including our own. Because of this, Islamic culture tends to seem isolated and rejectionist, with no relevance to a non-Muslim audience. In fact, of course, the Islamic Middle East had numerous artistic and other connections with Europe and with the rest of Asia, and these are illustrated by the display.

Our wish is that visitors from the Middle East will leave the Gallery with a sense of pride in their own artistic heritage; that Muslim visitors from other regions, including Britain, will have gained an insight into the Islamic culture of the Middle East, to which other Islamic cultures are so closely bound; and that everyone will understand that the Islamic art of the Middle East was important in its own terms, and because of its interaction with the art of cultures of the same period in other parts of the world.

Research

To develop the more detailed themes to be covered in the Jameel Gallery, to select the objects to be displayed, and to write the texts for the wall panels, object labels and other interpretative material, the curatorial team had to undertake a considerable amount of research. Our tasks included examining the mass of material in the Museum's stores and familiarizing ourselves with other museums' presentation of Islamic material, as well as reading up on individual aspects of the subject in libraries, and field trips to the Middle East. By September 2004 both the thematic outline and the object list were complete, and the conservation work and photography could be commissioned, while the texts were ready for editing by December 2005 and were handed over to the graphic designers in February 2006.

An opportunity to discuss the project with a group of curators in the same field came on 5 May 2004, when the Musée du Louvre in Paris held a day conference on new presentations of Islamic art in museums. I represented the V&A, while other presentations were made by curators from the Musée du Louvre itself, the David Collection in Copenhagen, the Gulbenkian Museum in Lisbon, the new Museums of Islamic Art in Athens and Doha, the Metropolitan Museum of Art in New York and the Museum für Islamische Kunst in Berlin. All these institutions were in the process of reinstalling their displays, and the presentations brought out the way the curators had responded to the nature of the collections in their care and the character of the building in which the display was to be mounted. The areas of debate were largely theoretical. Questions were raised about the validity of Islamic art as a category (which the V&A would defend, for the reasons set out above) and the division of the material by dynasty (which the V&A has largely avoided for the earlier period, for the reasons also set out above).

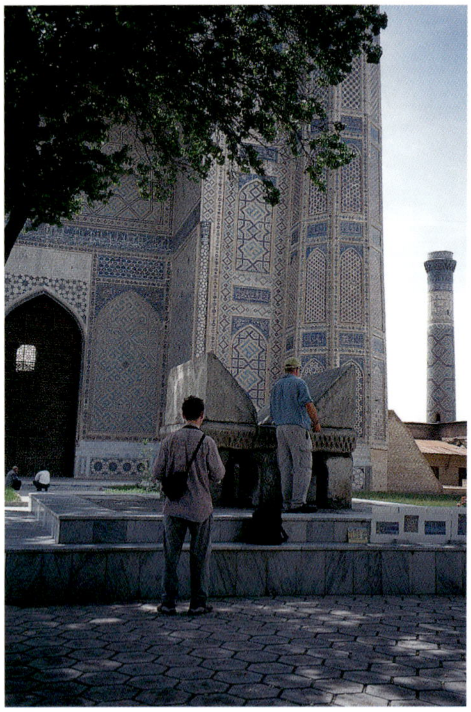

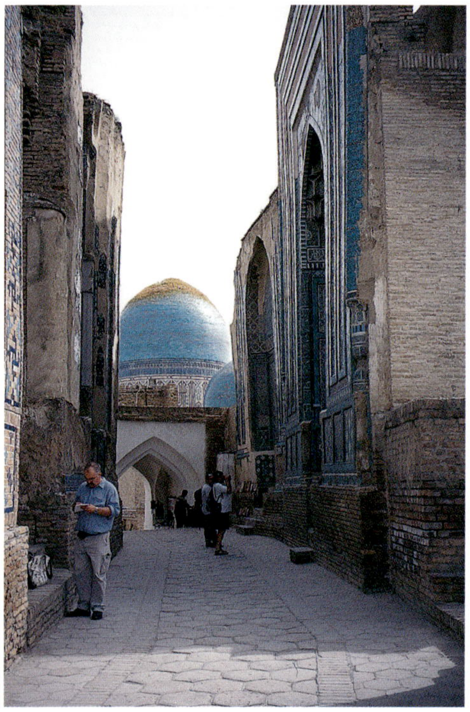

3.12 (*far left*) Tim Stanley (right) and Barry Wood (left) examining the huge Qur'an stand at the Bibi Khanim mosque in Samarqand, May 2004

3.13 (*left*) Tim Stanley at the Shah-i Zindah mausoleum complex in Samarqand, May 2004

Later that month three members of the curatorial team – Rosemary Crill, Barry Wood and I – spent 15 days in Uzbekistan, visiting Tashkent, Samarqand, Shahri Sabz, Vabkent, Ghijduvan, Bukhara, Khiva and Rishtan, Marghilan and other towns in the Farghana valley. As well as viewing museums and historical sites such as the mosque of Bibi Khanim and the Shah-i Zindah cemetery in Samarqand (illus. 3.12, 3.13), we visited craft potteries in Ghijduvan and in Rishtan and the Yadgarlik ikat factory in Marghilan, which uses traditional production techniques. An important

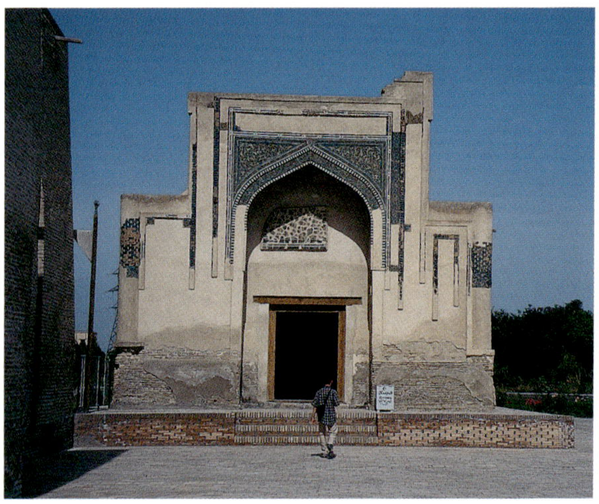

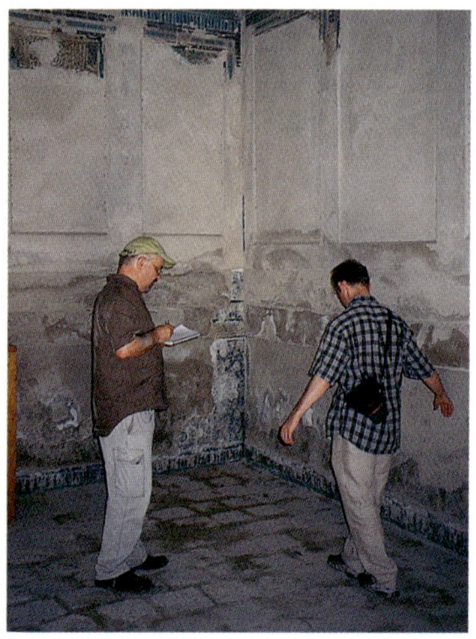

3.14 (*far left*) The tomb of Buyanquli Khan in Bukhara, May 2004

3.15 (*left*) Tim Stanley and Barry Wood pacing out the interior of Buyanquli Khan's tomb, May 2004

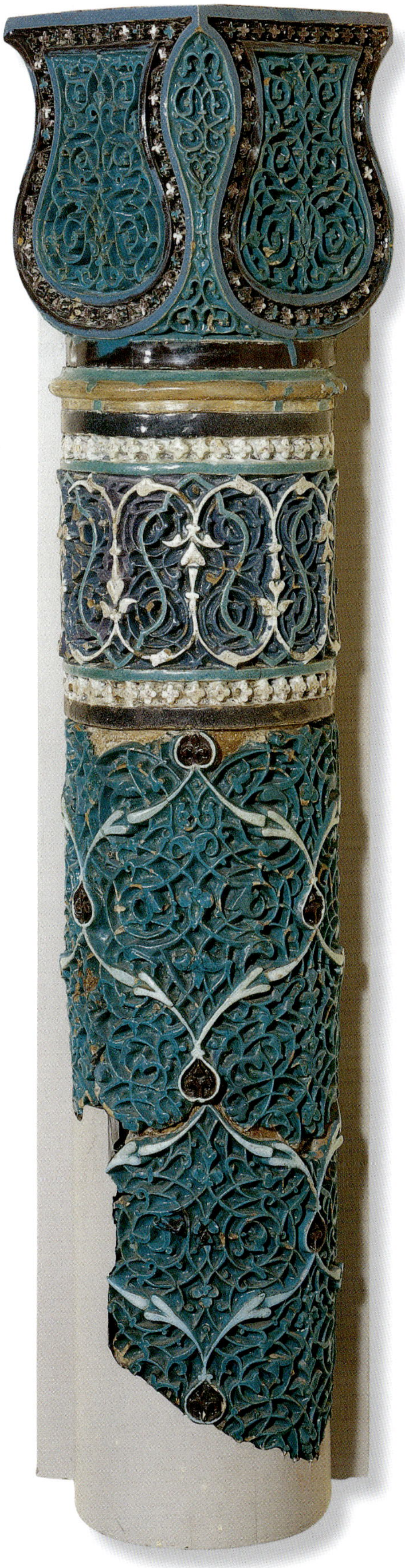

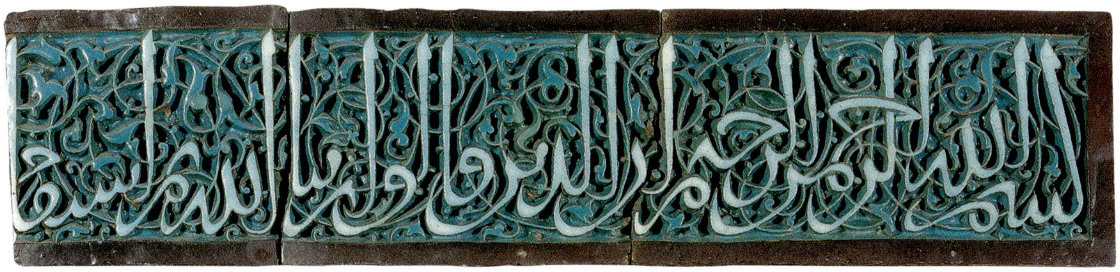

3.16 Tilework from the tomb of Buyanquli Khan. V&A: 567–1900 and 586–1899 (*left*) and 2033–1899 (*above*)

focus of the visit was the tomb of Buyanquli Khan, a descendant of Genghis Khan, in Bukhara, which is thought to have been erected about 1360 (illus. 3.14, 3.15). This building is one of the very few decorated with a remarkable type of tilework that was deeply carved with inscriptions and decorative motifs before turquoise and other coloured glazes were applied. Two large groups of these tiles were purchased by the V&A in 1899 and 1900, and a selection forms part of the display in the Jameel Gallery (illus. 3.16).

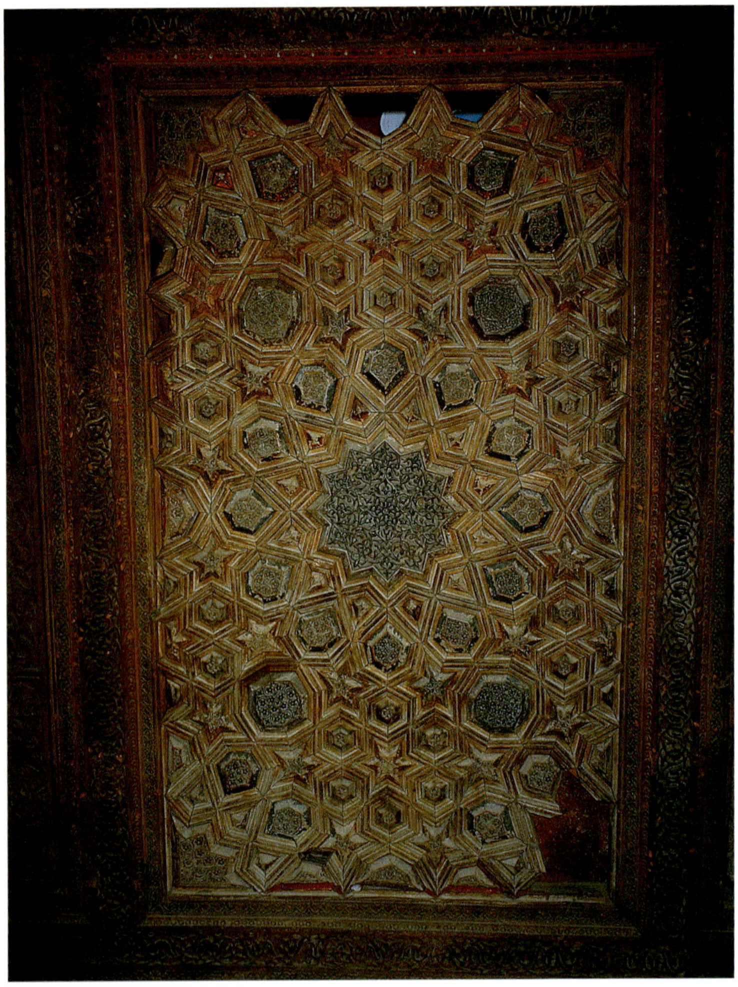

3.17 Part of the 14th-century tomb-marker from the grave of Sayf al-Din Bakharzi, now in the museum at the shrine of Baha' al-Din Naqshband, Bukhara

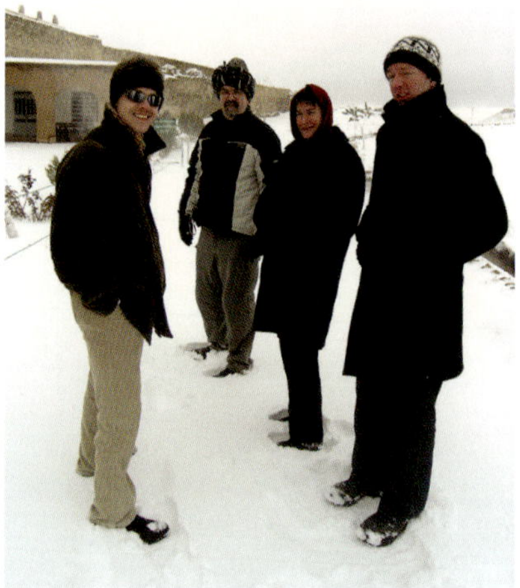

3.18 Members of the Gallery team visiting Takht-i Sulayman, Iran (left to right: Barry Wood, Tim Stanley, Rosemary Crill and Chris Bagot), November 2004

An unexpected bonus came when we visited the tomb complex of Baha' al-Din Naqshband near Bukhara. In the newly organized museum there, we saw a large section of the carved (and once painted) wooden tomb-marker from the mausoleum of Sayf al-Din Bakharzi (illus. 3.17), which stands next to that of Buyanquli Khan. This showed us that a panel of similar work now on display in the Jameel Gallery (illus. 3.19) came from the same tomb-marker.

In November 2004 the same team, together with Oliver Salway and Chris Bagot from Softroom and Nighat Yousuf, the Gallery educator, visited Iran. Our first target was the shrine complex at Ardabil, for which the Ardabil carpet (illus. 1.9) was made. We then travelled via Tabriz and Maraghah to the mountaintop archaeological site of Takht-i Sulayman, which we visited during a snowstorm (illus. 3.18). The Mongol-period palace on this site was the source of two wonderful tiles in the Gallery (illus. 3.20, 3.21). From Takht-i Sulayman, we went to Bakhtaran

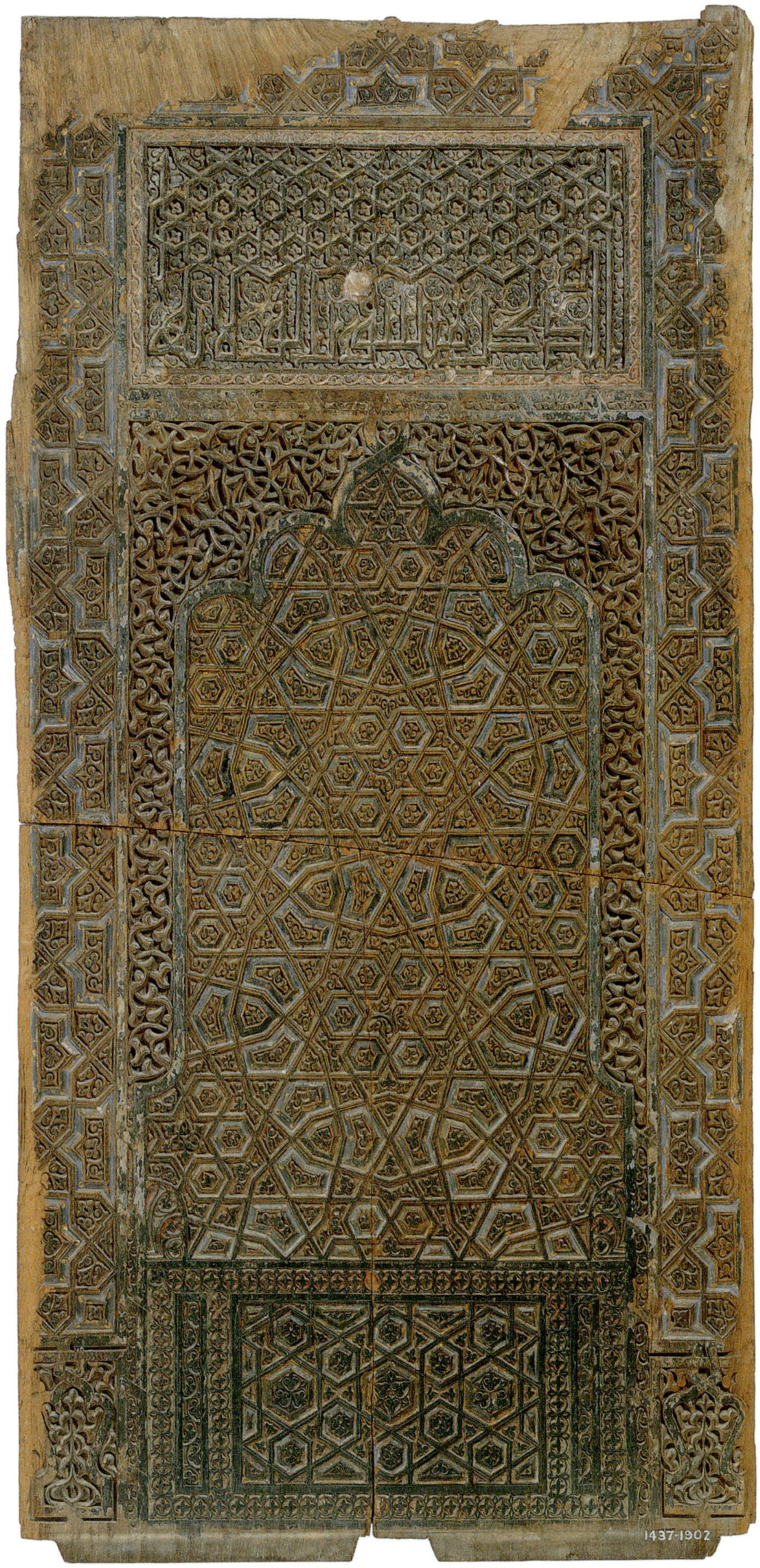

3.19 A panel from the tomb-marker shown opposite, now in the V&A.
V&A: 1437–1902

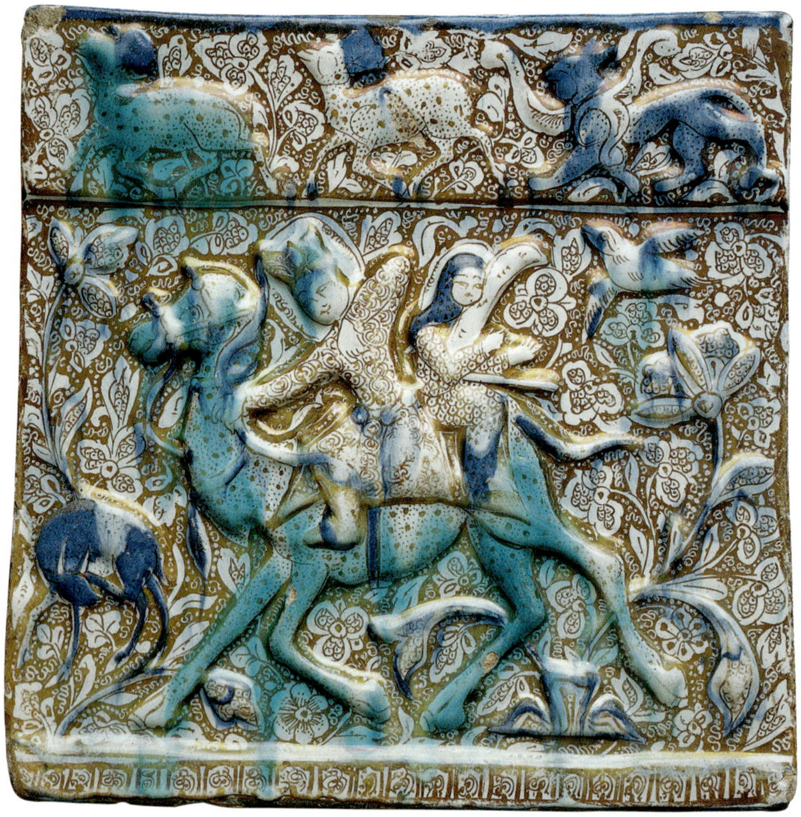

3.20 Lustre tile from Takht-i Sulayman, Iran, 1270s. V&A: 1841–1876

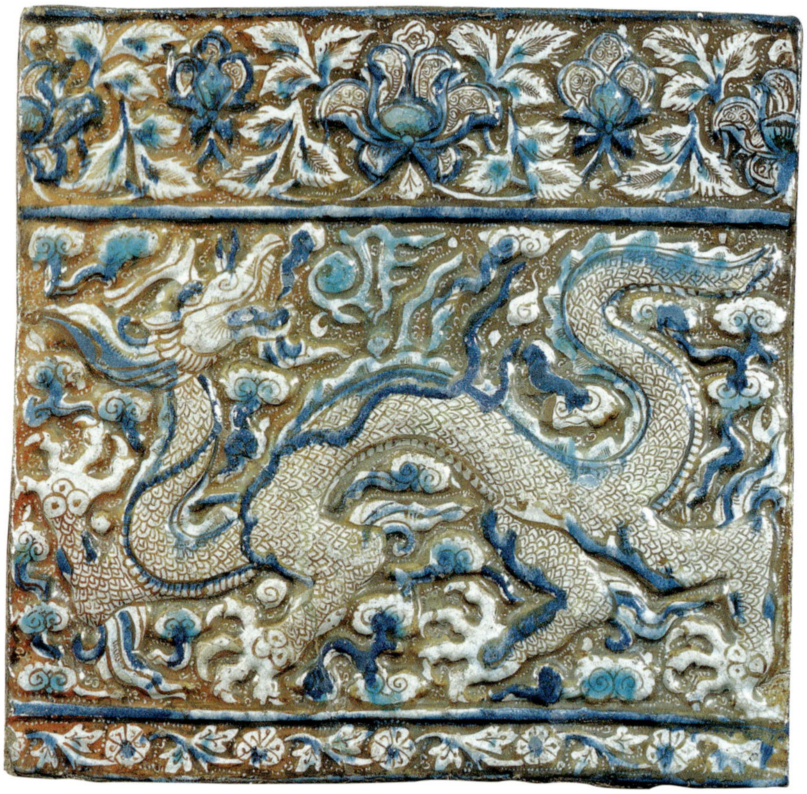

3.21 Lustre tile from Takht-i Sulayman, Iran, 1270s. V&A: 541–1900

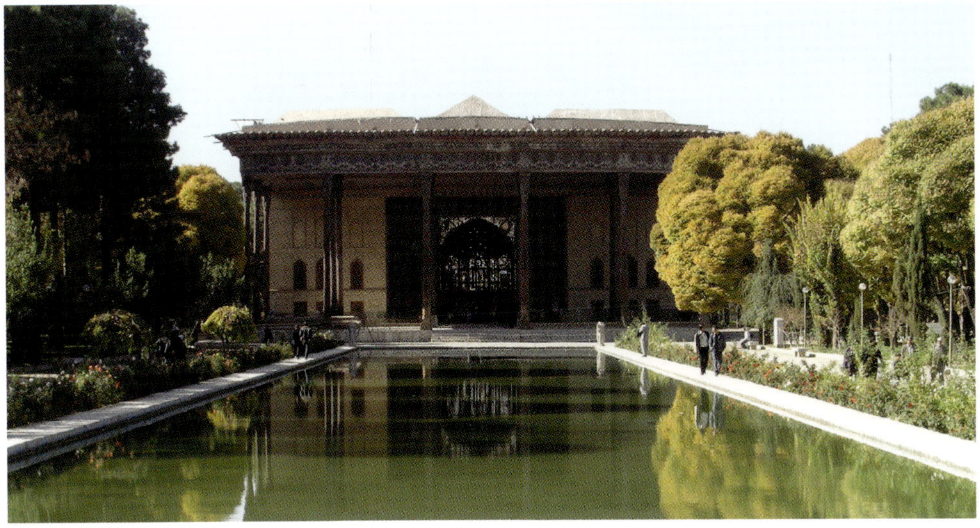

3.22 The Chihil Sutun pavilion, Isfahan

(formerly Kirmanshah) to see the pre-Islamic rock carvings at Taq-i Bustan and Bisutun, and then across the Zagros mountains to Isfahan and Yazd. The surviving Safavid pavilions of Isfahan, the Chihil Sutun (illus. 3.22) and the Hasht Bihisht, provided us with information on the original disposition of a tile panel that the V&A owns (illus. 3.23), and this is reflected in its display in the Gallery (illus. 4.12). The journeys from Isfahan to Yazd and from Yazd to Tehran allowed us to visit a number of monuments in smaller settlements along the way, such as the tomb

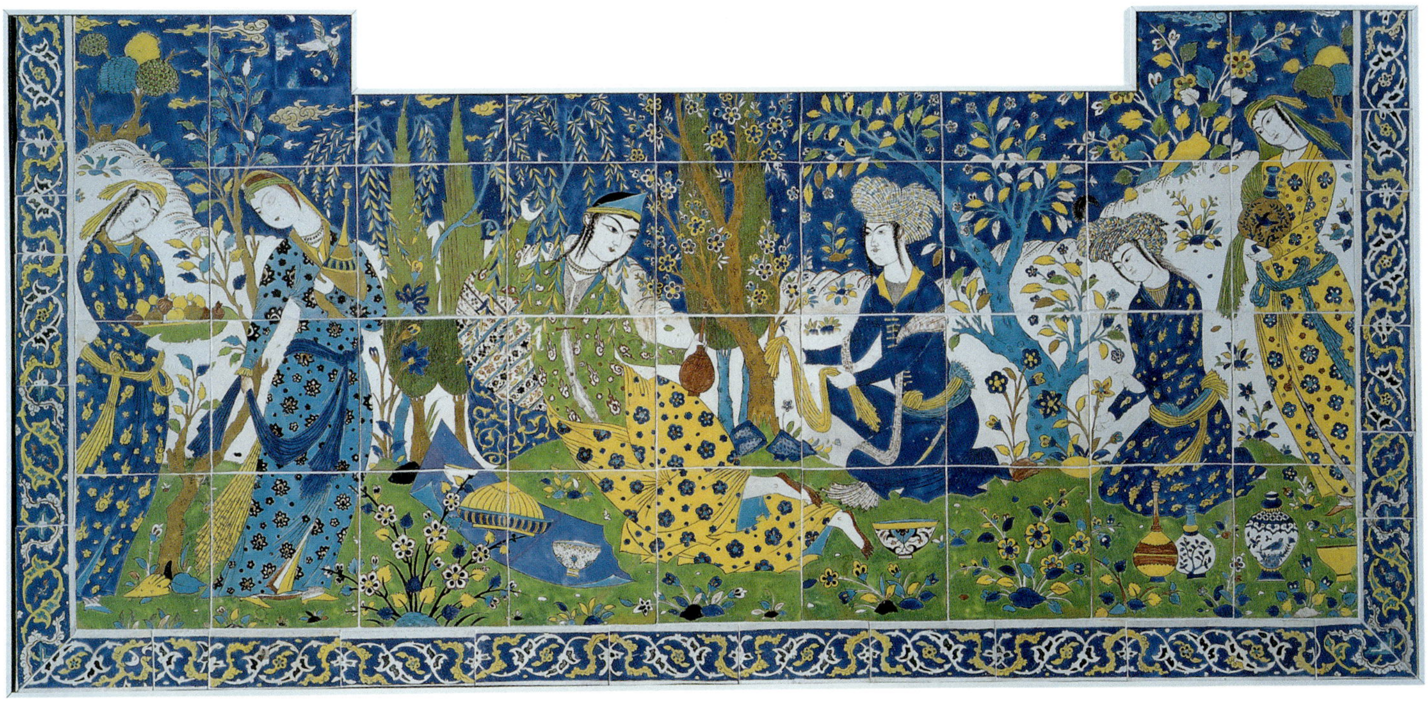

3.23 Tile panel, Iran, 17th century. V&A: 139–1891

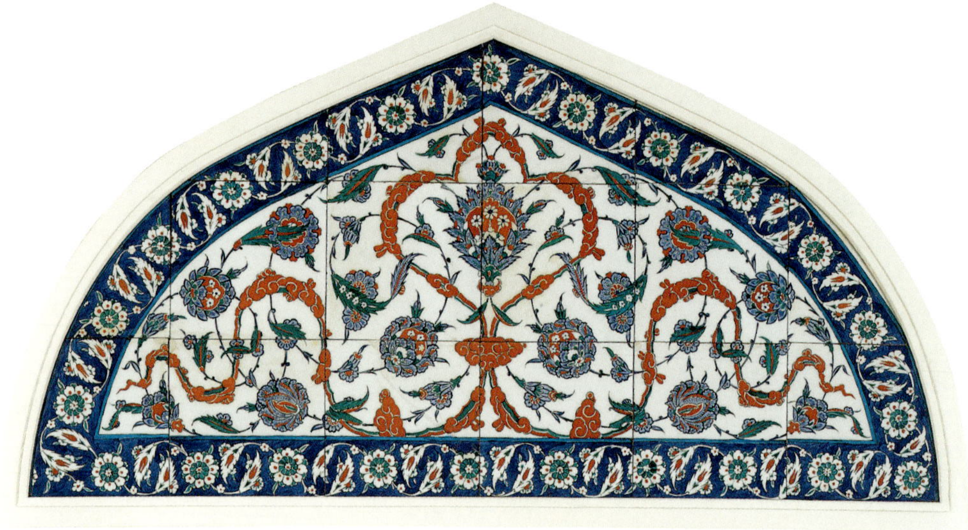

3.24 Tile lunette, Turkey, *circa* 1572. V&A: 1889–1897

complex of 'Abd al-Samad in Natanz. At our last stop, Kashan, we were able to watch velvet and other silk textiles being woven by hand in a craft workshop.

In early 2005 a number of short field trips were undertaken by individual curators to Istanbul, Cairo and Morocco. Among the sites I visited in the first two cities were the huge mosque of Piyale Pasha in Istanbul, from which a lunette tile panel in the Jameel Gallery is said to come (illus. 3.24, 3.25), and, in Cairo, the mosque that Sultan Qa'itbay built beside his tomb, where a minbar very like that in the Jameel Gallery still stands (illus. 3.26). In Morocco, Mariam Rosser-Owen

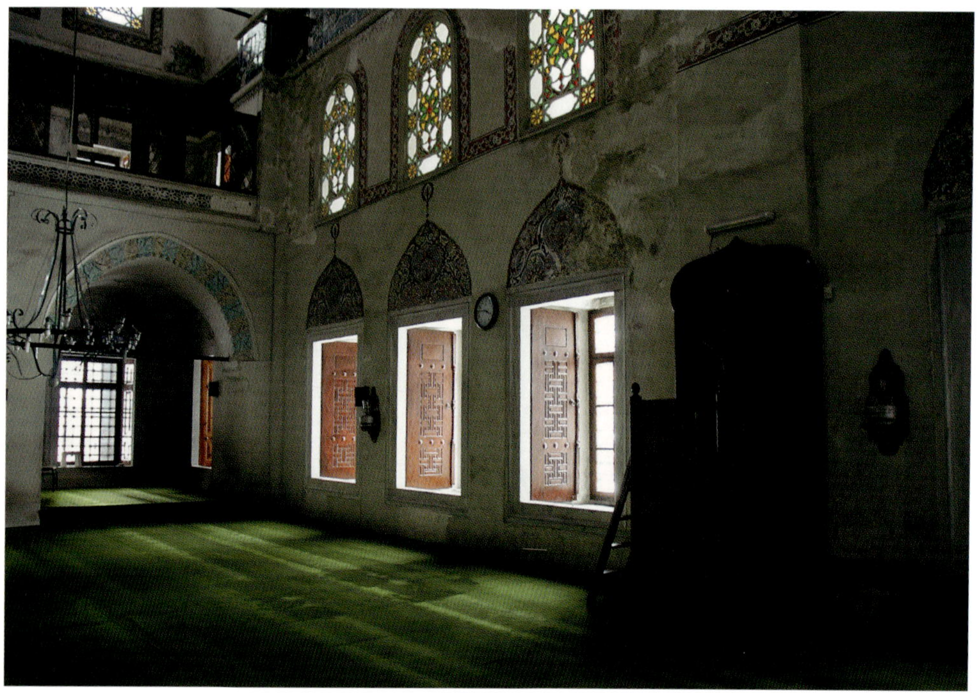

3.25 (*left*) Interior of the Piyale Pasha mosque, Istanbul

3.26 (*right*) Interior of the mosque attached to the tomb of Sultan Qa'itbay in Cairo

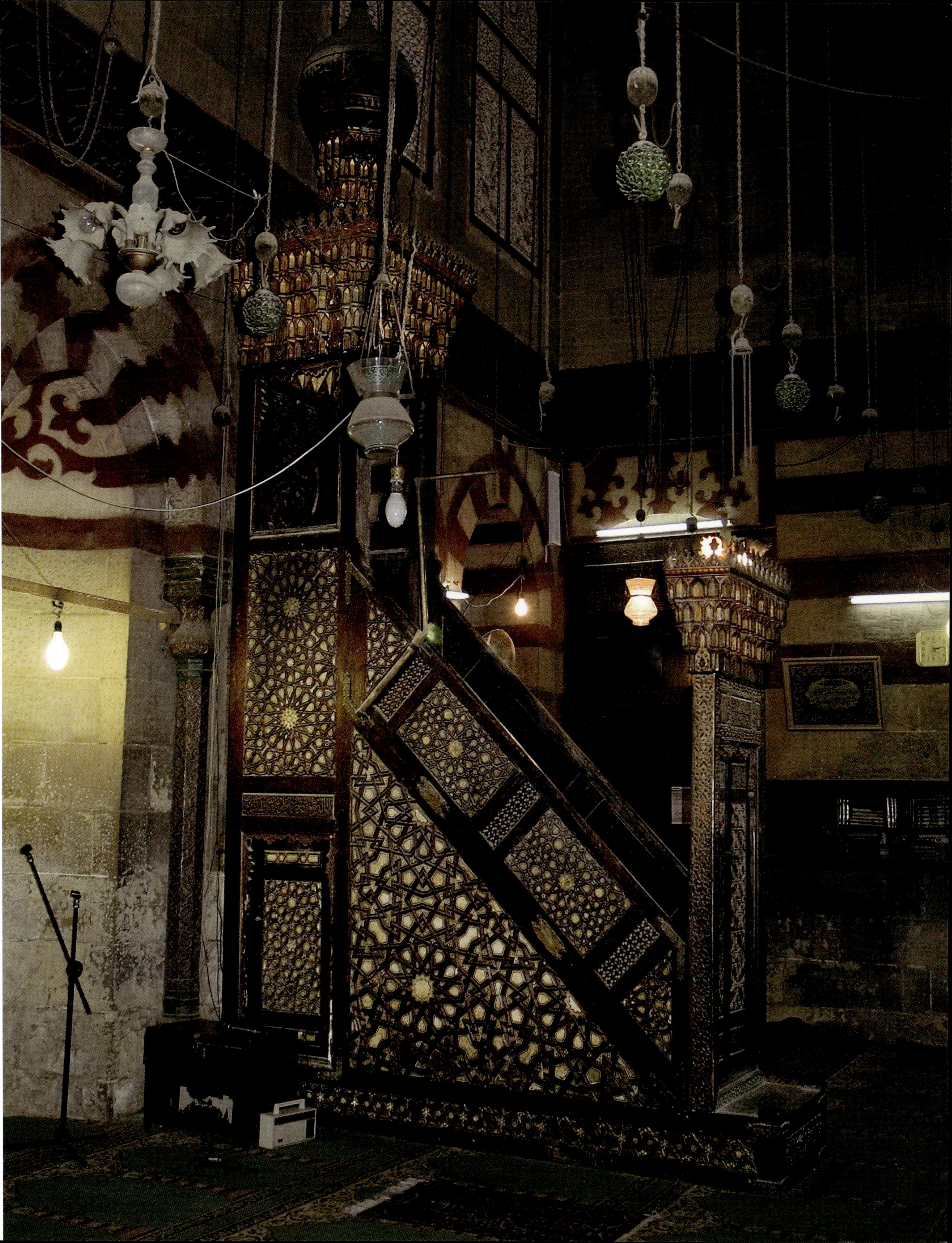

carried out more sustained research on six sections of a wooden calligraphic frieze in the V&A's collection (illus. 5.11). Panels of this type have been described at various times as Moroccan, Spanish, Syrian and Egyptian, but initial research pointed to Morocco as their most likely provenance, since inscribed woodwork is a consistent feature of monumental architecture there.

Parallels, at least in terms of the Kufic style of script employed, were indeed found in the carved woodwork on monuments of the early fourteenth century in Fez. One example is the Funduq al-Tastawniyyin, which provided lodgings and a place of business for merchants from Tetouan (illus. 3.27). The background decoration in these fourteenth-century examples was, though, much more elaborate and much denser than that in the V&A's specimens. The same was true of the Kufic inscriptions in stucco and cut tilework on fourteenth-century buildings of Fez. It was therefore necessary to find earlier parallels, from the Almoravid and Almohad periods (1055–1147 and 1147–1269 respectively), of which the Almohad city gates still standing in Marrakesh and Rabat are magnificent examples. These were built between 1150 and 1200 and feature long Kufic inscriptions that form the

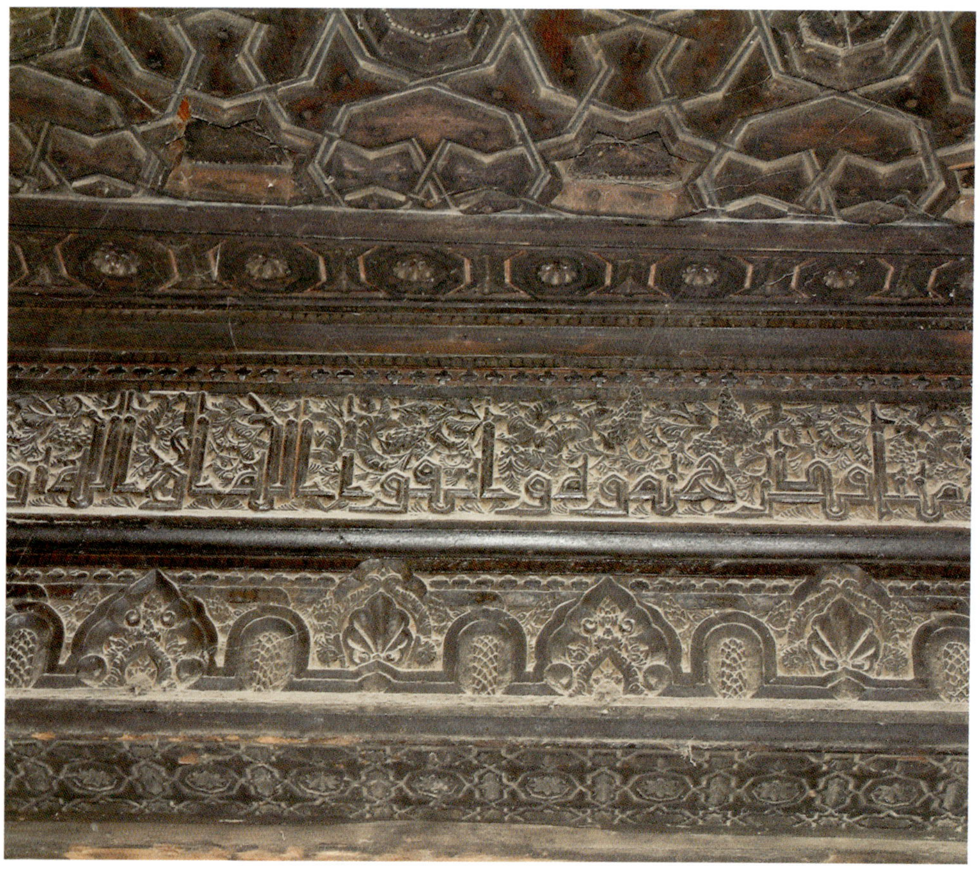

3.27 Detail showing the inscription on the ceiling of the Funduq al-Tastawniyyin, Fez

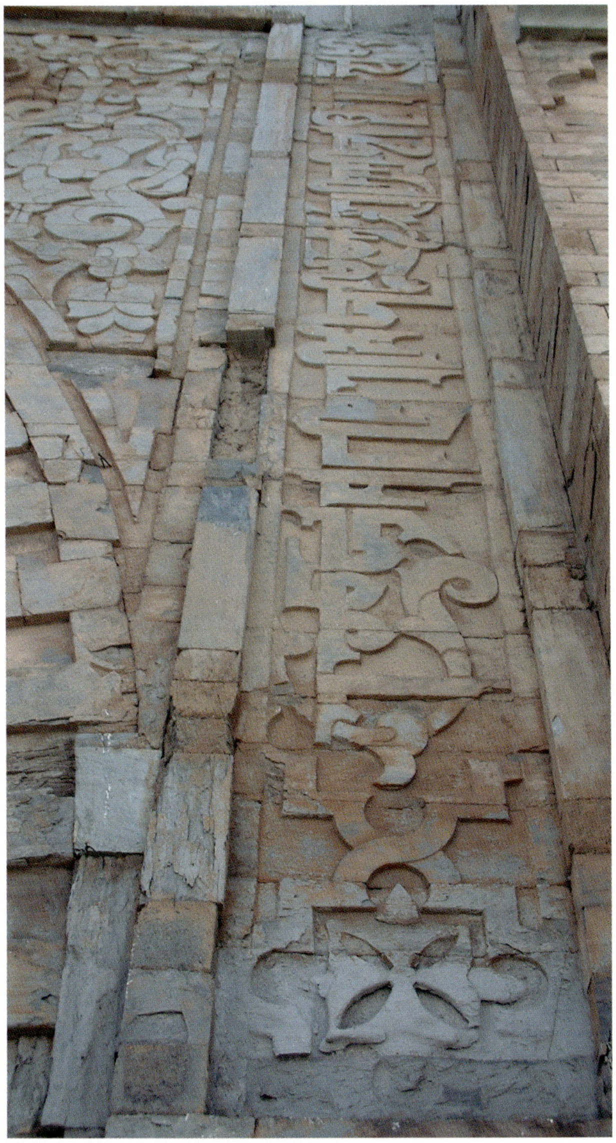

three sides of a square frame around the gates' main arch (illus. 3.28). The form of the script and the sober use of simple floral motifs provide the closest parallel to the design of the V&A's wooden beams. These can therefore be attributed to Morocco in the Almohad period.

The themes

The result of these deliberations is a concept for the Jameel Gallery that moves from the information-rich thematic treatment in the southern half of the room to a more relaxed, pattern-rich display in the northern half. The northern half of the room is, as has already been mentioned, devoted to two broad geographical regions, the Ottoman empire in the north-east quadrant of the Gallery, and Iran in the Safavid and Qajar periods in the north-west quadrant. To an extent, a similar arrangement exists in the southern half of the Gallery. When entering the Gallery from the south-east, the access point closest to the Museum's main entrance, visitors are greeted by

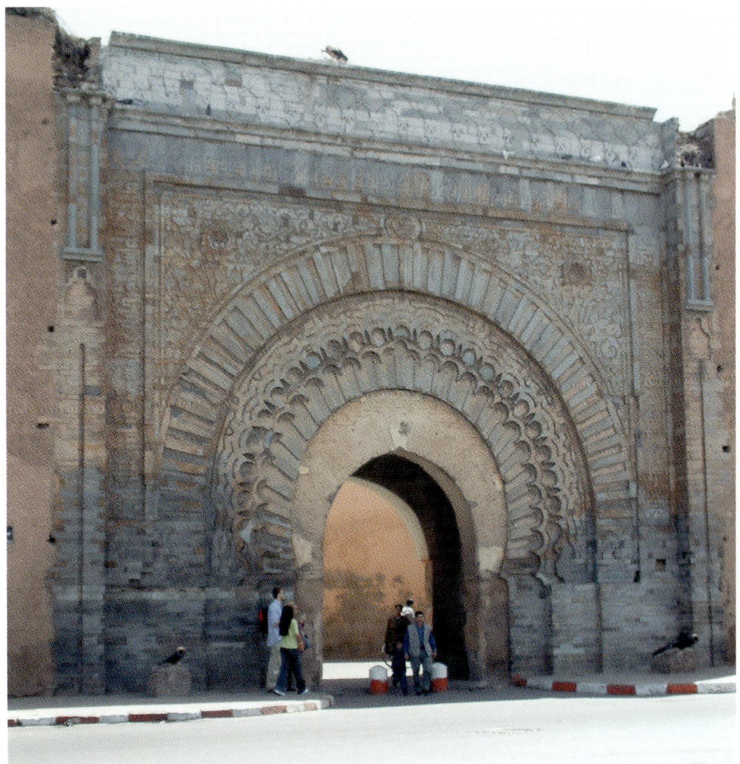

3.28 The Bab Agnhawa, Marrakesh, detail showing the inscription

3.29 The Bab Agnhawa

an introductory section on their right and the interactive map on their left (see Chapter 6). These interpretative elements tend to emphasize political history, and the surrounding displays reflect the role of the region's courts in the formation of the Islamic art of the Middle East, including secular objects from Mamluk Egypt and precious items of rock crystal and ivory made for courts in Cairo and in Córdoba in Spain in the tenth and eleventh centuries (illus. 1.1, 3.8).

The equivalent introductory section at the south-west entrance introduces the religious input into this formation process. It is surrounded by Qur'an manuscripts, the minbar of Sultan Qa'itbay, a large ablutions basin of carved marble, and displays of scientific instruments used for religious purposes, as well as textiles, tiles and sculpture associated with burial practices. The two sequences of themes – one covering religious art, the other secular art – merge in the displays devoted to Mamluk patronage, which are placed centrally at the southern end of the Gallery. These move from the minbar, through a range of smaller items made for religious buildings, to the secular objects already referred to.

The introductory themes in the south-east quadrant of the Gallery are not, however, all devoted explicitly to the arts of the court. Examining them in some detail shows how the displays and their interpretation can give a sense of interaction between the arts of the Middle East and those of other regions.

To the right of the entrance is a case showing items that illustrate the transition from the art of the Middle East in the pre-Islamic period to that of the Islamic period. The main issue is how the traditions of Antiquity were continued into the Islamic period, and how changes gradually accrued over time so that Islamic objects became distinct from those made in the pre-Islamic Middle East. To the right of the same entrance, a sequence of four cases contain groups of objects in several media that explain the main themes current in Islamic art before 1500: calligraphy, plant-based ornament, geometry, and human and animal figures.

Opposite is the display mentioned above showing courtly objects made from precious materials. It is continued by a display of later objects of base metal that had been made precious by the addition of gold and silver inlay. The great skill employed in making these allowed for a remarkably graphic depiction of many of the themes of courtly art. Together, these two groups – the precious objects and the inlaid metalwork – pick up the theme of transition to a distinctively Islamic art, for, while the rock-crystal and ivory objects can be seen as continuing both Roman and pre-Islamic Iranian traditions, the inlaid metalwork is an innovation in the art of the Middle East that had taken root by the end of the eleventh century.

Another 'Islamic' innovation, which began in Iraq a little earlier, in the tenth century, was the shift to the use of ceramic tablewares, and the flowering of ceramic art in the Middle East is the subject of the display on the inner side of the same case. If they could afford it, people used imported Chinese wares. If they could not, they bought locally produced wares, which at first simply imitated features of the imports. Very soon, however, the new demand spurred further innovations, such as the invention of lustre.

The influence of Chinese wares was sustained over a long period, and it received a great boost when in the thirteenth century the Mongols created a world empire that encompassed large parts of the Middle East as well as China. The Chinese began to produce blue-and-white and other types of porcelain for the Middle Eastern market, and local potters reacted by producing their own versions of these wares. Objects illustrating this process are shown at the north end of this case. Opposite is a display that illustrates a similar relationship between the Middle East and Europe. They include, for example, a number of outstanding specimens of so-called 'Veneto-Saracenic' metalwork, both those made in the Middle East for the European market in the fifteenth century, and sixteenth-century copies that were made in Europe.

The final element in the Gallery is the temporary display case in the south-west quadrant. Here we intend to show selections of material that are not well represented in the rest of the display, especially costume and manuscripts. Indeed, it is because both textiles and books are light-sensitive that the contents of this case will have to be changed on a regular basis. Loans from other institutions and private collections will be shown here, as well as pieces from the V&A collections.

With the opening of the Jameel Gallery of Islamic Art, the V&A has successfully completed another stage in one of the most important projects in the Museum's history, the coordinated redevelopment of all its public spaces. For the Museum's collection of Islamic art from the Middle East, however, this achievement is, if anything, more significant. More than half a century ago, in 1950, the finest part of this collection was given a prominent place in the Museum, but this prominence then faded, as the gallery aged and the light levels were severely restricted. Now, thanks to the decision to create a team of specialist curators within the new Asian Department, and, more importantly, thanks to the generosity of the Jameel family, a new gallery has been created that shows the Museum's impressive collection in a setting of fitting quality. The lights have been turned back on.

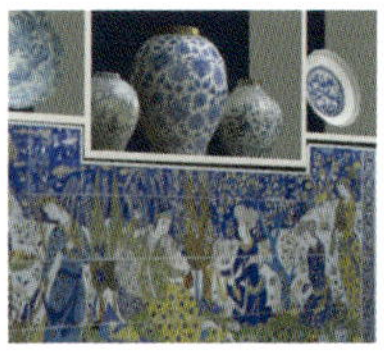
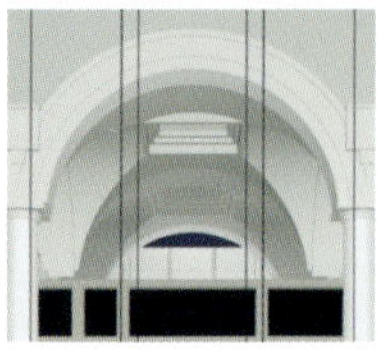
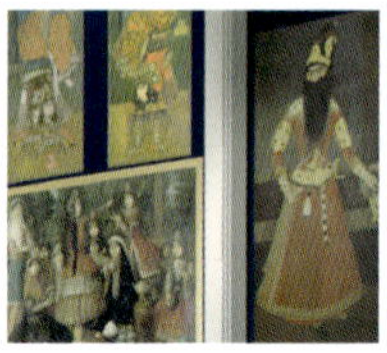

4 THE DESIGN OF THE JAMEEL GALLERY

Oliver Salway

Softroom, a London-based architecture practice, was appointed as lead designer for the Jameel Gallery in July 2003, following a two-stage invited competition. The first stage, involving a dozen or so design teams, called for an outline response, while the second stage asked for key ideas from two teams to be developed further. Since establishing Softroom in 1995, I and my fellow director Christopher Bagot had built up a diverse portfolio of work, including prior experience of temporary exhibition design. We had also previously encountered the challenges of integrating a contemporary aesthetic with the Victorian architecture of South Kensington, at the Prince Consort Restaurant in the Royal Albert Hall. However, we had never before worked with historical objects to create a permanent museum display, nor did we have a detailed knowledge of Islamic art or architecture.

The design brief

The Museum's design brief contained extensive requirements regarding the many technical aspects of museum display, including object conservation, visitor accessibility, content interpretation, graphic design and display-case construction. Many of these stipulations related to knowledge recently gained by the Museum during the creation (and subsequent operation) of the ground-breaking British

4.1 Computer-generated view of the Gallery from the Museum shop

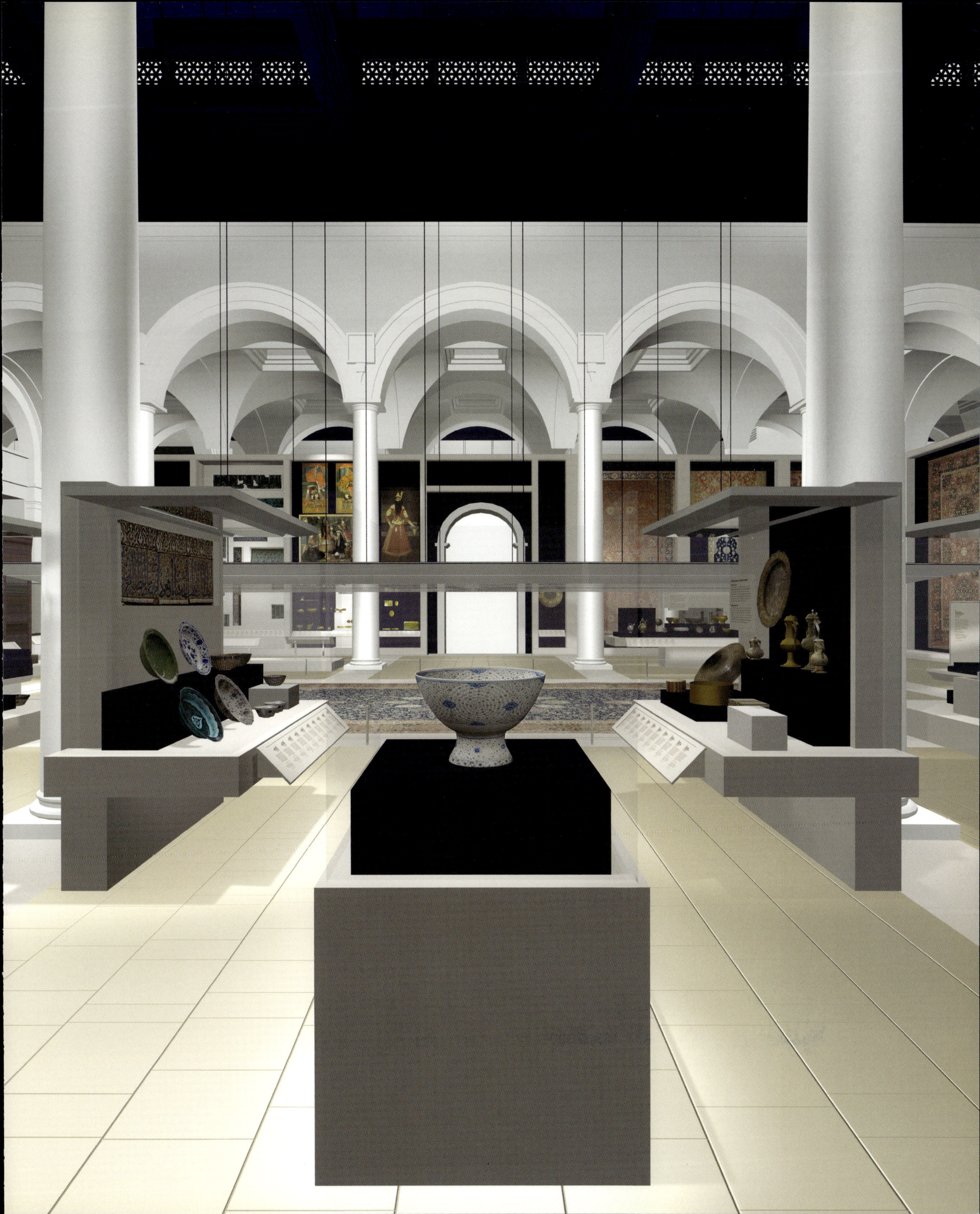

Galleries, which were to act as a benchmark for future projects. It was therefore Softroom's intention from the outset to create an innovative gallery, but one that built upon existing expertise.

A central aspiration of the brief was that the Gallery should evoke a subtle sense of Islamic space, without resorting to pastiche. In response, a contemporary visual aesthetic for the Gallery needed to be generated. We felt that the design must avoid the pitfall of attempting to dilute traditional forms in order to render them 'modern'. One clear reason for this is the direct proximity that the new elements would have with the artefacts on display. Many of these objects are supreme examples of genres that had been refined over centuries. By contrast, the design language of the exhibition would need to be rapidly defined over the course of a few months.

The design should also not contradict the curatorial messages of the Gallery, which aim in part to confront stylistic preconceptions about Islamic art. To focus too strongly on the dominant style of one period or region would be to risk bias, yet to collage indiscriminately would also be unacceptable. At the same time, the visual experience of any Islamic culture is indeed one of great diversity: the inheritance of pre-existing traditions, imperial domination, the migration of artisans and cultural exchange via trade have all played their part in the creation of a visual identity of beguiling complexity.

As one means to unlock the puzzle, the project's sponsor was emphatic that the designers should visit key sites within the Islamic world. These trips, taking in Egypt, Syria, Turkey and Iran, provided us with the opportunity to appreciate the context in which the artefacts had been produced and enjoyed. The photographic record of these tours resulted in an extensive resource against which we could subsequently evaluate our designs. Clearly, these brief excursions could never replace a lifetime of scholarship into the subject. However, whereas a little knowledge may be dangerous, a degree of first-hand experience has proven invaluable.

Overall, the demands of the brief required of its designers a degree of modesty, both in terms of playing a supporting role to the exhibits, and in recognition of our limited understanding of the cultural sphere. At the same time, the design had to be bold and confident, to stimulate and enchant visitors to the Gallery.

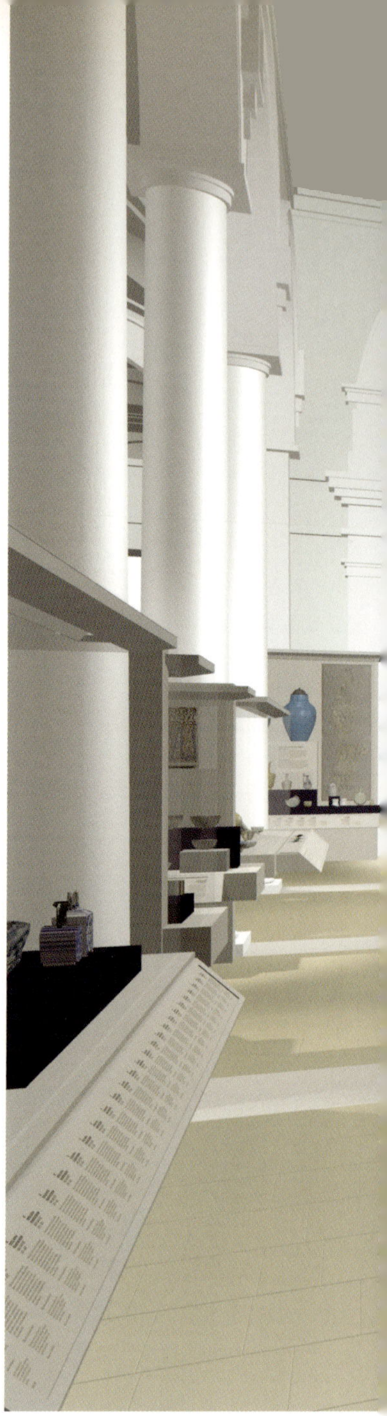

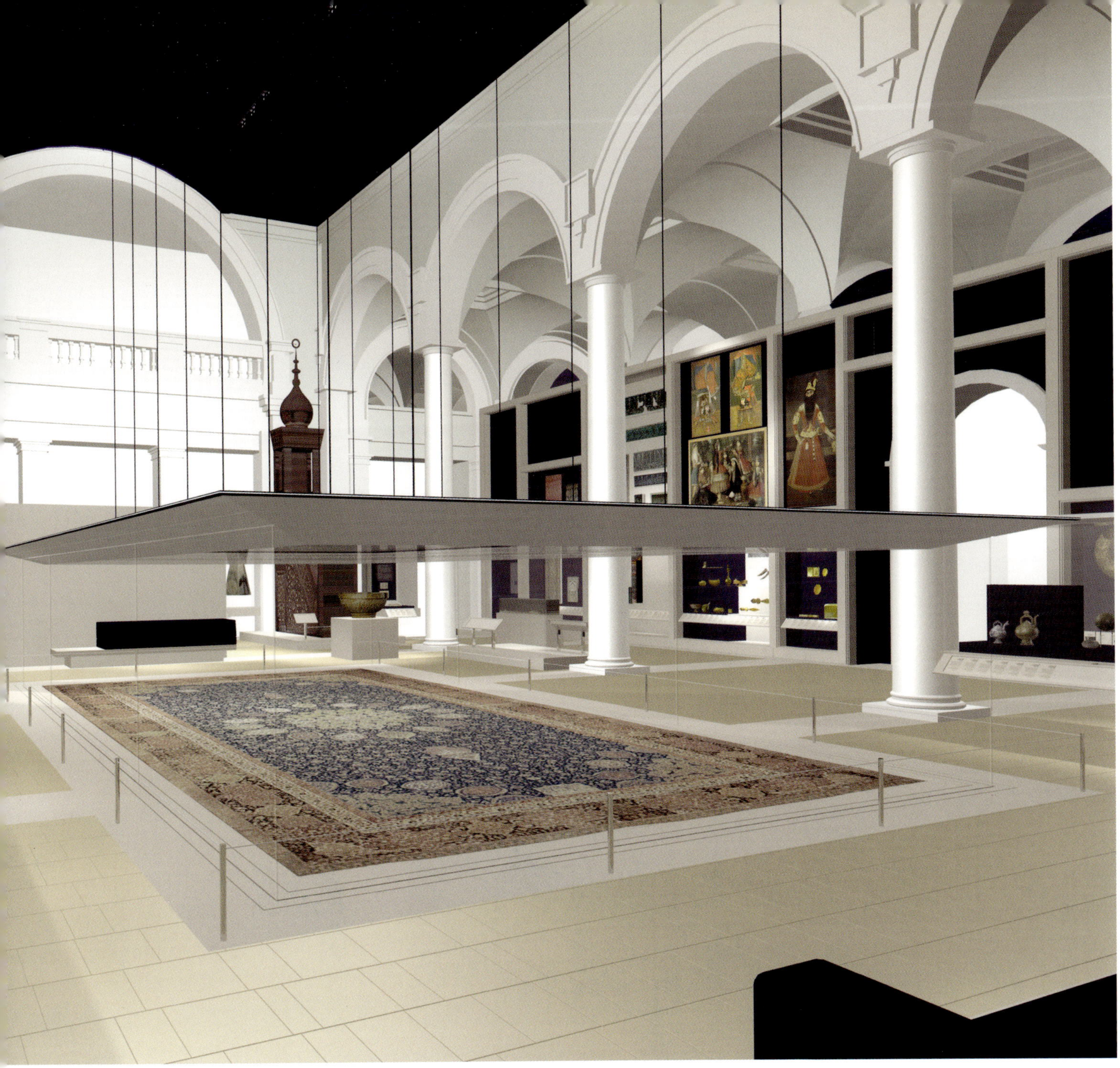

4.2 Computer-generated view of the Jameel Gallery, looking south to show the Ardabil carpet

The challenge of the existing architecture

While a central consideration was that the Gallery should be evocative of the spaces of the Islamic Middle East, a major constraint was imposed by the existing Italianate architecture of the Museum (illus. 4.2). The treatment of the gallery design represents an attempt to reconcile the two. Fortuitously, the Jameel Gallery is able to make a virtue of the classical form of its setting. A point of reference is the Umayyad Mosque in Damascus (illus. 4.3). There, the colonnades of the prayer hall are the product of the reuse and adaptation into an Islamic space of what was once a Roman temple and then a Christian church.

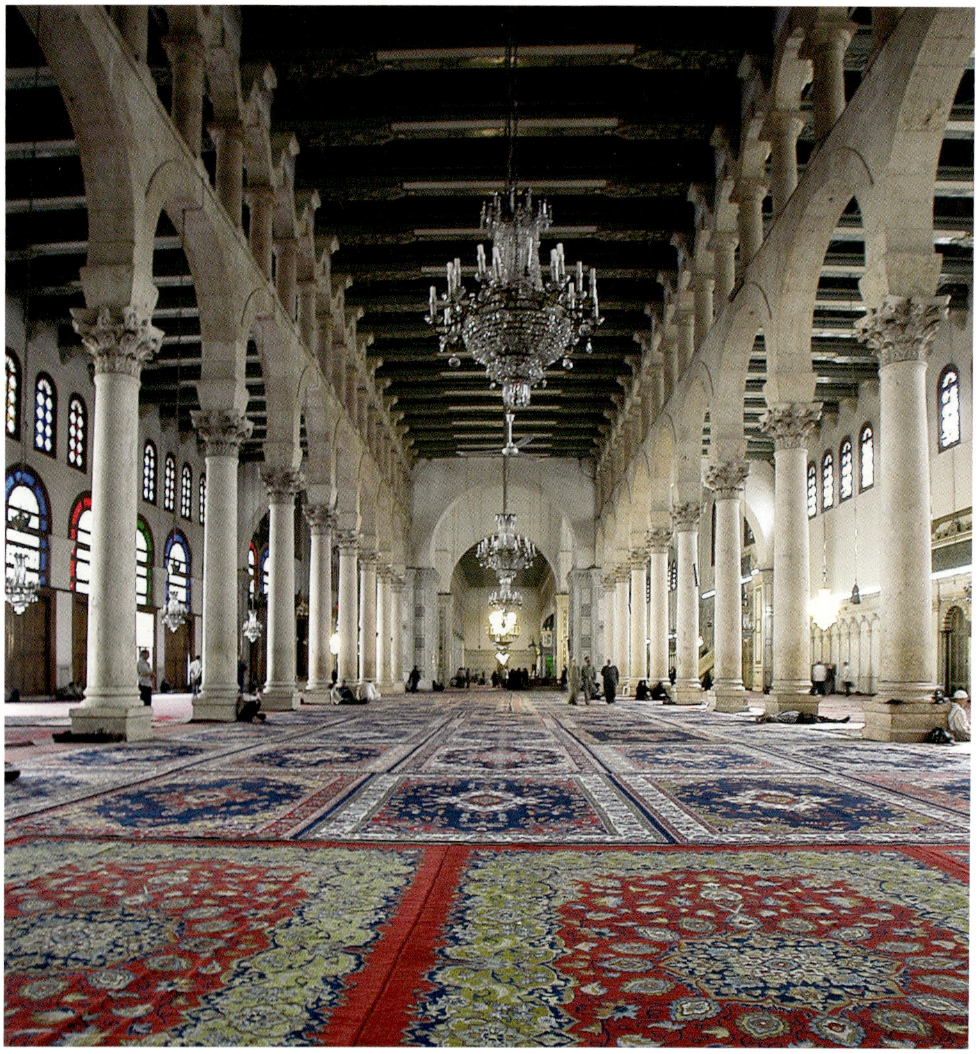

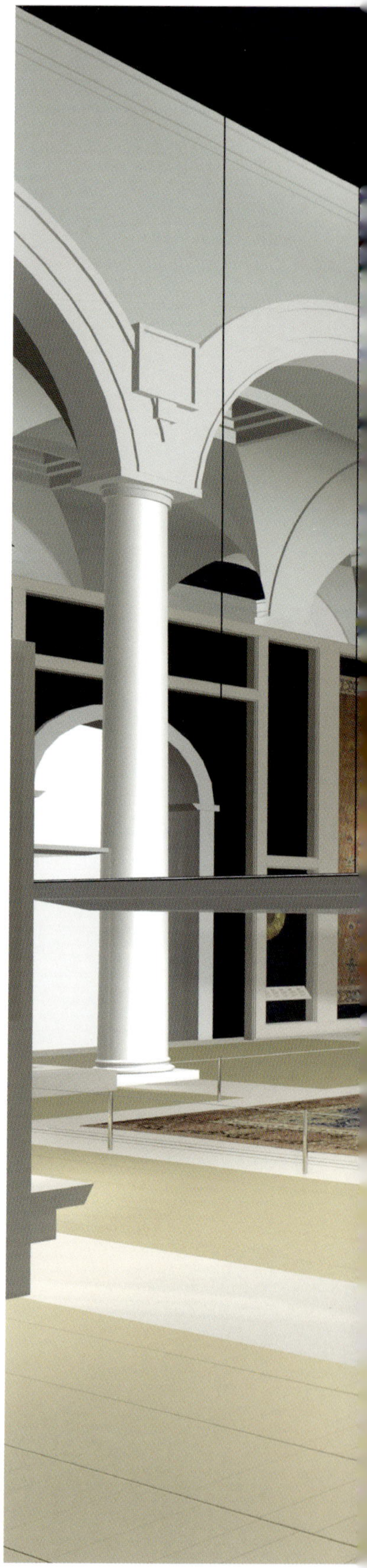

Unlike the enfilade of spaces that comprise the British Galleries, the Jameel Gallery is a single room with a strong character. Although there might have been curatorial advantages to creating a sequence of discrete spaces, it would have been architecturally inappropriate to heavily subdivide the room. A conscious decision was taken to maintain sightlines across the Gallery, and not to obstruct the reading of the composition of arches, architraves and columns already in place. In this way, the free-standing elements of the exhibition design are of a 'loose fit' around the historical structure (illus. 4.4).

4.3 (*above*) Interior view of the Umayyad Mosque, Damascus

4.4 (*right*) Computer-generated view of the Jameel Gallery, from the south-east entrance

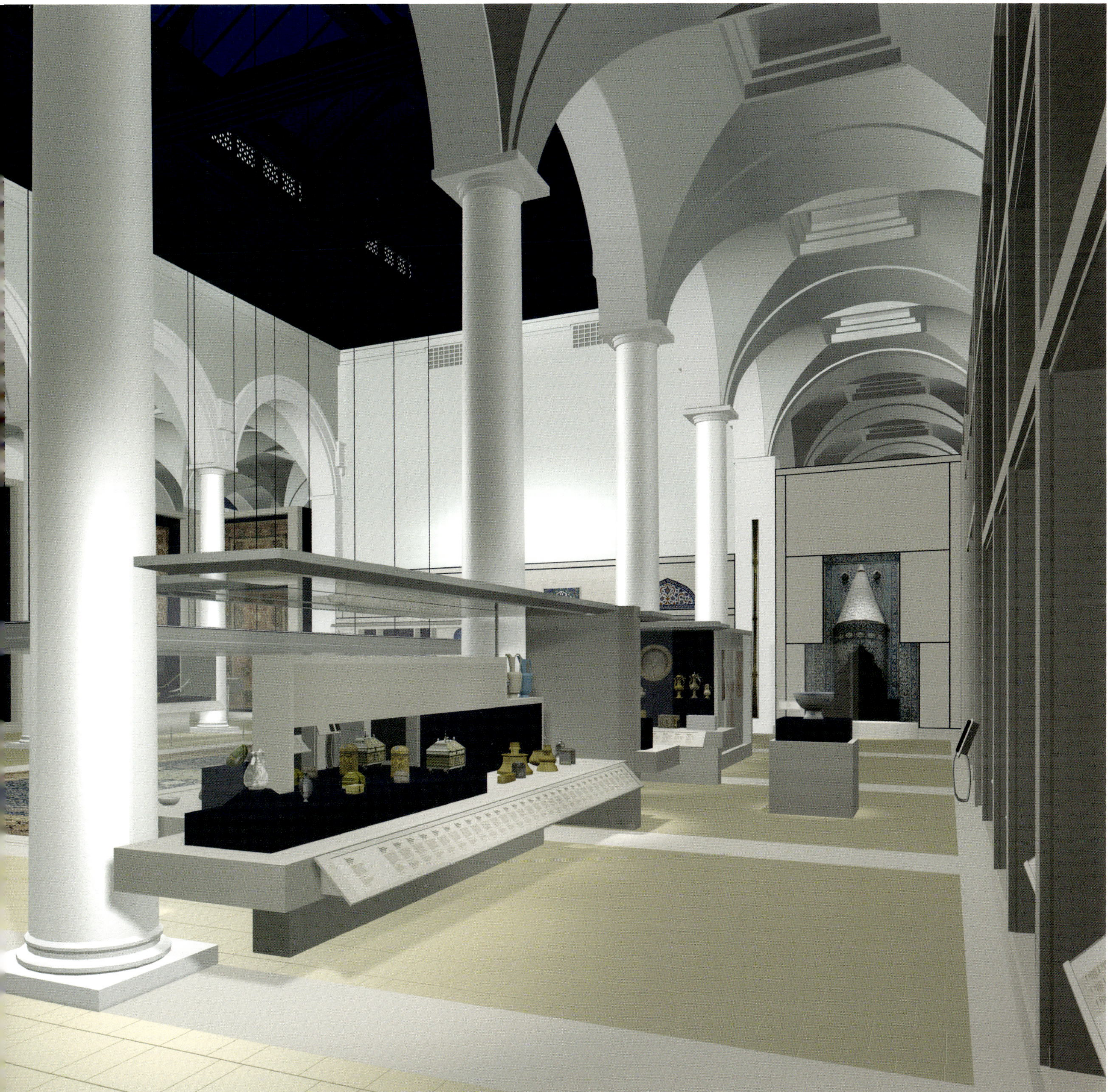

The gallery design accommodates the directives of the Museum's FuturePlan – a comprehensive renovation of the Museum, which includes an aim to liberate circulation routes across the site. As such, the Jameel Gallery takes its place within a suite of galleries dedicated to the arts of Asia. Connections to the neighbouring galleries have either been maintained or opened up (illus. 4.5). This allows for physical and thematic connections to be made between the displays in the Museum's main South Asian gallery to the west and its main Chinese gallery to the east. Of particular interest is the ability to step directly from the world of the Mughal empire in South Asia to displays dedicated to that of the Safavids, their counterparts of Iran, through the arched opening in the west wall of the Gallery.

Significantly, the maintenance of several large apertures into the Gallery space – of great benefit to the creation of an open and inviting atmosphere within the Museum – has impacted heavily on the resolution of the exhibition design. Where the environmentally controlled British Galleries permit a great many objects to be presented on open display, this is simply not possible in the Jameel Gallery. The space is intrinsically interconnected with the naturally ventilated main public spaces of the Museum and cannot avoid light-spill from the daylit ironwork gallery at high level on the south side. These factors require that all but a very few robust exhibits be encased in hermetically sealed environments free from dust, and shielded from stray light that might otherwise perceptibly fade over time the textiles on display.

The challenges posed by the objects

Primarily, the Jameel Gallery must provide an optimum balance between the often contradictory demands of displaying and conserving the objects that it houses. Of these, few can be more taxing than the centrepiece of the display, the Ardabil carpet (illus. 1.9). A key stipulation of the brief was to find an innovative solution for displaying this carpet, one of the Museum's larger and more fragile masterpieces.

For many years the Ardabil carpet had been hung in a huge upright case on the north wall of the Gallery. Originally the Gallery had been dramatically daylit from a central skylight in the nave and lanterns along the vaulted aisles, but these had subsequently been enclosed, making the space appear gloomy and uninviting (illus. 1.19). The dim level of artificial light remaining in the Gallery had resulted in the vertical glazing of the Ardabil's case distractingly acting as a mirror to reflect the semicircle of bright light from the ironwork gallery at the opposite end.

4.5 Computer-generated view of the Jameel Gallery from the reopened west entrance

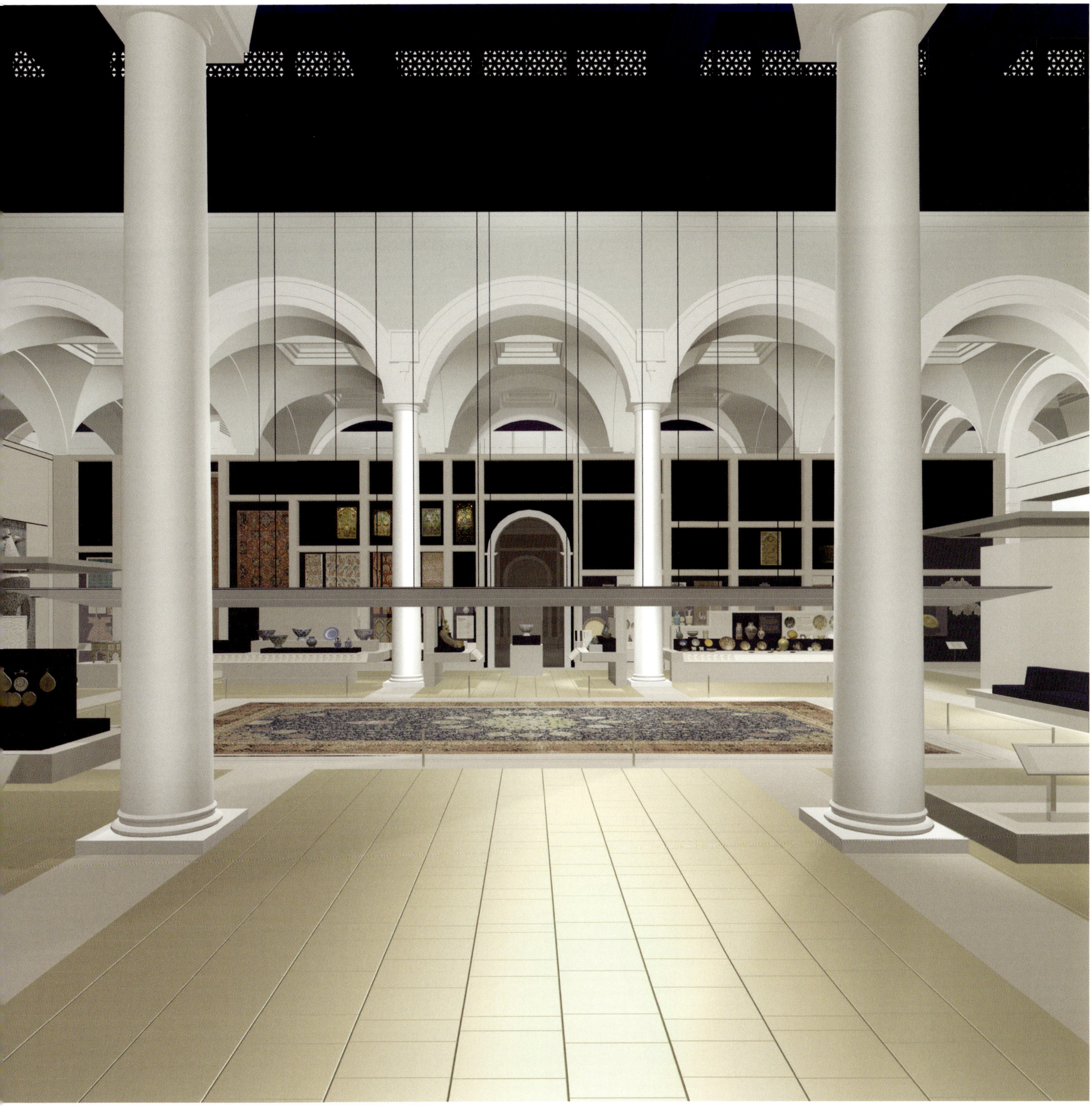

The first, and perhaps boldest, move in the design was to propose placing the carpet centrally on the floor. One reason for this was to emphasize the fact that the Ardabil is not a wall-hanging but a floor-covering, designed to be used and appreciated at ground level. When it is laid out flat, the viewer can experience the way the complex geometries of its design shift and change as you circulate around it.

As part of the feasibility analysis of the project, several options for encasing the carpet at low level were initially explored. Perhaps the obvious response would be to set the carpet beneath a glazed floor. However, this was not considered appropriate, because spanning the vast dimensions of the exhibit would have needed glass that was very thick (and hence of a strong green hue) and regularly supported by a grid of beams, disrupting the view of the carpet. The traffic of visitors' feet across the glass would inevitably have resulted in the glass becoming heavily scratched.

In the finalized gallery design, the Ardabil carpet sits in a case beneath a suspended canopy (illus. 4.2), which serves several purposes. The first is to provide an enclosure for the multitude of tiny light sources that give a controlled, even level of illumination, at the same time as protecting the textile from much of the stray incident light in the room. Second, an emphasis on the horizontal plane of the canopy distracts the eye away from the vertical glazing of the giant case. By suspending the canopy from fine rods from the ceiling, the glass need only support its own weight and can therefore be of minimal thickness, which in turn permits the colours of the carpet to be read as accurately as possible. This low-level ensemble is redolent of the dramatic chandeliers and glass lamps to be found in the great Islamic religious spaces, notably the mosque of Sultan Hasan in Cairo (illus. 4.6) and the Süleymaniye mosque in Istanbul.

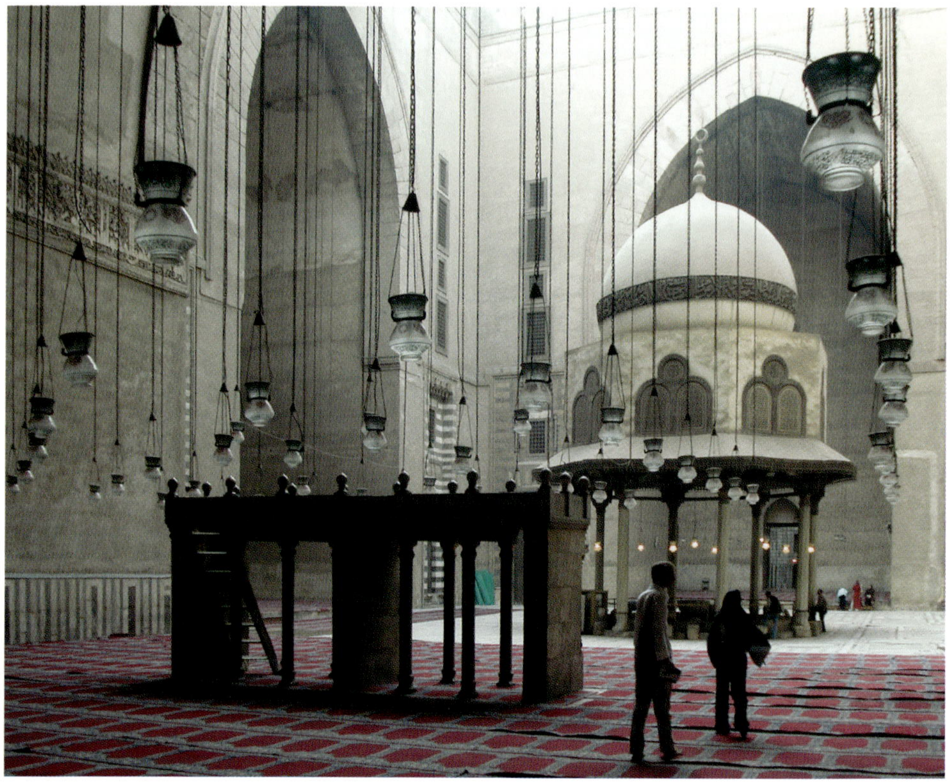

4.6 Interior view of the Sultan Hasan mosque, Cairo, showing mosque lamps with hanging chains

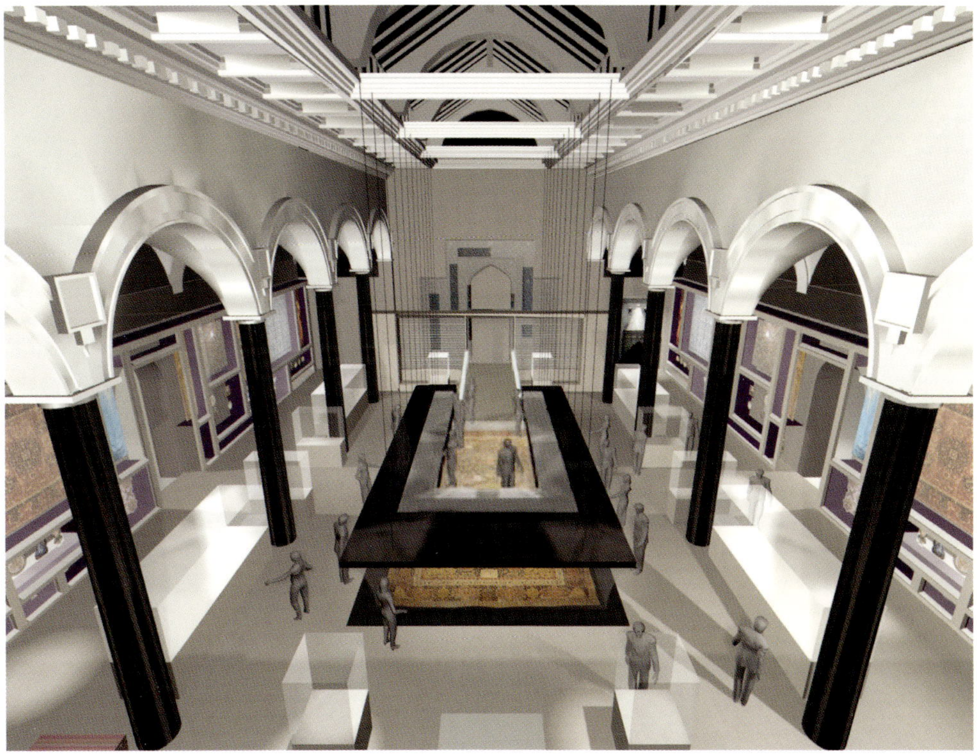

4.7 Early concept drawing for the Ardabil carpet case, showing viewing from the roof of the case; this scheme was later superseded

The glazing is treated with an anti-reflective coating, to mitigate the reflections that had so dogged the previous display. The stone paving is carried through from the main floor of the Gallery to the interior of the case. Working together, these measures help to create the impression that the carpet is in fact on open display on the floor, protected only by a delicate cord barrier around the perimeter.

Early concept designs for the case envisaged that access would be provided for visitors to the top of the canopy, from where they would have been able to look down on to the centre of the carpet through a large glazed panel (illus. 4.7). However, the problem of scratching the glass remained, and to make the experience accessible to all users, ramps would have wrapped around half of the Gallery, leaving many other exhibits viewable only from a slope. An alternative proposal, using steps and a platform lift, was considered potentially intrusive. The serene nature of the realized display seems entirely in accordance with the mood of the Gallery.

The very scale of the Ardabil carpet meant that it became the generative device for the planning of the remainder of the Gallery. The decision was taken to maximize the usage of the available wall space by creating a gridded framework around three sides. Niches within the grid house many of the two-dimensional

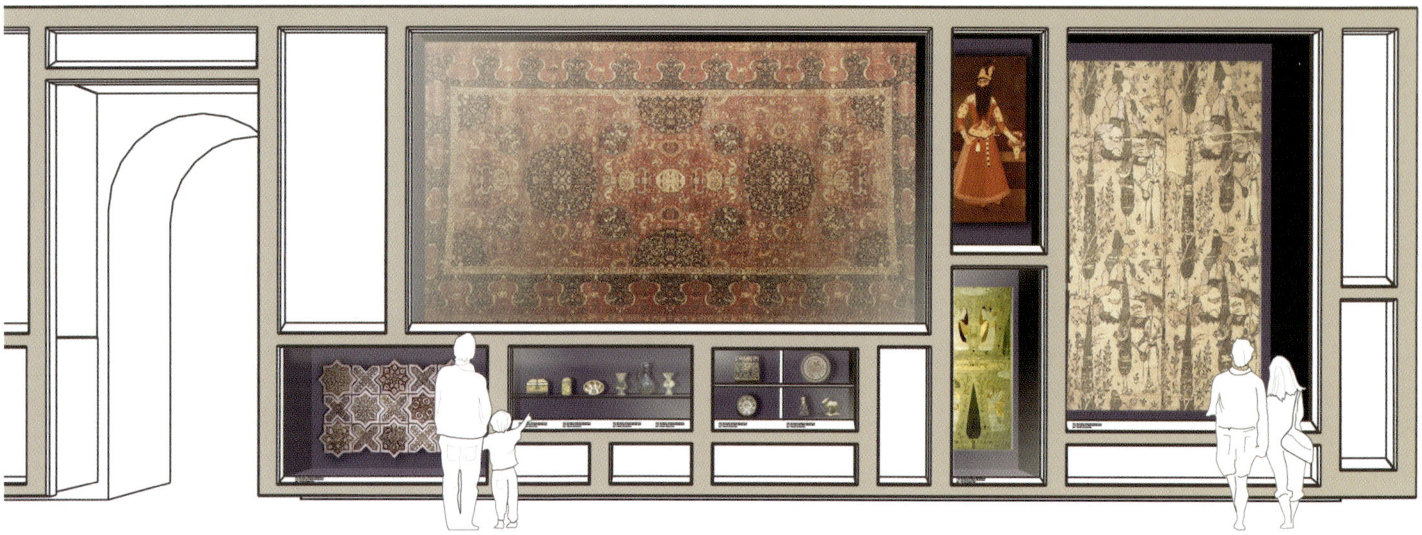

4.8 Initial study of wall-cases showing the grid system

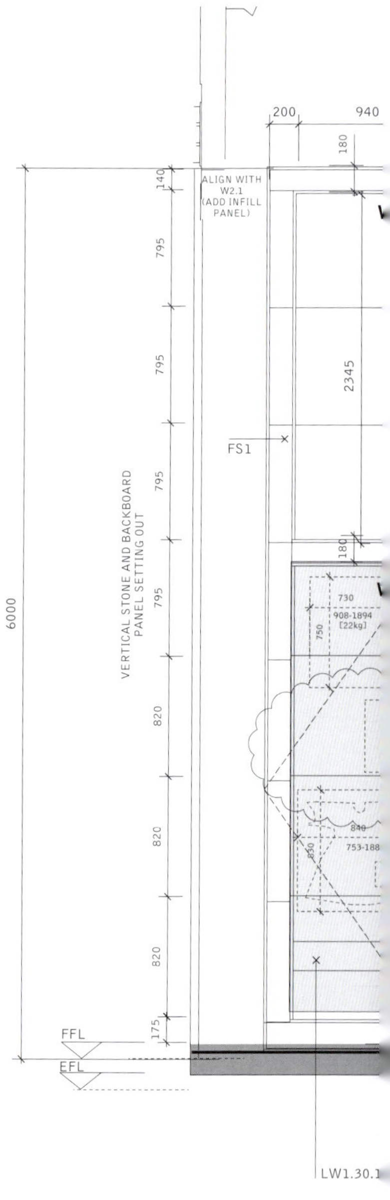

objects. The great size of the Chelsea, Morris and 'medallion Ushak' carpets, which must be hung vertically rather than laterally to avoid damage to their structure, demanded that the frame be taken up to a height of six metres, matching the height of the colonnade. Elsewhere, displays are on more than one level, with smaller objects at eye level, and bolder exhibits, such as the large Qajar oil paintings, shown above (illus. 4.8, 4.9). The grid itself echoes devices frequently employed to control blocks of differing patterns in traditional Islamic architecture, while the horizontal delineation of its cladding is a subtle nod to the banding frequently found in Ottoman architecture.

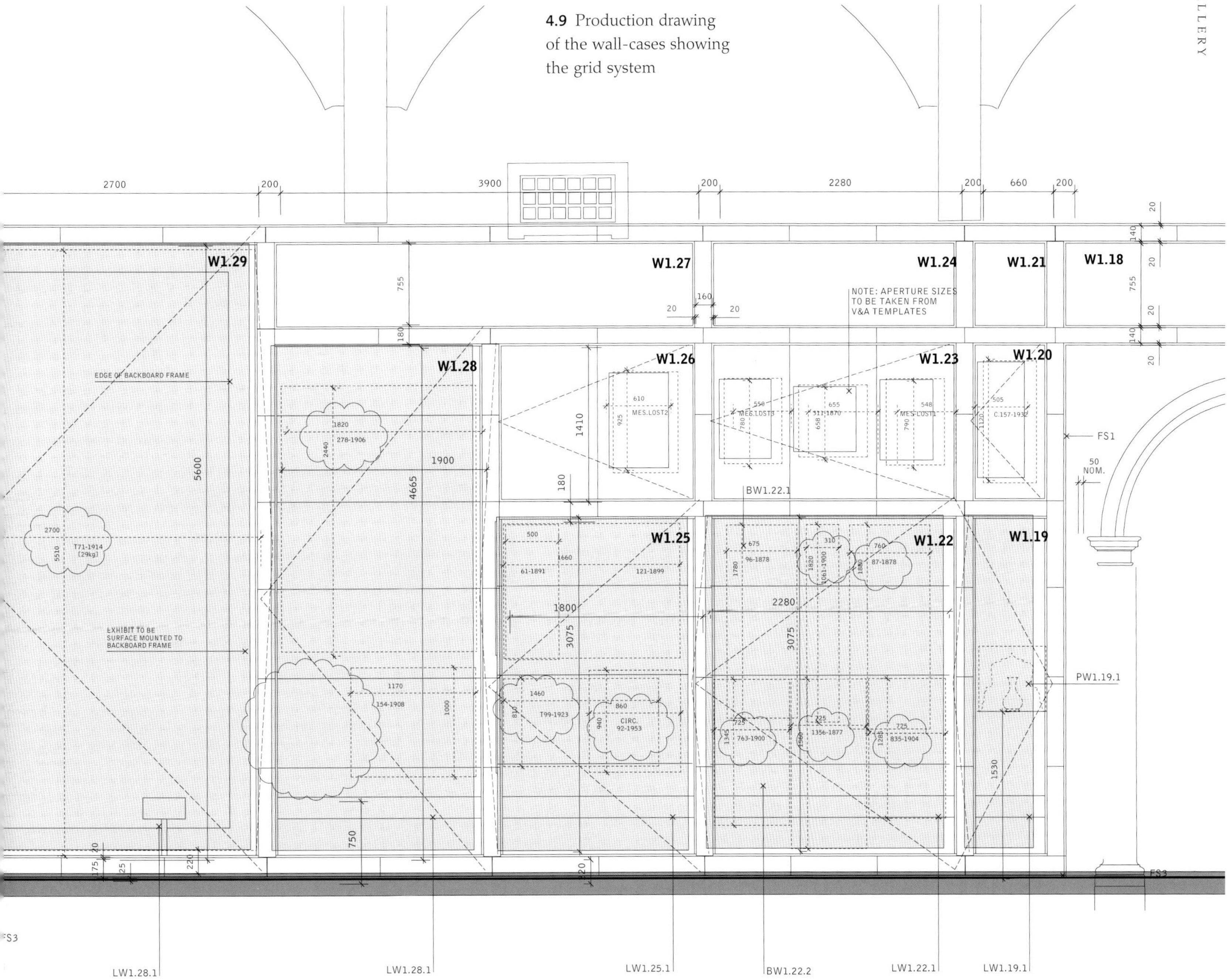

4.9 Production drawing of the wall-cases showing the grid system

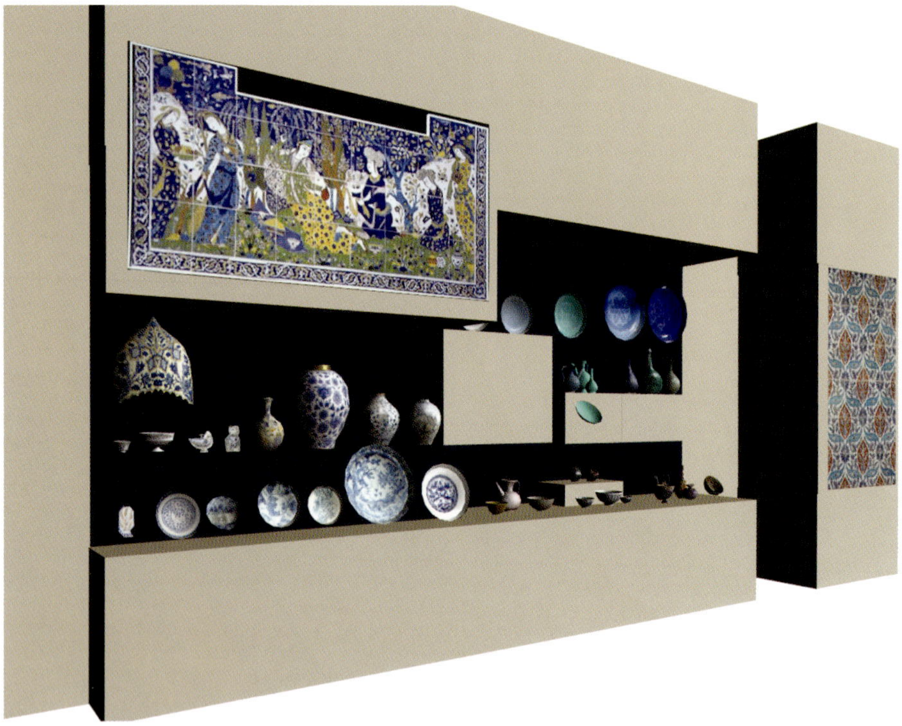

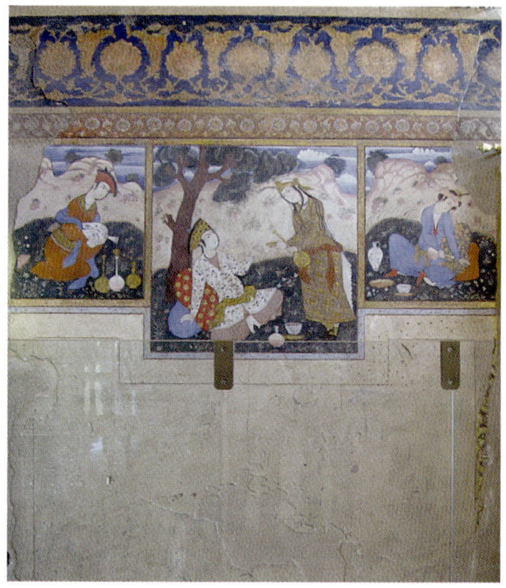

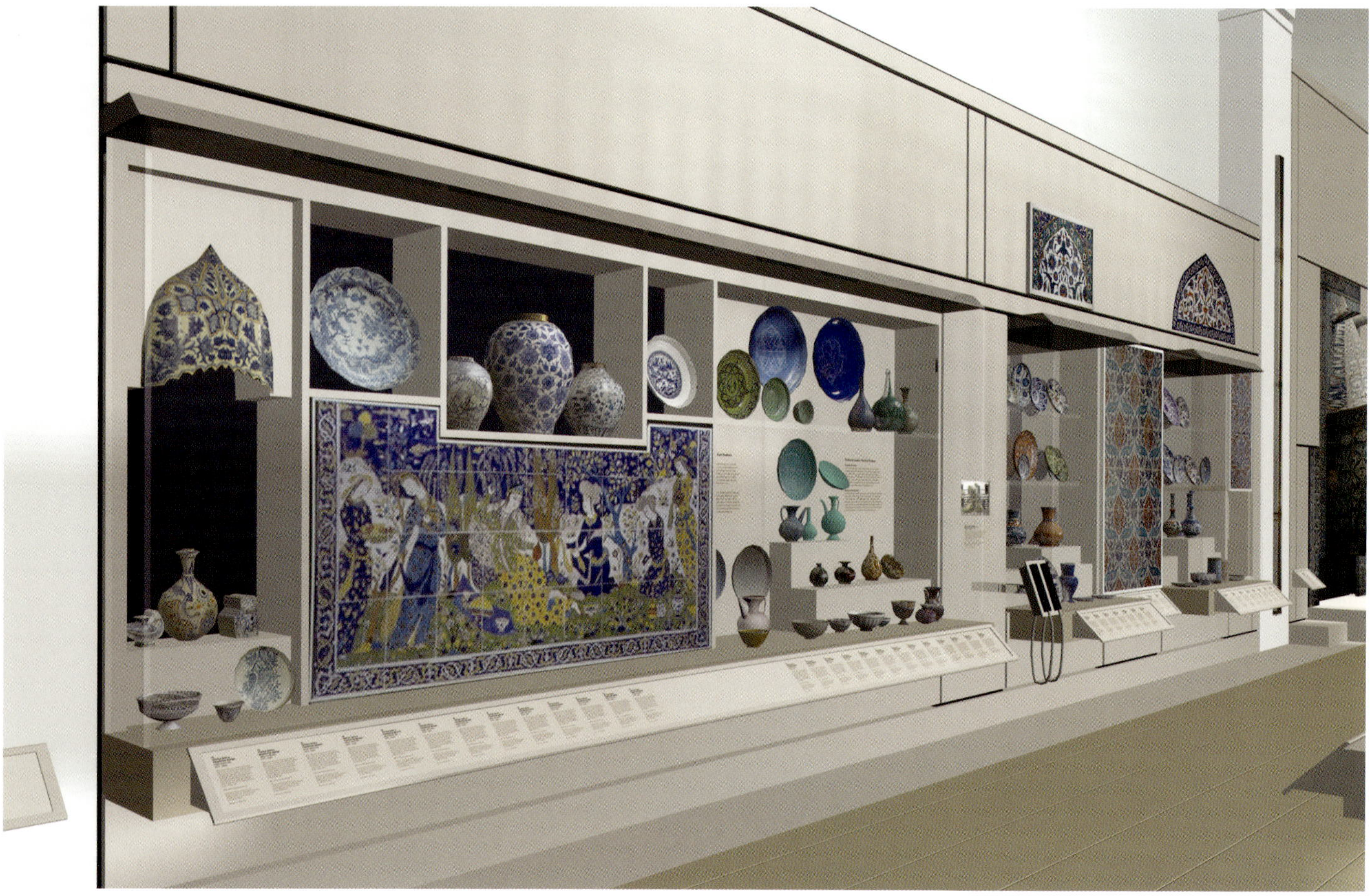

4.10 (*far left*) Early computer-generated view of the display of Safavid ceramics

4.11 (*left*) Painted dado in the Chihil Sutun, Isfahan

Where possible, reference has been made to the original context of exhibits. For example, the minbar is situated to the right of the arched opening on the south wall, in keeping with the location of minbars in mosques seen in Cairo and Istanbul. The Safavid picnic-scene tiles are shown beneath a tripartite arrangement of niches, as are similar dados found in the palace of Chihil Sutun in Isfahan (illus. 4.10–4.12).

Working with the curators

Regular discussions were held between the curatorial and design teams to ensure a smooth integration of the Gallery's content with its design aesthetic (illus. 4.13). Central to this process was the publication of a 'framework document', listing the catalogue of exhibits and explaining the rationale for their arrangement. A detailed list of individual objects and their display needs was also maintained.

It was understood that visitors might arrive through any of the four entrances to the Gallery. Thus the largest, architecturally scaled objects were placed for maximum effect where they might be the focus of a vista across the space – the Ottoman tilework chimney-piece and the Chelsea carpet each being prime examples, sited at the end of each of the aisles (illus. 4.4). A trail of 'star objects' from the collection was laid out around the Gallery, to serve as an enticing route for visitors to follow through the space. Hence the positioning of the Fatimid rock-crystal ewer near the main entrance, and the Ottoman 'Golden Horn' footed bowl halfway down the first aisle, clearly visible through the archway from the adjacent Museum shop (illus. 4.1).

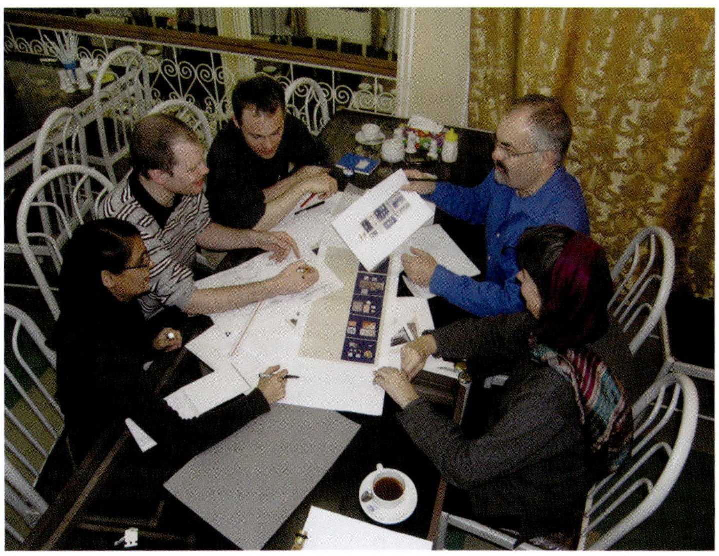

4.12 (*left*) Computer-generated view of the amended display of Safavid ceramics

4.13 Team discussion, Maraghah, Iran (clockwise from left: Nighat Yousuf, Oliver Salway, Barry Wood, Tim Stanley, Rosemary Crill), November 2004

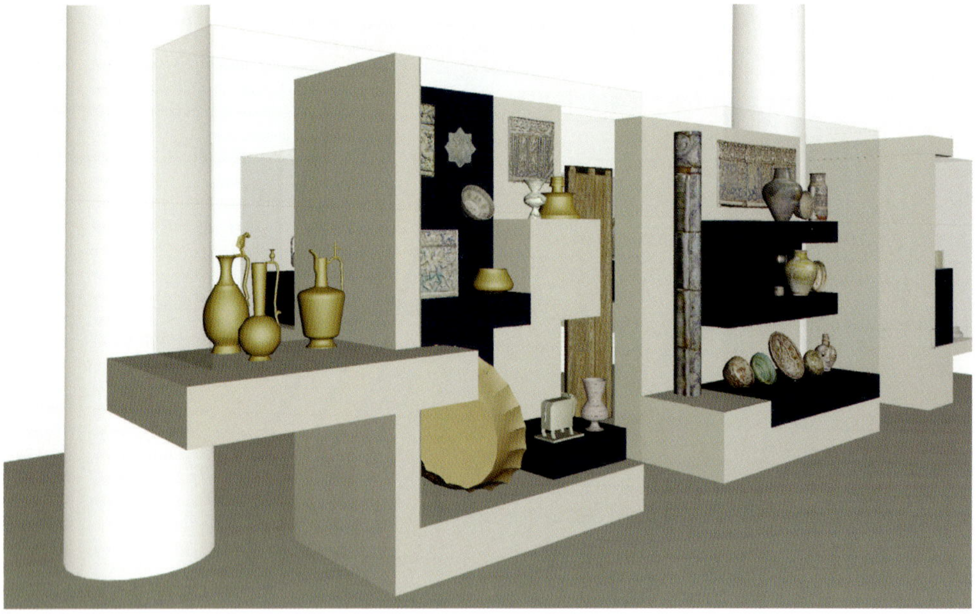

4.14 Computer-generated view of an early layout of Case F2

4.15 Computer-generated view of the final layout of Case F2, 'Art for the Court'

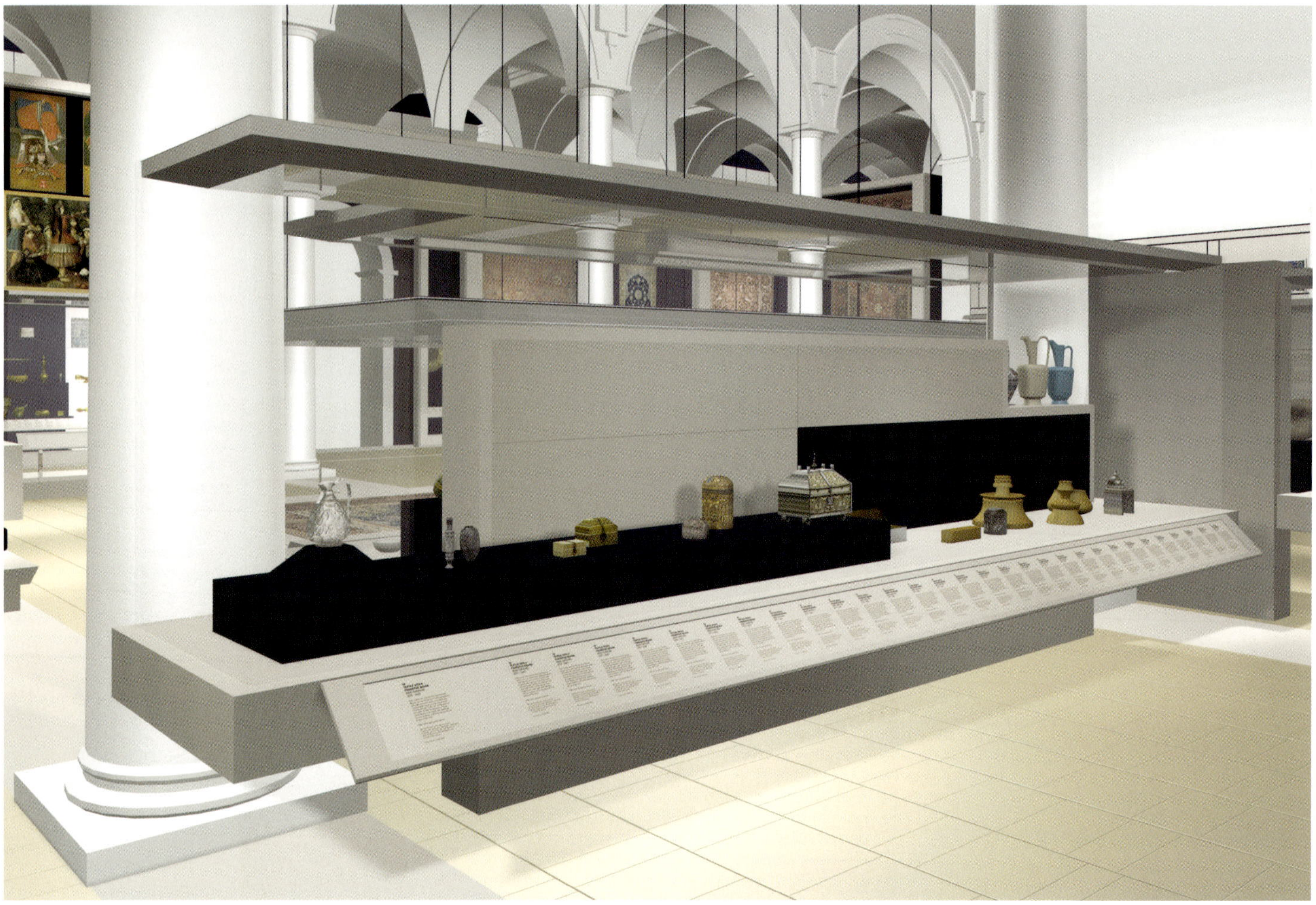

Significantly, the majority of the key artefacts were on tour around the globe as the design work progressed. In their absence, dimensionally accurate 3-D virtual models of each and every one of the 400-plus exhibits were made from photographs at an early stage. Being able to confidently position each object onscreen and see a good representation of its form and materiality proved extremely important, allowing for a very direct form of communication with the curatorial group as the content of the cases evolved (illus. 4.14–4.16).

4.16 Production drawing of the final layout of Case F2

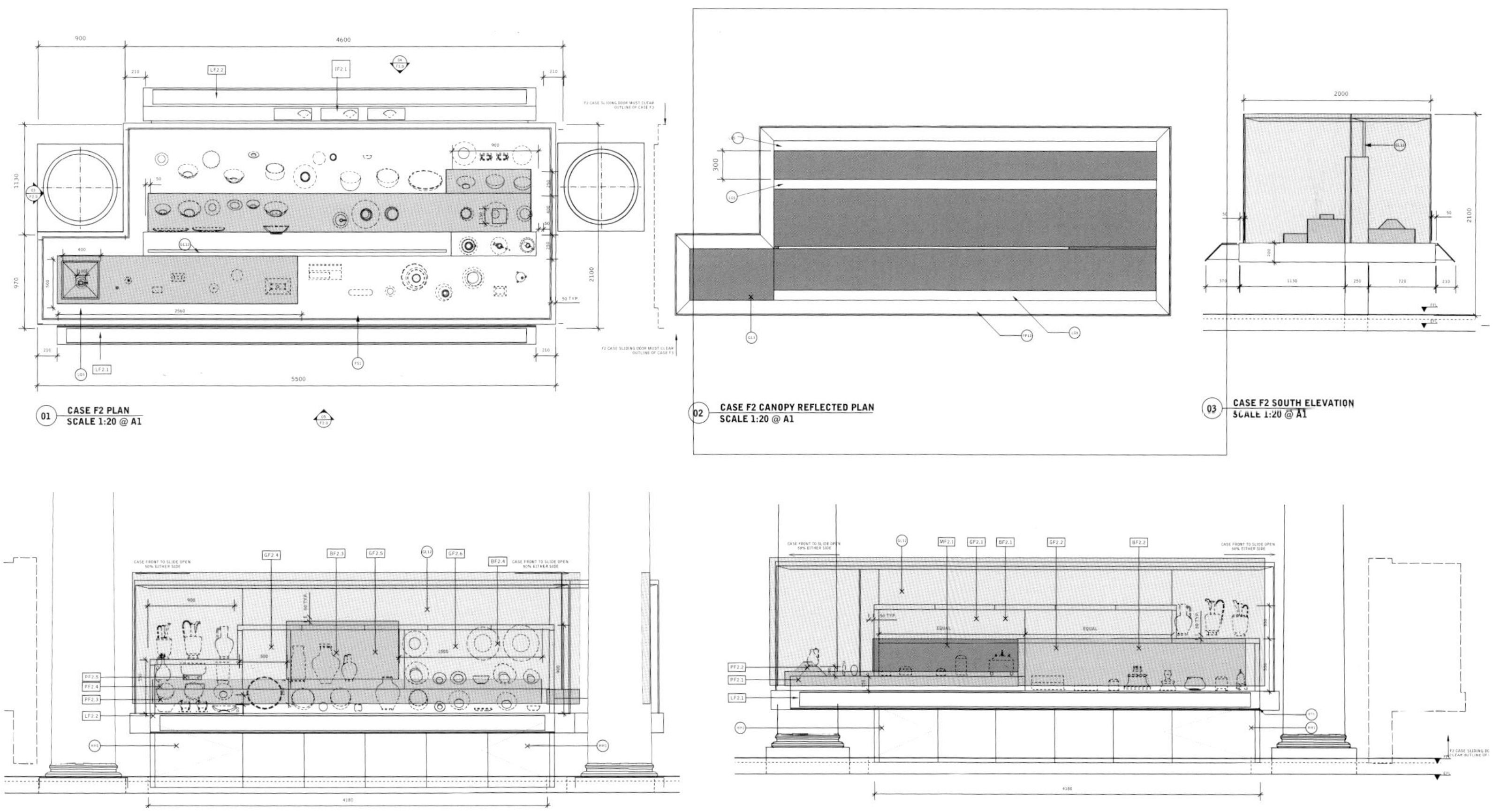

Lighting different types of object

Due to the fragile nature of the collection, the overall level of light within the Gallery is kept low. However, a primary goal was to banish the unenticing and oppressive feeling of the previous display. As a consequence, in laying out the Gallery, a practical division of objects was made on the basis of their sensitivity to light, with textiles kept to the aisles and niches, and the hardier, more light-fast exhibits, such as the many ceramics, being prominently displayed in more brightly lit locations.

Whereas the previous display had suffered from the problem of light reflecting in the glazing of the cases, in the new lighting scheme by DHA Designs the cases are generally lit from within by concealed fittings. As with the case of the Ardabil carpet (illus. 4.2), the majority of the free-standing display cases have a delicate canopy housing fibre-optic lighting, which provides an even level of illumination across the bed of the case and over the text panels on the vertical faces. A combination of top, front and under-lighting with point sources is used in order to pick out detail according to the differing forms and materiality of the objects that are on display (illus. 4.17).

However, not all of the exhibits are encased. Due to their grand scale and relative durability, a few items – such as the minbar – can survive as open displays. Such objects are lit conventionally by spotlights, mounted on discreet runs of track located between the coffers of the ceiling. Others, including the marble ablution basin from Hama, are under-lit from within their plinth, to best reveal the form. In addition, a group of stucco panels, displayed at high level within the wall-case grid, are backlit to reveal their inset stained-glass designs. A concealed fluorescent wash enables the pattern to be read from all points of the Gallery, while a directional spotlight to one side adds a more dramatic effect, redolent of a beam of sunlight.

While work on the Gallery continued, detailed scientific tests were conducted by the Museum on the light-fastness of the different dyes used in the woollen pile of the Ardabil carpet. These revealed that, at the proposed 50-lux level of illumination of the carpet, there was a risk of the darkest blue colour fading perceptibly over the next 25 years. To prevent this, it was decided that the carpet would be illuminated to 50 lux for 10 minutes in every half-hour throughout the day. This radical solution represents the best compromise between preventative conservation and display, and even adds somewhat to the overall mystique of the exhibit.

4.17 Lighting designer David Robertson of DHA Designs demonstrates lighting for a mock-up of case F2 (left to right: David Robertson, Tim Stanley, Claire Thompson, Paul Leng, Oliver Salway)

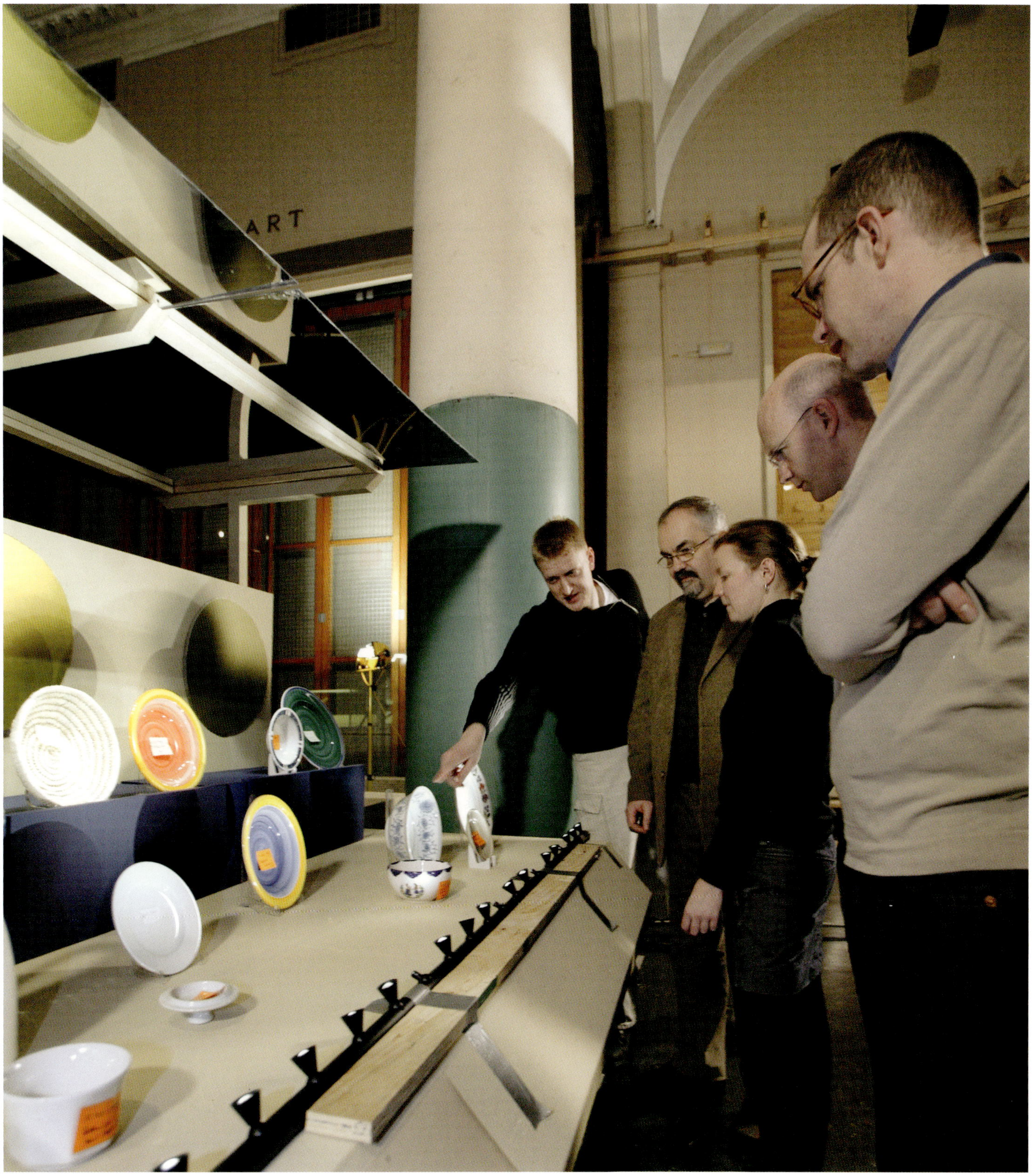
ART

The materials used for cases and flooring

The criteria for selecting the materials to be used as finishes in the Gallery were in part practical and in part formed by a wish to resonate with those found in authentic Islamic spaces. In order to withstand a high volume of visitors for at least a quarter of a century (the expected minimum lifespan of the Gallery), all surfaces must be extremely durable. The delicacy of the exhibits, and the unified nature of the gallery space, implied that a restricted palette would best suit the requirements of the display.

For the flooring, a warm-toned but very hard limestone was selected (illus. 4.18), with contrasting bands of a paler limestone used to pick out the structural grid of the space – a practice witnessed in the palaces of Iran. The tones reflect those found across the Middle East and give a sense of lightness to the Gallery. The floor slabs were laid out perpendicular to the long axis of the Gallery, with stones of irregular width echoing the pattern in the courtyard of the shrine at Ardabil, where the carpet may once have been placed.

The columns have been treated with a white polished plaster finish, to render them as smooth as possible. As a reference to the forest-like columned interiors exemplified by the Friday Mosque in Isfahan or the Great Mosque of Córdoba, mirrors in the blind lunettes of the aisles, above the wall cases, amplify the vaulting of the Gallery, creating an ambiguity concerning the true extent of the space.

To counteract the potential for the hard finishes to create a distracting echo within the space, acoustic consultants Soundspace Design assisted in the addition

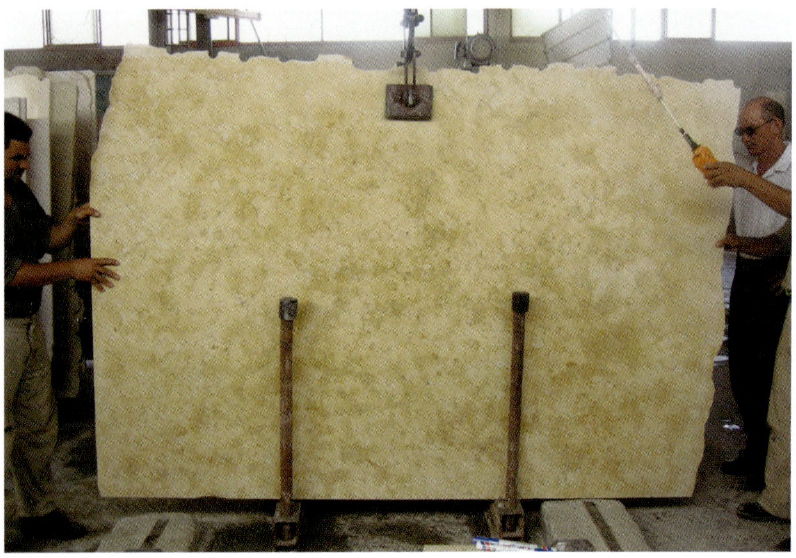

4.18 A slab of the limestone selected for the Gallery floor

of sound-absorbent fabric. Padded material is concealed beneath the overhangs of the free-standing display cases and in the empty bays of the wall-case grid. The entire upper surface of the Ardabil carpet case is perforated and lined to act as a giant baffle against unwanted reverberations. These measures help to give the Gallery a calm and contemplative atmosphere.

The exposed wall surfaces at high level are painted in a soft, pale-green hue with the plasterwork mouldings painted white for contrast. Elsewhere, the dominant colour used throughout the Gallery is a dark midnight-blue, chosen for its ability to recede behind exhibits such as the metalwork, and to reflect the use of blue pigment on many of the ceramics and the central ground colour of the Ardabil carpet. In a dramatic step, this colour is carried over onto the soffit of the nave roof. There are many examples of rich dark-brown or green ceilings in wood or metal to be found in the domestic architecture, mosques and markets of the Islamic world. The intention here was to suggest this effect without direct mimicry, which a shift in colour has permitted.

Beneath the pitch of the nave roof, the original clerestory glazing (in-filled with asbestos cement panels in the past) has been reopened. The rigours of object conservation demand that only a very small percentage of the incoming light may be permitted to penetrate the Gallery. For this reason, each window has an applied film to screen ultraviolet radiation, a diffusing inter-layer in the glass to scatter direct sunlight, and a metal grille. The grille has a laser-cut pattern that alludes to the wooden *mashrabiyyah* screens used in the Middle East to provide privacy, shade and ventilation (see illus. 4.1). The pin-prick pattern of light that it lets through is just enough to animate the upper level of the Gallery and provide a connection to the outside world.

To ensure consistency across the Gallery, wherever possible objects are either placed directly on stone display surfaces or raised on midnight-blue steel plinths. In the selection of stone, slabs with a muted tone and natural variation were preferred, in sympathy with the exhibits, many of which have gently patinated with age.

Two deep leather-upholstered benches, again midnight-blue in colour, enable visitors to rest and view the Ardabil carpet from either end. Behind them, stone-clad walls screen the display cases beyond. Decorating their faces with Islamic patterns and applying them using sandblasting had been considered. However, after full-sized mock-up panels were prepared, concerns arose about the ability of contemporary technology to convey accurately the subtlety of the original carvings, and the idea was dropped in favour of leaving the natural stone finish.

Gallery fit-out and the display cases

A key strategic decision was to split the fitting-out works of the Gallery into two distinct packages. Responsibility for the overall building works, including the roof, floor and decorations, was undertaken by Beck Interiors, a firm with extensive experience of museum renovations. For the display cases themselves, Italian specialists Laboratorio Museotecnico Goppion were appointed. Goppion had successfully delivered the extensive and complicated display-case works for the British Galleries at the V&A and recently rehoused the Mona Lisa at the Musée du Louvre. Their considerable expertise was brought to bear on the many challenges presented by the Jameel Gallery.

Of paramount importance was the need for the display cases to meet the conservation requirements of the exhibits. In tandem with this, they must provide a superlative viewing experience for the visitor. The quality of materials and construction must therefore be second to none. The cases must also provide a safe and reliable working environment for the Museum staff whose task it is to install and maintain the displays. From the outset, the target was to standardize the fabrication and opening mechanisms of the cases, in order to ensure consistency of appearance and facilitate their operation. Simple doors, as opposed to more complex mechanisms, are favoured by Museum staff and were generally adopted as the access method.

Wherever possible, tried-and-tested technology has been employed, to limit the risks associated with innovative design. This was a deliberate attempt to counterbalance some of the challenges inherent in the exhibition design. The sheer scale of the Ardabil carpet case and the wall-case framing pushes modern glazing techniques to their limit (illus. 4.19). In addition, a determination on the part of the designers for the free-standing cases to float above the floor involved skilful engineering by both Goppion and consultants Arup to devise structures that utilize the build-up of the raised floor to conceal dramatic cantilevered supports.

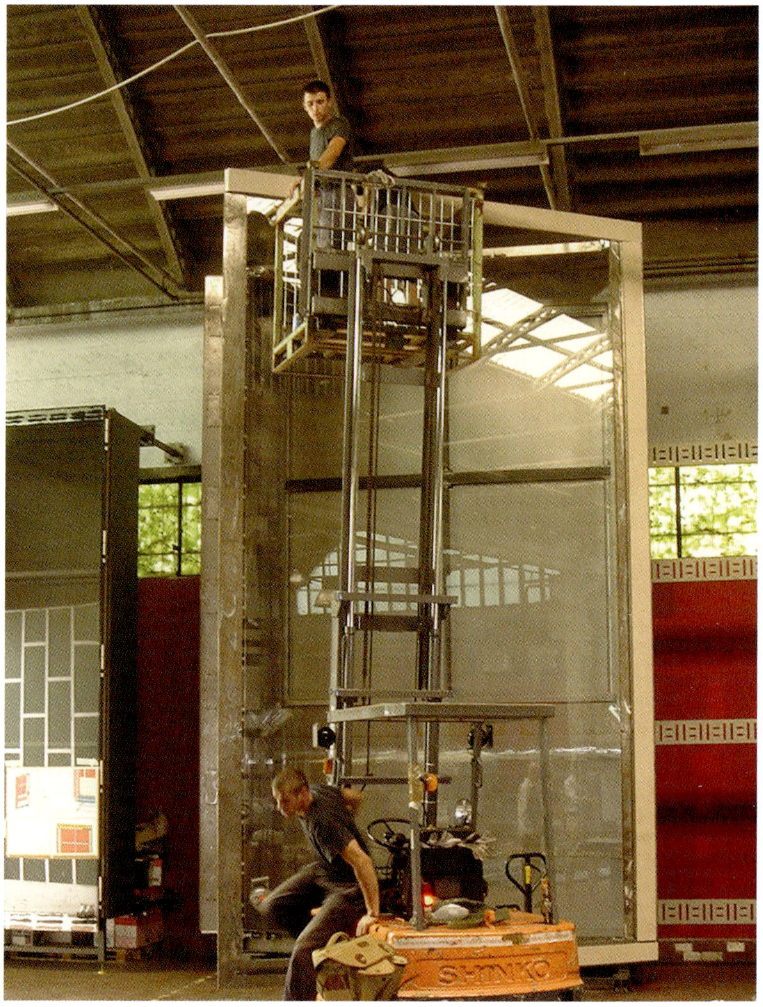

4.19 Construction of a wall-case at the Goppion workshop, Milan; this is the largest glazed display case ever to have been made for a museum

The graphic style for labels and text panels

A consistent source of complaint among museum visitors is that the graphics used for object labelling are illegible. Since the textual interpretation of the displays plays such a key role in shaping the enjoyment of an exhibition, it was a primary consideration of the design team to build upon the experiences of the Museum in this regard.

Graphic consultants Martin Jacobs Art Direction + Design developed a consistent strategy for type within the Gallery, in accordance with the Museum's evolving in-house guidelines regarding type sizes and techniques. To create a sense of rhythm and diversity, two typefaces were used throughout: a serif font (Jude) for headings, and a sans-serif font (Interstate) for the body text, chosen for its clarity and legibility at small scales (illus. 6.2, 6.3).

4.20 Plan of the final layout of cases within the Gallery

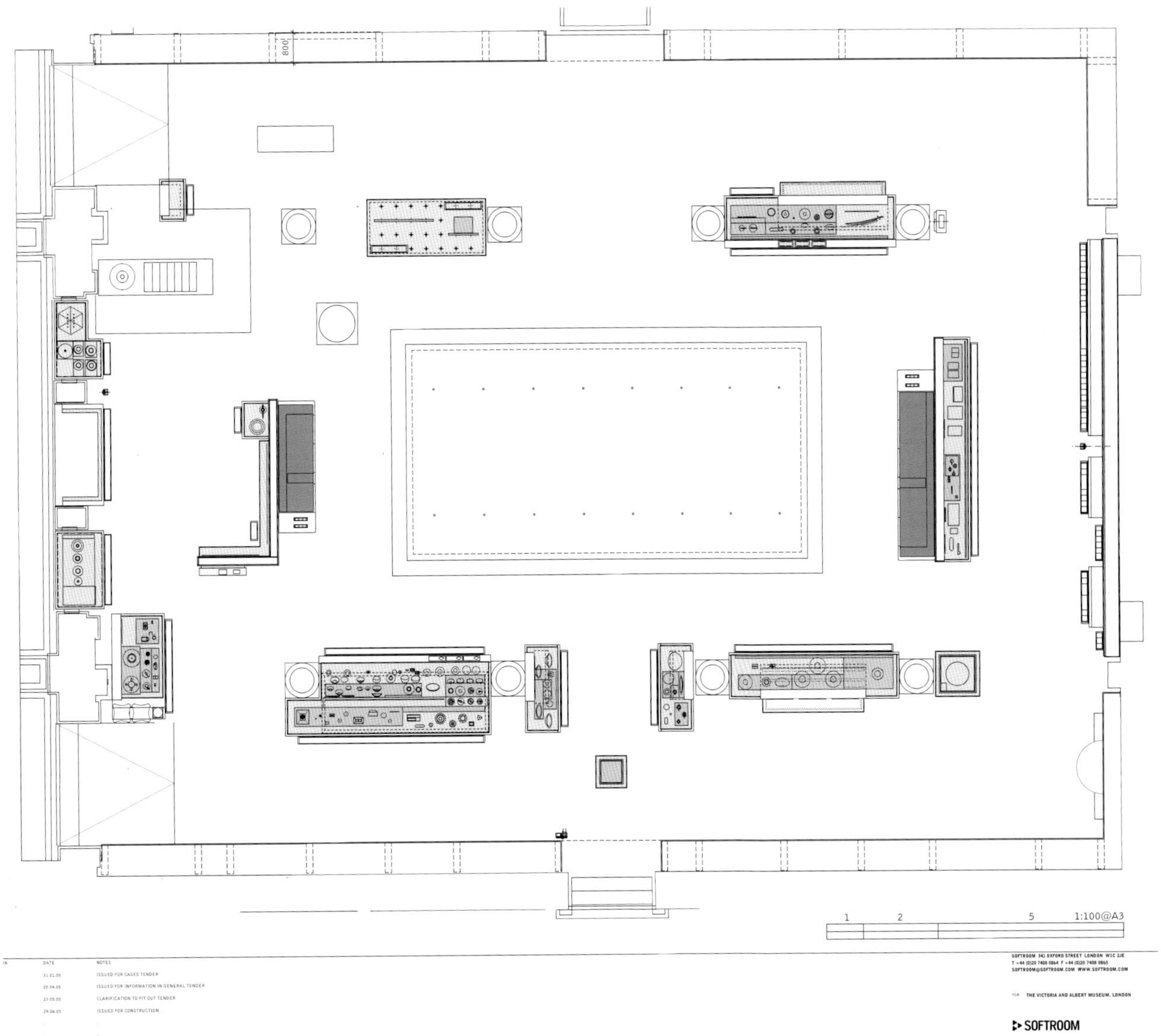

The colour palette of the graphics follows the midnight-blue and pale stone tones of the Gallery architecture. On larger text panels, the text is reversed out, with stone-coloured letters on a dark-blue ground, enabling the text to float behind the exhibits on the backboards of the cases. At all times, the issue of accessibility by all visitors was a prime consideration. Following on from the Museum's investigations into the ideal positioning of labels, all texts relating to objects are confined within a band at roughly table height. To avoid shadowing on to the labels, the graphic strips are gently backlit.

Although the Jameel Gallery houses a permanent display, it is in the nature of museum displays that the exhibition contents are not immutably fixed. Objects may be loaned for temporary shows, or rotated with others to prolong their life. For this reason, the Museum prefers to use graphic systems that can be quickly replicated in-house. The designers studied the facilities of the Reprographic Department to this end, as well as compiling a manual of standards to be followed in the future.

Summary

At the conclusion of the design process, the overwhelming lesson is that the design of an exhibition space – such as that created for the Jameel Gallery – is a careful balance of a diversity of factors. The architectural design must harmonize with the message of the displays, while the needs of conservator and visitor must be equally resolved. The experience also serves as an illustration of how introducing new designers to the exercise can invigorate the task. At the same time it underlines the importance of capitalizing on the wealth of knowledge of those within the Museum and of the external consultants and experts in manufacture.

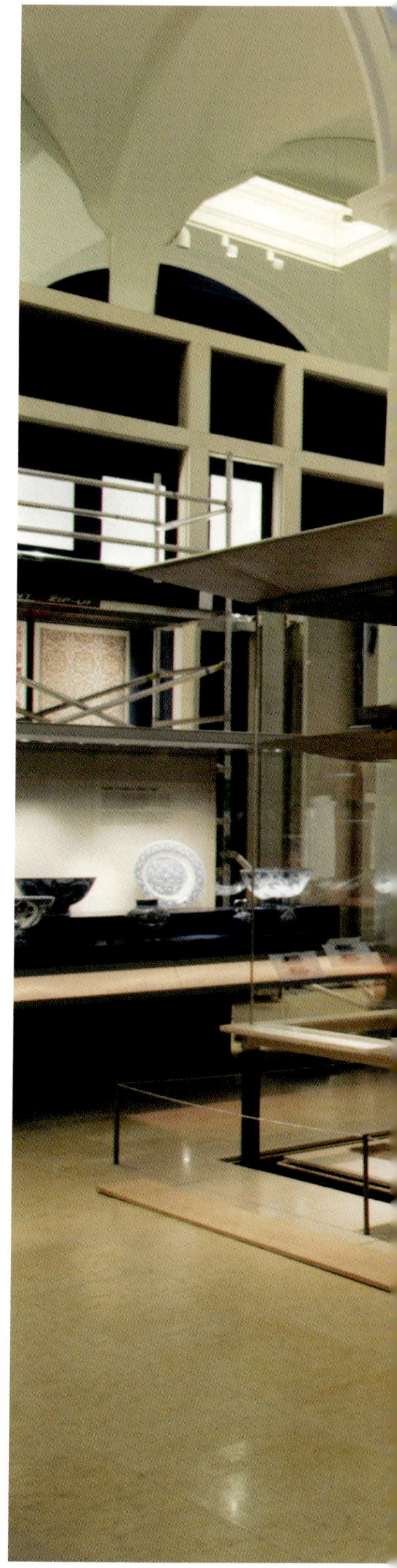

4.21 View of the Gallery during installation, showing the Ardabil carpet case in a partially raised position, 9 June 2006

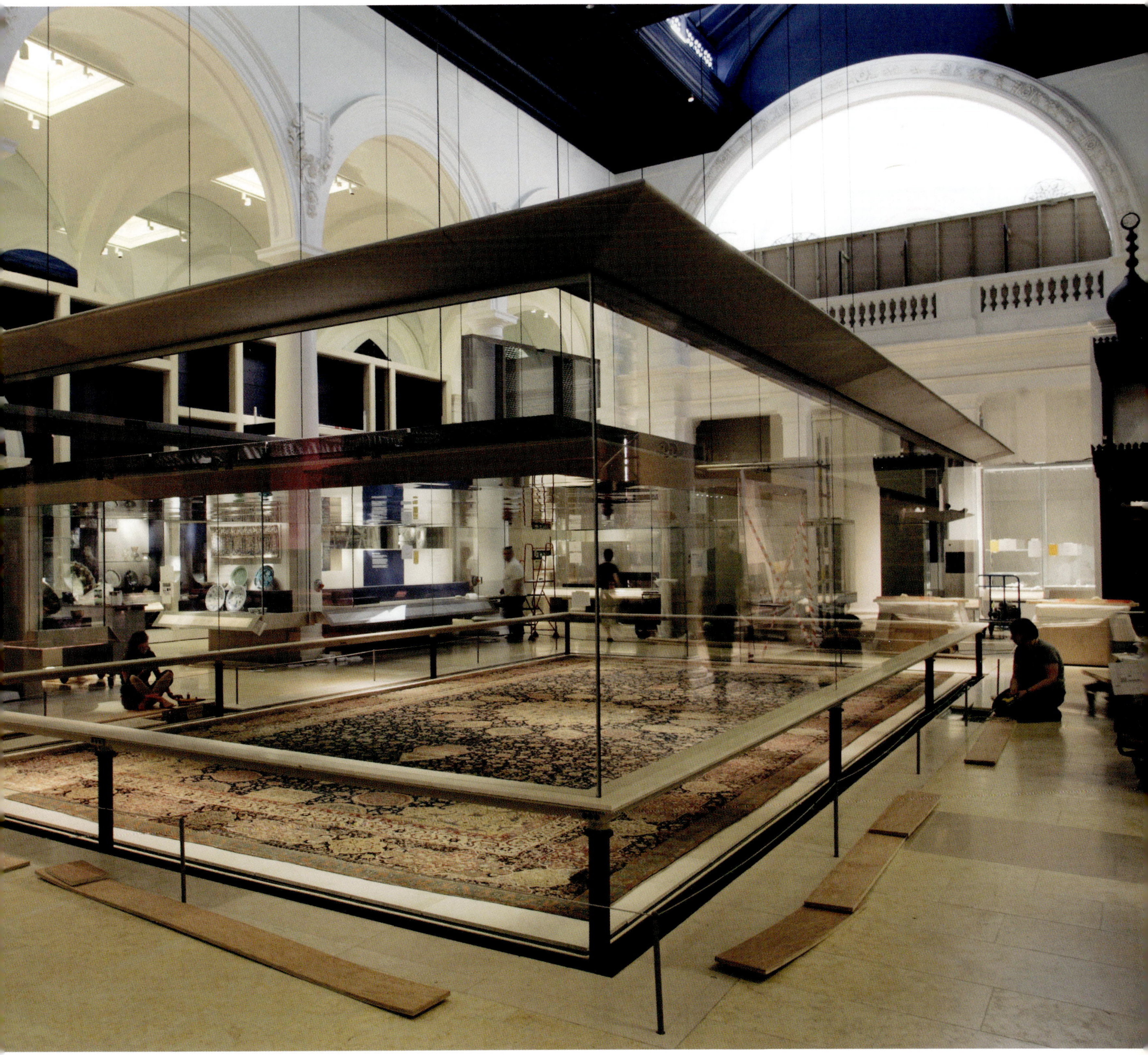

4.22 (*right*) View of the Gallery at the start of construction, 27 October 2005

4.23 (*below*) View of the Gallery under construction, 20 January 2006: the raised floor and the grid system for the wall cases are in place, and the channel for the Ardabil carpet case's lifting mechanism is visible

4.24 (*opposite, top*) View of the Gallery under construction, 9 March 2006: the wall-case doors are in place and the structure for the top of the Ardabil carpet case is suspended from wires

4.25 (*opposite, bottom*) View of the Gallery under construction, 20 April 2006: the completed Ardabil carpet case and free-standing cases

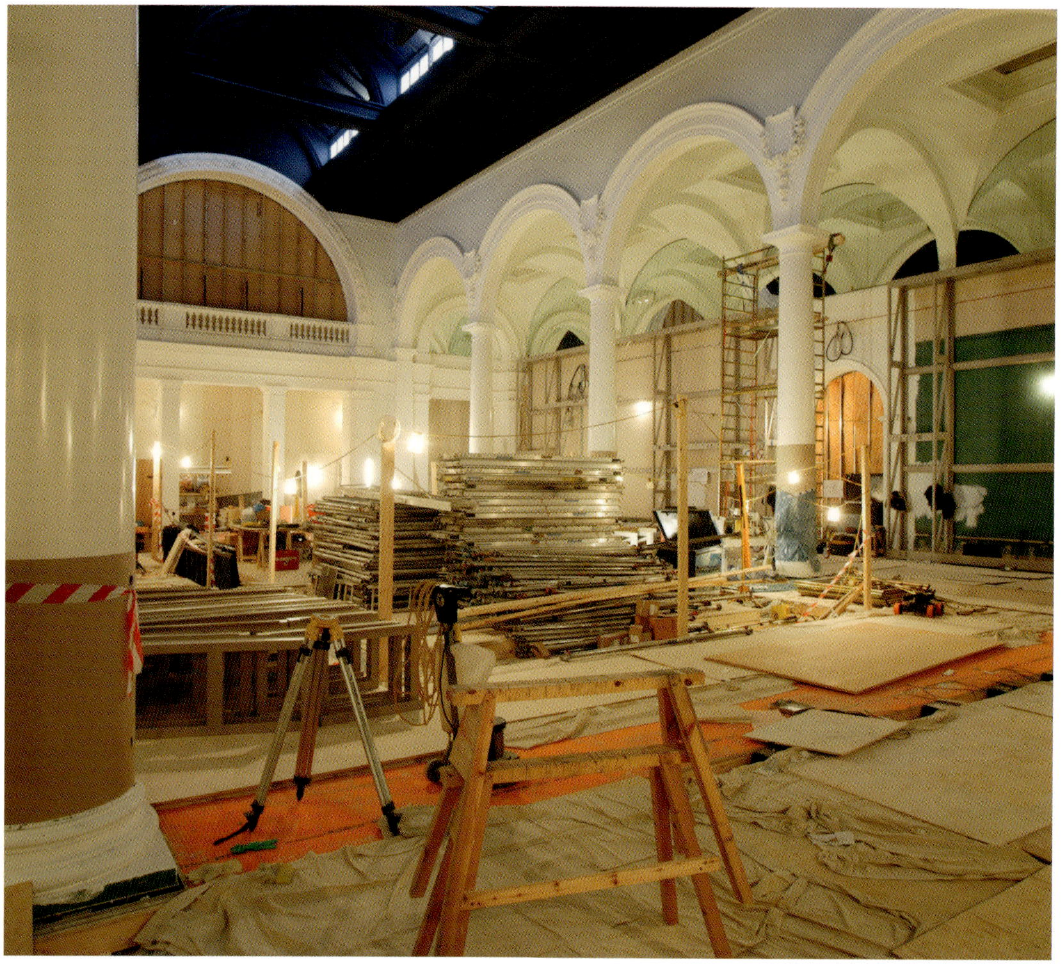

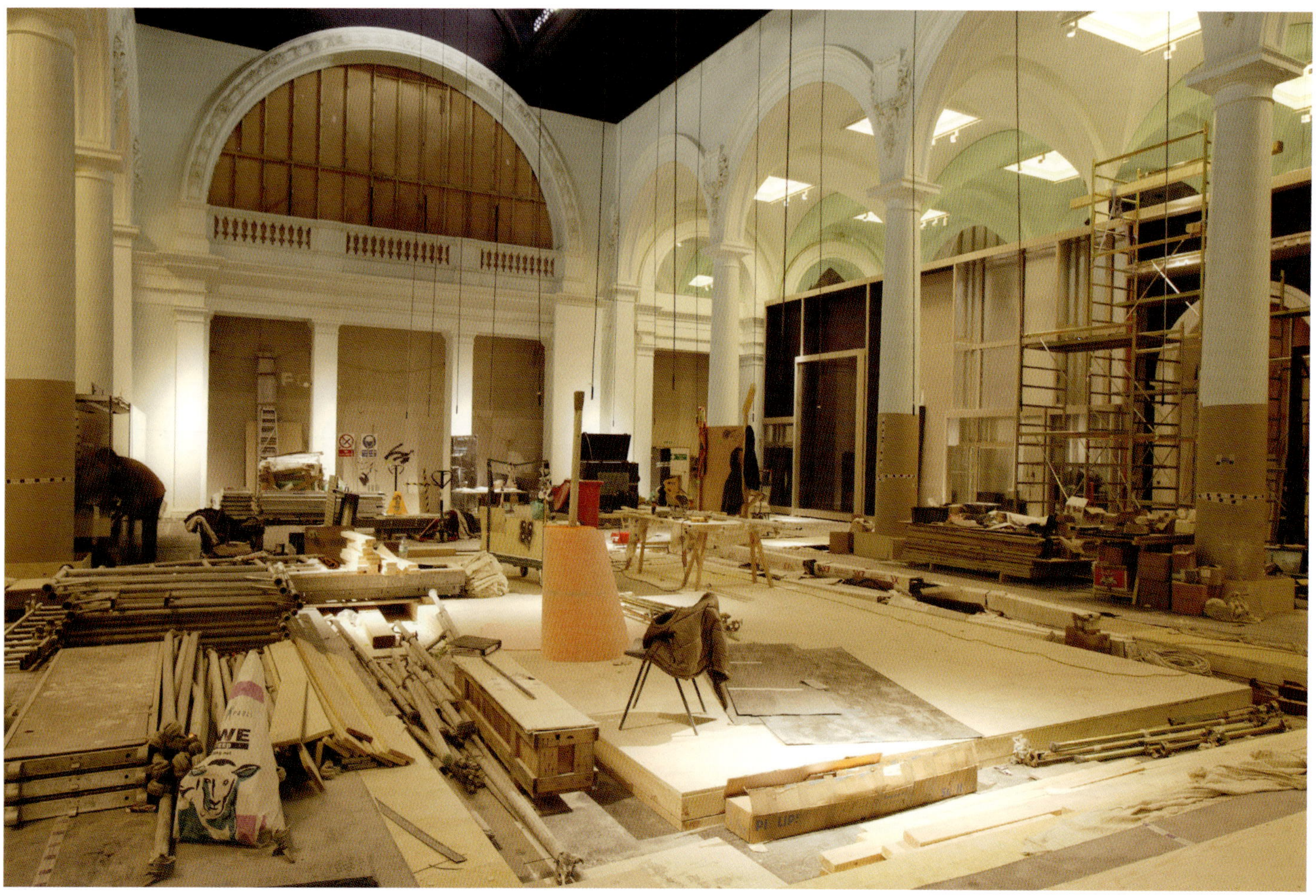

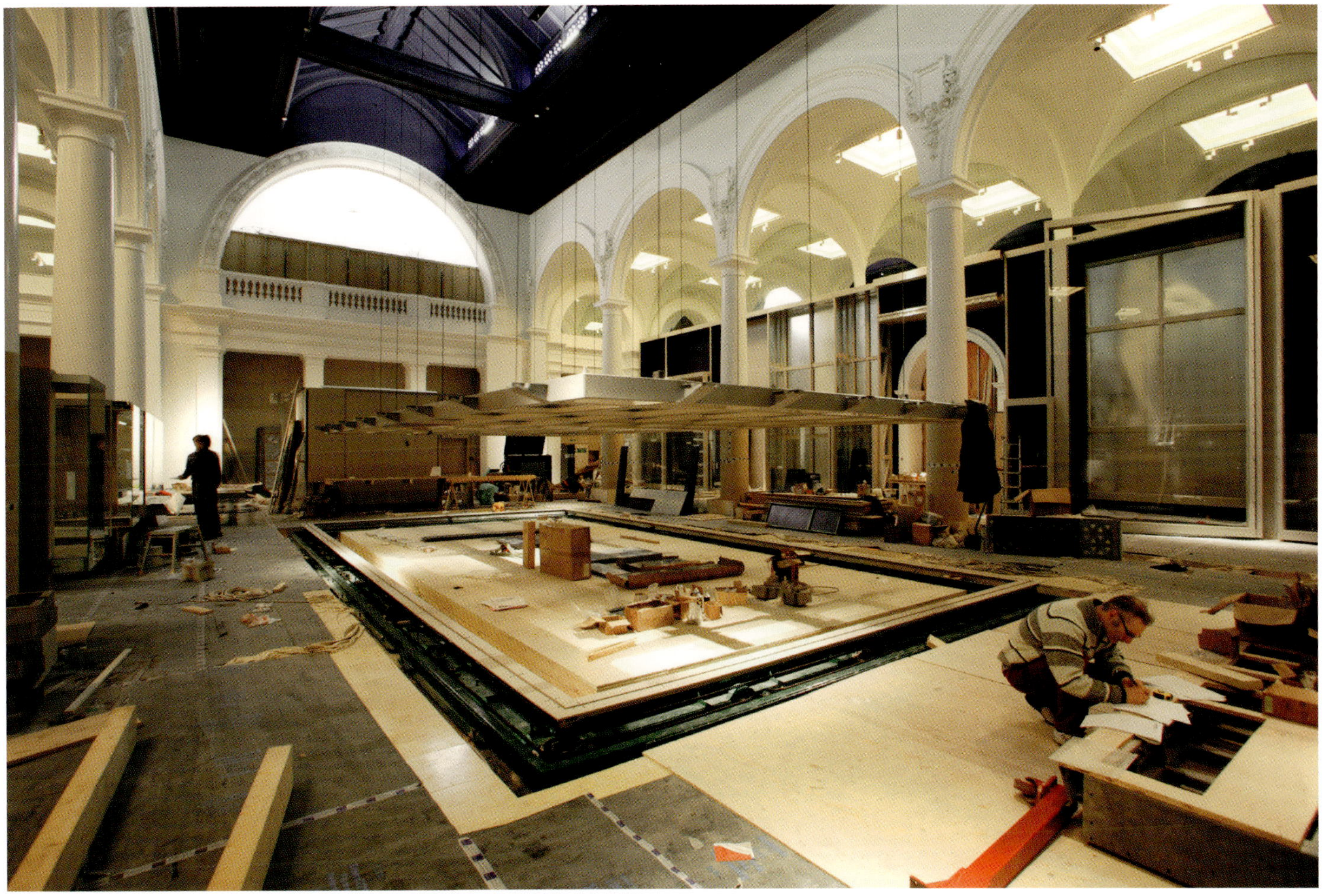

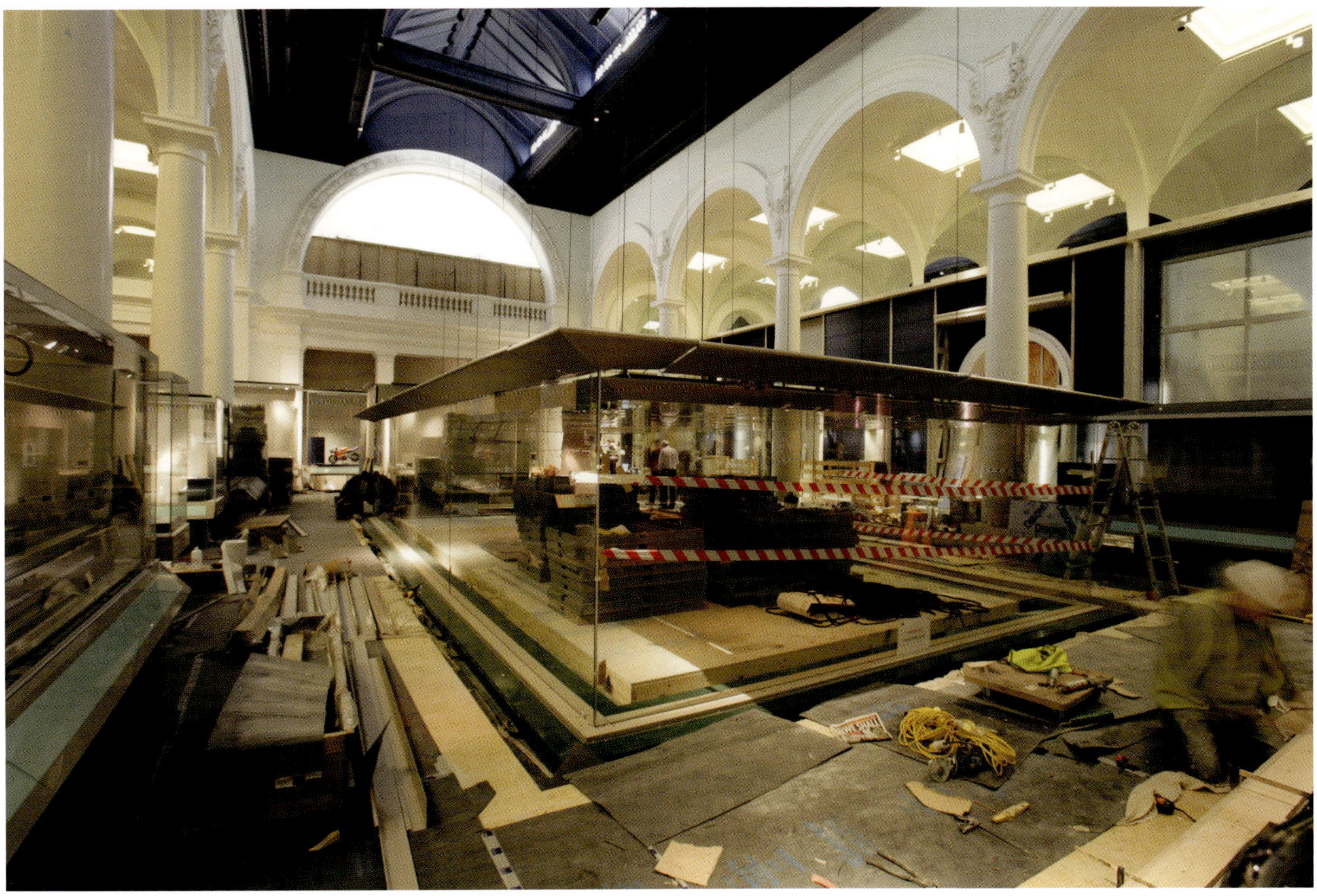

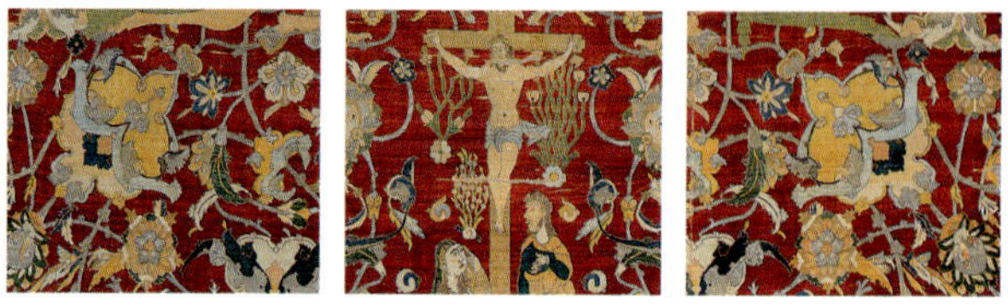

5 THE CONSERVATION PROGRAMME

Introduction

Mike Wheeler

The refurbishment of the Islamic Gallery presented a unique opportunity to assess and conserve the pieces previously on show, as well as to prepare new material for display and public access. This mammoth task included the conservation of more than 400 objects, about 100 of which had already been treated for the *Palace and Mosque* exhibition. Treatment included the conservation of paper and books, sculpture, metalwork, ceramics and glass, as well as furniture and important textile items such as the Ardabil carpet. In some instances conservation entailed restoration of missing areas, as well as more routine cleaning and stabilization. Case studies of a few complex objects in different media are outlined on the following pages.

The process of conservation offers the possibility for extremely detailed examination of items, adding to information about the objects, as well as helping to establish their origins and provenance. In the case of the Nasrid capital from the Alhambra palace and the Moroccan carved-wood panels, microscopic examination has revealed fresh information concerning the pigments used in the original colour scheme. Investigation of the Safavid cope has also enabled new conclusions to be drawn about the origins of this vestment.

5.1 Detail of the Nasrid capital showing blue paint (see illus. 5.17). V&A: 341–1866

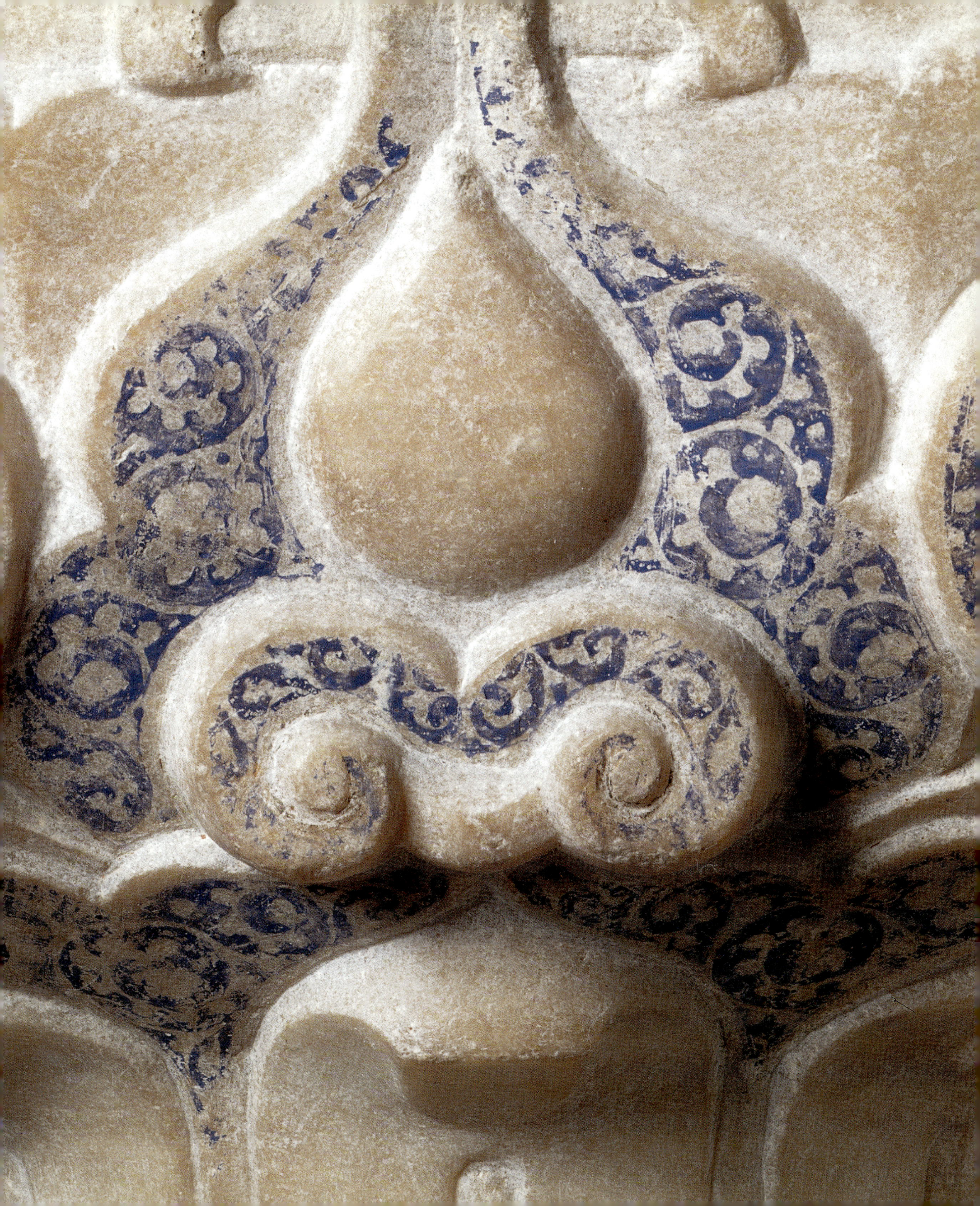

The conservation of the fifteenth-century Mamluk Qur'an necessitated resewing, but not reproducing the original style of binding. This is intended to indicate the original format and show its manner of use, while reinforcing the fact that it is an incomplete volume. The decision to reconstruct the format was taken as a result of close collaboration between V&A book conservators and Tim Stanley, Senior Curator for the Middle East collections. Similar curatorial collaboration resulted in the successful restoration of missing parts in a thirteenth-century fritware bowl from Iran, and in the reconstruction of the glass vessel known as the Buckley ewer.

In all of these cases, care has been taken by the Museum's conservators to respect the context and integrity of the original pieces. Restoration has only been carried out in instances in which it has been agreed by the conservator and the curator that the aesthetic integrity of the piece would be seriously compromised if it was left undone, and in instances in which reconstruction does not interfere with the future retrieval of information. The need for reversibility of all treatments carried out is fundamental to the underlying principles of conservation.

Although it is intended that many of the important pieces will be on semi-permanent display, it is also the intention to have changing displays and a rotation of objects to allow visitors to see new items. This policy, together with reduced light levels, helps to protect vulnerable objects with fugitive dyes and pigments, which might be damaged by prolonged exposure to light. Other preventive conservation measures in the Jameel Gallery include the use of microclimates in showcases, to protect moisture-sensitive objects that might easily be damaged by fluctuations in temperature and relative humidity.

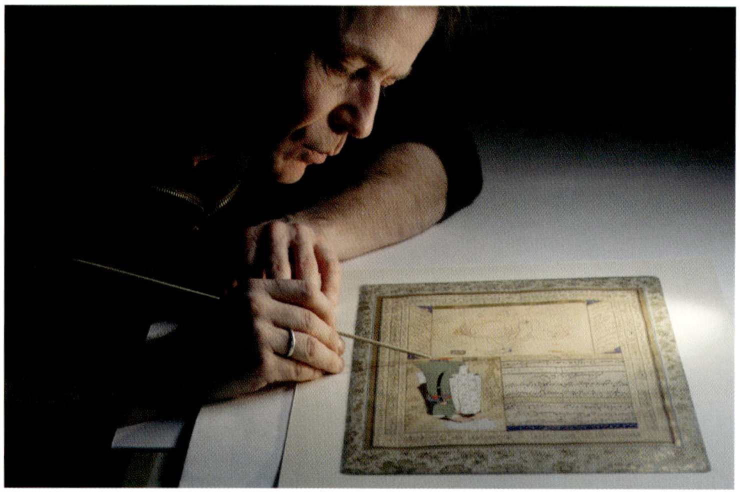

5.2 Conservator Mike Wheeler examining the pigments on a Persian album page. V&A: L.6964–1880

Reconstructing missing parts

Juanita Navarro and Fi Jordan

Ceramic and glass objects that have been broken into many fragments are likely to have missing parts. These range from small chips along break-lines and rim edges to whole sections of the object being lost. The conservation treatment of an early thirteenth-century fritware bowl and a tenth-century glass ewer illustrate two different approaches to reconstructing areas of loss on ceramics and glass objects.

An early thirteenth-century fritware bowl (V&A: C.125–1931)

The inside of this lightweight fritware bowl depicts three seated figures, dressed in finery and drinking wine. The painted decoration is seen through a clear glaze. A single band of script on the outside, in sgraffito (incised through the glass), gives a conventional benediction for the owner ('May the Creator protect its owner, wherever he may be') and two quatrains from a love poem.

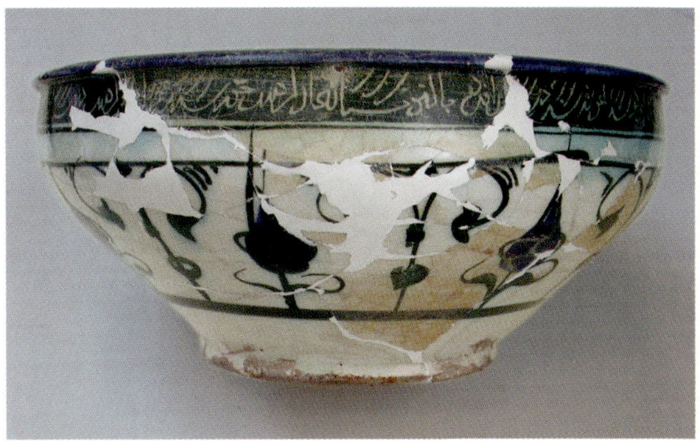

5.3 The outside of the 13th-century bowl after bonding and filling, but before retouching.
V&A: C.125–1931

5.4 The outside of the bowl after retouching the filled areas

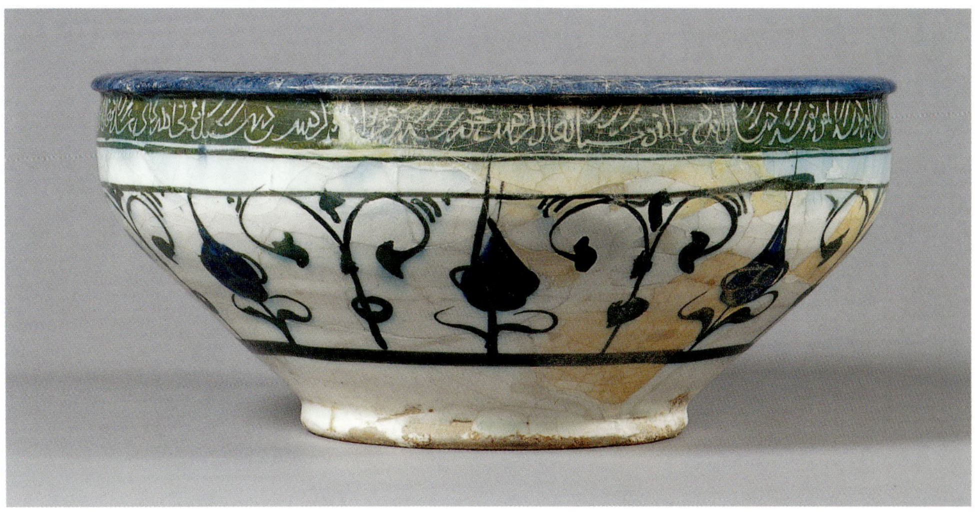

It is not unusual for Islamic ceramics to have been badly broken in the past. Not only had this bowl been broken into 117 pieces, but there were also many gaps. Additionally the fragments appeared to have been buried in different conditions (such as dry, wet and corrosive). This had resulted in the unequal degradation of the glaze surface and in some staining of the porous body, as may be seen by the different textures and colours of the fragments (illus. 5.5).

Before any conservation treatment starts, the different alternatives are always considered. Is the conservation necessary? Should the missing areas be filled in? Is there enough remaining evidence to retouch the fills accurately?

Conservation was needed because the old organic adhesive had become brittle, losing its bonding strength and thereby putting the bowl in danger of further damage. Additionally, some of the fill material had become soft and slightly powdery, and the old paint was yellowed and unsightly. Structurally, the bowl needed at least to be dismantled, cleaned and rebonded. This necessary process would leave visually distracting gaps, especially to the faces. It was decided that the gaps should be filled in and retouched. It was possible to integrate the image on the front, to complete the gaps in the benediction and poetry with accurate script, and to complete the decorative band outside, which was repetitive and could be suitably copied. Therefore the gaps were filled (illus. 5.3, 5.5) and retouched (illus. 5.4, 5.6). The bowl now looks complete and can be enjoyed in a condition that is nearer to its original splendour. The retouching is unobtrusive and may be distinguished only on close examination.

5.6 The inside of the bowl after retouching the filled areas

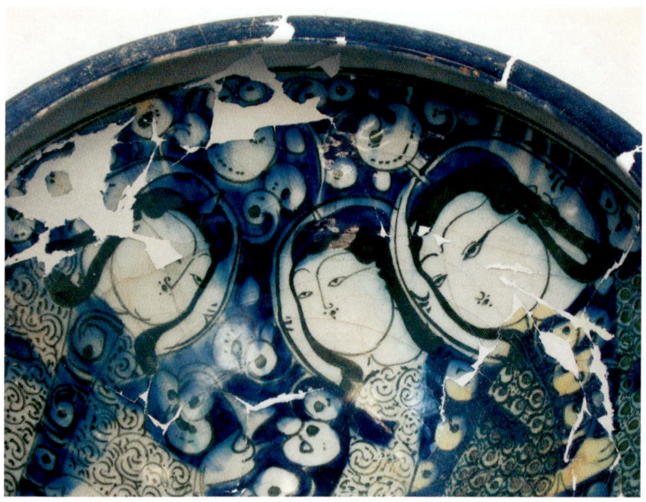

5.5 (*left*) The inside of the bowl after bonding and filling, but before retouching

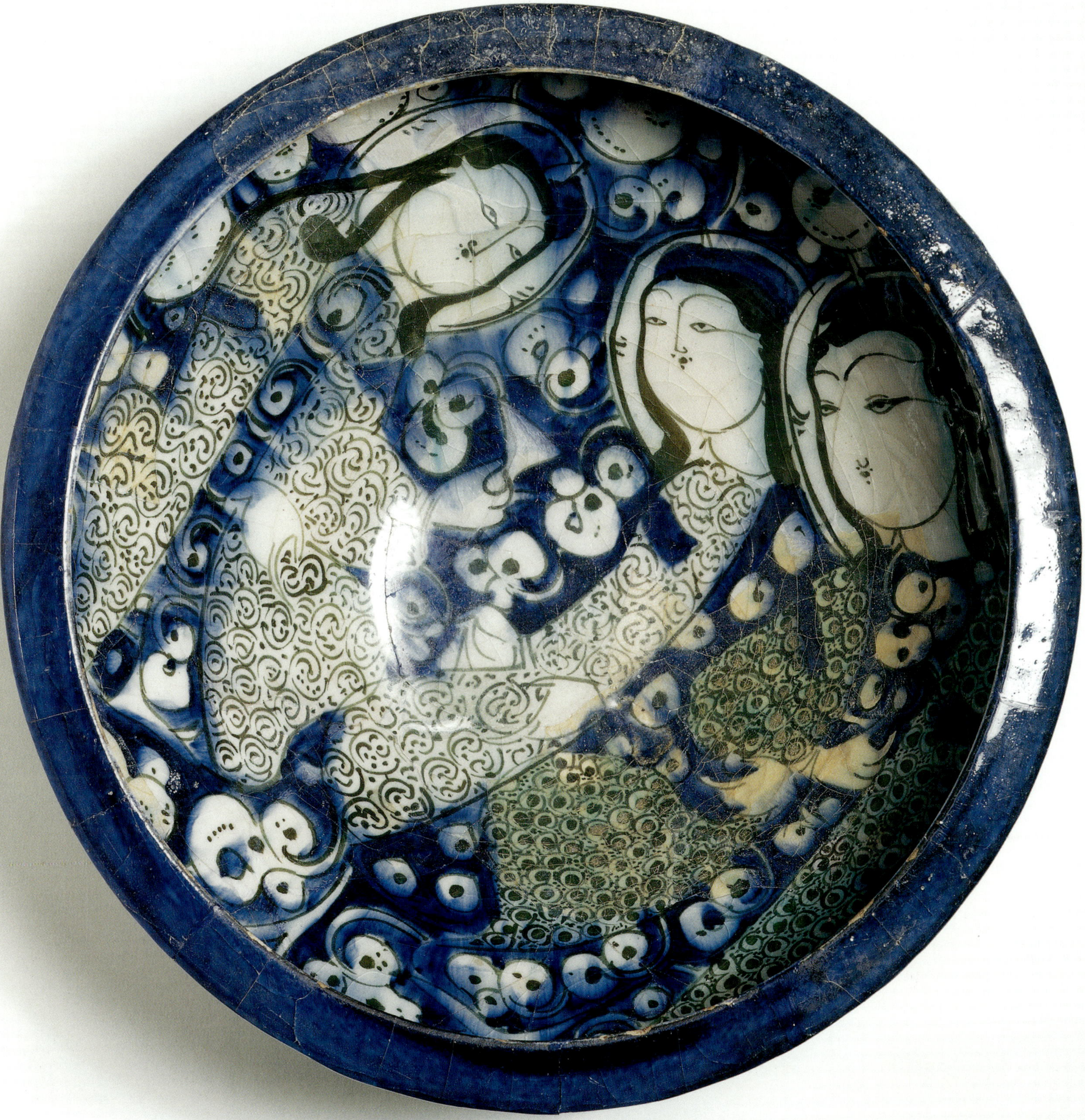

The Buckley ewer (V&A: C.126–1936)

This tenth-century glass ewer had been broken into numerous fragments with approximately one-third of the object missing. An earlier method of restoration, which involved the bonding of fragments on to an inner opaque resin support with a metal strap on the handle, detracted from the design and clarity of the glass. The restoration materials used had also deteriorated and discoloured, adding to their intrusiveness and making the object unstable to handle (illus. 5.7).

The fragments were dismantled and a new display method was sought. The ewer would not be displayable without some form of support, either through the reconstruction of missing parts or a purpose-built mount.

The extent to which the areas of loss were filled differs from those on the early thirteenth-century fritware bowl. In this case, a partial reconstruction was deemed appropriate. Given the fragile nature of the glass, the complex procedures required to reconstruct the complete object would have placed it at risk of further damage. Large areas of the carved relief decoration are missing and, in the absence of evidence, ethically inappropriate to reproduce.

During the reassembly of the glass fragments, small gaps were filled to provide additional support to the structure. The conservator had to bear in mind the risks of applying too much pressure when bonding and filling the vulnerable glass. In restricting the fillings to essential areas only, the risks were limited. As the object was left with large areas of loss, it required a further method of support – a clear perspex mount was designed to fit accurately within and below the ewer.

The chosen treatment enables the ewer to display its translucent quality, inherent fragility and the skill of the craftsman. The fillings to the small gaps are coloured, shaped and polished to blend with the glass surface. With a clear support mechanism, this partial reconstruction aims to be unobtrusive and to deceive the eye into completing the missing outline of the glass (illus. 5.8).

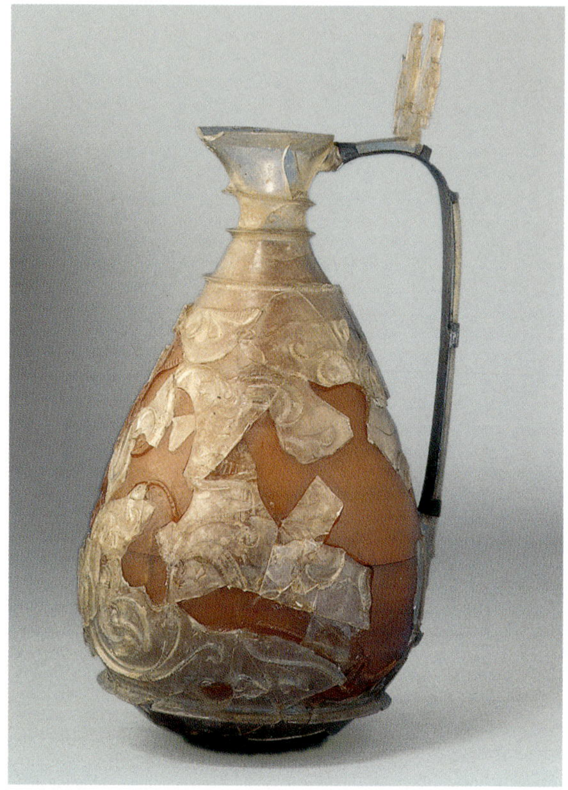

5.7 The Buckley ewer with its old resin mount. (V&A: C.126–1936)

5.8 The Buckley ewer with its new perspex mount

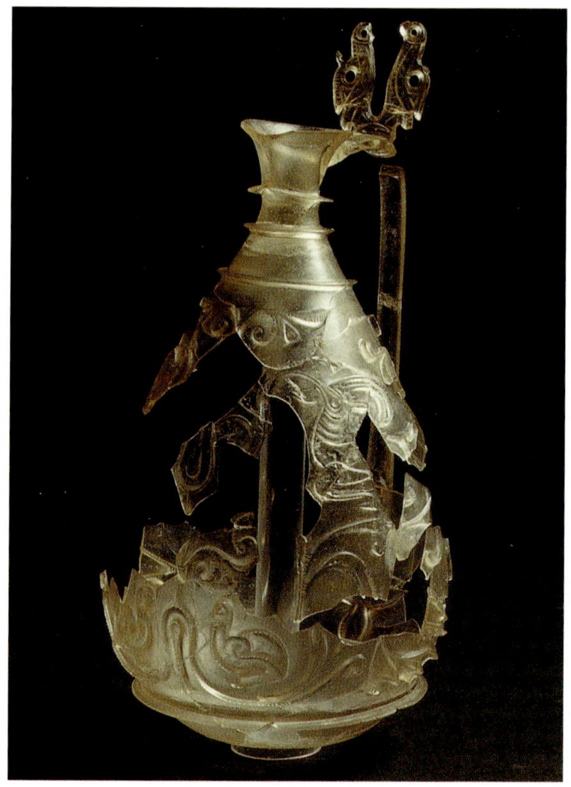

A thirteenth-century inscribed panel from North Africa (V&A: 378A–1907)

Shayne Rivers

Conservation aims to ensure the long-term preservation of the V&A's collection. In the case of this painted wooden panel, the most important aspect was to preserve the painted decoration.

Wood expands and contracts in response to changes in relative humidity (RH). The more the RH fluctuates and the wider the range, the more the wood moves in response. The paint layers also move in response to fluctuations in RH. However, wood only expands and contracts in one direction (across the grain, not along it), while the paint layers expand and contract evenly in all directions. Even though the amount of movement is comparatively small, over time and with enough fluctuations the paint will inevitably begin to flake off the wood.

When conserving this painted panel, the first task was to check the surface carefully. This required a bench microscope to allow the conservator to identify any loose or flaking areas and then to re-adhere them, a process called consolidation (illus. 5.9). The conservator (Nigel Bamforth) chose a consolidant that was compatible with the original materials, that had good long-term stability, and that could be removed to allow further treatment if it proved necessary in the future. He used as little consolidant as possible – just enough to adhere the flakes without changing the overall appearance of the surface.

Once the painted decoration had been consolidated, it was strong enough to be cleaned. Dust was removed using a soft brush in combination with a low-suction vacuum nozzle. After careful tests, the surface of the paint itself was cleaned using cotton swabs slightly dampened with de-ionized water. Finally, white spirit was used to reduce old wax deposits on the Kufic script.

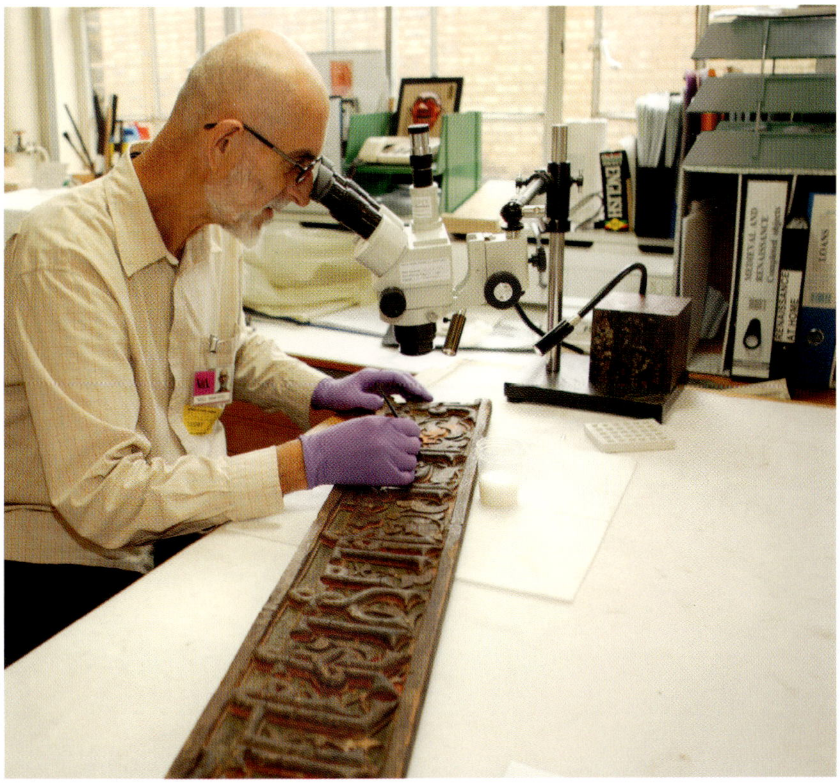

5.9 Conservator Nigel Bamforth examining the surface of the wooden panel. V&A: 378A–1907

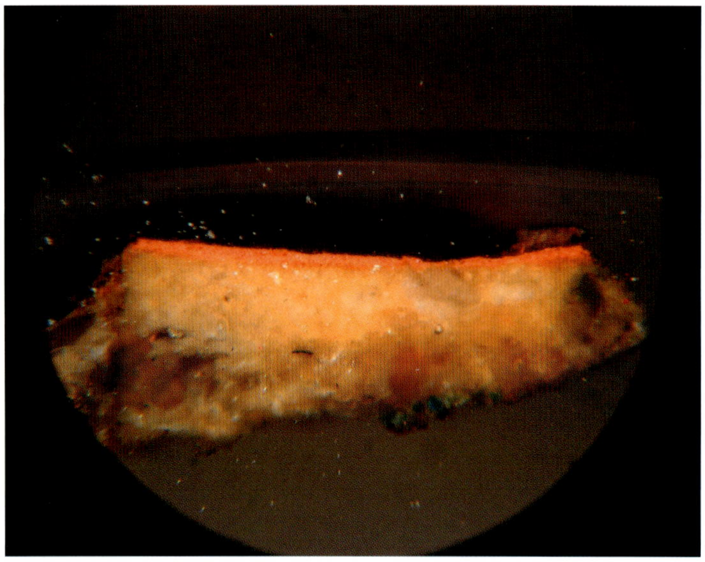

5.10 Close-up detail of traces of paint on the surface of the panel

Secrets of the paint revealed

It is often the case that, because a conservator examines the object in such detail, he or she makes discoveries about provenance or manufacturing techniques that might not otherwise be noticed. Under the microscope, it was apparent that there were at least three layers of paint on the panel, and that the older, lower decorative schemes were different from that on the top. A few samples (each less than one millimetre wide) were taken from the different decorative elements of the panel. These were embedded in a resin block, which was then abraded and polished. The V&A's object analyst (Lucia Burgio) used a microscope to view the paint layers from the side, which revealed that although the Kufic script had always been black, the other decorative elements had had different colour schemes at different times (illus. 5.10).

In the past, this might have led the Museum to consider whether to remove the later paint layers to reveal the original decorative scheme. On an object as old and rare as this panel, however, information about changes in decorative schemes is as valuable as knowledge of the original design. The V&A values all the information contained in the paint layers and we aim to preserve it in its entirety. Digital imaging can be used to give an idea of the previous colour schemes (illus. 5.12).

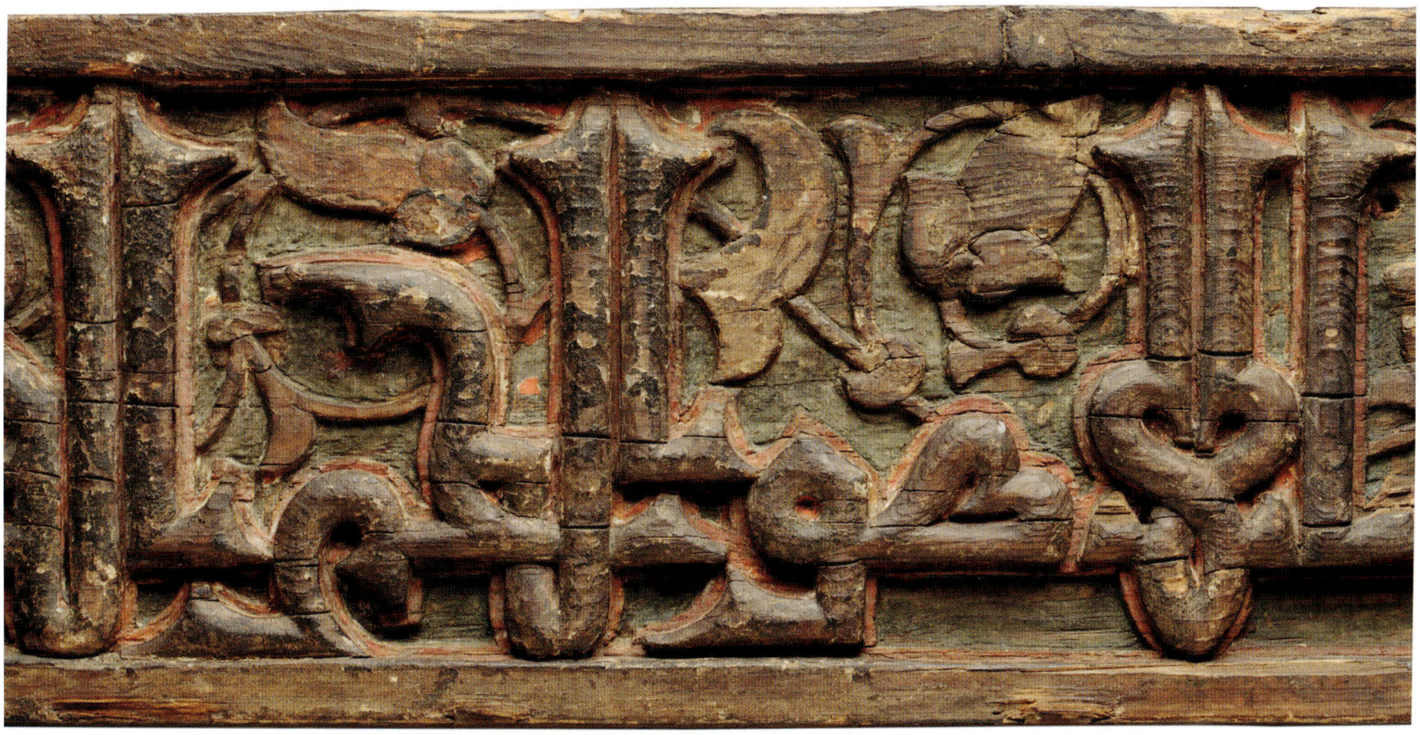

5.11 Detail of the panel after conservation

5.12 Digital reconstruction of the panel as it may originally have appeared

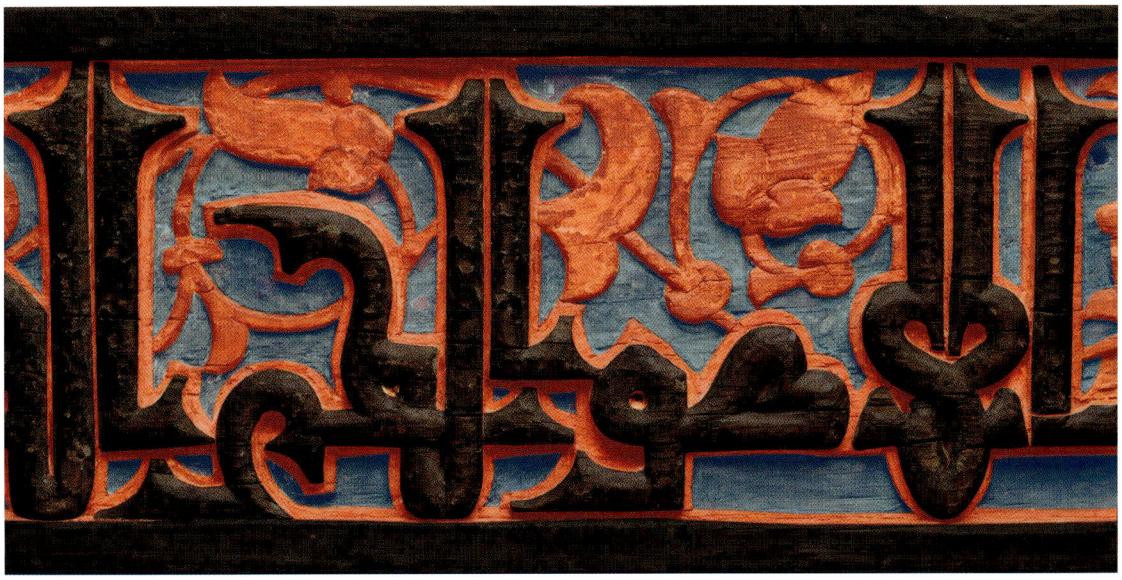

The Mamluk Qur'an leaves (V&A: 7217–1869)

Karen Vidler and Jane Rutherston

The manuscript comprises 20 non-sequential leaves from the final sections of a Qur'an copied in the Mamluk empire, probably Egypt, in the fifteenth century. The object was selected for inclusion in the Jameel Gallery because it represents an outstanding example of Mamluk religious art. It is of an unusually large format, being from the second-largest Mamluk Qur'an known, and has not previously been published (illus. 5.15).

On initial assessment by Book Conservation, the condition was found to be very unstable (illus. 5.13). The huge leaves of the poor-quality paper had no support, and because of their weight and size, over its history the handling of the leaves without appropriate support had resulted in tears appearing from the centre back folds into the gutter margins in some gatherings (groups of leaves). Bad handling and degradation of the weak paper fibres had resulted in numerous tears along most edges, with weakness, skinning, areas of loss and tears to the back folds (illus. 5.14). Seventeen of the leaves have a pink hue where a red pigmented surface size had been applied with uneven brush strokes. There was no evidence of the previous sewing structure or indication of the style of binding used. In addition, one of the leaves had at some time been cut down, presumably to be mounted for display as an example of calligraphy.

5.15 (*right*) A page from the large Mamluk Qur'an after conservation. V&A: 7217–1869

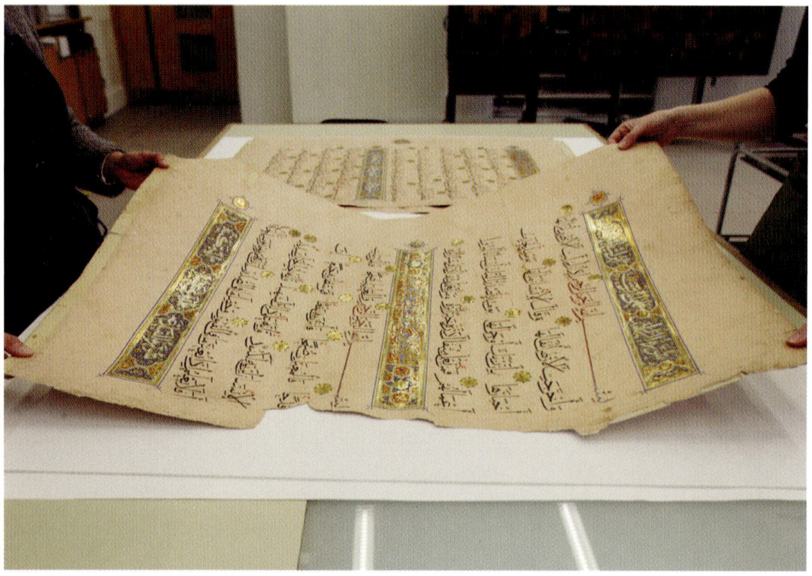

5.13 (*below left*) Conservators turning the leaves of the Mamluk Qur'an before conservation

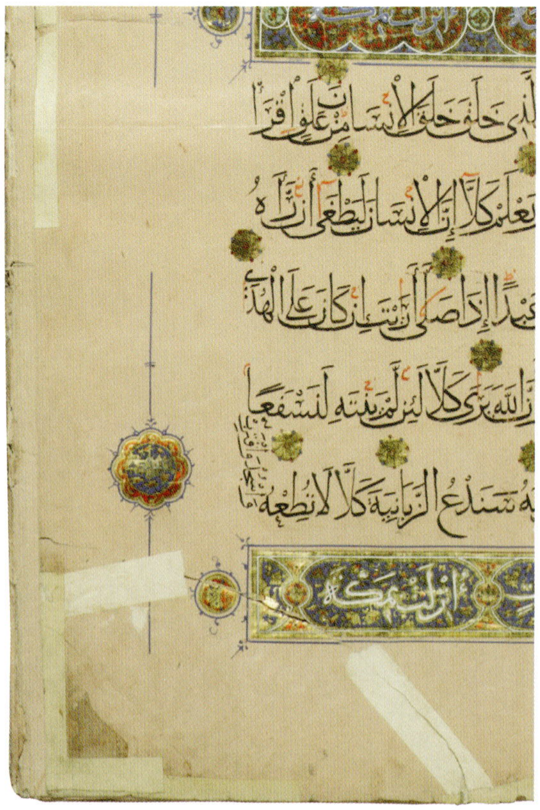

5.14 (*below*) Folio 18v of the Qur'an before conservation

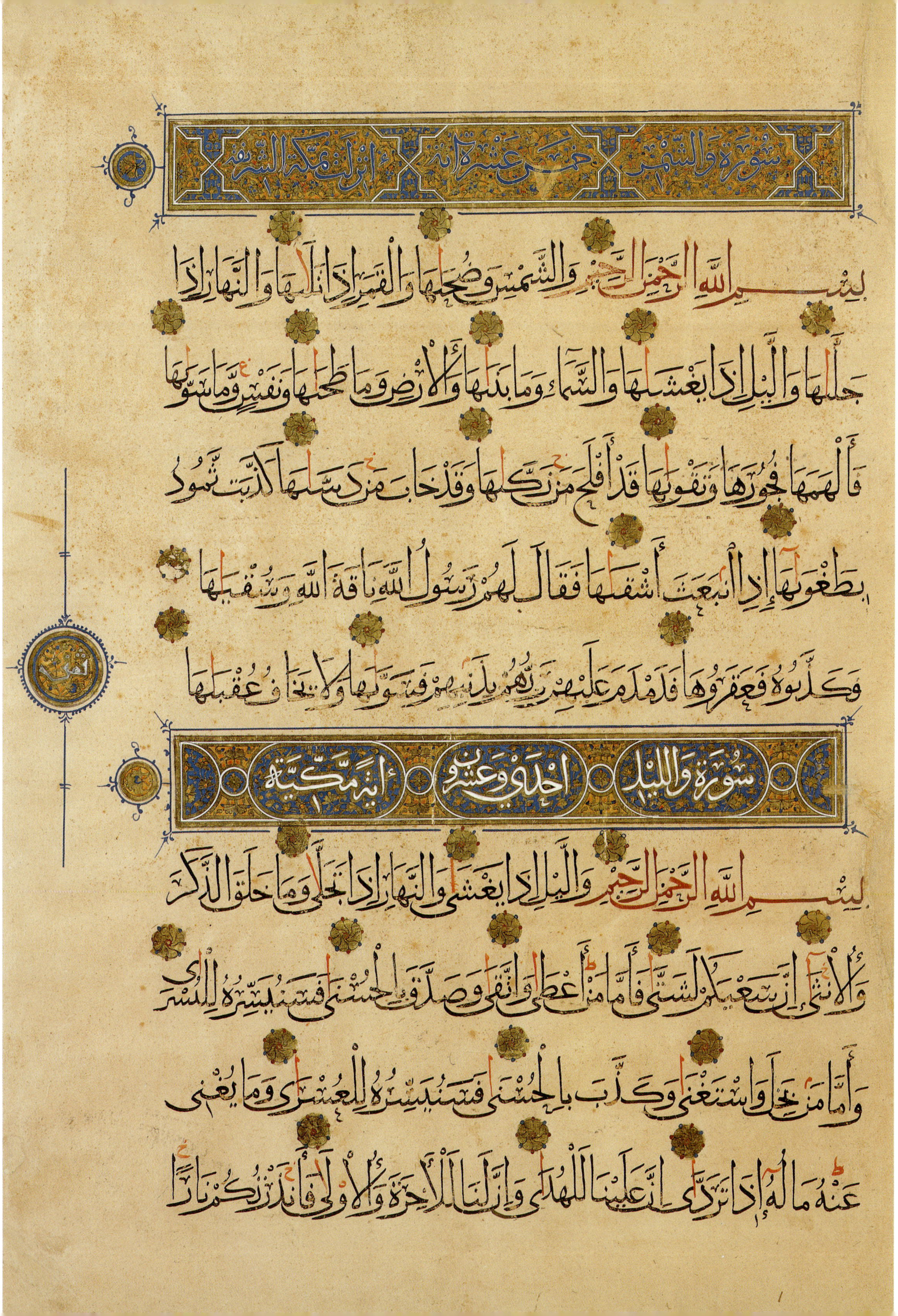

سورة والشمس خمس عشرة آية أنزلت بمكة الشريفة

بسم الله الرحمن الرحيم والشمس وضحاها والقمر إذا تلاها والنهار إذا
جلاها والليل إذا يغشاها والسماء وما بناها والأرض وما طحاها ونفس وما سواها
فألهمها فجورها وتقواها قد أفلح من زكاها وقد خاب من دساها كذبت ثمود
بطغواها إذ انبعث أشقاها فقال لهم رسول الله ناقة الله وسقياها
فكذبوه فعقروها فدمدم عليهم ربهم بذنبهم فسواها ولا يخاف عقباها

سورة والليل إحدى وعشرون آية مكية

بسم الله الرحمن الرحيم والليل إذا يغشى والنهار إذا تجلى وما خلق الذكر
والأنثى إن سعيكم لشتى فأما من أعطى واتقى وصدق بالحسنى فسنيسره لليسرى
وأما من بخل واستغنى وكذب بالحسنى فسنيسره للعسرى وما يغني
عنه ماله إذا تردى إن علينا للهدى وإن لنا للآخرة والأولى فأنذرتكم نارا

After discussion with Tim Stanley, several decisions on treatment methodology were agreed:

- To commission Griffin Mill to make a suitable toned paper for in-filling missing areas
- To tone a variety of Japanese papers for reinforcing tears and repairing and recreating back folds
- To tone the Japanese paper using acrylic or watercolours
- To remove old repairs
- To indicate missing leaves by including a hooked guard to extend the leaf
- To resew gatherings using a link stitch (illus. 5.16).
- Not to bind the gatherings
- To house in a bespoke portfolio.

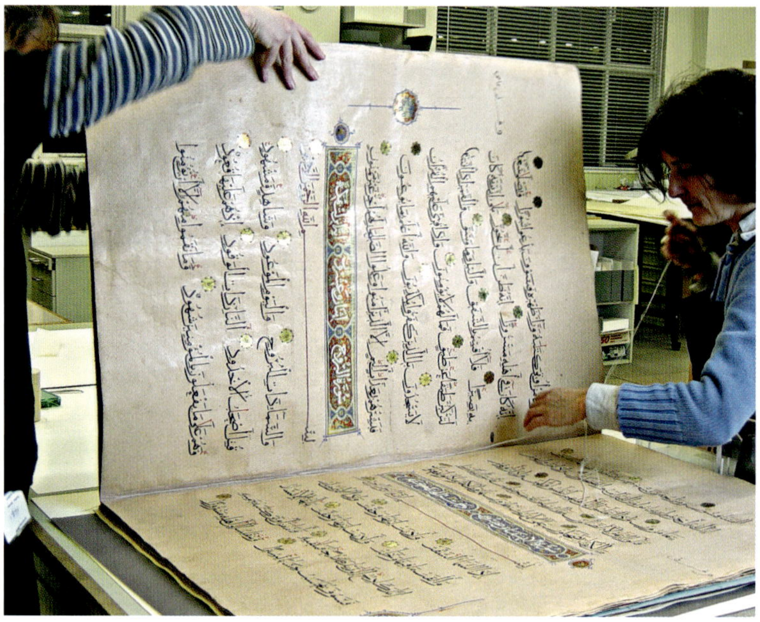

5.16 Conservators Karen Vidler (left) and Jane Rutherston (right) sewing the Qur'an pages

The solutions reached in order to undertake conservation of the manuscript enabled the conservators to achieve their main objectives:

- To stabilize the condition of the folios
- To strengthen the folios, enabling them to be turned without further damage occurring
- To gather the extant folios into a text-block format
- To provide the Qur'an with support for handling
- To house the Qur'an in a suitable conservation-quality enclosure
- To enable the Qur'an to be accessible to the public.

The appearance of the leaves, once treated, was much improved and it is now possible to handle them with ease and without the assistance of a second person supporting them on turning. The simple sewing structure has kept open the option of changing the sewing and including a binding at a future date, should such a decision be made. The lack of adhesive allows for easy reversal of sewing and separation of leaves. Should further leaves be acquired in the future, they could be incorporated without complicated disbinding that could cause damage.

A Nasrid marble capital (V&A: 341–1866)

Víctor Hugo López Borges

During the conservation treatment of this Nasrid capital (illus. 5.17), several thorough examinations were carried out, focusing mainly on the layer of paint, and this provided important new information towards the documentation and authentication of the object.

This Hispano-Islamic capital has its provenance in the palace of the Generalife in Granada, which was built in 1273–1302 by the second emir of the Nasrid dynasty, Muhammad II, and renovated by Ismail I in 1319. In the Generalife (from the Arabic *Jannat al-'Arif*, or 'Garden of the Architect'), which was designed as a summer retreat for the royal household within the Alhambra complex, the architecture blends perfectly with gardens, orchards, pools and fountains.

5.17 Overall view of the Nasrid marble capital. V&A: 341–1866

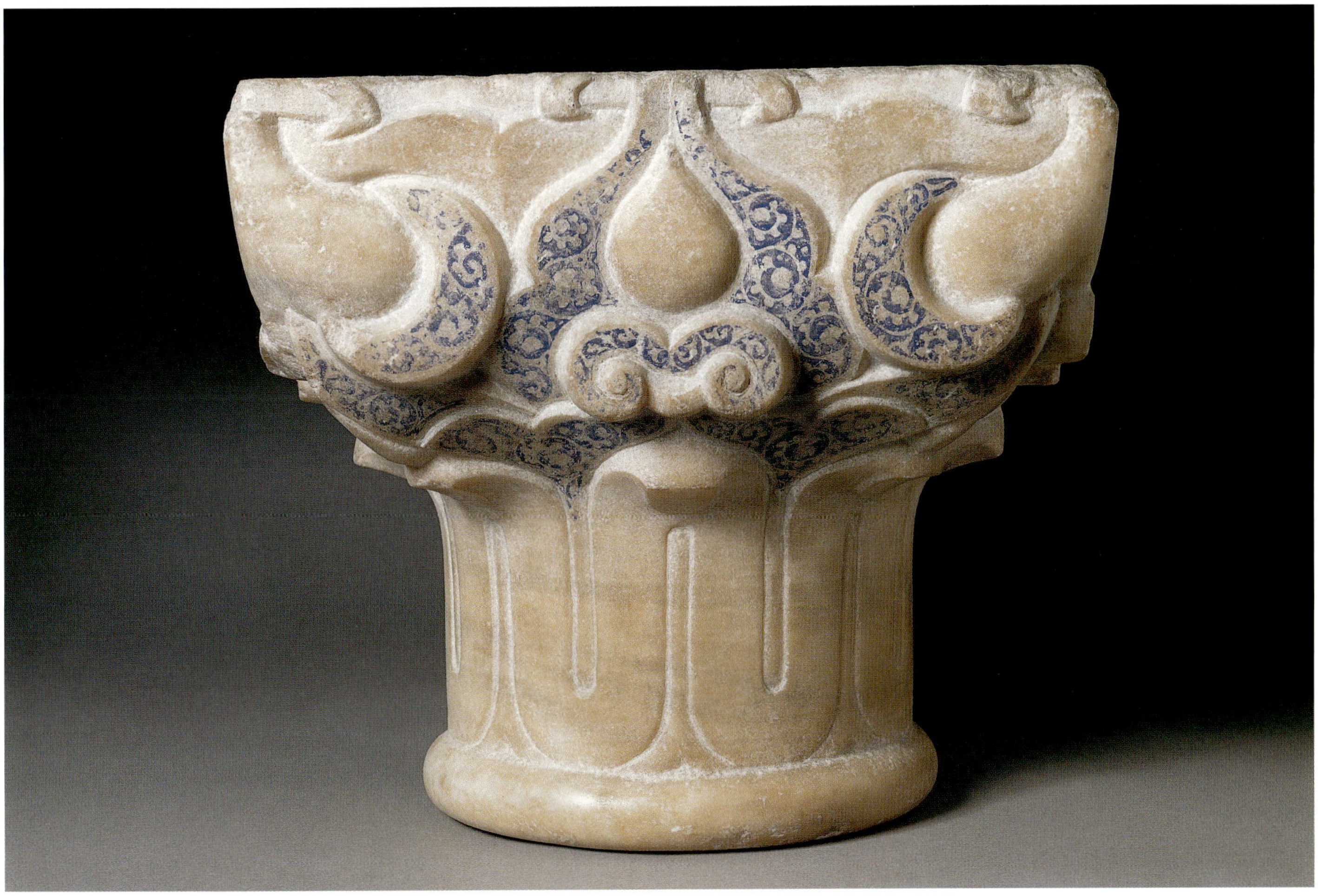

The style of this capital is representative of one of the most popular Nasrid creations, the capital of palm leaves. It could be classified as a capital of transition, where bold and archaic carved decoration becomes denser and smaller. Although the exact original location is not known, this capital relates stylistically to the ones in the Patio de la Acequia, the 'courtyard with the water-channel'.

The material used for the carving is probably Macael marble, from quarries in Almería. But the most striking detail is the applied decoration, which resembles 'ataurique', the typical intricate vegetal decoration found on Nasrid plasterwork. The first examination established that the marble was structurally sound, although eroded throughout. The applied blue polychromy was stable, still well bound and directly applied on the marble (illus. 5.1).

Further examinations were necessary, using ultraviolet light, pigment analysis and optical microscopy. Under UV light a greenish fluorescence was observed, showing the presence of an aged binding medium indicating the old nature of the polychromy. Under the microscope examination, small traces of red pigment were discovered consistently framing the blue decoration, and this leads us to believe that it was a part of the decorative scheme, now lost. Samples were taken from the blue and red decoration to be analysed by polarized light microscopy. The results identified the presence of lapis lazuli for the blue and cinnabar or dry-process vermilion for the red, both pigments that were very widely used during the Nasrid period.

Regarding the technical details of the application, it could be seen that the outline of the decoration was traced freehand without any previous pouncing (some pentimenti or corrections could be seen) and using the tip of a very fine brush. Once this outline was dry, the inner spaces were painted in with a thicker brush; it is possible to see how the two different layers overlap each other without mixing. This technique may be connected to Islamic traditions mentioned in a late sixteenth-century work in Persian, the *Qanun al-Suwar* of Sadiq Beg, also known as Sadiqi, who distinguished between *dam-shu* (painting with the tip of the brush) and *miyan-shu* (painting with the middle of the brush). Sadiq Beg also makes reference to the complexity of using lapis lazuli as a pigment, which requires special ways of application and binding. This supports the evidence we see in the painting method used on the capital.

A brass lamp-holder (V&A: 109–1888)

Phil Sofer and Sophy Wills

One of the more challenging objects selected for the *Palace and Mosque* tour was a large brass mosque lamp-holder. This late fifteenth-century object had already had an eventful history, surviving a fire and subsequent burial, to be partially reconstructed in the nineteenth century. Its chequered past has resulted in the embrittlement of the metal so that some parts, such as the remains of the upper dome, cannot be handled safely.

As is to be expected in an object with this history, the surface was covered in many areas with green copper corrosion products. Where these patches were compact and shiny in appearance, they were not an immediate cause for concern. However, in some areas small patches and pits of powdery white-green corrosion products appeared to have erupted through, and analysis identified these as atacamite and paratacamite, which are copper chlorides, products of 'bronze disease'. Although the lamp-holder is brass, it is still subject to this aggressive progressive corrosion mechanism, caused by the presence of chlorides, possibly introduced by salts from the soil where it was buried. What was certain was that action needed to be taken, as this corrosion process is self-perpetuating: the corrosion products, together with moisture from normal atmospheric conditions, will promote further corrosion.

The lamp-holder was required for the touring exhibition, so the challenge was to transport a bulky and heavy, yet fragile object – with a significant corrosion problem that would be exacerbated by any exposure to ambient humidity levels – to four museums on three continents without any further deterioration occurring. A combination of approaches was needed, from interventive treatment to stabilize the bronze disease, to a very detailed plan for packing and handling of the object while on tour, and rigorous control of the environment. Detailed discussions between Metals Conservation, Conservation Science, packing specialists, couriers and curators both from the V&A and the borrowing institutions resulted in a complex plan of action.

Interventive treatment

As the surface of the object was solvent-cleaned to remove dirt, dust and old museum coatings, it became evident that the bronze disease extended over at least 60 per cent of the lamp-holder (illus. 5.18). Recognized treatment methods would

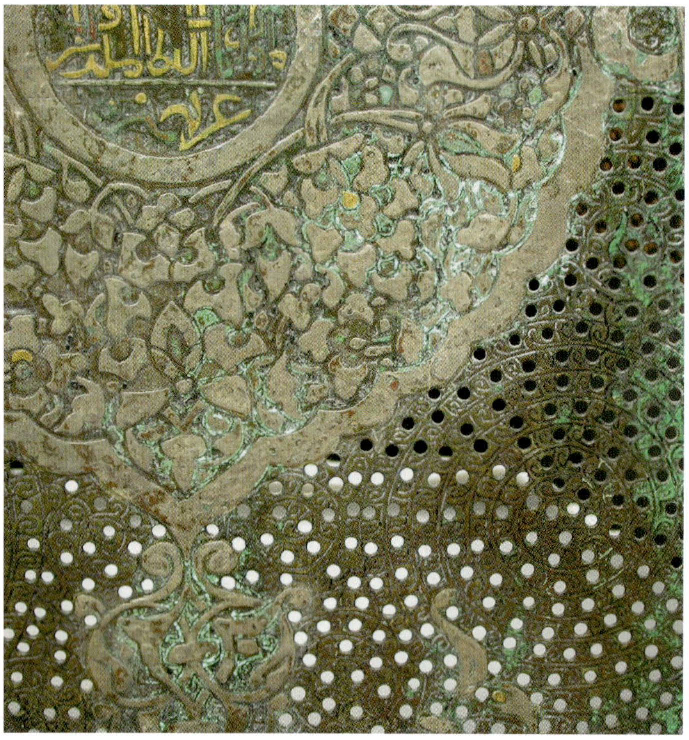

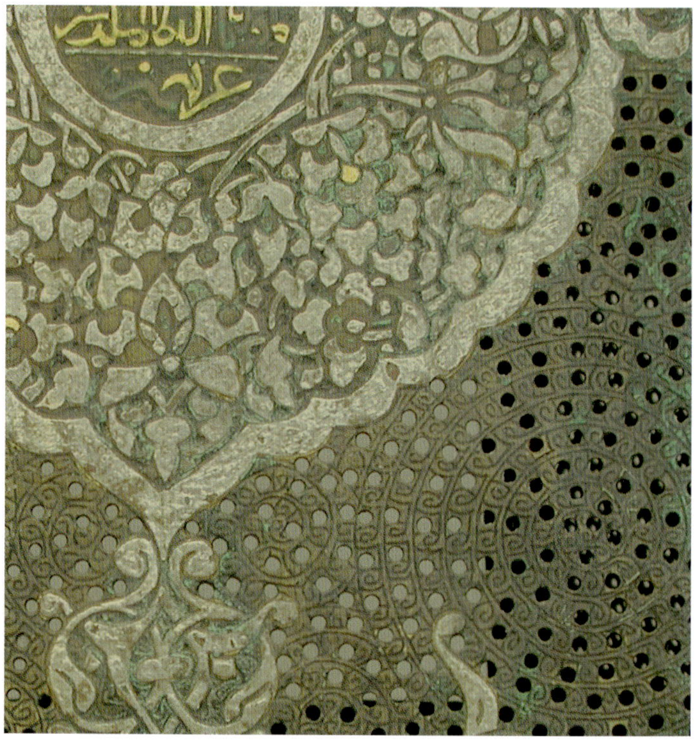

involve treating each individual pit with a chemical; this changes the copper chloride to more stable, non-harmful compounds. This method has been proved to be successful on objects where the bronze disease is localized; but it does cause surface colour change. It was considered unfeasible here because of the scale of the problem, and so a less interventive treatment regime was devised.

The aim was to take away the catalysts of the bronze disease by removing the copper chlorides and then protect the surface from moisture, so that the corrosion mechanism would be halted. The whole surface of the object was examined under a high-powered microscope, and where copper-chloride corrosion products were visible, these were removed (illus. 5.19) using microscalpels originally designed for eye surgeons. The surface was thoroughly cleaned and any traces of ambient moisture removed using solvents. It was then coated inside and out with two coats of an acrylic lacquer.

5.18 (*above left*) Close-up detail of the bronze mosque lamp-holder before treatment, showing white areas of bronze disease. V&A: 109–1888

5.19 (*above*) Close-up detail of the lamp-holder after treatment to remove bronze disease

Environmental control

There were three environments to be controlled: the packing case during transport, the display cases at the various venues, and the open environment as the object was unpacked before installation or packed for transit to the next venue. The first two were controlled by creation of a micro-environment. Within the packing case, the object was wrapped in a double layer of light-gauge polythene, creating an airtight microclimate. Within this was placed a combination of silica gel and molecular sieve in bags, both of which remove water molecules from the air. For an object of this size and weight, the use of timber for the packing case was unavoidable; but timber and particle boards all emit acidic organic vapours that attack metal objects. To neutralize this problem, timber surfaces were treated with a museum-tested sealant, or coated with a self-adhesive aluminium foil to prevent any gases escaping from the wood. All other packing materials used had been tested to ensure that they were pH-neutral.

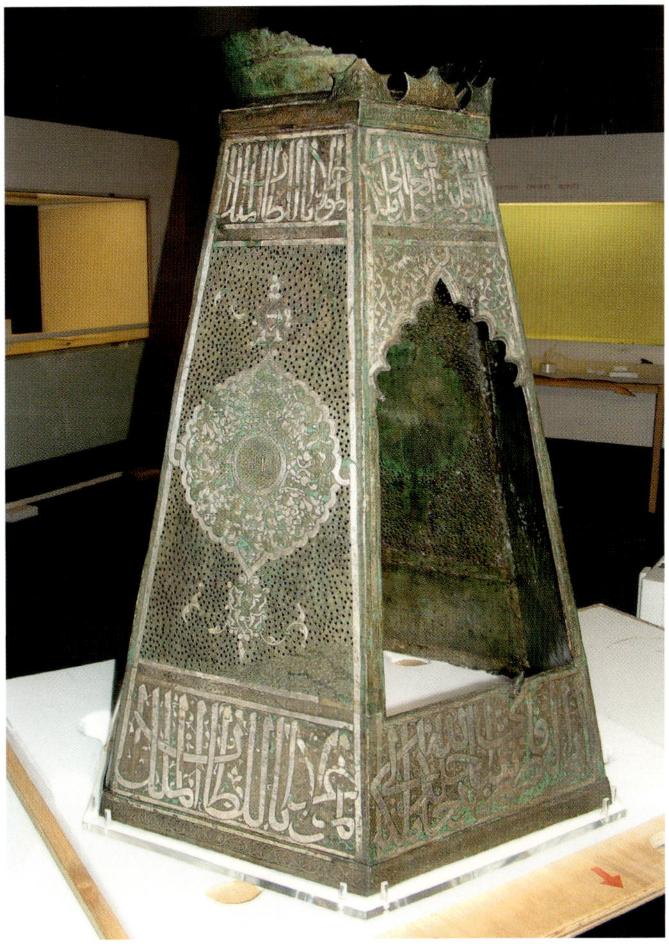

5.20 (*right*) The lamp-holder on its base for packing

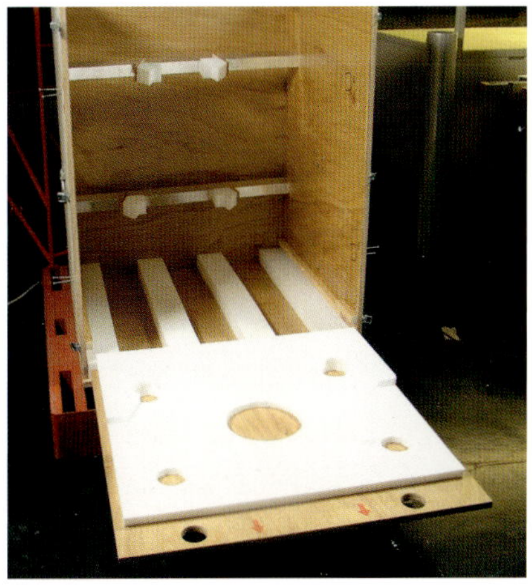

5.21 (*far right top*) The specially designed crate for the lamp-holder

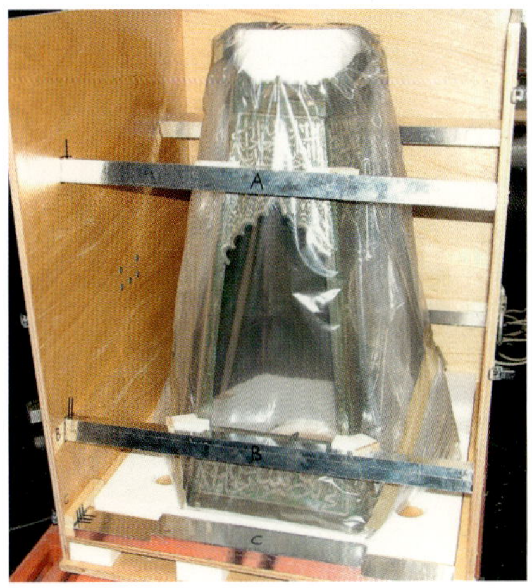

5.22 (*far right*) The lamp-holder in its crate for travelling

The construction of the display cases at the venues was also governed by the need to avoid materials that would emit harmful vapours (and this could include museum objects made of organic materials such as wood or leather) and by stringent control of the relative humidity through the use of desiccants. When the object was moving from one micro-environment to another, the only control possible was time – couriers were told that the object must be unpacked in front of the display case and placed inside immediately, with the display case closed as quickly as possible, to minimize exposure to an uncontrolled environment.

Packing and handling

The object travelled on a perspex base, fitted on to a tray that slides out of the packing case (illus. 5.20). At each venue the object could be slid out of the case and lifted into the display case using the perspex base, thus keeping handling to a minimum. The lamp was stabilized with four timber battens with foam corner sections shaped specifically to the contours of the object to prevent lateral and upwards movement during transit (illus. 5.21). They were positioned so that they braced the object at its strongest points (illus. 5.22).

With the object already sealed in a micro-environment, this crate was then closed, each edge was fitted with gasket seals to make it airtight, and it was then placed in an outer crate, also fitted with gasket seals; this was lined with 100 millimetres of foam insulation on all sides to help reduce vibration. Comprehensive packing notes and photographs showed exactly how to deconstruct (or reconstruct) the case to minimize risk of damage to the object, and to minimize the time that the object spent in an uncontrolled environment.

With these controls in place, the lamp's progress was monitored through the use of environmental data loggers inside both the packing case and the display cases. Progress was further monitored by the completion of questionnaires by couriers, giving information such as times when cases were opened and closed; where the packing crates were stored before transit; the type of transport (plane, truck); and the length of journeys. This data will be analysed and reports written, so that we may use the lessons learnt for the future.

A seventeenth-century Safavid cope
(V&A: T.477–1894)

Marion Kite

A cope dating from about 1605, and often known as the Marcy-Indjoudjian cope, has long been recognized as one of the most important examples of Safavid pile-weaving of the early seventeenth century (illus. 5.24). It is knotted using 11 colours of silk, and silver and silver-gilt metal threads are woven into the design to form the scrolling stems of the floral motifs and the ground of the orphrey (the decorative band around the front opening of the cope). The weaving is remarkably fine and has approximately 650 knots to the square inch (6.45 square centimetres). It combines Christian iconography with typical Safavid floral motifs, and it is unique in that it was woven as a cope rather than being made into a vestment from some other textile.

5.23 Detail of the Safavid cope with traces of Armenian letters at right edge.
V&A: T.477–1894

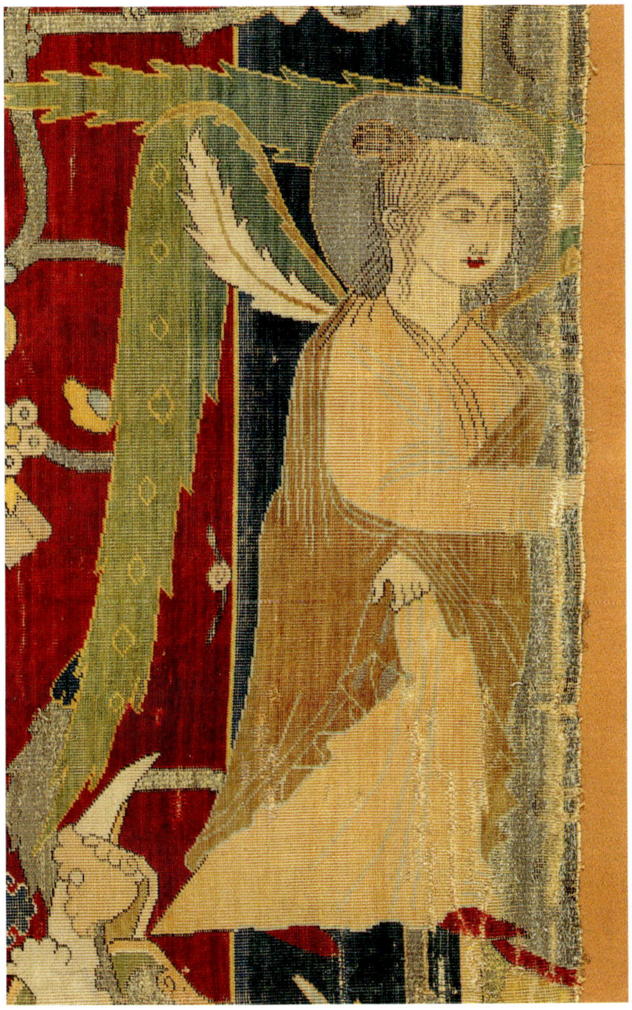

The practical conservation was complex, due to the fragmentary state of the vestment and lack of cohesive structure. Each of the individual pieces of the cope required an overall adhesive support to prevent loss of knots before the pieces were realigned in their correct positions and couched on to a linen fabric support. Previously, the cope had been mounted in its cropped form. The orphrey was for the most part missing, and space had not been allowed to indicate where the boundaries of the orphrey would have been. For the current work, the original size of the cope was calculated by taking measurements from various points where small fragments of the outside edge of the border remained, and the support linen was marked out to the original size of the cope.

Technical examination, conservation research and discoveries made during the current work have enabled new conclusions to be drawn that define more clearly the origins of this vestment. Dye analysis has completed the documentation, and the discovery of part of an inscription in Armenian script has strengthened the case for an Armenian origin for the vestment. The text was discovered on a worn section of the orphrey next to the figure of the Archangel

Gabriel (illus. 5.23), and with the assistance of Dr Vrej Nersessian from the British Library it has been possible to partially reconstruct this text. It is logically possible that a companion text was originally present beside the figure of the Virgin, but no trace of this remains.

The use of digital image manipulation has enabled a visual reconstruction of the complete cope to be made, permitting the colour balance and design to be interpreted and appreciated in a form closely resembling how it would have been seen when first made (illus. 5.25, 5.26).

5.24 The Safavid cope after conservation. V&A: T.477–1894

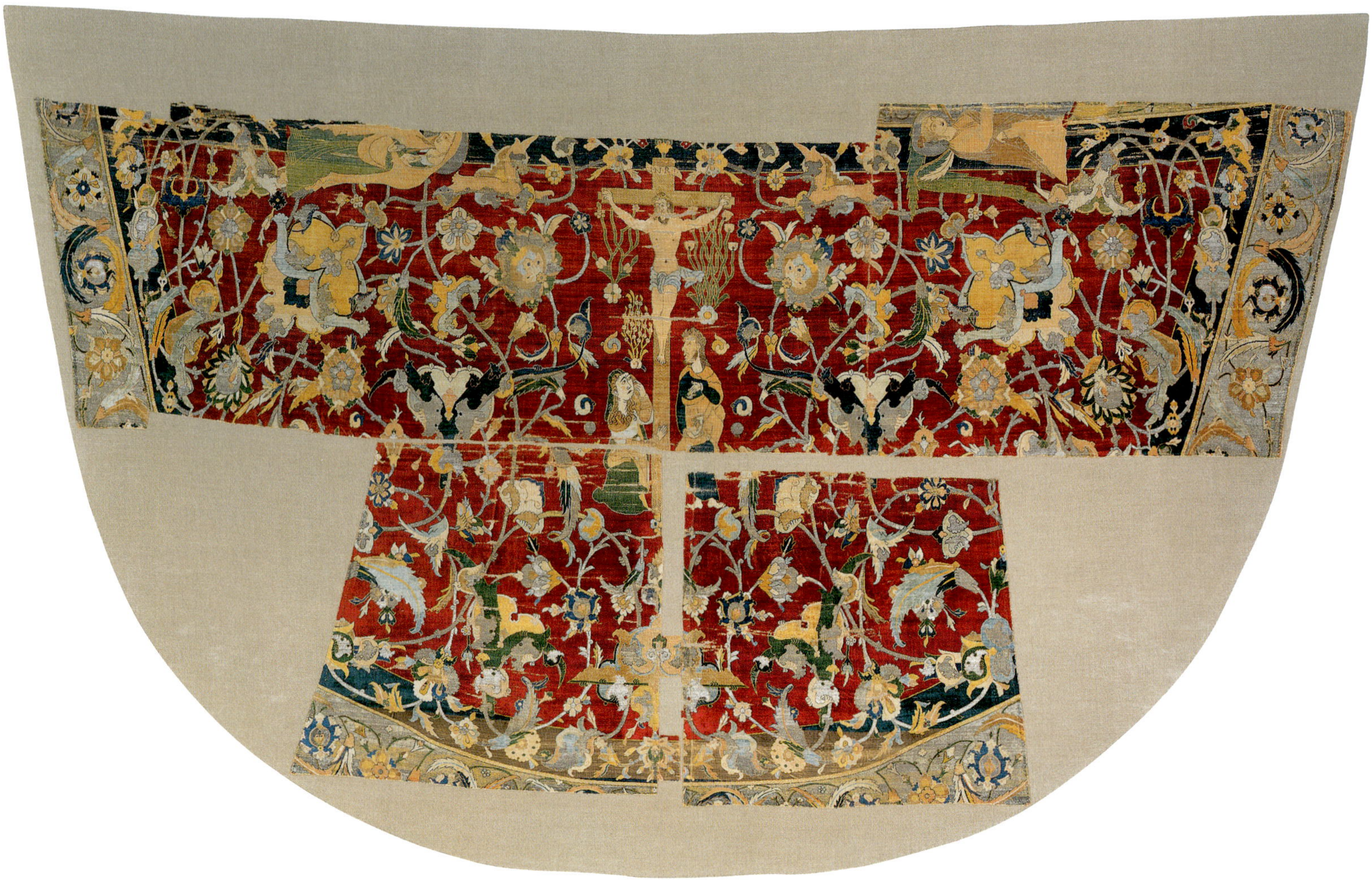

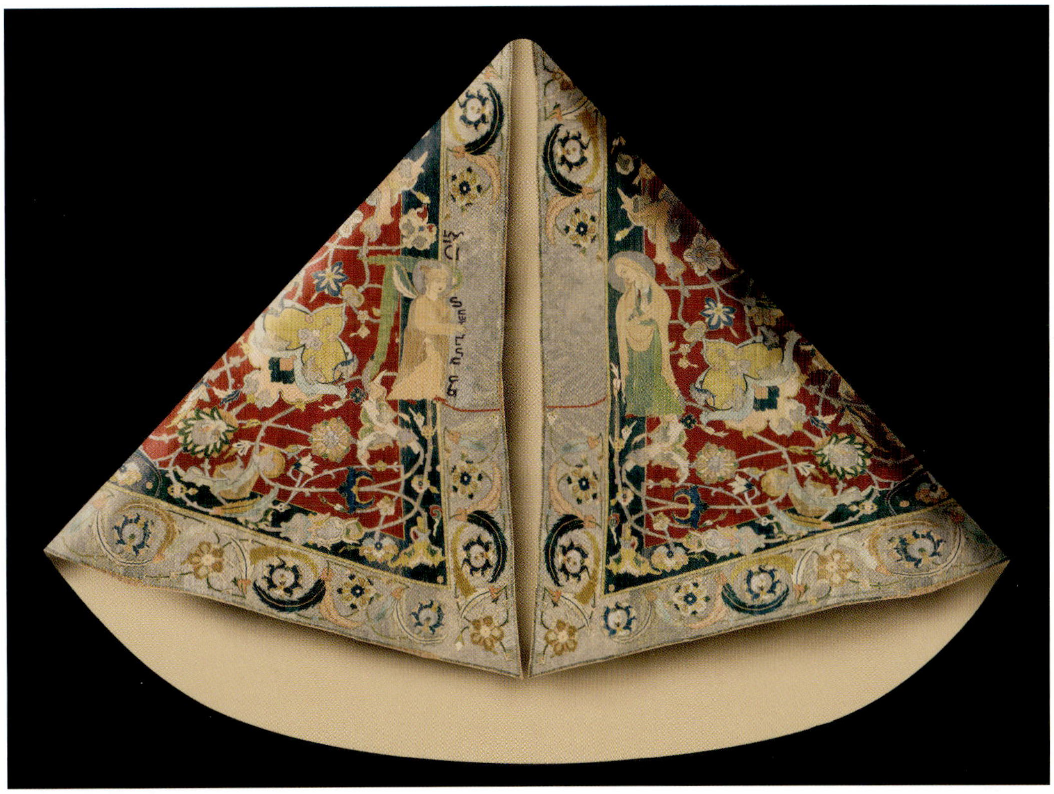

5.25 Digital reconstruction of the cope as it would have been worn: front

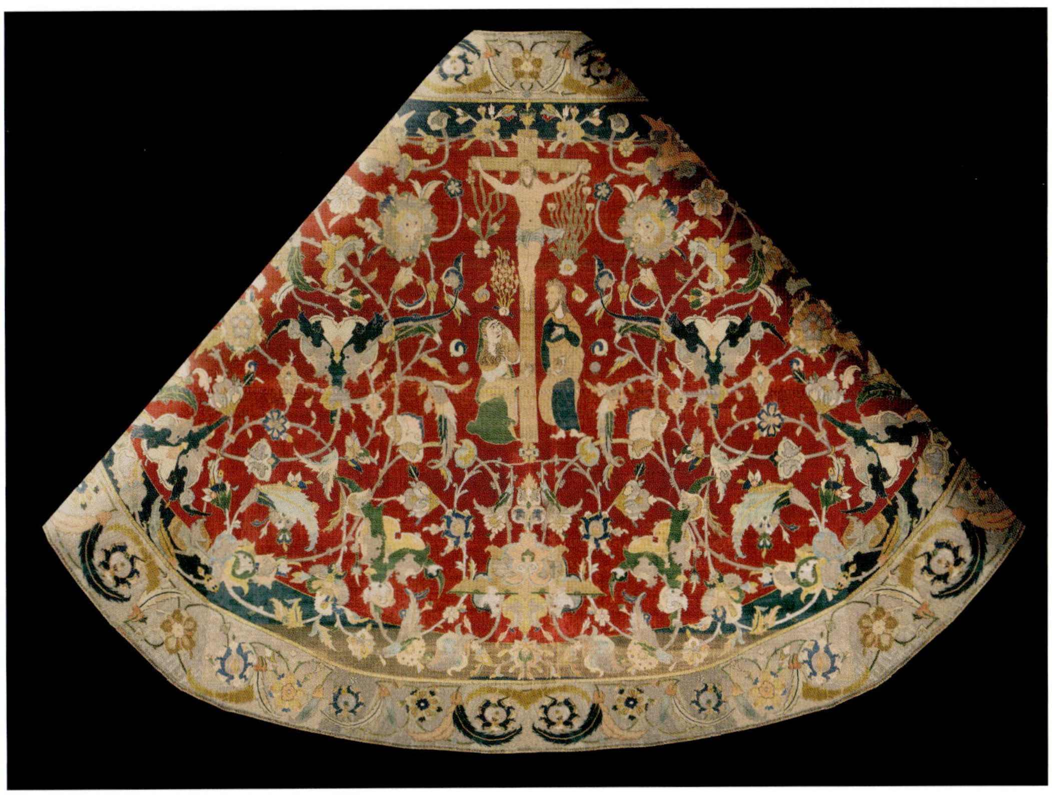

5.26 Digital reconstruction of the cope as it would have been worn: back

6 Gallery Interpretation

Nighat Yousuf

Dedicated to the memory of Margery Clinton, a talented ceramicist who contributed to the development of the Gallery touch objects and understood the importance of the hands-on experience in museums.

Interpretation is the means by which we explain the Museum's objects and displays to our visitors. The use of interpretation in the Jameel Gallery is based on the principles applied during the British Galleries project, which led to a restructuring of the way the V&A offers interpretation in its galleries. In planning the British Galleries, the focus was on the needs of the visitors, in addition to the selection and display of objects, design and interpretation. Visitor-centred gallery development became a major consideration for gallery redesigns and new developments at the V&A, moving away from a focus solely on the selection of objects towards a more integrated approach, which includes visitor requirements.

The V&A's audiences

The V&A's public includes a wide range of audience types and learning styles, so certain target audiences were selected early on in the Jameel Gallery project in order to identify visitor needs. Audience research carried out at the time of the creation of the British Galleries identified eight distinct types of visitor: this has now been refined down to six. The research looked at audiences in terms of their

6.1 Visitors studying a model of the Alhambra in the V&A's Architecture Gallery

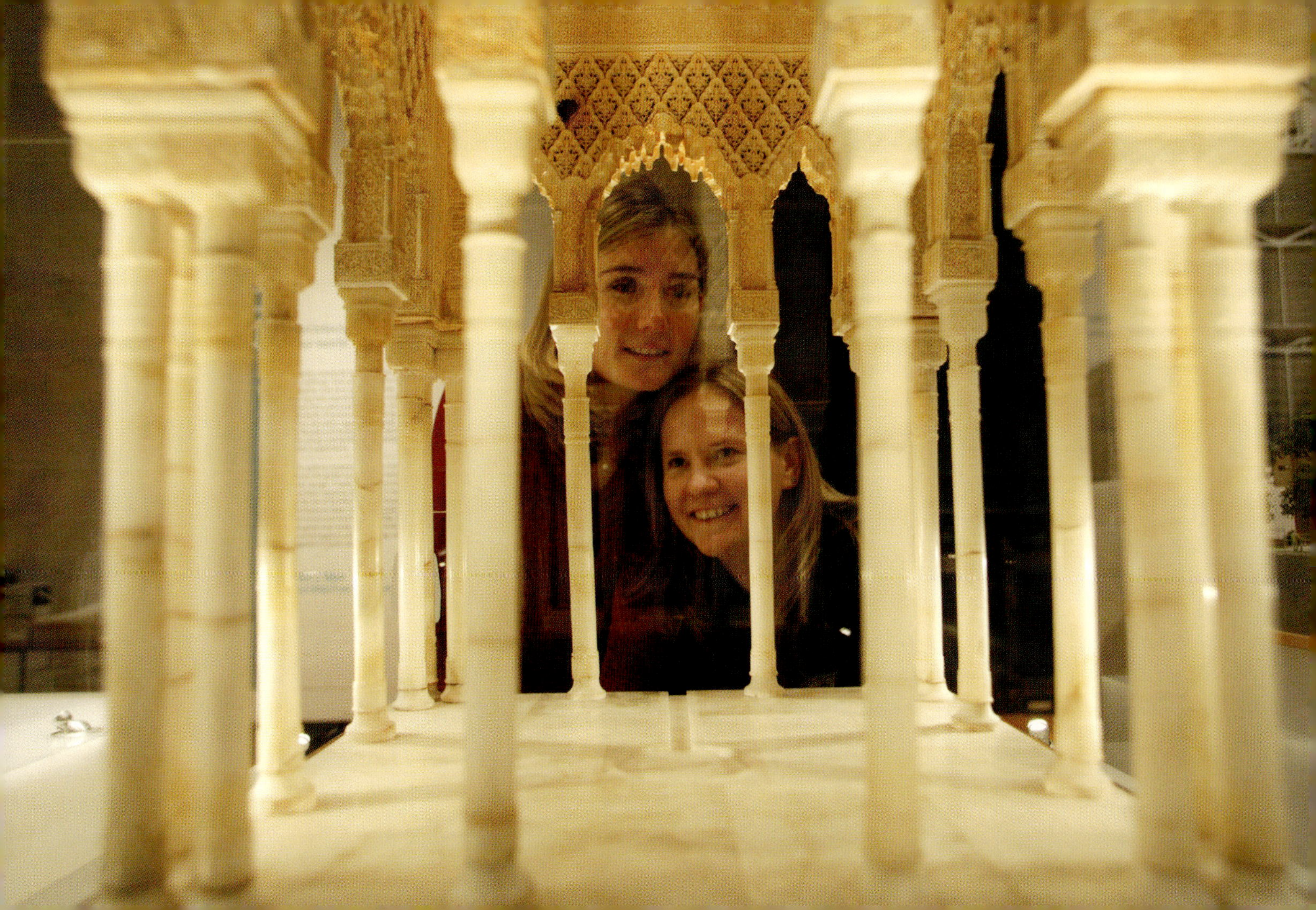

visiting 'styles', both social and intellectual, and their needs, rather than from a traditional marketing perspective based on social and demographic data. The six types of V&A audiences can be categorized as follows:

- Schools
- Students
- Families
- Professionals in the creative industries
- Adult independent visitors not in other categories
- Groups.

There is inevitably some overlap within these groups – someone may visit on one occasion as part of a student group and on another as part of a family or as an independent visitor. Issues of social class and cultural diversity are considered for all gallery and exhibition programmes laterally across all six categories. We usually concentrate on two of these groups as primary audiences for new galleries, depending on the type of material on display. For the Jameel Gallery, families and adult independent visitors were chosen as the two main target groups. The central location of the Gallery on the ground floor, near the main entrance and the shop, suggested that the majority of visitors would fall into these types.

In the late 1940s when the previous display in what is now the Jameel Gallery was created, design was based on a traditional chronological and taxonomic display arrangement with a very academic labelling system. Designing exhibitions to enable parents to explain the themes to their children, or to allow children to learn in relation to their own physical and intellectual needs, was not considered. Today family groups are one of the fastest-growing sections of the museum audience in Britain. Families represent the most important and core visiting unit, but they choose where to go carefully and match the museum provision to their own needs. Families are categorized by the V&A as one or more adults visiting with one or more children under the age of 16, visiting on their own (i.e. not in a school group). Families want to spend time together in a worthwhile pursuit, and the children (especially the youngest child) generally drive the visit, an observation that was highlighted in the visitor-shadowing exercise.

Adult independent visitors not in other categories are predominantly friendship and family groups where all members are aged 16 and over. This category also includes individual overseas visitors (i.e. those not arriving in organized tours). They manage their own learning and are not restricted by conventional subject boundaries. Their interests and experiences are wide-ranging and varied.

In addition to the families and adult independent groups, it was felt necessary to focus on an audience type defined by its cultural identity. In view of the subject matter of the Gallery, we therefore added Muslim community groups as a third key target audience. These could be UK-based or from overseas, and would include voluntary associations, adult and community groups. The Jameel Gallery should have particular appeal for a Muslim audience, and the V&A is striving to attract a more culturally diverse audience to all its galleries. The redesign of the Middle East gallery is particularly relevant to the British multicultural population, and to current interest in Islamic culture, given the contemporary global political environment and media sensitivities surrounding Muslim society. The V&A therefore has an opportunity to present positive aspects of Islamic art and culture.

Learning styles

The classification of learning styles adopted by the V&A during the development of the British Galleries is based on four learning styles identified in recent academic studies: analytical learners; common-sense learners; experiential learners; and imaginative learners (see the boxed text below).

- *Analytical learners*: are best at understanding a wide range of information and putting it into a concise, logical form. They learn by thinking and watching, prefer interpretation that provides facts and sequential ideas, want sound logical theories to consider, and look for intellectual comprehension. This is a group for whom traditional art and design museums with lots of objects and information on labels cater well.
- *Common-sense learners*: learn by thinking and doing, prefer to try out theories and test them for themselves and look for solutions to problems. They are best at finding practical uses for ideas and theories.
- *Experiential learners*: use concrete experience and active experimentation, learning by feeling and doing. They enjoy imaginative trial and error, prefer hands-on experience and look for hidden meaning.
- *Imaginative learners*: are best at viewing concrete situations from many different points of view. They learn by feeling and watching and by listening and sharing ideas. They prefer interpretation that encourages social interaction, and like to be given opportunities to observe and gather a wide range of information and to look for personal meaning.

Text adapted from B. Serrell, *Exhibit Labels: An Interpretive Approach*, Walnut Creek, CA, Alta Mira Press, 1996, pp.51–9.

Effective learning makes use of all four modes flexibly in whatever combinations suit the situation. Traditionally, museums have catered well for analytical learning, and present some stimuli for common-sense learning, but experiential and imaginative learning have often been overlooked. Museum professionals need to understand the range of learning styles to cater for diverse audiences. Visitor-shadowing exercises for curatorial team members were arranged to give curators an idea of the variety of audiences and the different combinations of learning techniques they used when visiting the Museum. Discussions with the concept team of findings from their observations were carried out with reference to the various learning styles. This enabled the curators to gain a greater understanding of the learning needs of visitors other than their professional and academic peer groups, who tend to fall mainly into the 'analytical' group of learners.

Analysis of learning styles helps to determine the types of interpretative devices that are suitable for the gallery. All learning styles should have equal status in a museum environment. Ideally, the interpretative approaches used would cater for the full range of learning styles, but this can be difficult in reality, given practical limitations such as space, design constraints and finances. The aim is to ensure that anyone from a target audience could go around the gallery and find something to meet their needs and appeal to their preferred learning style. Recommended selections of interactive devices were suggested to the team, based on their relevance to display arrangements, learning styles and distribution within the gallery. The original selection of interpretative devices was reduced as the gallery design evolved and object selection was refined. The chosen interactive devices were then notionally placed in the gallery with regard to display limitations, access requirements and an even distribution within the space.

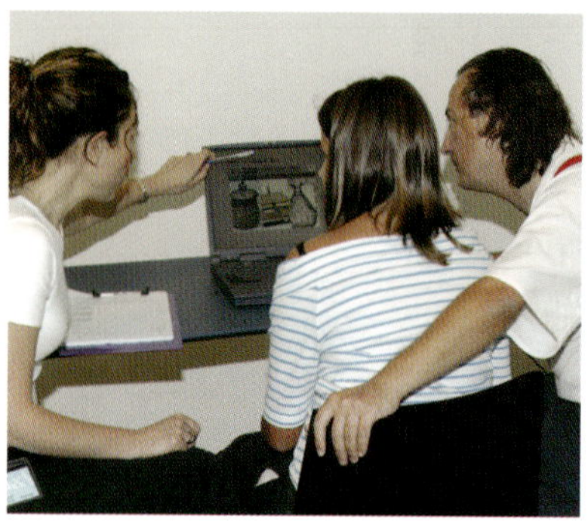

6.2 Evaluating the style-guide prototype with members of the public

Evaluation processes

Throughout the development of the Jameel Gallery, a systematic evaluation programme was implemented to engage with our audiences and to enable the gallery development team to make informed decisions at critical stages in the process. Findings from the earliest stage of the cycle – known as 'front-end' evaluation – informed the interpretation scheme, as well as the development and implementation of the wider gallery concept. The aims of the front-end evaluation were:

- To look at prior knowledge and preconceptions of the proposed themes
- To look at preferred approaches to learning about the gallery themes
- To test knowledge of specific terms and technical vocabulary
- To assess the recognition of key objects and images.

The study comprised two phases. Phase 1 assessed visitors' prior knowledge, interest, experience and attitudes towards Islamic art, and used techniques such as personal meaning mapping (an exercise designed to explore what associations the words 'Islamic art' have for the general public) and word-sorting exercises (for example, of key terminology). Phase 2 assessed participants' responses to specific issues and exhibition ideas in order to focus on key issues raised by visitors in the first phase and explore them in greater depth. The researchers chose quotes from respondents in Phase 1 to be discussed by focus groups in Phase 2, so the data from Phase 2 was entirely visitor-generated, with no intervention by researchers. A total of 36 visitors were sampled for Phase 1 of the study and another seven visitors for Phase 2.

The full report from the evaluation was published on the V&A web-site. Noteworthy key points from the study, which have been addressed in the design of the Gallery, include the following:

- The words and phrases that people initially used were generally based on widely disseminated stereotypical views of both the Islamic world and Islamic art. To address this, the terminology used in the Gallery is explained through appropriate text and labelling, because even terms with high levels of recognition (such as 'Ottoman' and 'Persian') produced poor understanding.
- Visitors expect a clear hierarchy of information to give them a framework within which to navigate the Gallery both physically and intellectually. Visitors were not confident in their understanding of the themes, which emphasized the need to have explanatory material in the Gallery. A text and labelling hierarchy was carefully planned to define and guide the visitor through

1 **Carpet with Animals Fighting**
Iran, probably Isfahan
1550–1650

This is one of a small group of carpets of very high quality, which includes the so-called Emperor carpet in Vienna. This example is remarkable for the white ground of the border and the liveliness with which the animals were drawn.

Silk warp (Z2S) and weft, wool pile

Museum no. 601-1894

2–3 **Lengths of Velvet with Flowers**
Iran, probably Isfahan
1600–1700

When Shah Abbas I made Isfahan his capital shortly before 1600, he developed the city as a centre of luxury textile production. Silk velvets were made in abundance, both for local use and for export. Many had floral patterns, some composed of fantastic blossoms (2), others of flowers closer to nature (3).

Silk velvet

Museum nos. 286-1894, 717-1899

4 **Fragment of Silk with Animals Fighting**
Iran
1500–1600

The type of animal combats found in the background of the Chelsea carpet are the main motif on this silk. One row shows a cheetah attacking a wild ass. The other has an ox being mauled by a lion-like beast with a fantastic tail. This fragment was part of a cope, a Christian church vestment.

Silk thread in lampas weave

Museum no. T.111-1929

5 **Carpet Fragment with Animals and Angels**
Iran
1500–1700

The carpet from which this fragment came belongs to a disputed group. Many doubt its attribution to Safavid Iran, even though the design is composed mainly of characteristically Safavid elements. The wolves at the top, however, are unusual.

Silk warp and weft, wool pile, metal-wrapped thread

Museum no. T.77-1919.
Given by Charles T. Garland

6.3 A typical object label

Inlay of Silver and Gold

Objects made from base materials were often transformed by sophisticated forms of decoration. An important example is brassware decorated with inlaid surface ornament.

For larger motifs, small areas of brass were chiselled out and filled with thin sheets of silver, gold and copper. Details were added by chasing the surface of the softer metals, and contrast was created with a black filler. The results were, for metalwork, an unusually graphic form of decoration, often of great quality.

Inlay first became popular in eastern Iran in the mid-12th century. The technique then spread westwards, and by 1250 was in use across the Middle East. Its popularity declined after 1500.

Inlaid brasswares survive in large numbers, but the valuable inlay has often been picked out.

6.4 A typical information panel

potentially unfamiliar terminology (illus. 6.3, 6.4). Visitors are provided with information about the objects, presented in layers of progressive detail. Text, labelling, images, maps and films are incorporated into the Gallery experience. The subject areas of the Gallery also have clear content titles so that visitors can distinguish and prioritize sections in visiting terms. The gallery themes are key to visitors' understanding of Islamic art and these are also summarized in a gallery book for visitors' reference.

- One of the key misconceptions that the Gallery aims to dispel is the commonly held view regarding the ban on the use of images in Islamic art, and it is important to address this clearly. Muslims did – and do – own pictures, and in particular pictures of Islamic sites and personalities. This subject is addressed as one of the major themes in the Gallery and is reinforced in the text and labelling, as well as being emphasized in the interactive style guide.
- An important finding related to the understanding of objects is that recognition of objects as 'Islamic' is based on patterns and colours. This supports the use of a style guide as a major interpretative element of the Gallery.
- Western art historical terms such as 'arabesque' and old regional names such as 'Persia' should be avoided. Evaluation findings stressed the importance of using intelligible, contemporary language.

Development of gallery themes

The educator on the concept team acts as an audience representative, devises and recommends specific interpretation and makes this relevant to the themes and messages in the Gallery, as well as to the needs of the target audiences. In order to build on the findings of the front-end evaluation and incorporate them into the layout of the Gallery, a series of workshops were carried out with the concept team to refine the themes of the Gallery with its audiences in mind. Key messages to be conveyed were established with the team to provide a framework for displaying the objects. Accessibility issues for the disabled and for children were also explored and strongly influenced the team's design decisions.

Interpretative devices

A series of suggested interpretative devices were set out in the framework document. Selections were based on the needs of specific target audiences – for example, many children have a preference for experiential learning and enjoy using hands-on interactive devices. The concept team considered the use of a number of interpretative devices as the project evolved, and a small range of low- and high-technology devices, including audio-visuals, was finally agreed upon.

Interactive design and development were carried out with the concept team. A multimedia manager translated the team's concepts into a technical brief, for tendering out to external agencies for shortlisting and selection after interviews and presentations. All the interactive elements were designed to be used on the V&A's web-site as well as in the Gallery.

Style guide

As the front-end evaluation had shown, many visitors felt bewildered when confronted by such an unfamiliar area as Islamic art. It was therefore important to give visitors the framework to recognize significant stylistic features. Following the model for style guides in the British Galleries, a computer kiosk providing an interactive guide to Islamic style was developed with the design company Nykris (illus. 6.6). This consists of a touch-sensitive screen that provides visual examples of key Islamic styles, with brief explanations of the main features of those styles. Users can choose to learn about a particular style or dynasty, and can also test their knowledge in a quiz (illus. 6.2, 6.5, 6.7).

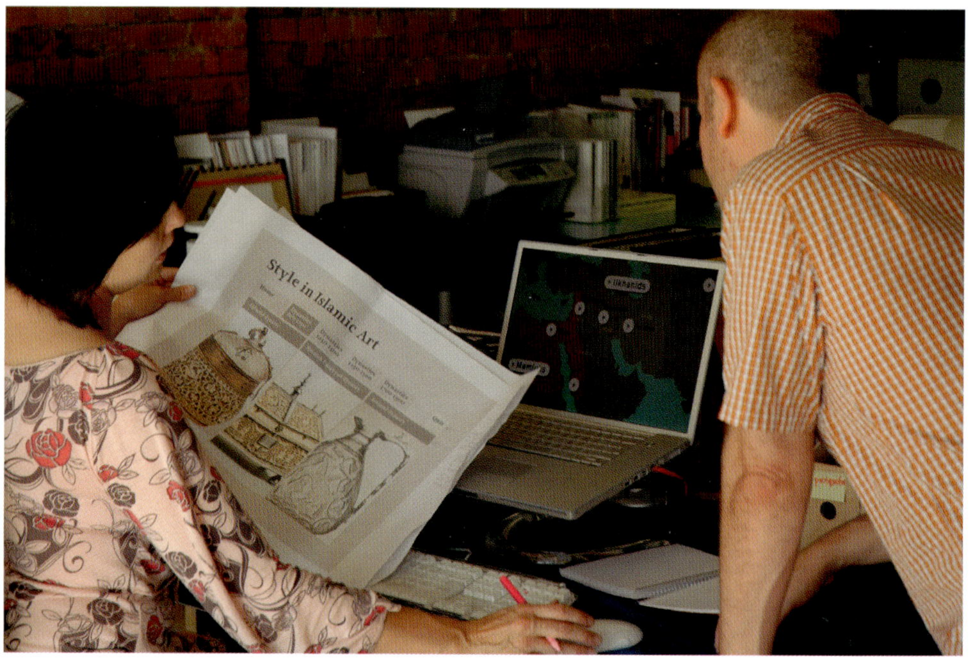

6.5 The Nykris team at work on the style guide (left: Nikki Barton, right: Martin Godfrey)

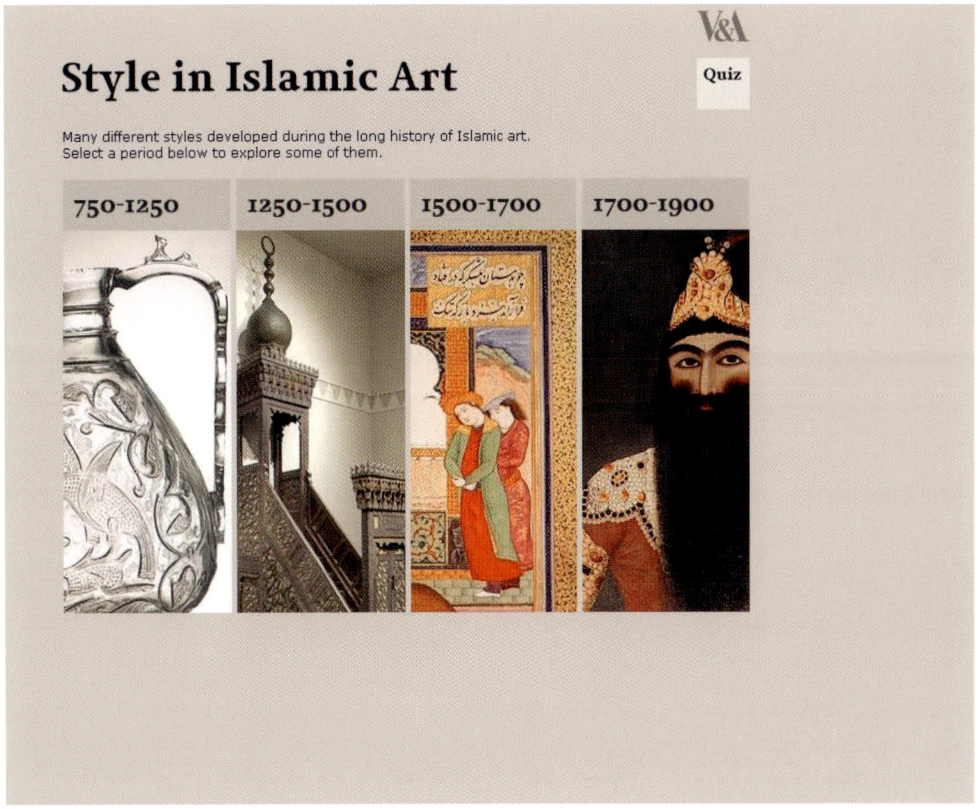

6.6 The Islamic style guide: a sample screen

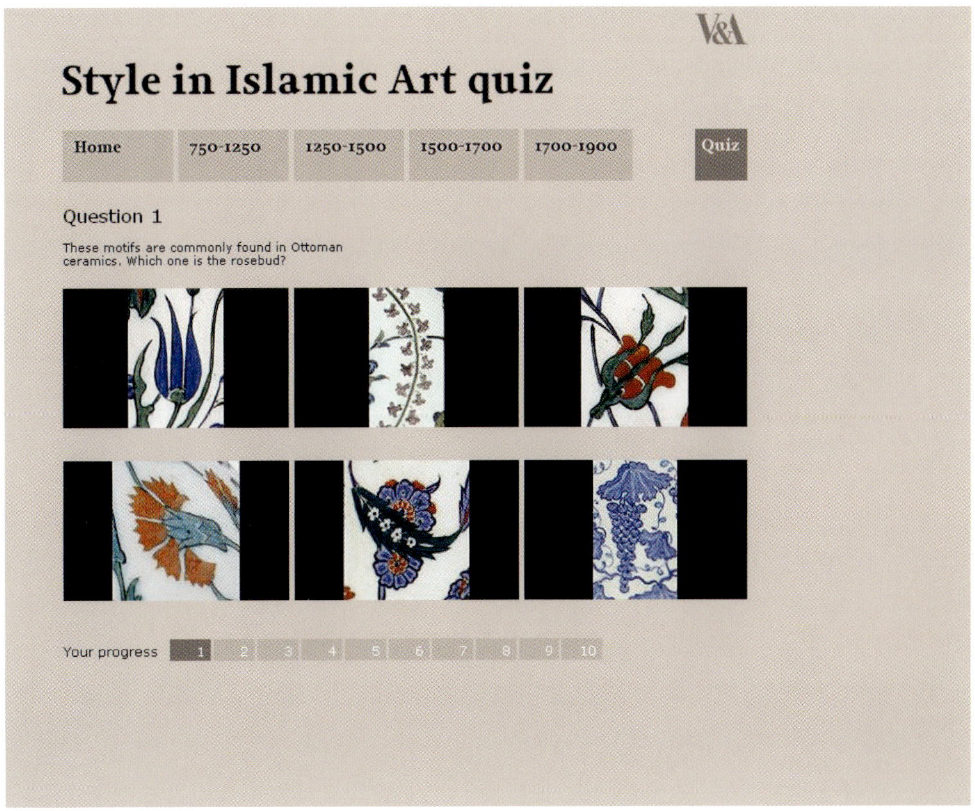

6.7 The style-guide quiz: a sample screen

Map and time-line

The animated map, in contrast to the style guide, is a new type of interpretative tool for the V&A. The evaluation had shown that most visitors were unclear about the geography and history of the area covered in the Gallery: this map, also developed by Nykris in consultation with the concept team, shows the spread of Islam from the seventh to the twentieth century, and gives information about key cities and dynasties (illus. 6.8). Visitors can touch the screen to learn more about a particular period, city or dynasty, or they can play the whole two-minute sequence to gain an idea of the ebb and flow of Islamic history. The map is accompanied by a static time-line printed on the adjacent wall, showing key events in both Islamic and world history.

Audio programmes and videos

Like all the interpretative devices, each audio and video programme was designed to relate to particular messages conveyed in the Gallery. The audio and video programmes were packaged together and contracted out to a single specialist company, Atacama, which was experienced in filming for museums in the Middle East (illus. 6.9).

Two three-minute videos were commissioned by the V&A for the Gallery. One video deals with the 'Art for Religion' theme, focusing on the mosque as a place of worship and religious ritual. Displays relating to religious art are put into context, as mosque architecture, ceremonies and related objects are shown in the film. The other video examines palaces relevant to the 'Art for the Court' theme. The architecture, ceremonies and related objects have been filmed partly to emphasize messages about figurative art playing its part in Islamic art. The films have narration and soundtrack available through handsets; subtitles, Braille and large-text transcripts are also provided to increase accessibility.

The team provided Atacama with an outline of the areas we wished to cover and with specialist background material. The script was refined with the concept team. Atacama filmed on location throughout the Middle East, at the V&A and in Sheffield's Millennium Galleries, where objects were on display during the last leg of the *Palace and Mosque* touring exhibition.

The audio programme focused on readings of Persian poetry inscribed on, or relating to, several of the objects in the Gallery. Original and translated extracts were provided so that Atacama could develop the scripts further. Both English and Iranian narrators were used. Prototype testing of audio-visual equipment was also built into the design processes.

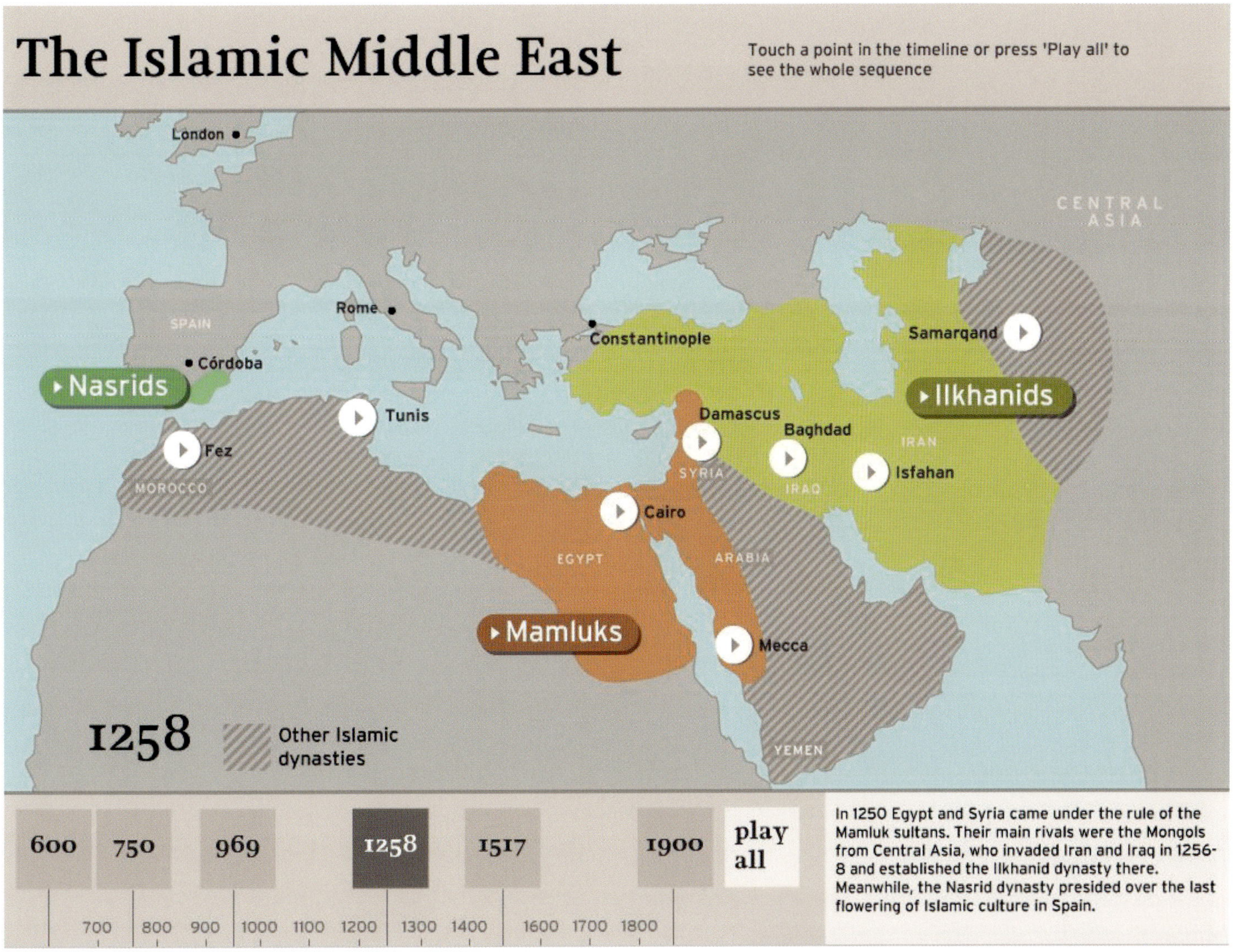

6.8 The interactive map: a sample screen

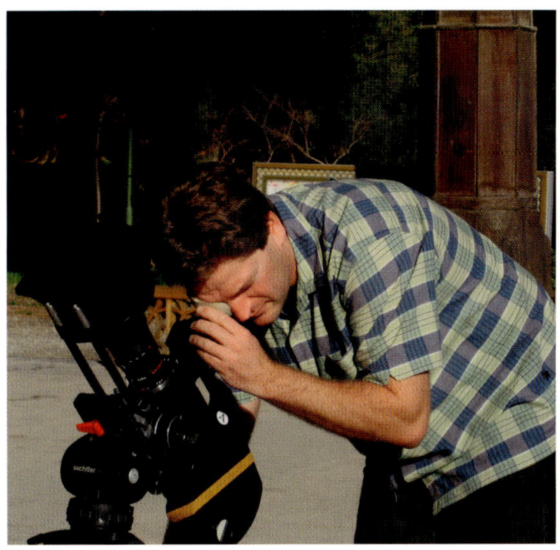

6.9 Mark Whatmore of Atacama filming in Iran for the Jameel Gallery videos

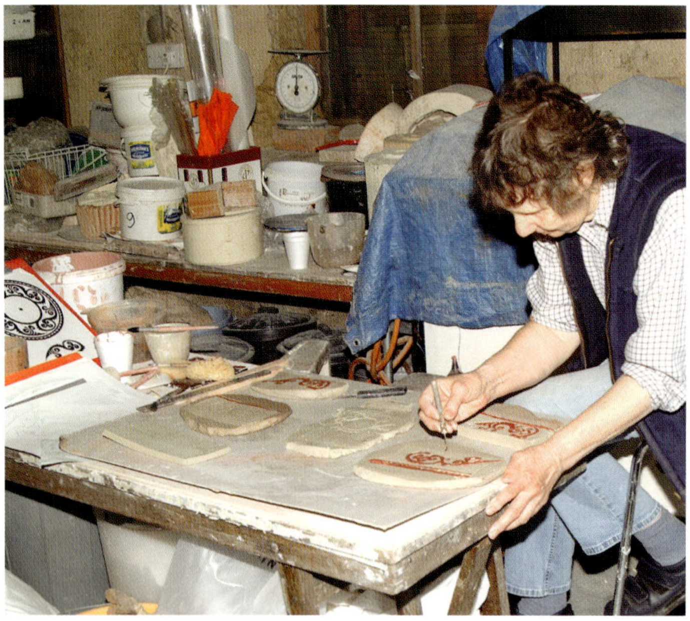

6.10 Ceramic touch objects being made by potter Alison Robinson

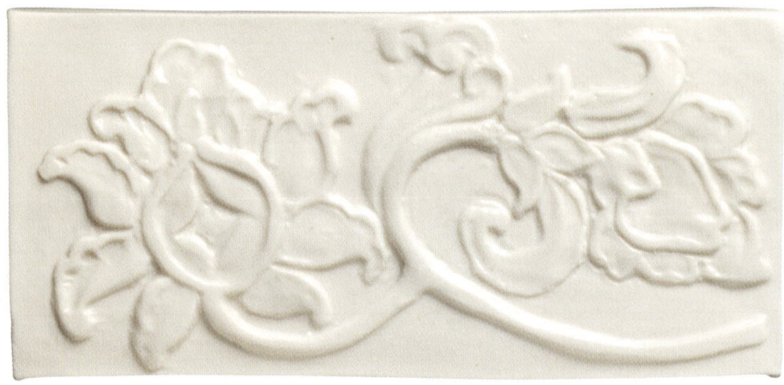

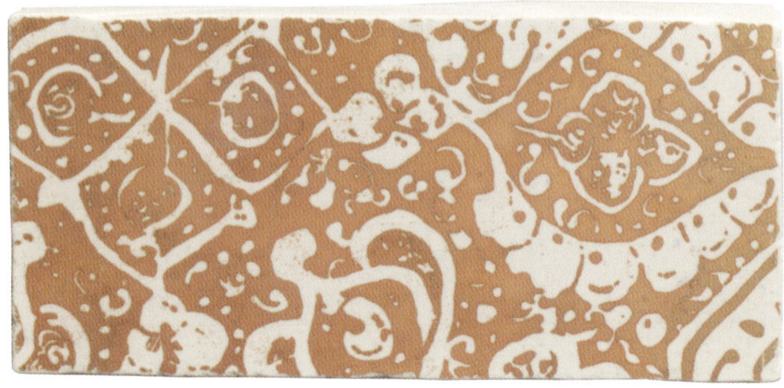

6.11 Three touch objects showing ceramic techniques. (*From top*) Earthenware with slip decoration, moulded porcelain, and fritware with lustre decoration; made by Alison Robinson (top and centre) and Margery Clinton

'Low-technology' devices

These include simple devices with no working parts, such as touch objects and replicas showing manufacturing processes. The selection was based on relevance to the display, clarity of purpose and location within the Gallery. The devices should not detract from the displays, while still being appealing to visitors. These factors contributed to decisions about the size, location and design of the interactive devices.

The final selection included a group of specially commissioned ceramic sherds to show different bodies and glazes (illus. 6.11); a replica of a section of carved tilework to demonstrate the unique technique used (illus. 6.13); and a book of some of the types of pattern seen in objects throughout the Gallery, made with raised surfaces (illus. 6.15). All of these are meant to be handled: the pattern book and carved tile in particular are intended for use by visually impaired visitors, and are accompanied by Braille texts.

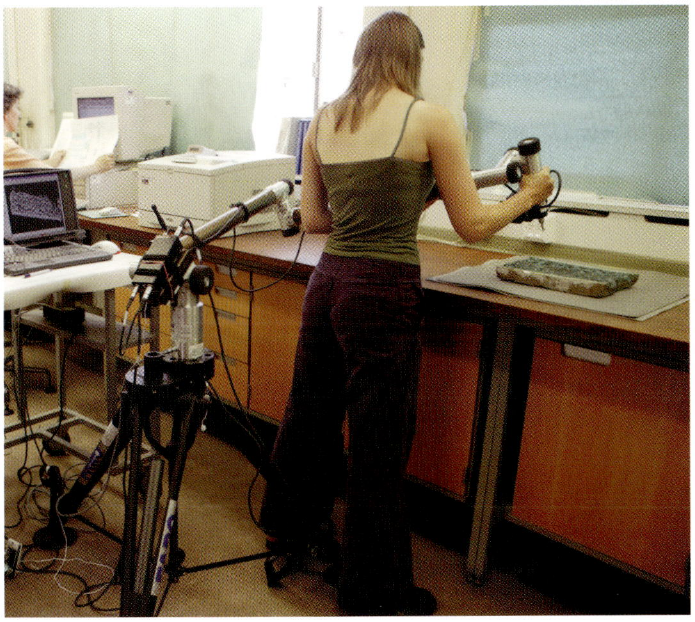

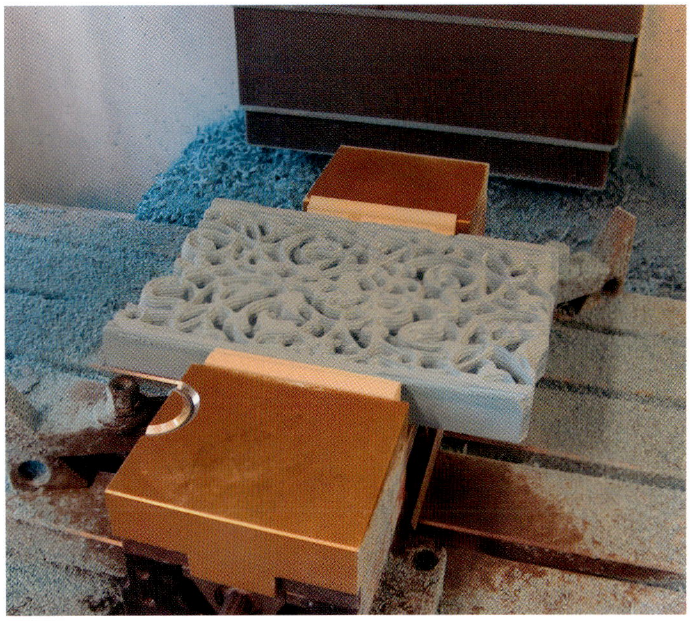

6.12 Annemarie LaPensee from Liverpool Museums Conservation Centre laser-measuring a tile from Buyanquli Khan's tomb

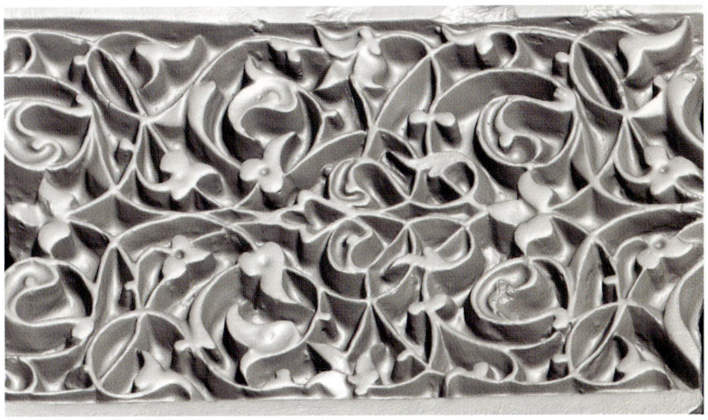

6.13 The finished reproduction of the tile as a touch object (before glazing) to show its deeply carved design

6.14 (*left*) The reproduction tile after initial glazing

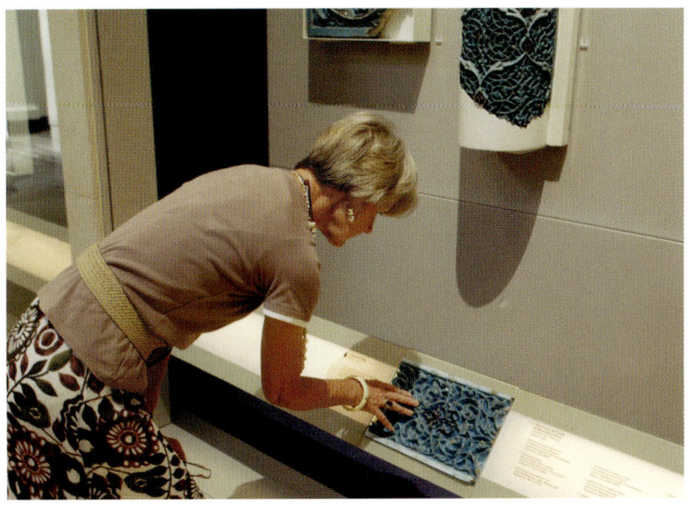

6.15 The 'touch tile' in place in the Gallery

Gallery and object books are interpretative aids which provide deeper discussion of some of the key issues that are likely to be of interest to visitors. The Ardabil carpet has a dedicated object book in which further information on the history and study of the object is given (illus. 6.16). These books are placed near seating and may be studied or browsed while the visitor is resting. Gallery and object books are also useful for visually impaired visitors, with Braille-provision text provided together with large-print text versions.

Access and disability issues, including the effectiveness of the touch objects and Braille signage, were reviewed at key stages of development with the V&A's disability and access officer, and with external specialists from organizations such as the Royal National Institute for the Blind and the Royal National Institute for the Deaf. Their recommendations informed the choice of materials and design of the touch objects. Modification and retesting were carried out before commissioning the final device.

Summary

The multicultural nature of today's society is particularly pertinent in responding to visitor needs for the Jameel Gallery. Museums strive to make provision for all parts of society; it is essential to be aware of the nature of potential audiences and to create galleries that interest as broad a range of visitors as possible. Inevitably people from different backgrounds have different perceptions and interests in relation to museum exhibitions. Social and cultural preconceptions embedded in everyday life must also be considered when interpreting the collection. Galleries should build on common areas of interest and should address stereotypes uncovered in front-end evaluation.

The V&A's major redesign and installation of the Jameel Gallery of Islamic Art has given us an opportunity to update the presentation of the collection, to provide a greater level of interaction with the visitor, to develop interest in – and promote a greater understanding of – the diversity of Islamic art and to inspire an appreciation of its beauty.

6.16 (*right*) Barry Ginley proof-reading the raised-pattern book with Braille text

6.17 (*far right*) The interactive map in use in the Gallery, with the time-line above

6.18 (*right*) Visitors watching the video in the Gallery

6.19 (*far right*) The Islamic style guide in use in the Gallery

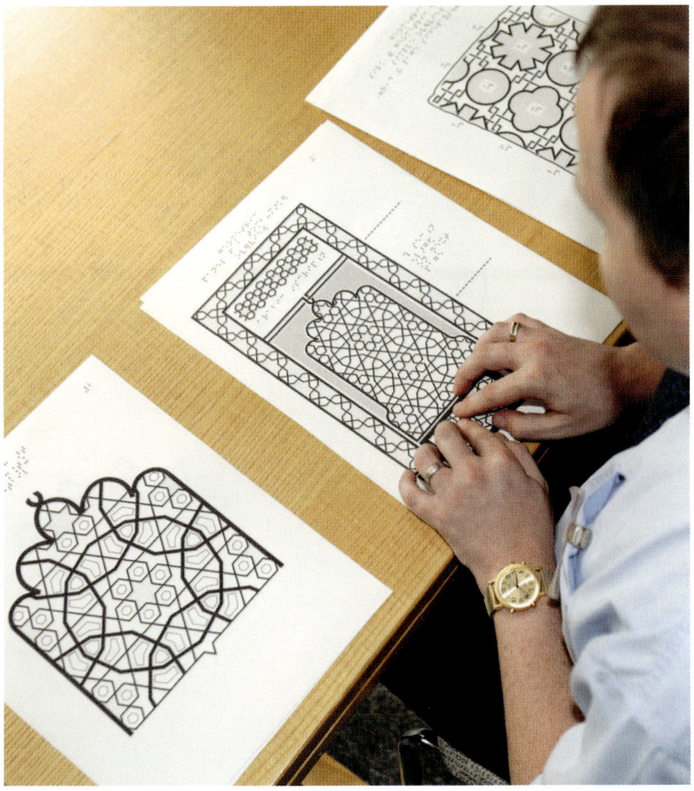

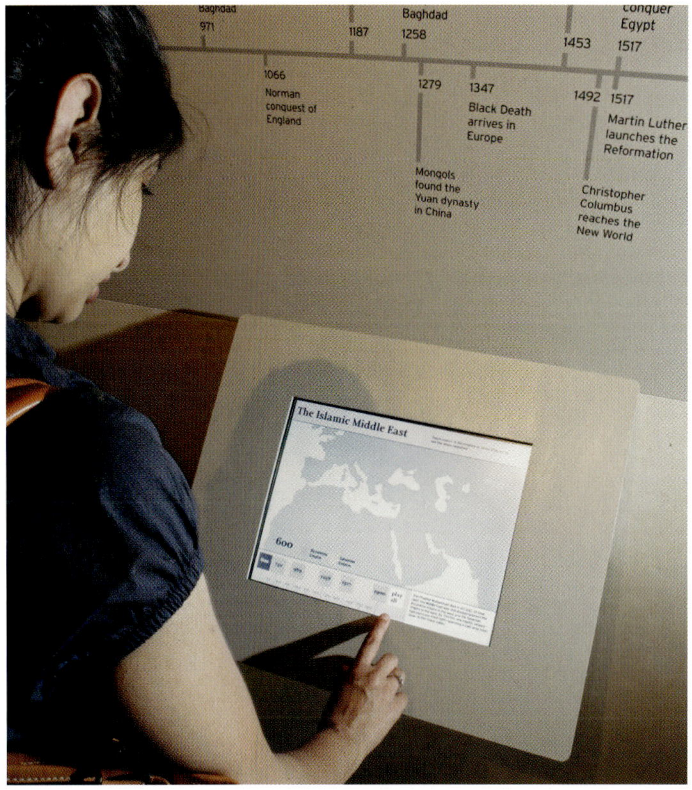
Baghdad
971
1187
Baghdad
1258
1453
conquer
Egypt
1517
1066
Norman
conquest of
England
1279
1347
Black Death
arrives in
Europe
1492
1517
Martin Luther
launches the
Reformation
Mongols
found the
Yuan dynasty
in China
Christopher
Columbus
reaches the
New World
The Islamic Middle East
600

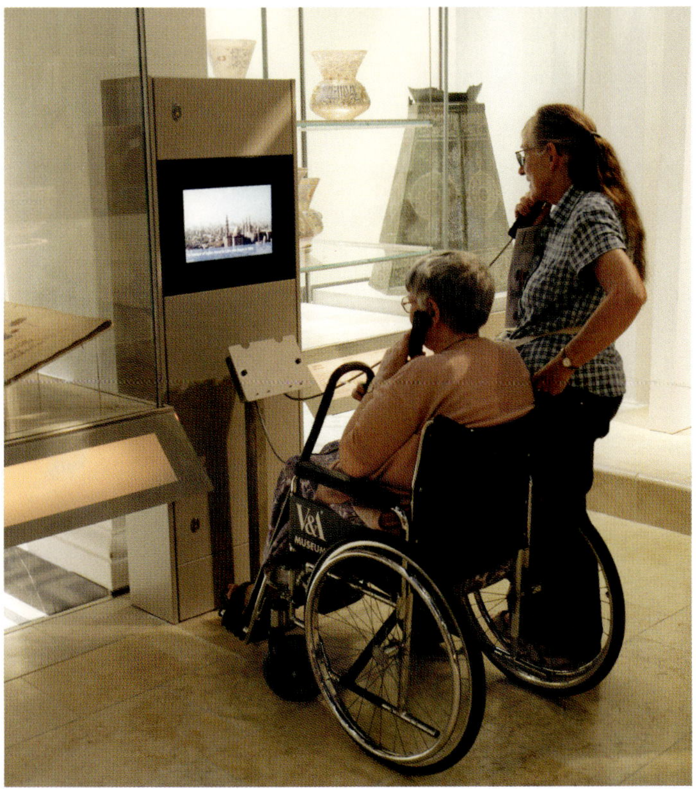

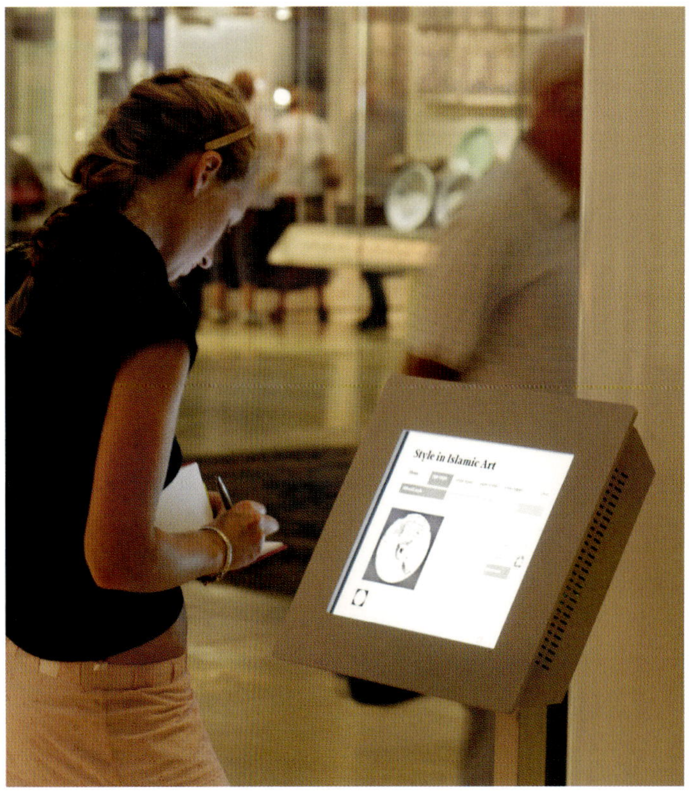
Style in Islamic Art

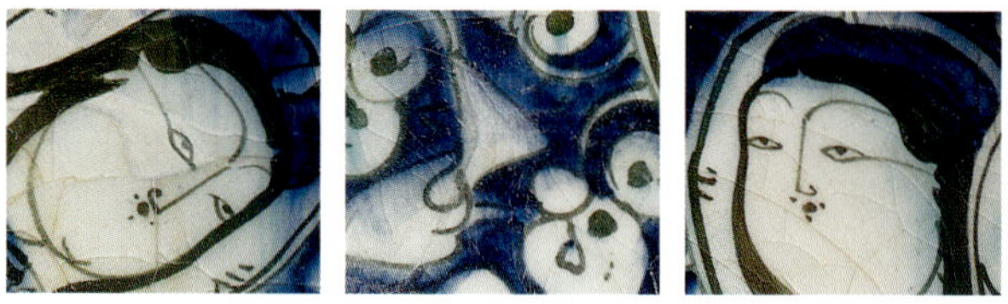

7 PROJECT MANAGEMENT FOR THE JAMEEL GALLERY

Claire Thompson

The Islamic Middle East gallery, located in Room 42 on the ground floor near the main entrance (illus. 7.2), was built in the 1899–1909 phase of building works to Aston Webb's design. At the heart of the V&A, next to the Central Court, the gallery – consisting of a central 'nave' spanned by a top-lit roof, flanked by groin-vaulted aisles, with arcades carried on Tuscan columns – was intended to evoke the architecture of Renaissance Florence. The floor area is approximately 550 square metres, with the gallery's height rising to approximately 13 metres at the centre. There are entrances on the south, east and west sides of the gallery, which has no general environmental control. All of these original features have informed the new design (see chapter 4).

A project as complex as the creation of a major new display of more than 400 objects needs careful advance planning and monitoring. As project coordinator, my role was to ensure that all the different elements of the project ran smoothly and on schedule. This ranged from dismantling the old gallery display and arranging storage for the objects, organizing the *Palace and Mosque* touring exhibition and leading its installation at all four venues, to keeping the curatorial team on track and ensuring that text for the graphic panels was delivered on time. My final task was to oversee the installation of all 400 objects in the new Gallery.

7.1 Installing the Ardabil carpet, June 2006

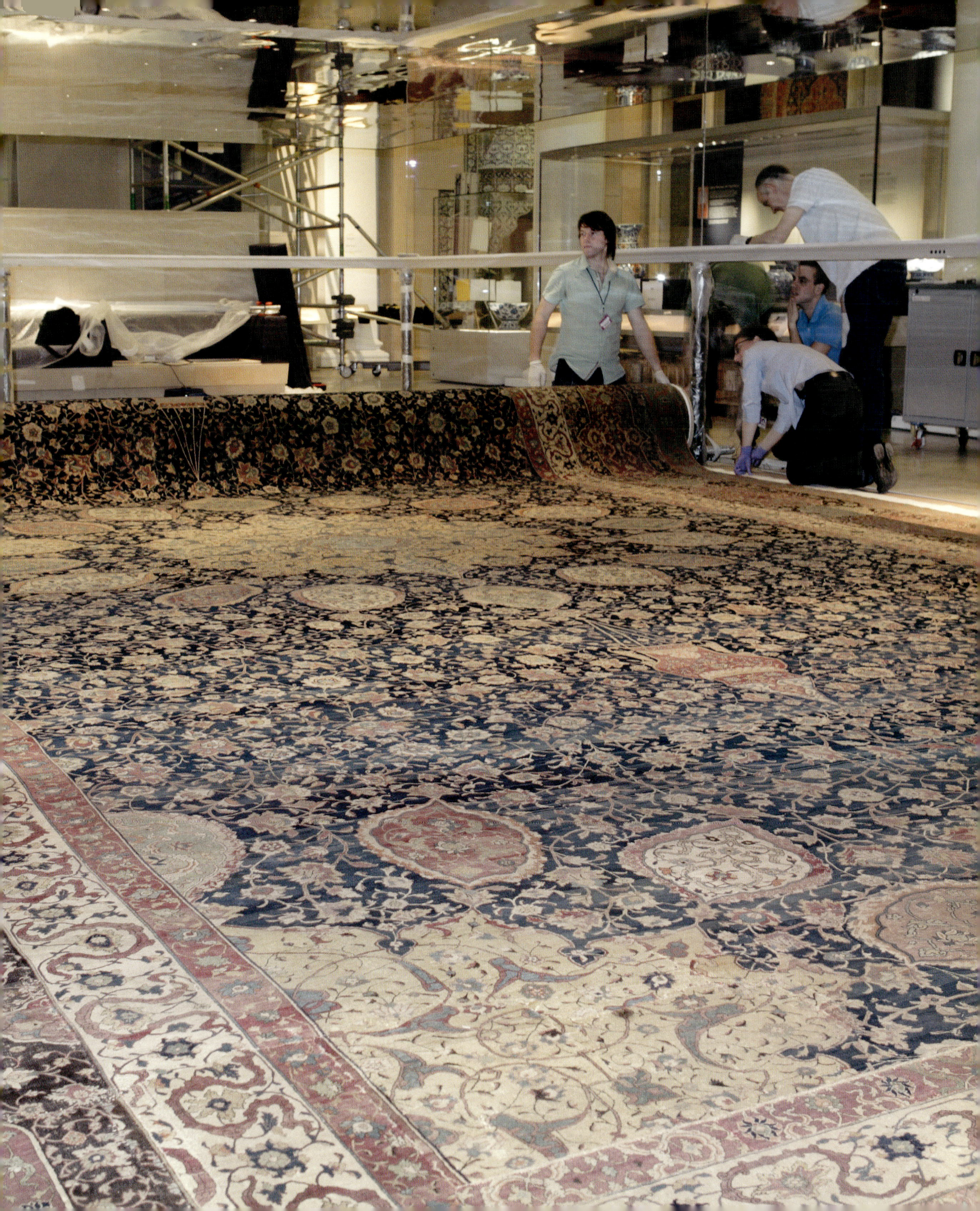

FUTURE PLAN: ISLAMIC GALLERY

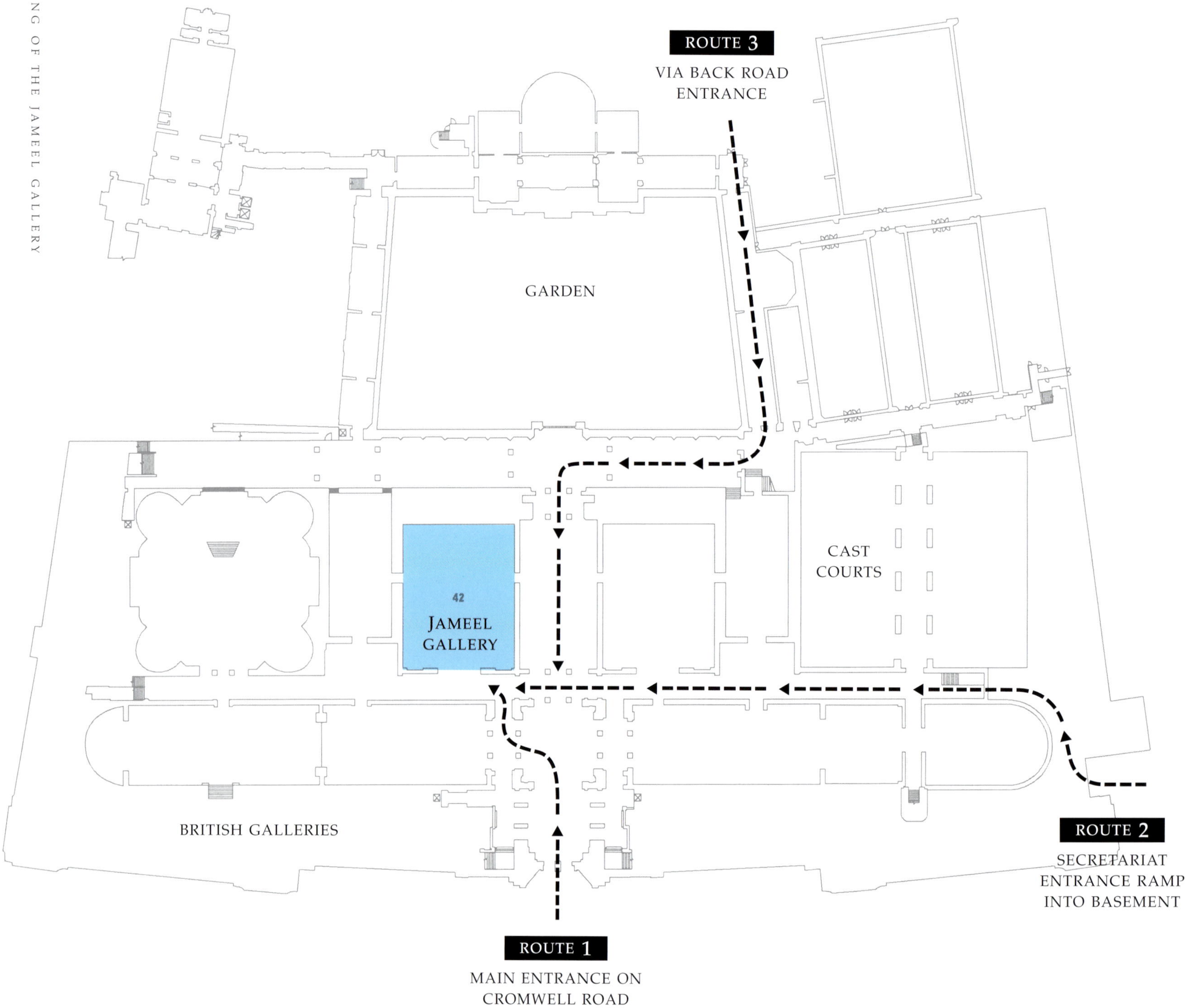

7.2 Plan of the ground floor of the V&A showing the location of the Jameel Gallery and access routes to it

7.3 Schematic diagram of the project team

The team

The long-planned renewal of the Islamic Middle East gallery was made possible in early 2003 thanks to the Jameel family's donation, and the V&A's first task was to set up a dedicated team responsible for the intellectual content and the structure and management of the refurbishment process (illus. 7.3).

The initial concept team was drawn from the Asian Department and consisted of Deborah Swallow (preceding Gwyn Miles, who took over as project director in 2004, and Moira Gemmill, from January 2006), Tim Stanley and Rosemary Crill, supported by the Middle Eastern section's assistant curators. New appointments were made at the outset to support the concept team – a project coordinator, project curator and gallery educator. This group formed the project team, which was supplemented as the project progressed by V&A staff working within the normal departmental structure (Collections Services, Public Affairs, Projects and Estates, etc.).

V&A MUSEUM: PROJECT TEAM ORGANIZATION FOR THE JAMEEL GALLERY PROJECT

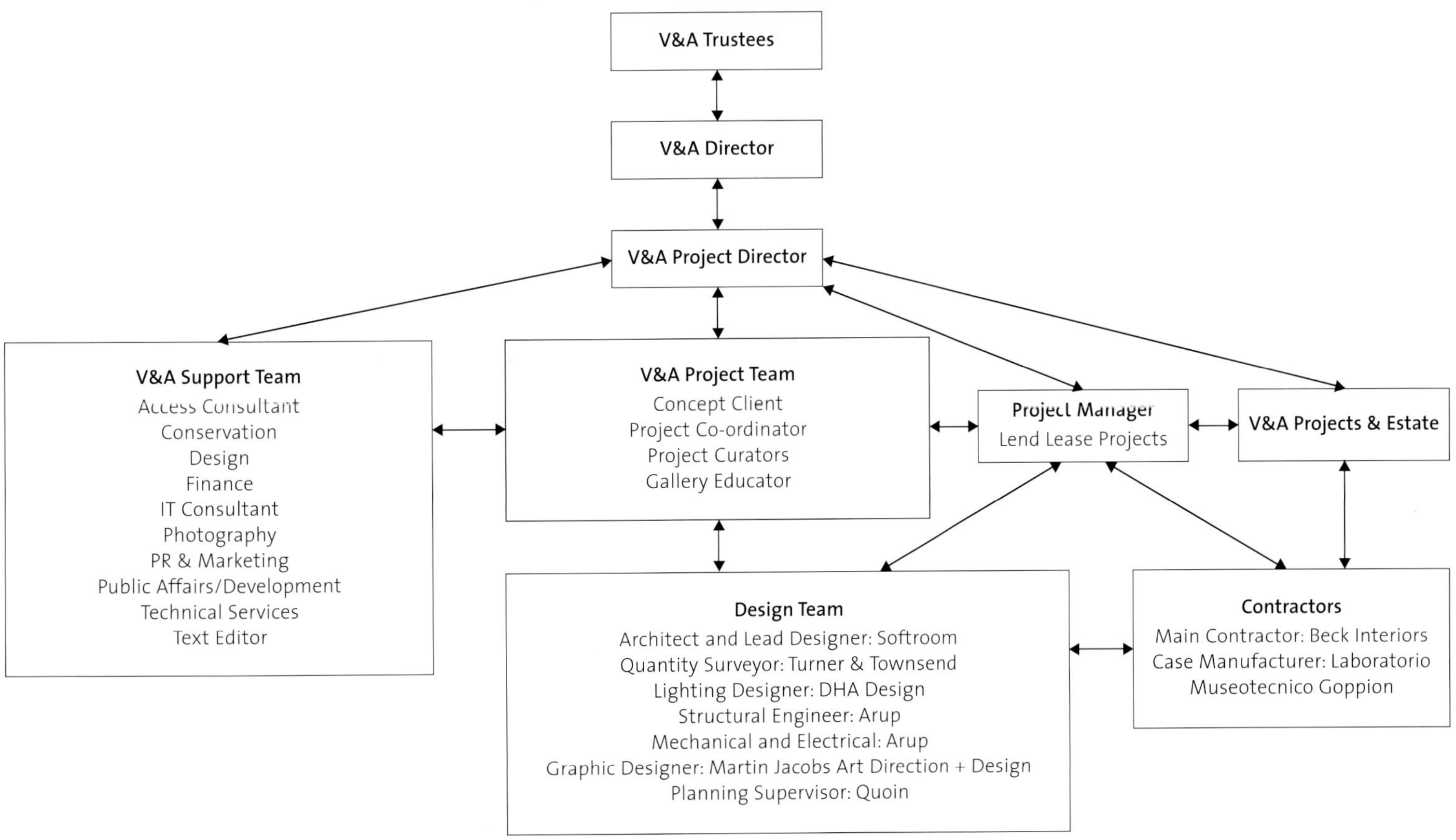

In early 2003 Lend Lease were appointed as construction manager and Turner & Townsend as quantity surveyor, so that the process of choosing the lead architect and other specialist consultants could begin. Following an open invitation in the *Official Journal of the European Communities*, after an initial shortlisting process, five companies were asked to tender for provision of both architectural and exhibition design. A paid pitch was then held to develop the ideas of two companies, and Softroom were chosen as lead designers in July 2003. The selection and appointment process quickly got under way for the remainder of the design team who would be responsible for the expression of the concept ideas in physical form: Arup as the structural, mechanical and electrical engineers, Quoin as planning supervisor, DHA Design as lighting designer and Martin Jacobs Art Direction + Design as graphic designer.

Systems and communications

In 2003 the project team's first task was to forge the narrative concept and the aims for the touring exhibition and new gallery, then to work out how to deliver them. Following the example of the V&A's British Galleries project, a framework document was developed, detailing the intellectual content of the Gallery, the objects required and the interpretation needed to make it accessible to the public. A key tool in this early stage was a programme breaking the project down into manageable and integrated tasks so that activities, roles and responsibilities were clear to team members (illus. 7.4). Armed with these two tools, discussions could be held to identify the objectives and the resources required to deliver the project by the agreed opening date of July 2006.

Islamic Project programme: exhibition and gallery development

ID	Task Name
1	**EXHIBITION**
2	Agree objects, write text, conservation, photography, mounts etc
3	Pack crates, shipments leave V&A
4	Venue 1 - National Gallery of Art, Washington
5	Venue 2 - Kimbell Art Museum, Fort Worth
6	Venue 3 - Setagaya Art Museum, Tokyo
7	Venue 4 - Millennium Galleries, Sheffield
8	Shipments return to V&A
9	
10	**GALLERY**
11	**Design milestones (RIBA work stages)**
12	Inception and Feasibility - Stages A, B and C
13	Scheme Design - Stage D
14	Detailed Design - Stage E
15	Production Information and Procurement - Stages F, G, H, I & J
16	Construction on site - Stages K and L
17	**Gallery milestones**
18	Gallery closure
19	Gallery handover to Lend Lease
20	Gallery handover back to V&A
21	Object installation
22	Gallery opening events
23	**Content issue**
24	Issue Framework Document
25	Issue Interpretation (incl. AV & IT) Document
26	**Photography**
27	Agree photography requirements and schedule work
28	Photography of objects for gallery
29	**Conservation**
30	Issue Object List to Conservation Departments
31	Condition assessment of objects
32	Agree schedule of conservation work
33	Conservation process
34	**Mounts / frames**
35	Agree requirements with designers and Tech Services
36	Mounts / frames production
37	**Gallery interpretation**
38	**2-D design concepts**
39	Outline design proposals
40	Design development to sign off
41	Production phase
42	**Interpretive text and object labels**
43	Writing and editing of label and panel text
44	Finalised copy on disc to Graphic Designer for formatting
45	Formatting, proofreading and signing off process
46	**Interactives (high and low tech)**
47	Agree requirements with designer and project team
48	Produce information as required
49	Production of interactives

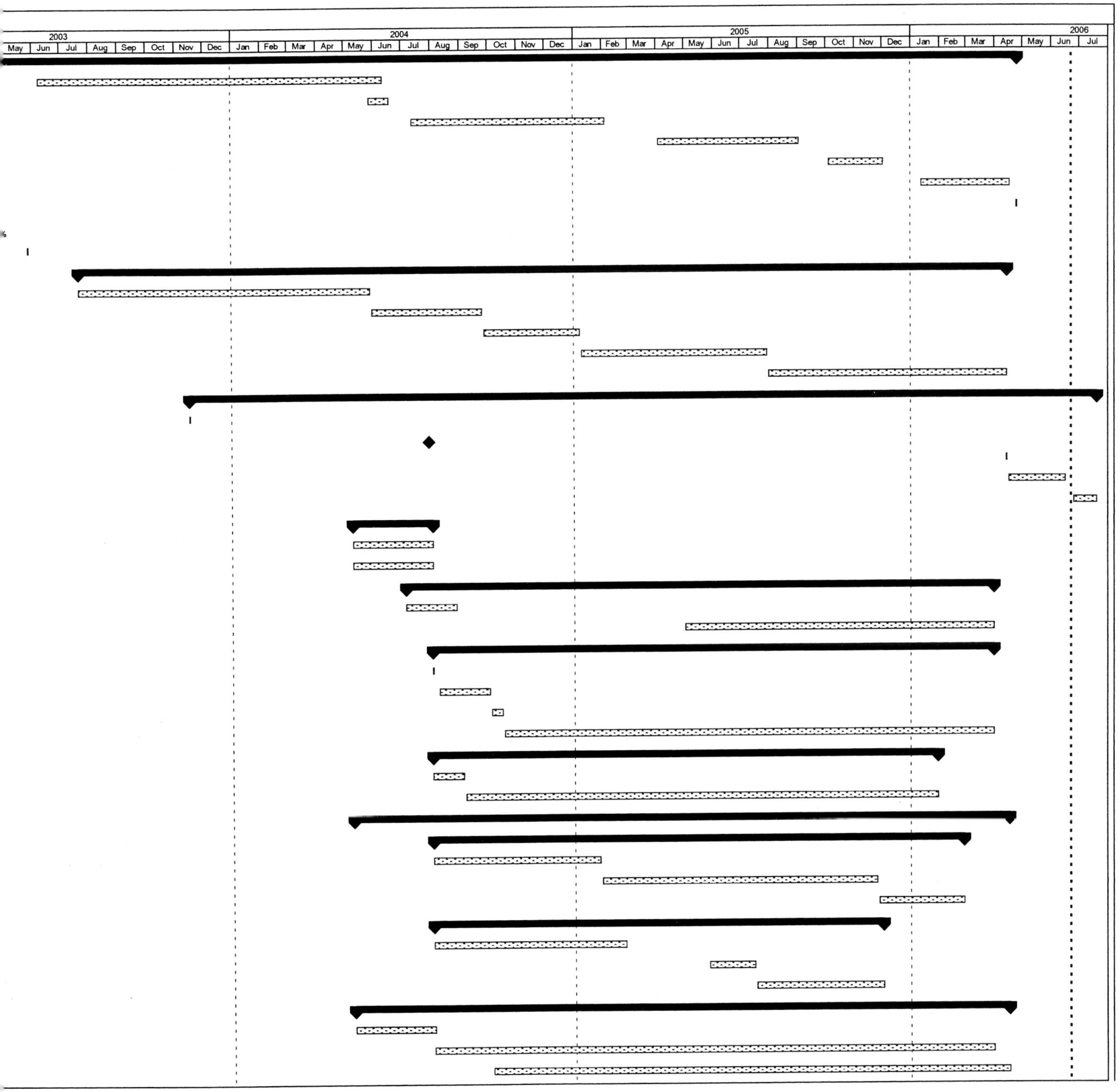

7.4 Chart showing the timetable of the project

Another tool that developed out of the British Galleries was Projexs, a project-specific information database used by our team, first for the touring exhibition *Palace and Mosque* and then for the Gallery. The team entered detailed information about every object – including photography and conservation requirements, object dimensions and display needs – while the database automatically drew down information from the V&A's central Collections Information System and fed it into the database to generate working lists for the conservation teams.

Throughout the project, regular meetings were an essential way to keep team members informed, distribute information, agree the way to drive the project forward and monitor progress. It was important that every team member understood what had to be delivered and when it was required, so they could best plan how these targets would be met. Good communication was vital to the successful delivery of the project, and a meeting structure was established early on.

The project team met fortnightly with the lead designers throughout the project to shape the intellectual content and layout of the Gallery, to coordinate and monitor V&A activities and to ensure good communication across the Museum. The graphic designers, interpretation specialists, technical liaison staff and others were invited to these meetings as the project required.

The Islamic Project Steering Group met monthly. Headed by the project director, its remit was to coordinate the project (that is, the Gallery, the touring exhibition and the associated publications) throughout its progress, agreeing and signing off developments and providing an opportunity for consultation with the sponsor's team.

The design team, headed by construction manager Lend Lease, brought the lead designers and specialist consultants together with the V&A's project coordinator on a regular basis to ensure harmony of design and construction. These meetings developed to include the main trade contractors as the work progressed on site.

The practical process

In August 2003 staff responsible for storage, collection records, object handling, packing, conservation and photography were brought together to plan the first practical step of de-installing the existing gallery. An off-site store was prepared to accommodate the objects, and when Room 42 was closed in November 2003, the decanting process began. Known as the 'Gateway' procedure, which is standard for every gallery closure at the V&A, this was a four-week process of auditing the 400 objects in the gallery, checking and updating their catalogue records, taking record photographs of each object, condition-checking, packing and then transferring them to storage (illus. 7.5–7.8). Detailed method statements were prepared before undertaking the de-installation of more challenging objects, such as the minbar and the large carpets displayed behind heavy glazing.

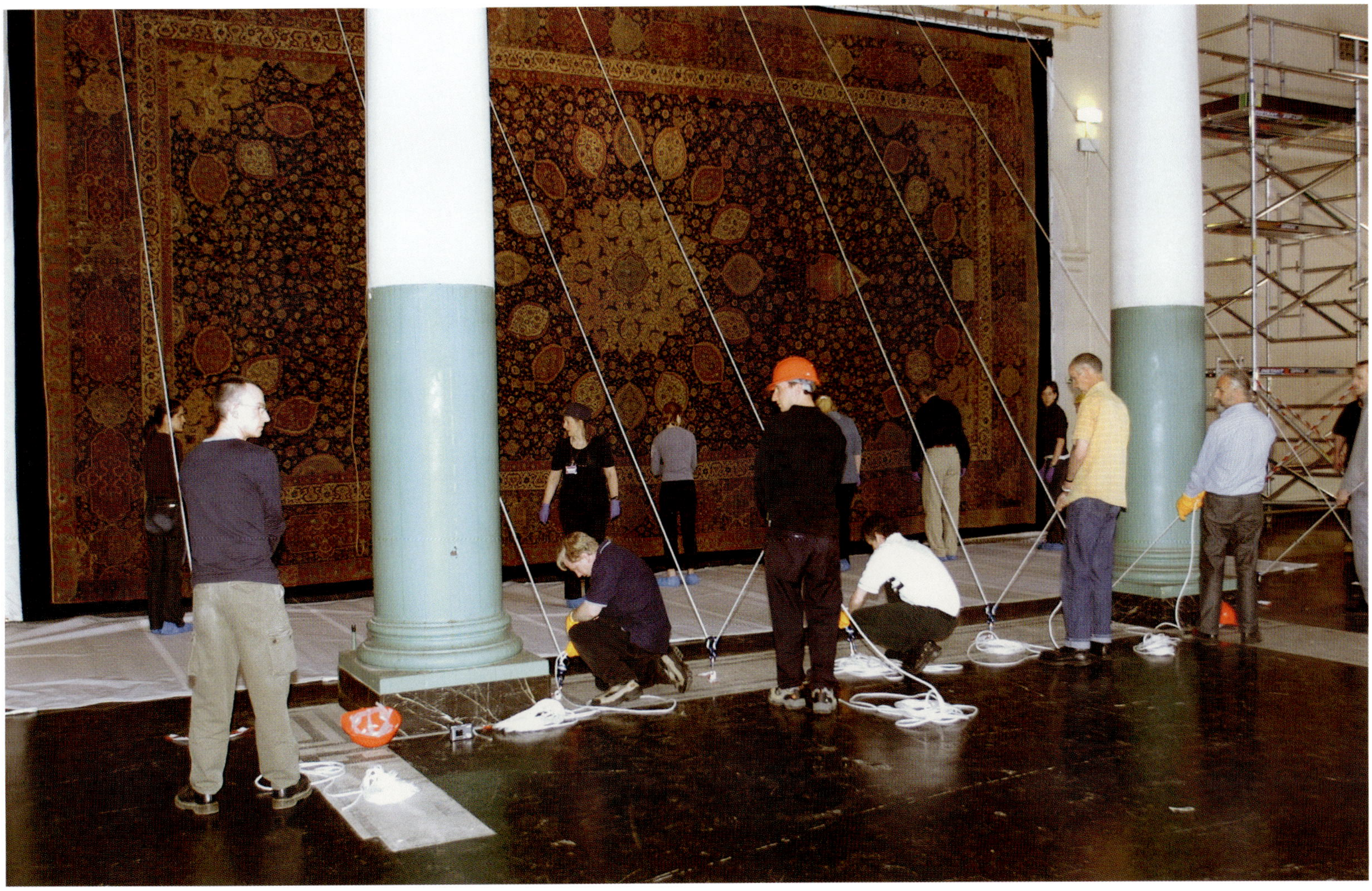

7.5 De-installing the old Islamic gallery: preparing to take down the Ardabil carpet

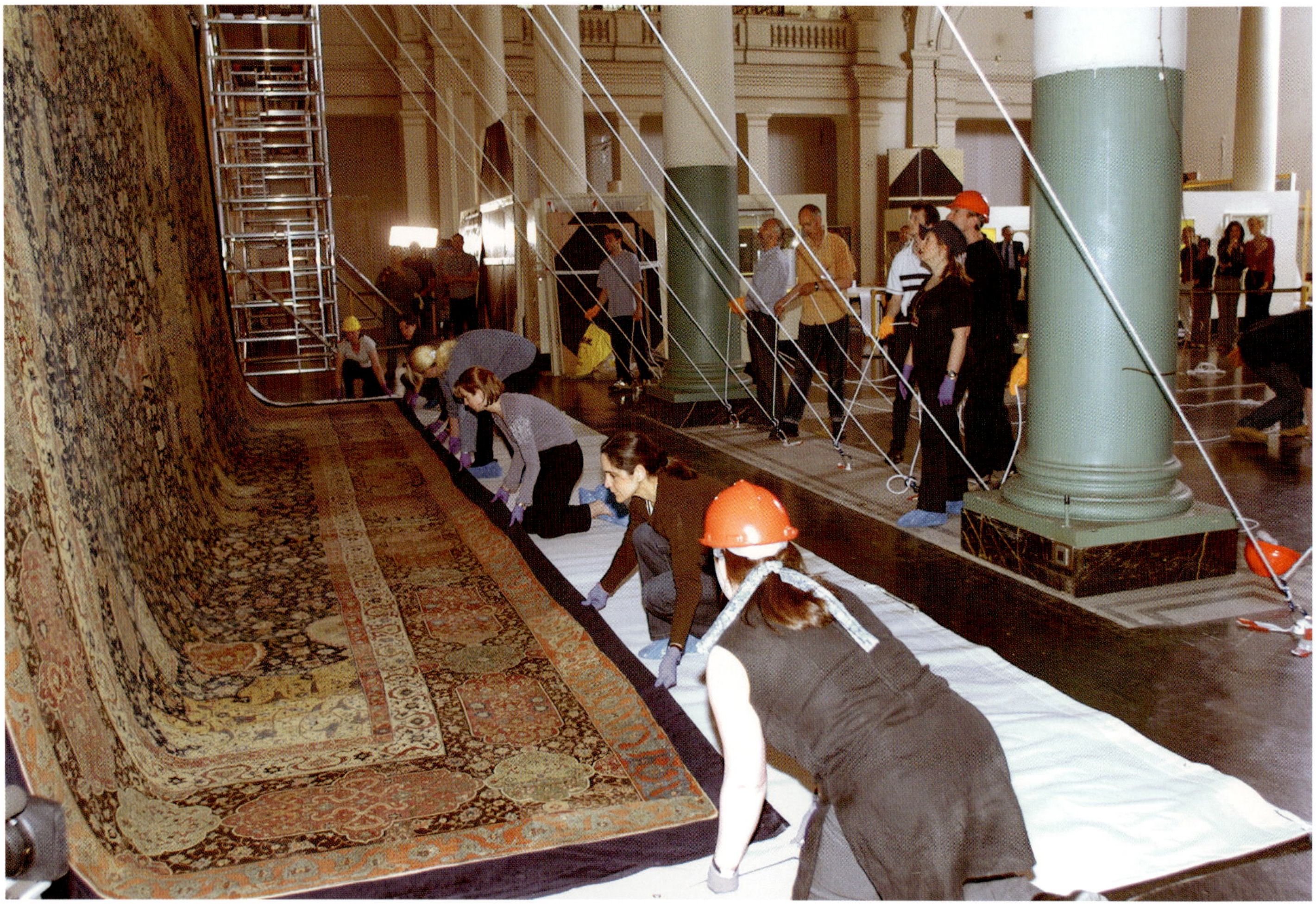

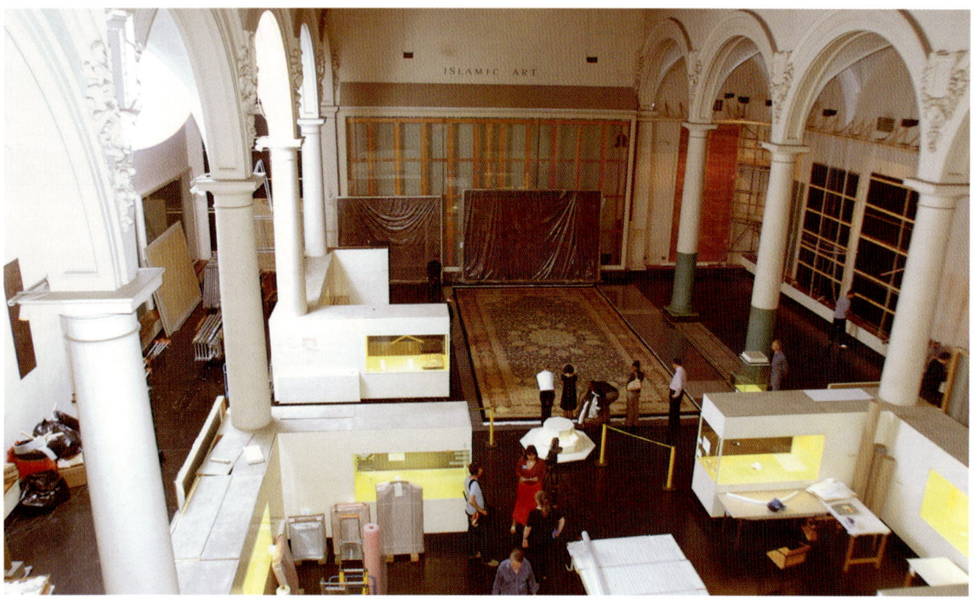

7.6 De-installing the old Islamic gallery: the Ardabil carpet being lowered

7.7 De-installing the old Islamic gallery: the Ardabil carpet lying flat

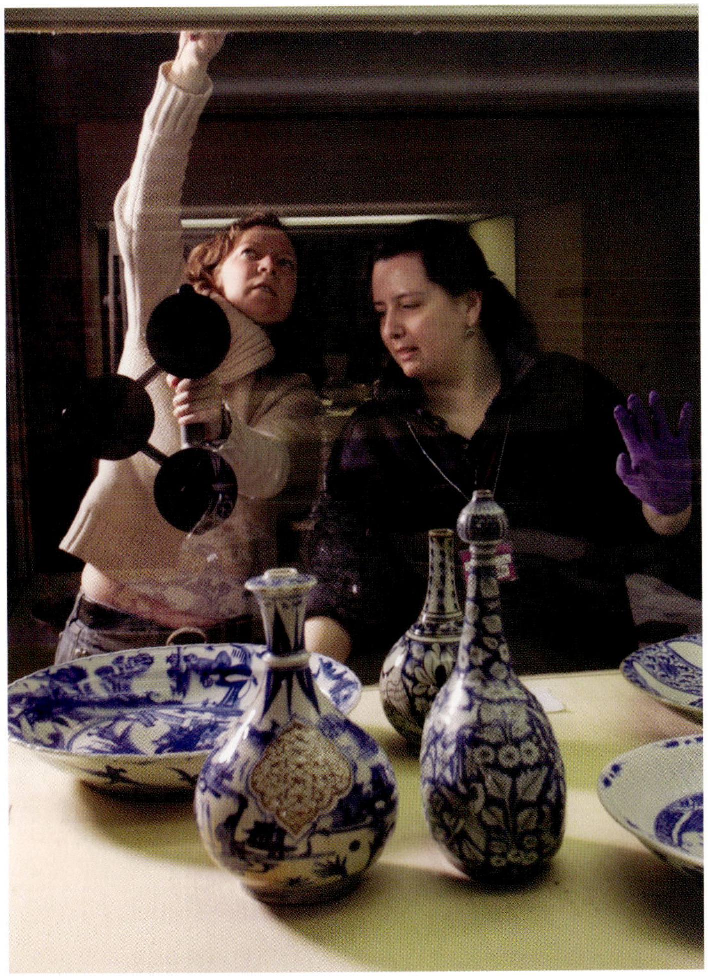

Preparing the touring exhibition

By the time of the gallery closure, the object list for the touring exhibition had been largely agreed. The 120 objects chosen were prepared for departure from the V&A, and in six months the conservation work was done, the mounts made, travel crates built and packing undertaken. Because of time and resource limitations, a number of large ceramic objects were sent out of the museum for conservation work. A star object of the show, the Iznik fireplace, needed six months of work on its own (illus. 7.9, 7.10) to turn it into an object suitable for travelling to four international venues.

Heritage Tiles were contracted to remove the fireplace from the corridor outside the Islamic Gallery, then conserve and remount the tiles on to a lightweight, demountable structure. Records from a previous move in

7.8 Claire Thompson and Mariam Rosser-Owen decanting objects from the old Islamic gallery

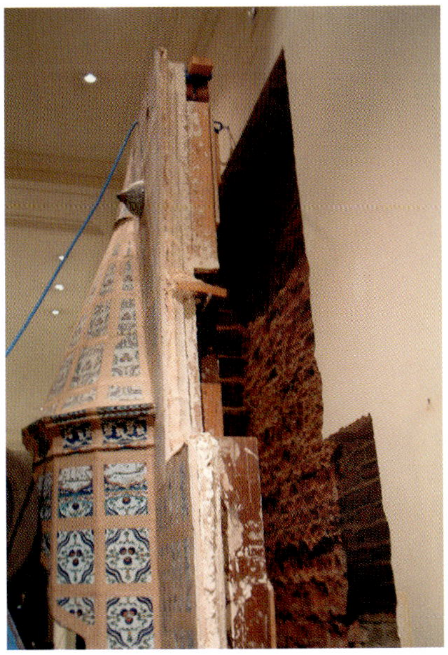

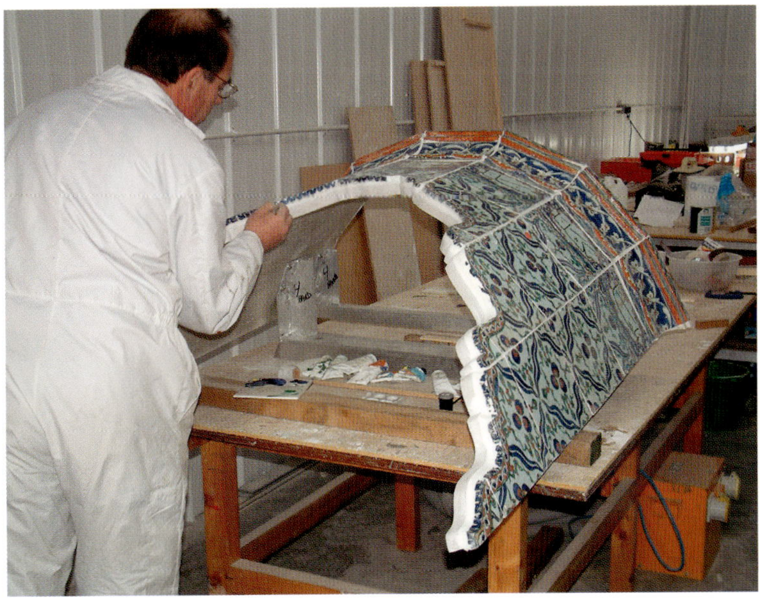

7.9 (*far left*) The Iznik fireplace being removed from the gallery by Heritage Tiles

7.10 (*left*) The Iznik fireplace undergoing conservation by Heritage Tiles

1987 suggested that the fireplace weighed around 1,500 kilograms. It was mounted as one piece on a timber substructure, with a mixture of lath and plaster, wooden splints, hessian, shellac and glue holding the tiles in place. Heritage Tiles separated each tile from the substructure and ground the thick plaster screed off each one. Following painstaking conservation, the tiles were then remounted on to strong, lightweight Hexalite backing panels, which were designed to hang on an aluminium frame. A replica hearth was made from MDF to replace the original heavy stone and marble hearth. The fireplace now breaks down into eight manageable pieces and weighs around 350 kilograms.

The touring show opened in Washington, DC, in July 2004 (see Chapter 2).

Focus on the Gallery

Once touring exhibition arrangements were well under way, attention focused in earnest on the Gallery. By August 2004 the Framework Document was agreed, enabling the team to set up the Projexs database. Object lists were then generated to kick off assessments of conservation, photography and display requirements, and the resources needed to undertake this work (illus. 7.11). The considerable challenge of moving more than 300 objects between storage, the mount-making workshops, photography and conservation studios was undertaken by the assistant curators. Short-term contract staff were needed to supplement the V&A's existing conservators and deliver the objects in time for the installation, which was due to start in March 2006. Object photography was scheduled in from May 2005 to March 2006, as it needed to fit around the ongoing conservation of objects. By March 2005, a year before installation, in-depth mounting and framing decisions had to be made to inform the detailed design of the display cases.

In the 12 months to March 2006 the team agreed object arrangements through mock-ups and detailed layouts, researched and wrote text, oversaw the development of the graphics and interpretative tools for the Gallery and planned the Gallery installation. Meanwhile we also put up and took down the touring show in Texas, Tokyo and Sheffield, with all the associated work that each new venue necessitated.

	No. of objects needed for gallery	*No. of objects prepared for touring show*	*No. of objects needing new photography*	*No. of objects needing new mounts or frames*	*No. of conservation hours to prepare for gallery*
Ceramics and Glass	228	46	65	116	2500
Metalwork	63	21	29	22	450
Textiles and Dress	47	16	21	39	3000
Furniture and Woodwork	16	5	11	9	100
Sculpture	28	3	5	16	450
National Art Library	14	7	3	7	250
Prints, Drawings and Paintings	9	4	0	5	0
Totals	**405**	**102**	**134**	**214**	**6750**

7.11 Chart showing the numbers of types of object in the Jameel Gallery

7.12 Chart showing the budget breakdown for the Jameel Gallery

GALLERY DESIGN AND CONSTRUCTION BUDGET Cost breakdown	Design team professional fees	20 %
	Fit out and exhibition installation	36 %
	Display cases	35 %
	Graphics	2 %
	Construction contingency	7 %
		100 %
MUSEUM ANCILLARY BUDGET FOR GALLERY Cost breakdown	Project staffing	30 %
	Administration costs	8 %
	Decant of old gallery and storage	5 %
	Object conservation	20 %
	Photography	4 %
	Frames and mount making	5 %
	High and low-tech interpretation tools	12 %
	Visitor evaluation	3 %
	Website	3 %
	Marketing and opening events	10 %
		100 %
TOURING EXHIBITION BUDGET Cost breakdown	Project administration	15 %
	Object conservation	15 %
	Photography	3 %
	Frames and mount making	7 %
	Crates, shipping, transport agents	45 %
	Insurance	8 %
	Publication	7 %
		100 %

Installation

The project team started working with Technical Services on the detailed planning of the object installation from late 2005. We calculated that 400 objects of varying complexity would take the team 10 weeks to install. Goppion's completion date was programmed for 13 April 2006, and so we planned to work from 18 April to 16 June, allowing a decent contingency period before the Gallery opening on 18 July 2006.

Of the 47 cases in the Gallery, 30 contained objects that were in Sheffield with the touring show, and we therefore concentrated at first on the large carpets, heavy tilework, high-level windows and textile displays (illus. 7.1, 7.13). When the touring objects returned to the V&A on 25 April, there were 50 crates to unpack before work could start on the rest of the Gallery. We worked in teams tailored to the task in hand. The curators worked on small object displays (illus. 7.14, 7.15), with a technician to install object mounts if necessary. For large and complex objects, assessments were undertaken to plan the work stages, equipment and manpower required. DHA Design focused and set light levels alongside installation, so that the exact placement of objects could be agreed as we went along.

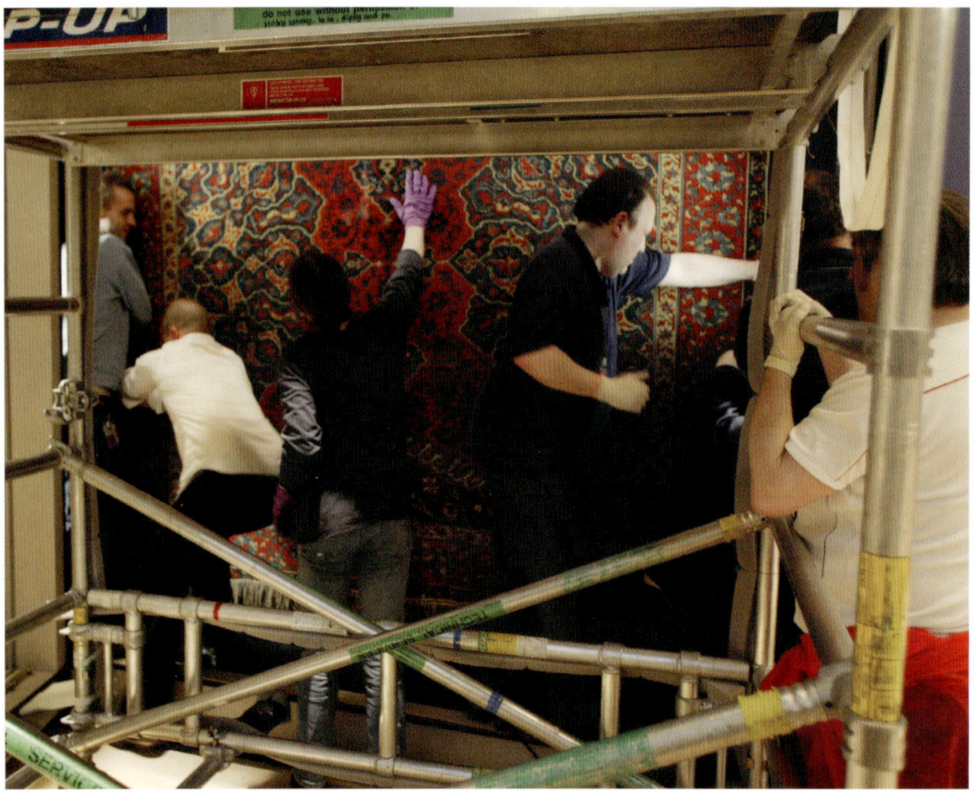

7.13 (*left*) Members of the Technical Services team installing the Ushak carpet, May 2006

7.14 (*above right*) Jenny Westwood installing the coloured glass windows, June 2006

7.15 (*right*) Ruby Clark placing a bowl in the ceramics display, June 2006

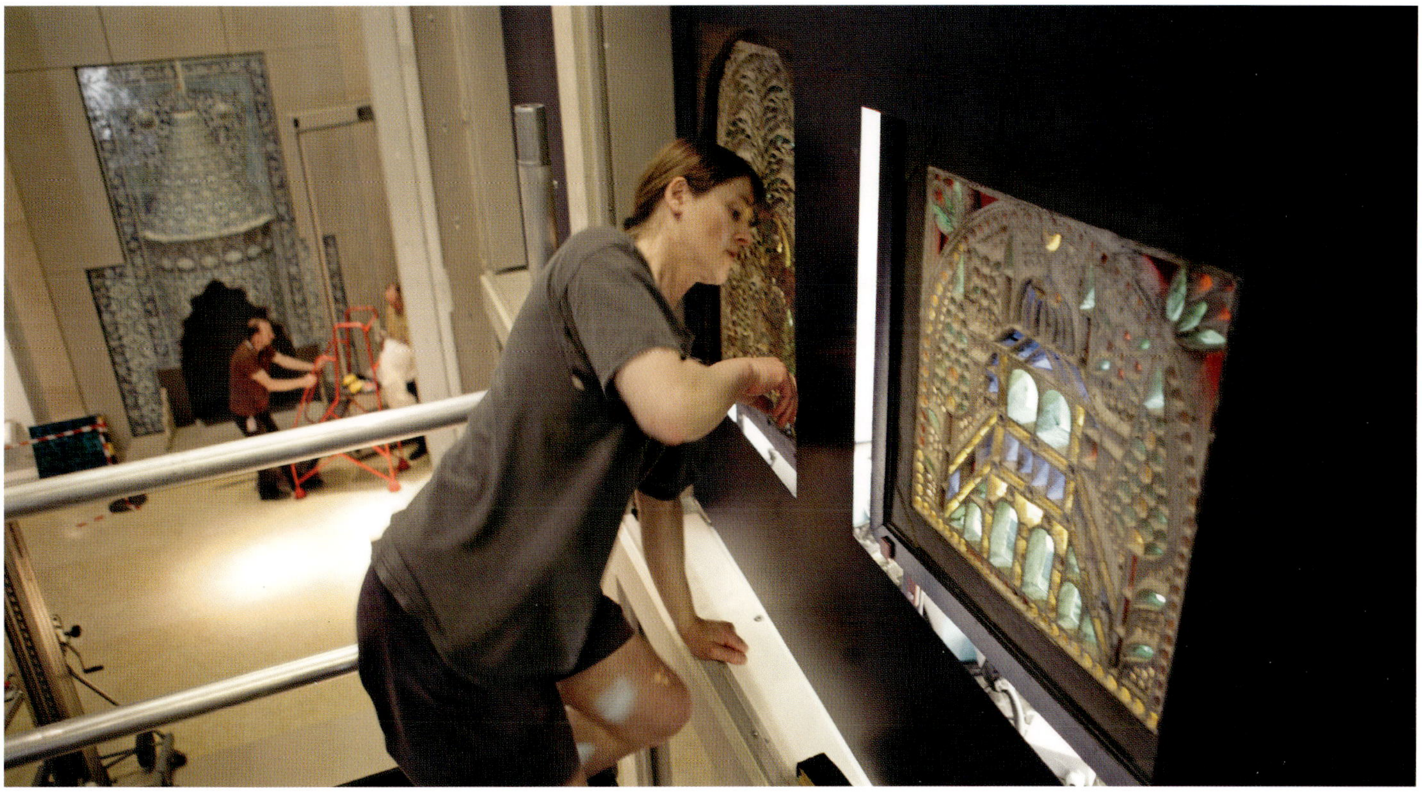

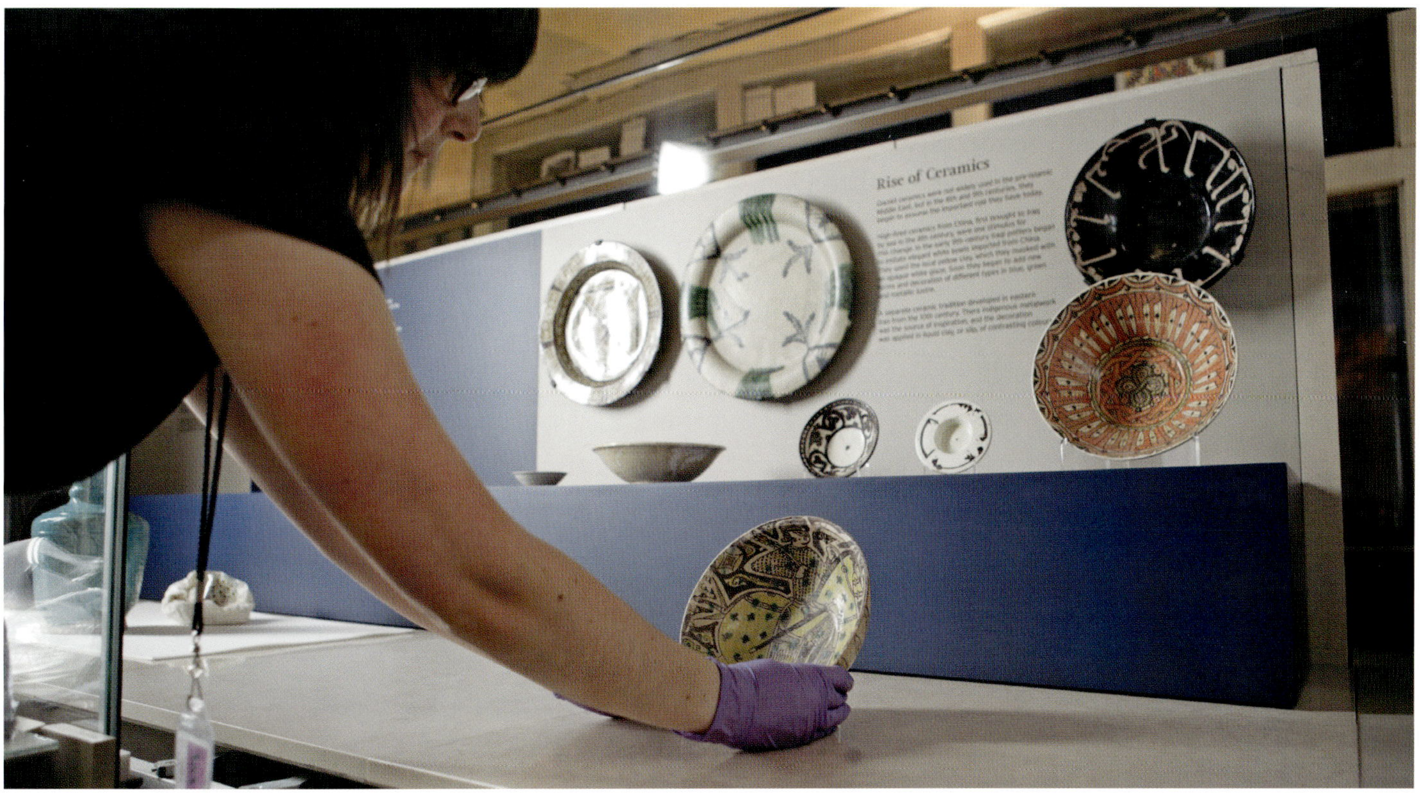
Rise of Ceramics

Lessons learnt

Our biggest challenge was the project's timescale. The project team was relatively new to the V&A and had to hit the ground running to deliver, from scratch, an international touring exhibition, two publications and a major new gallery in just over three years. In the early stages the project team was under pressure to keep up with the design team, which was focused solely on the Gallery. Careful prioritization and hard work were required to keep one step ahead, and in cases such as the Ardabil carpet's light-fastness testing, the V&A was very late in delivering vital information to the consultants.

The touring exhibition presented an interesting challenge. Initially it distracted from the delivery of our main goal: the permanent gallery. Yet it enabled narrative ideas to be thought through and allowed us to see the objects in a new light (quite literally, due to the darkness of the old Islamic gallery). From a practical point of view, we sometimes found it frustrating to have more than 100 objects on the other side of the world. However, in moving these objects between four venues, an intimate knowledge of them was gained, which came in particularly useful when designing cases for, and installing, the new gallery.

Because of the travelling objects in particular, and the needs of the project in general, it was vital to keep the object database up-to-date and accurate; and it took a concentrated effort to do this. Unfortunately, the database let us down in two ways: it lacked the ability to link object photos to their records, and, more importantly, we tried but failed (due to security issues) to make it electronically available on the Web. The project would have greatly benefited – and the vital flow of information would have been made far more efficient – if the consultants had had ongoing access to object dimensions and display needs.

Continuing problems were also caused by objects that suddenly 'grew' on being remeasured (many accepted dimensions having been inaccurately converted from feet and inches in the old Museum registers) or when mounts were added for display purposes. In future we need to deliver information to our designers with an understanding of precisely what is required.

On 18 July 2006 the project was delivered on time and within budget, with thanks to all those involved in making it possible.

Project team

Project Director: Deborah Swallow (until August 2004), Gwyn Miles (from August 2004 to December 2005), Moira Gemmill (from January 2006)
Concept Team: Tim Stanley (Concept Client) and Rosemary Crill (Senior Curator), Barry Wood (Project Curator), Mariam Rosser-Owen and Ruby Clark (Assistant Curators)
Project Coordinator: Claire Thompson
Project Educator: Nighat Yousuf

Conservation: Nigel Bamforth, Anne Bancroft, Amanda Barnes, Val Blyth, Lucia Burgio, Brendan Catney, Albertina Cogram, Nicola Costaras, Alan Derbyshire, Miriam McLeod, Frances Hartog, Diana Heath, Lynda Hillyer, Charlotte Hubbard, Fi Jordan, Marion Kite, Víctor Hugo López Borges, Sofia Marques, Graham Martin, Juanita Navarro, Albert Neher, Victoria Oakley, Laura Pretsell, Boris Pretzel, Shayne Rivers, Jane Rutherston, Sandra Smith, Donna Stevens, Gates Turner, Karen Vidler, Catia Viegas Wesolowska, Jo Whalley, Mike Wheeler, Sophy Wills, Natalia Zagorska-Thomas

Exhibitions and Loans: Jane Drew, Linda Lloyd Jones, David Packer, David Wright
Information Systems Services: Rosemary Faulkner, Peter Ford, Mark Hook, Paula Pinasco
Interpretation Editors: Lucy Trench, Mark Kilfoyle
Learning and Interpretation: Juliette Fritsch, Barry Ginley
Photographic Services: Ken Jackson, Maja Kardum, Mike Kitcatt, James Stevenson, Ian Thomas
Projects and Estate: Mick Figg, Barry Freeman, Moira Gemmill, Jane Scherbaum, Mandy Ward
Public Affairs: Sarah Armond, Helen Beeckmans, Camilla Graham, Debra Isaac, Patricia O'Connor, Jane Rosier, Henrietta Sitwell
Technical Services: Richard Ashbridge, Andrew Campbell, Wayne Chisnall, Matthew Clarke, Tim Couldwell, Aimee Frodsham, Jim Goddard, Robert Lambeth, Sue Ridley, Matthew Rose, Philip Sofer, Jenny Westwood
V&A Publications: Ariane Bankes, Geoff Barlow, Mary Butler, Clare Davis, Nina Jacobson, Clare Taylor

Principal consultants

Architect and Designer: Softroom (Christopher Bagot, Oliver Salway, Tyeth Gundry, Caroline Rabourdin)
Quantity Surveyor: Turner & Townsend
Structural Engineer: Arup
Mechanical and Electrical Engineer: Arup
Construction Manager: Lend Lease Projects
Lighting Designer: DHA Design
Planning Supervisor: Quoin
Graphic Designer: Martin Jacobs Art Direction + Design
Audience Research: Audience Focus Limited

Works packages

Fit-Out: Beck Interiors
Display Cases: Laboratorio Museotecnico Goppion
Low-Tech Interactives: Margery Clinton, Alison Robinson, RNIB, Liverpool Museums Conservation Centre, Martin Jacobs Art Direction + Design, The Big Push
Audio Visual, IT and Web: Atacama Ltd, Integrated Circles, Nykris

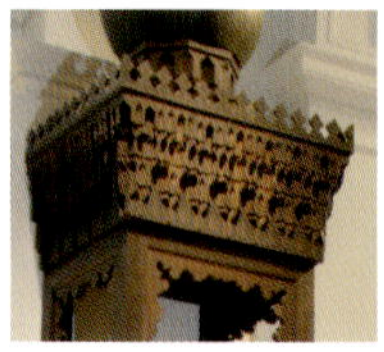
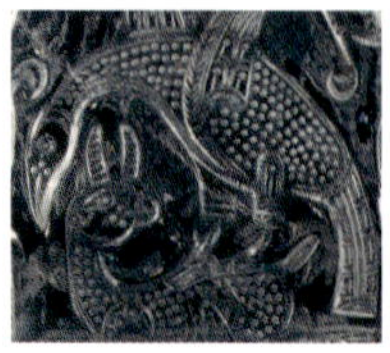
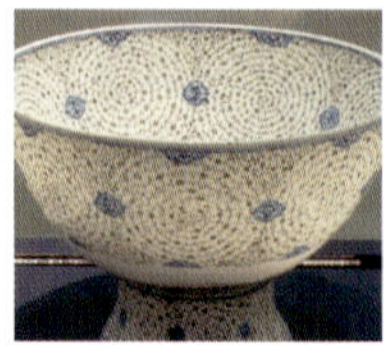

8 THE JAMEEL GALLERY: A PHOTOGRAPHIC TOUR

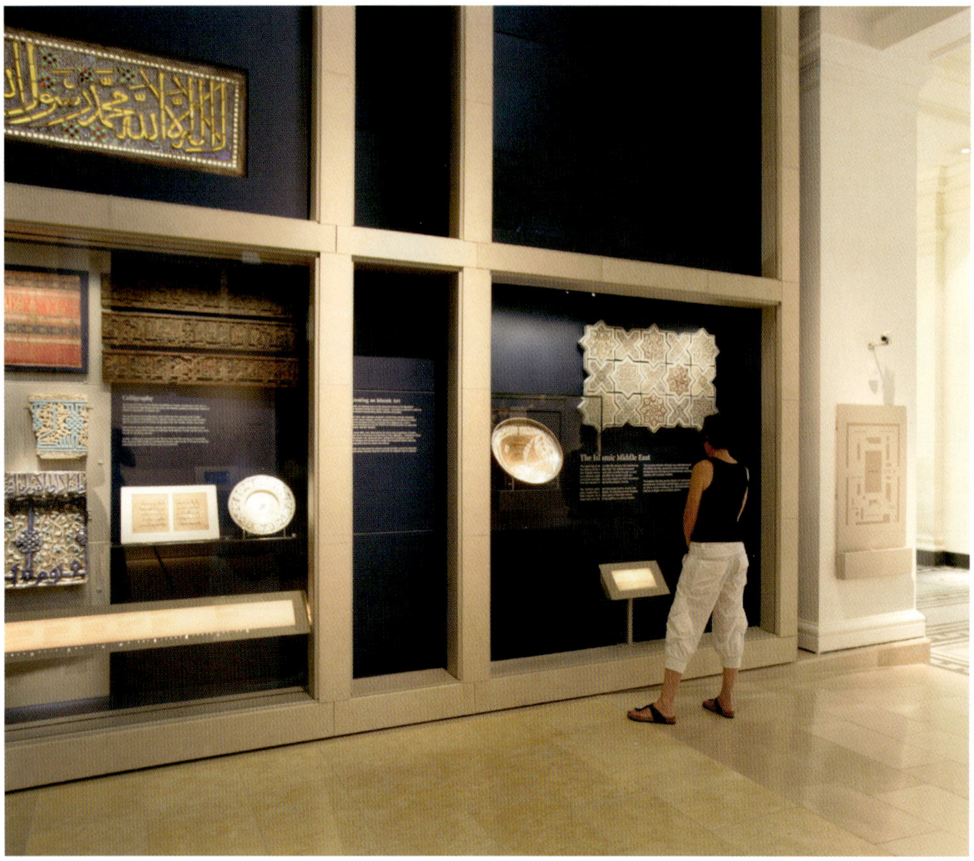

8.1 The introductory section at the south-east entrance to the Gallery

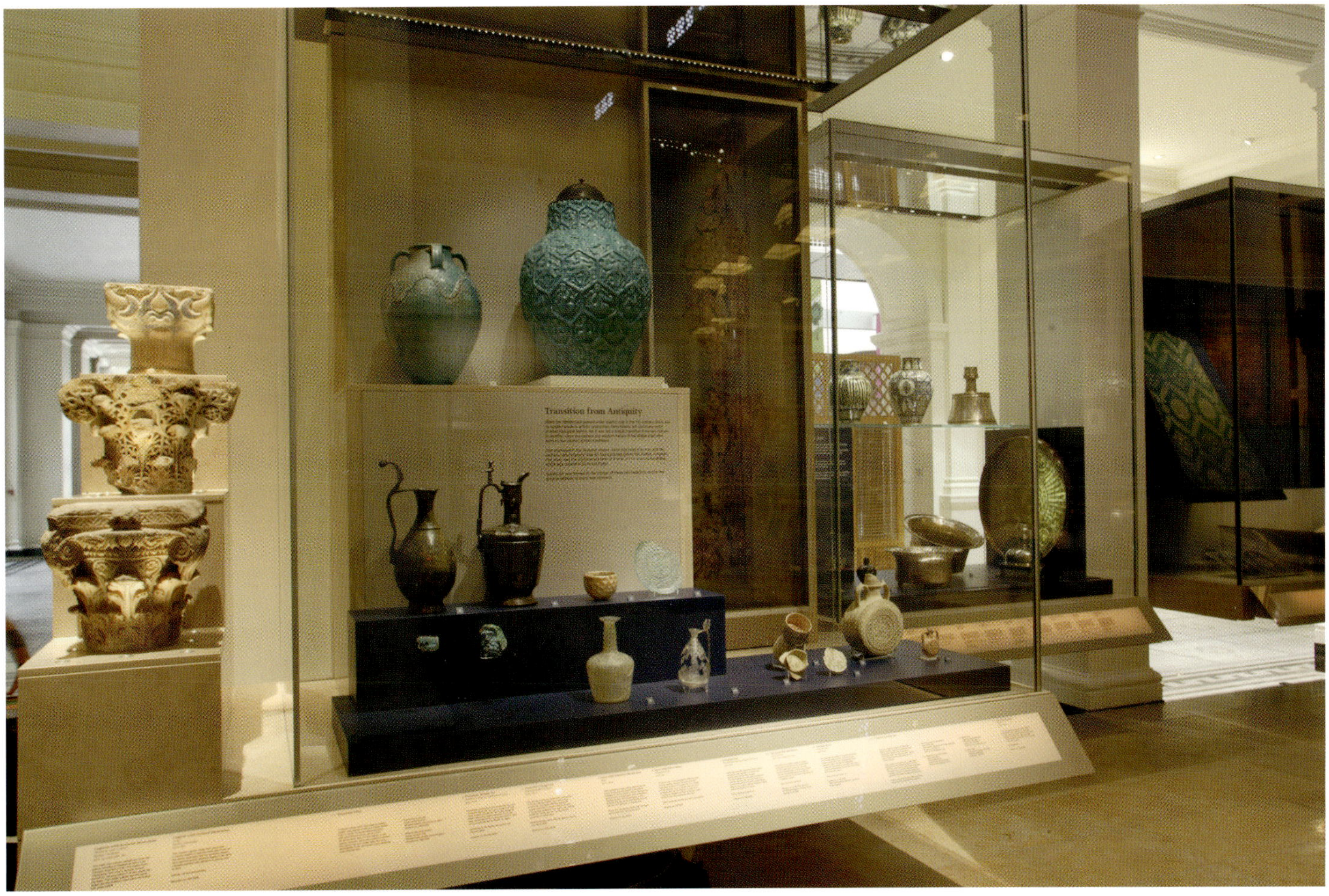

8.2 (*above*) Cases showing the transition from Antiquity to a distinctively Islamic art

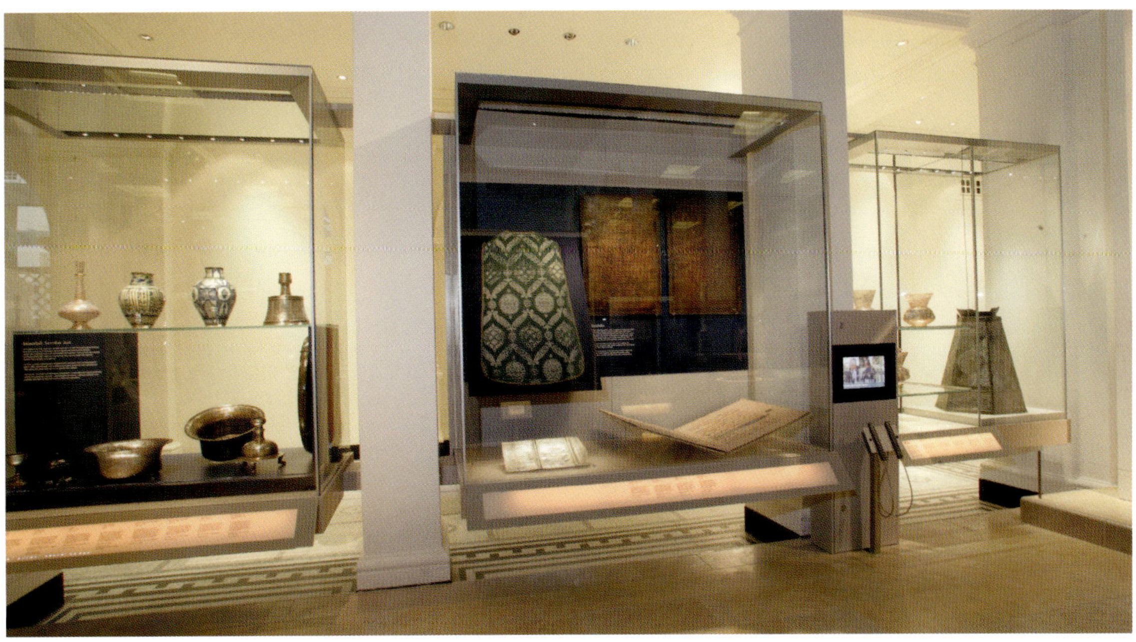

8.3 Part of the display on Egypt and Syria under the Mamluks

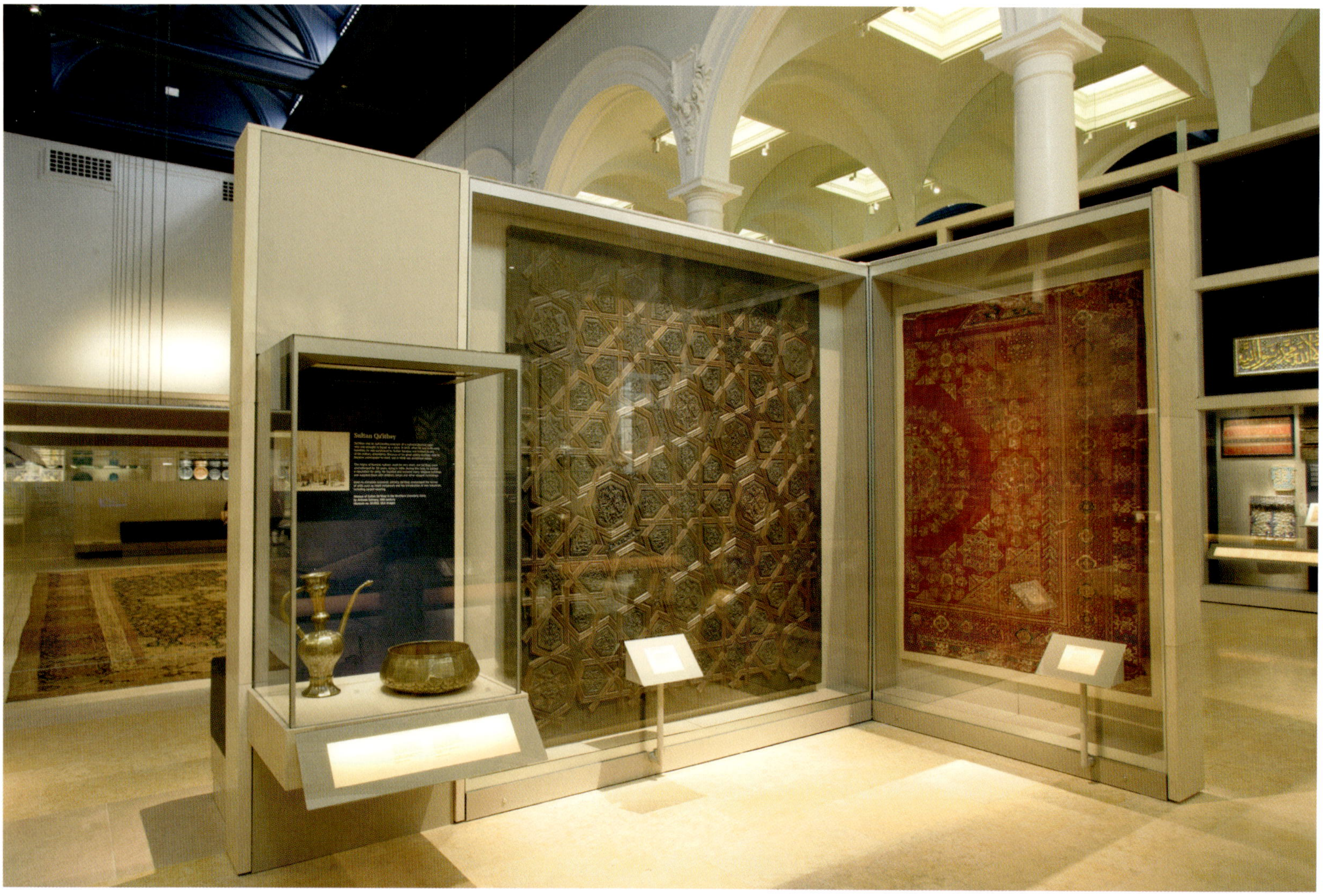

8.4 Part of the display on Egypt and Syria under the Mamluks

8.5 The section on Art for Religion at the south-west entrance, with Qajar paintings and the temporary display of Central Asian costumes also visible

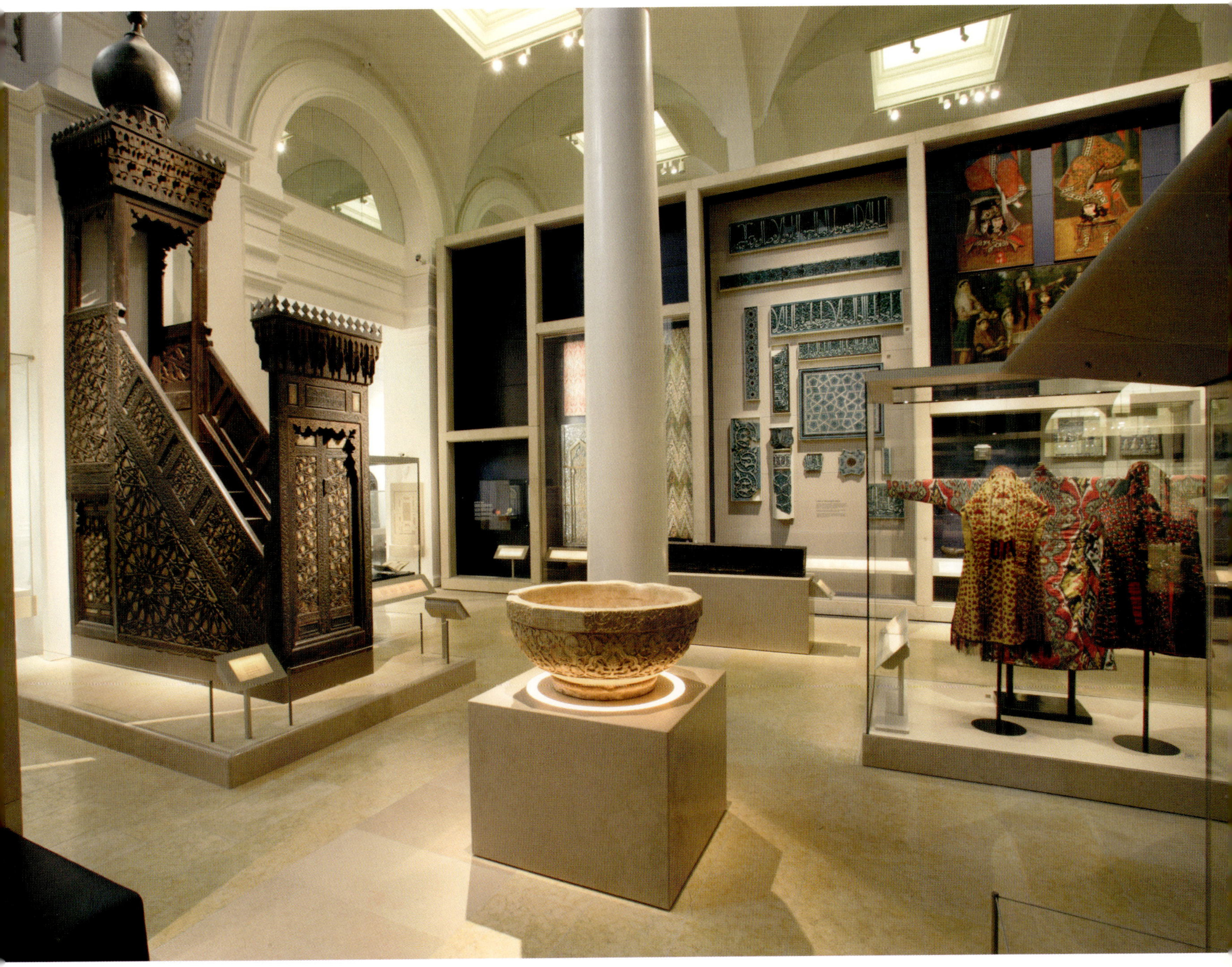

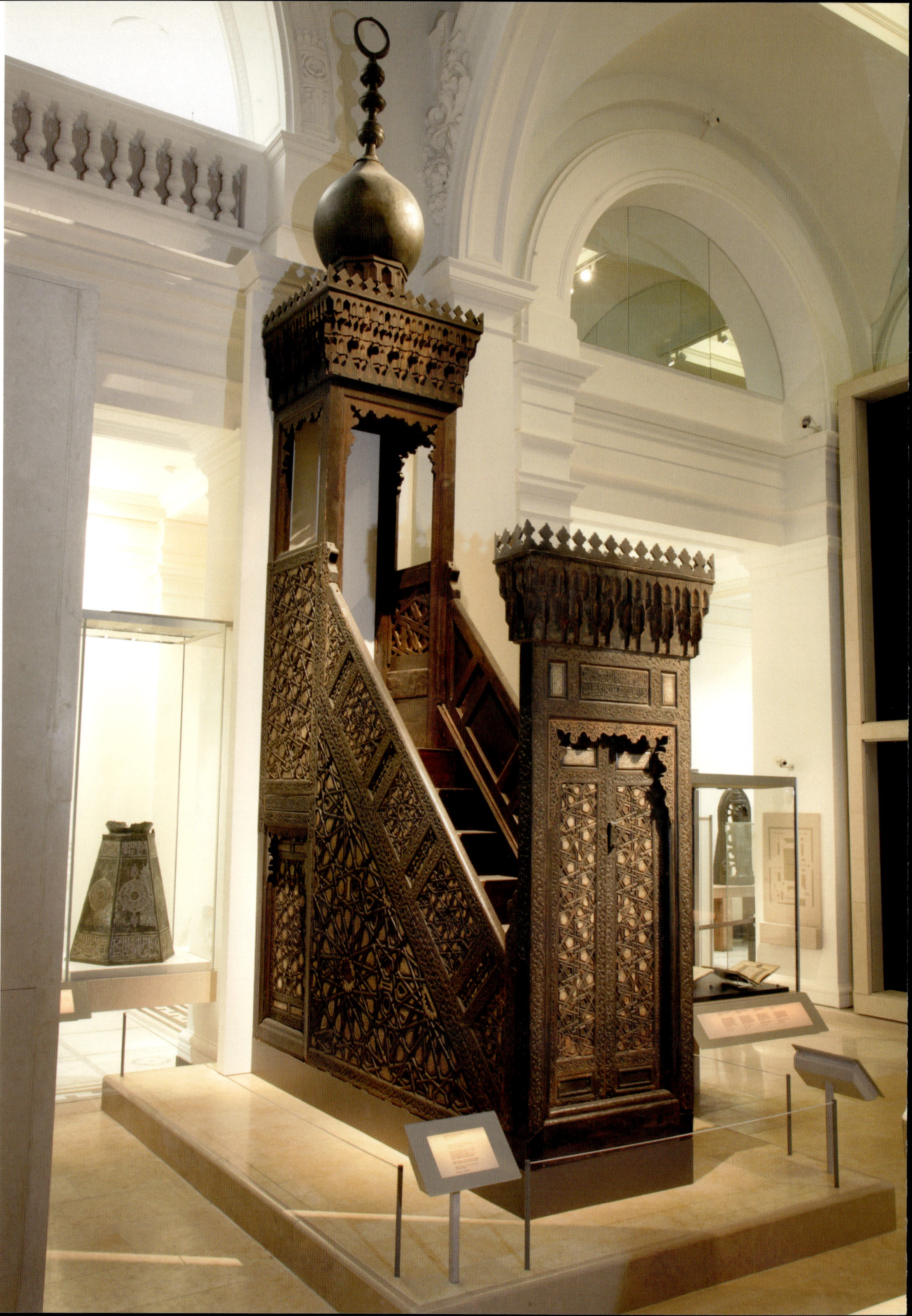

8.6 (*left*) The minbar of Sultan Qa'itbay

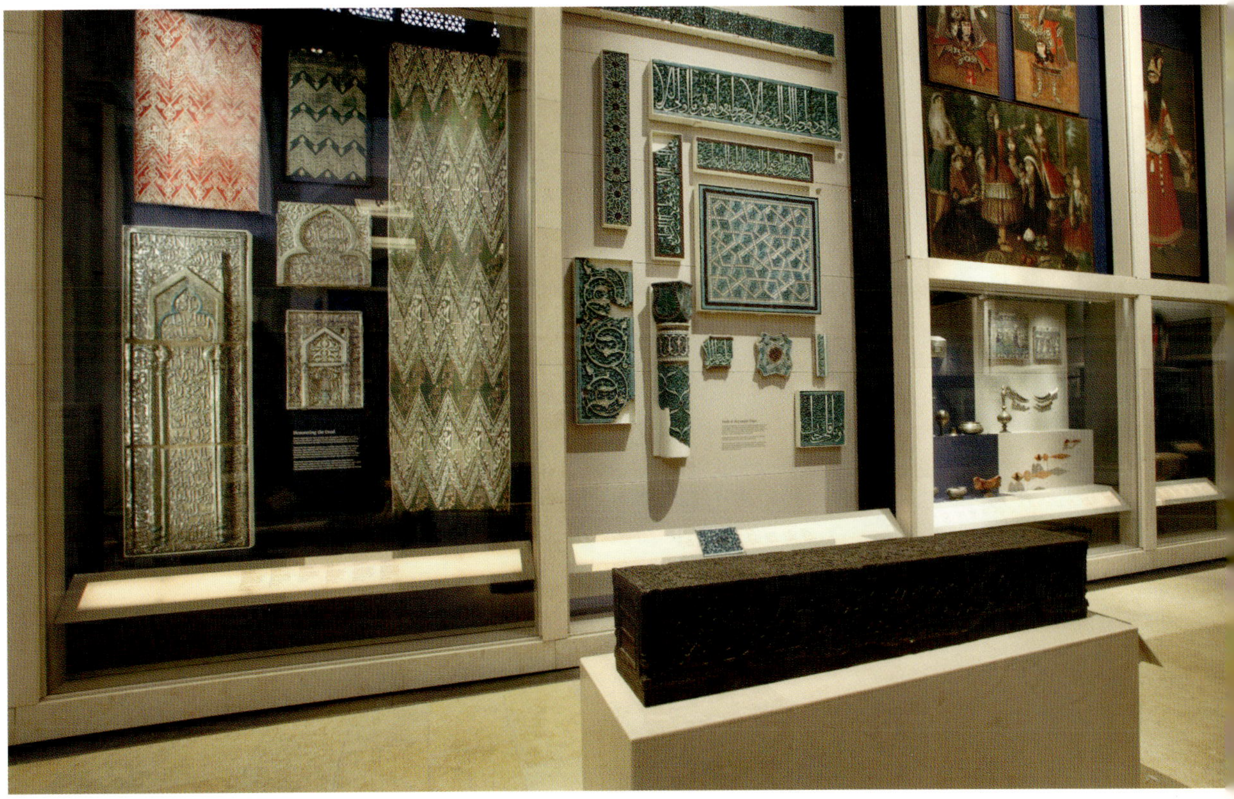

8.7 (*above*) The section on Art for Religion, showing religious textiles and commemorative tiles, the tilework from the tomb of Buyanquli Khan in Bukhara, and a tomb-marker from the same building. The Qajar display is visible on the right

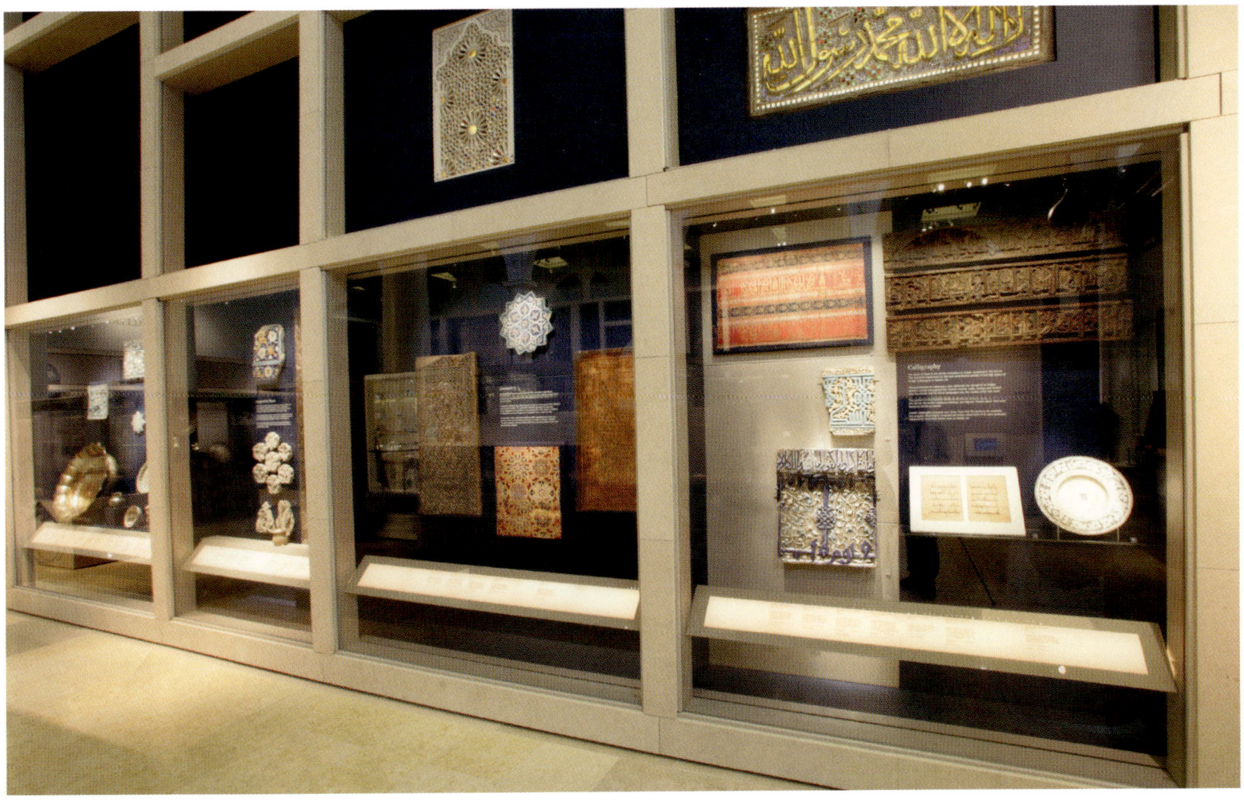

8.8 (*left*) Cases illustrating the content of Islamic art: (from the right) the use of calligraphy, geometric decoration, floral ornament and the use of figures

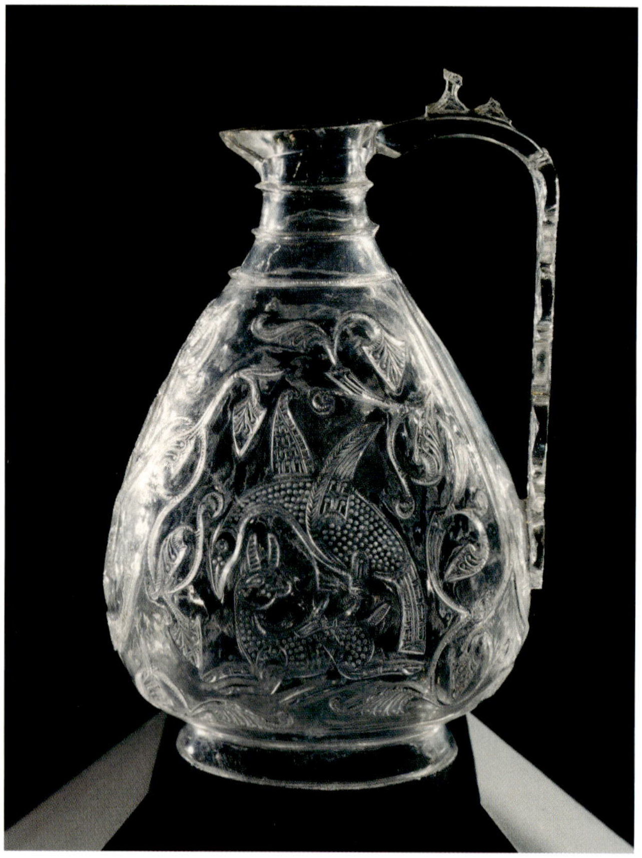

8.9 The rock-crystal ewer in its display case near the south-east entrance

8.10 The section on Art for the Court, showing rock-crystal, carved ivory and inlaid metalwork objects

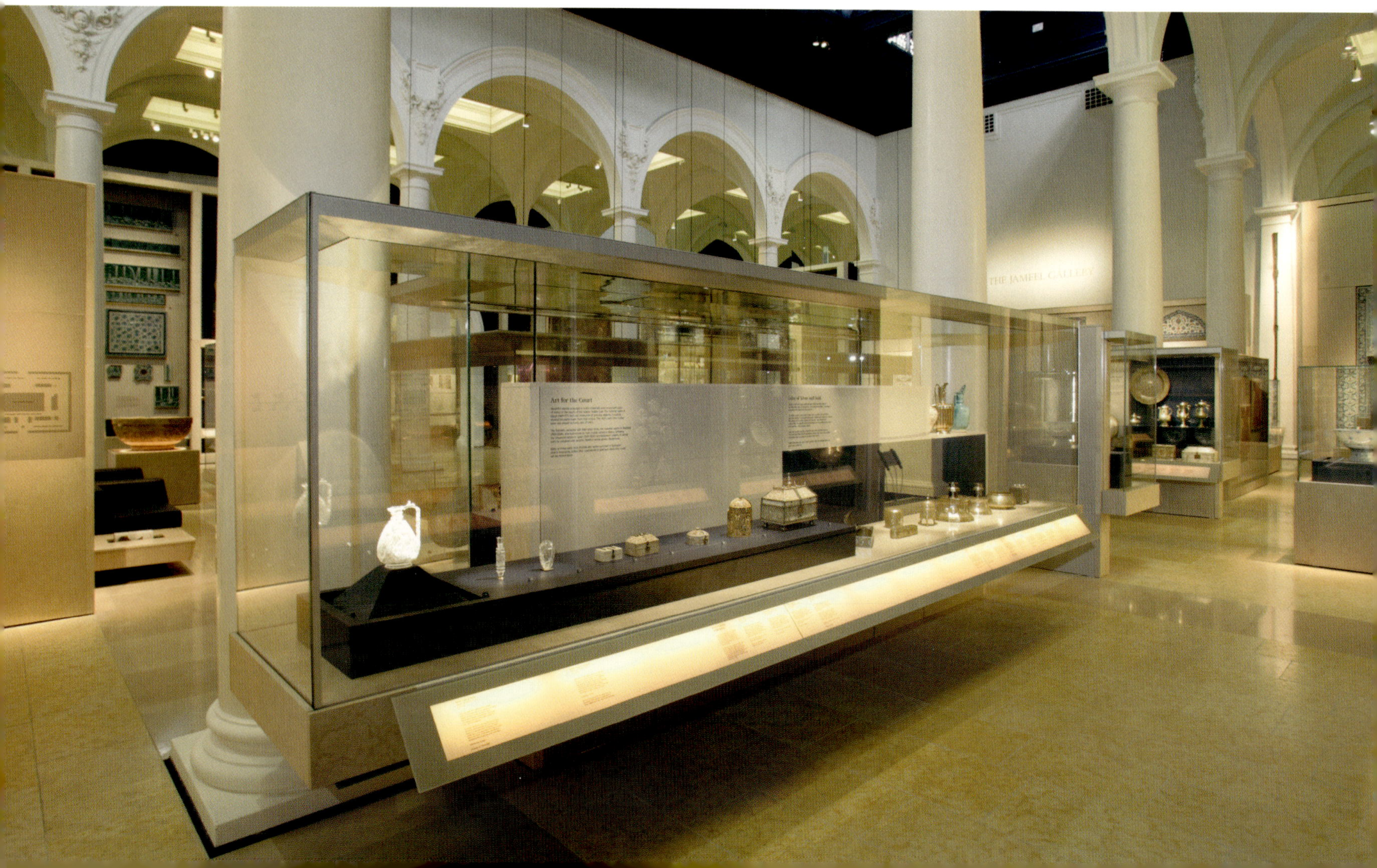

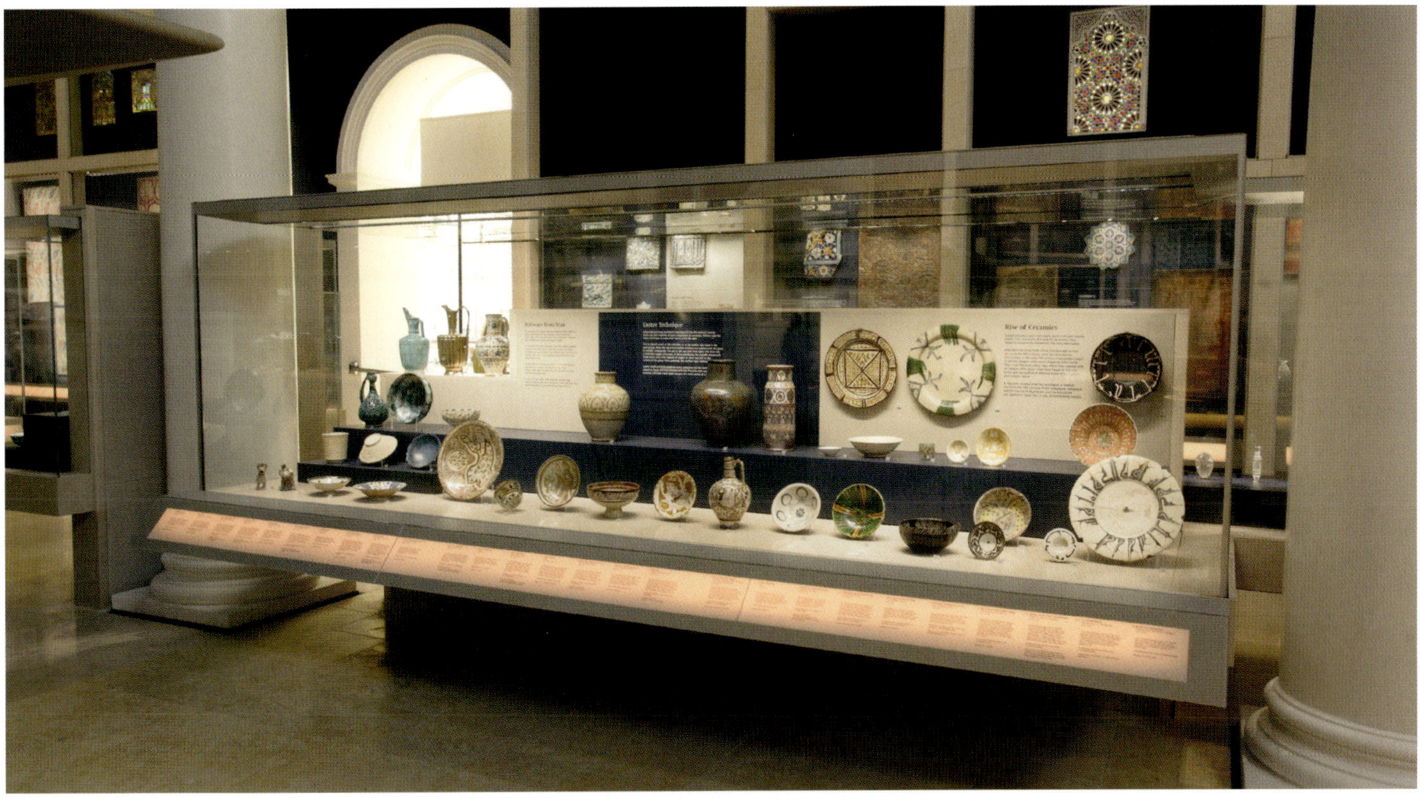

8.11 (*above*) The Rise of Ceramics display, showing the development of ceramics from the 8th century in Iraq to 13th-century Iran

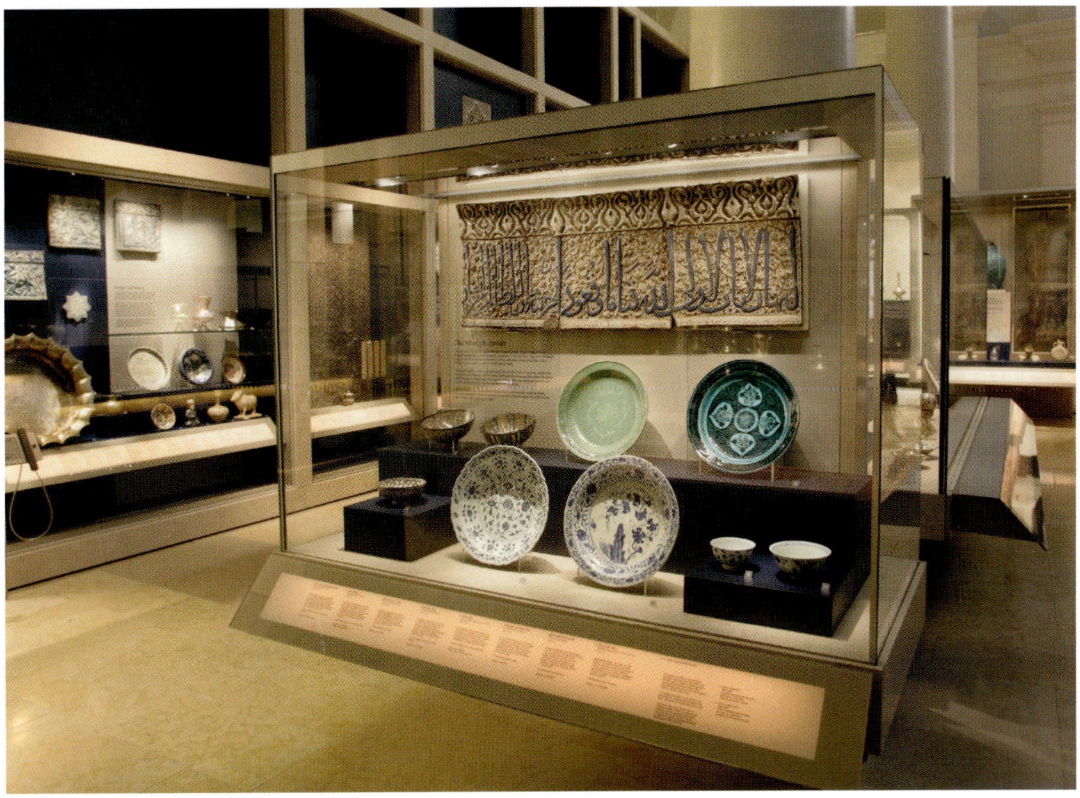

8.12 A case illustrating developments in ceramics in Iran after the Mongol invasion in the 13th century

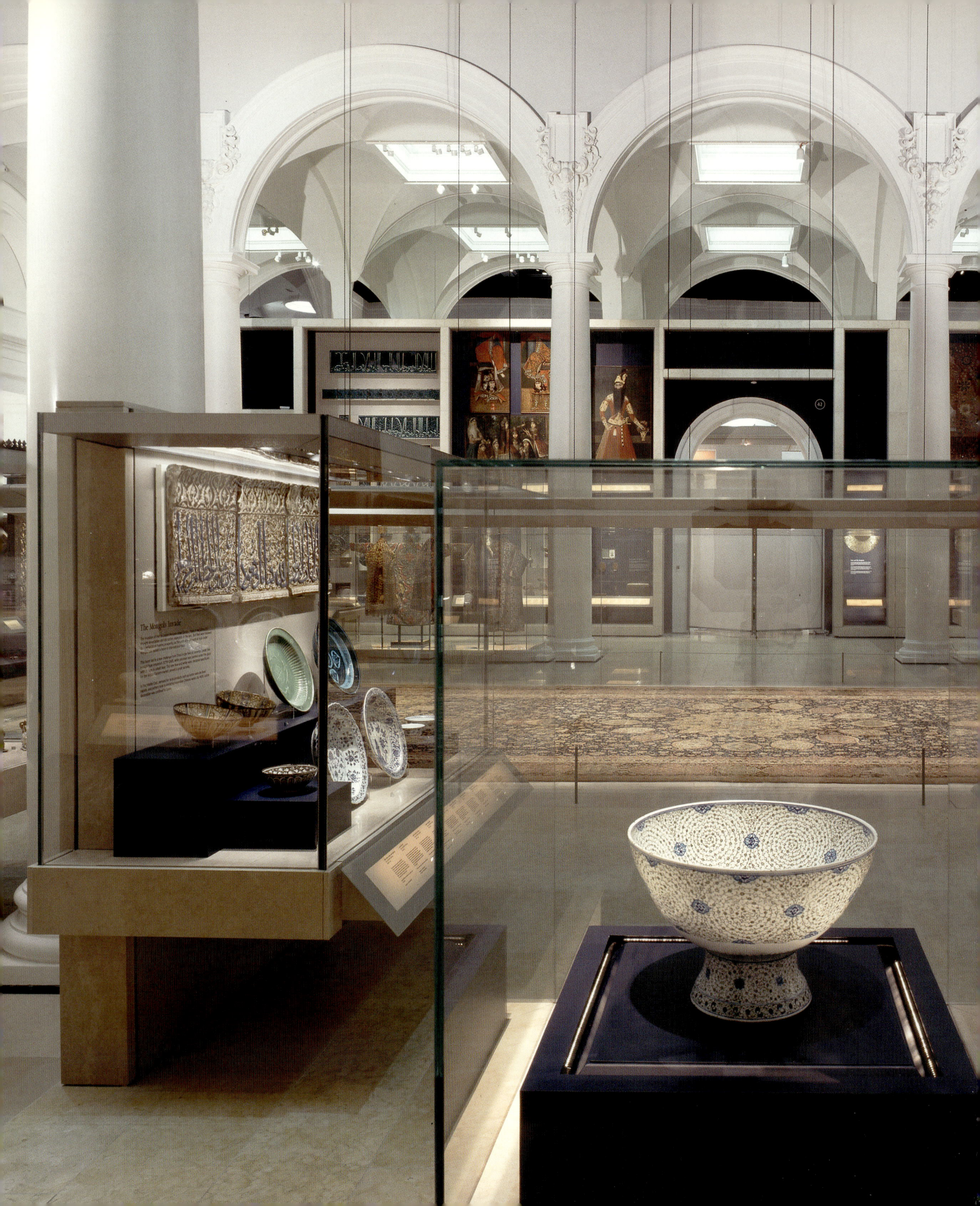

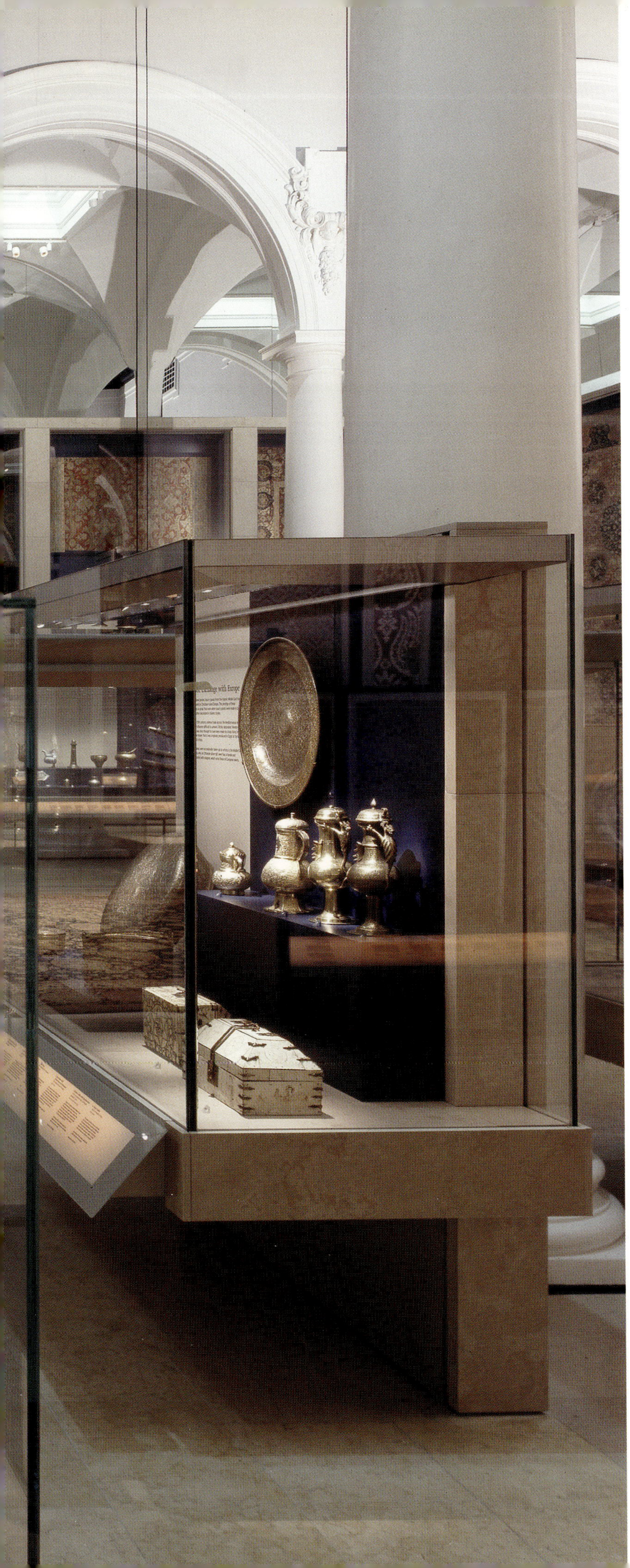

8.13 A view of the Gallery from the east entrance

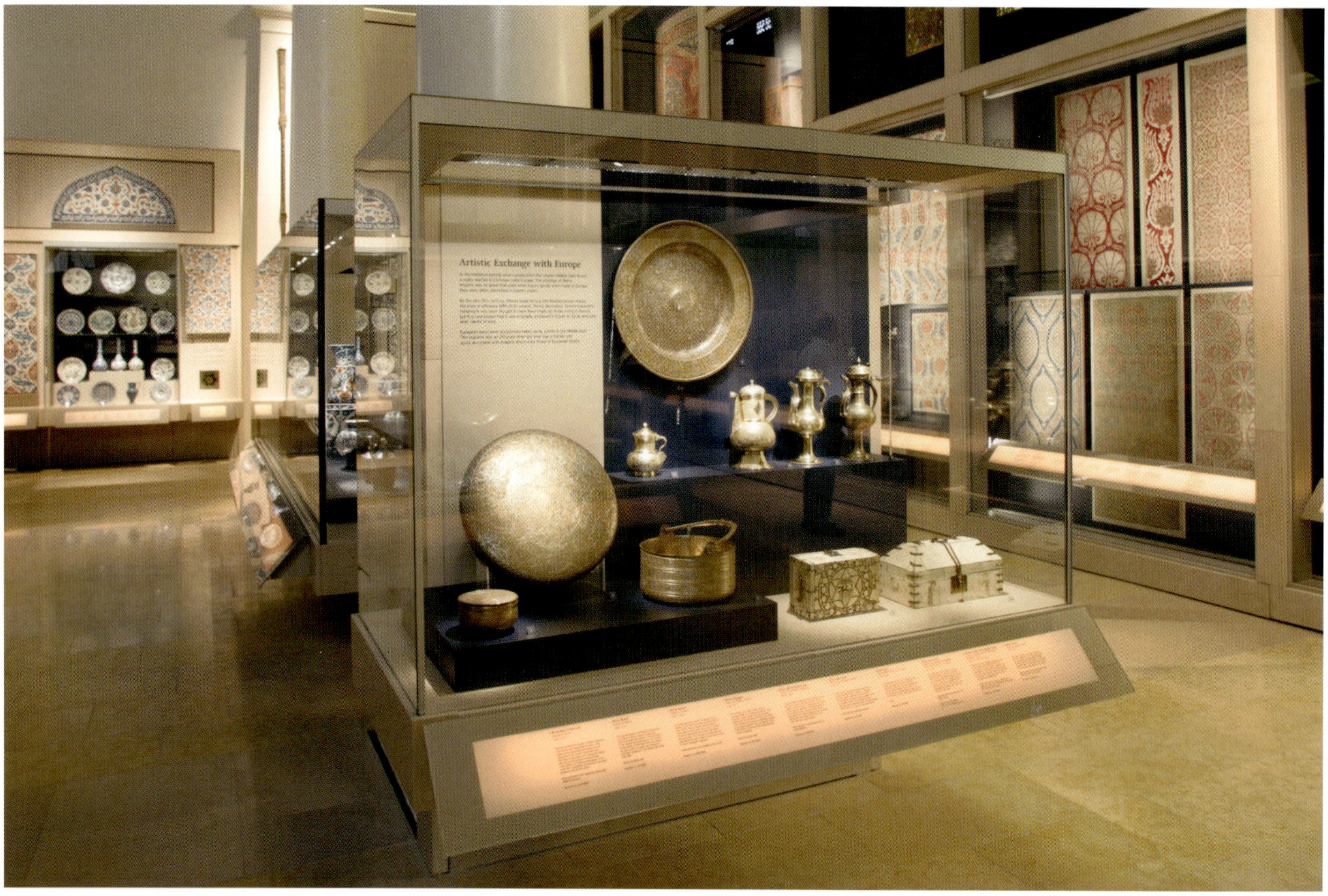

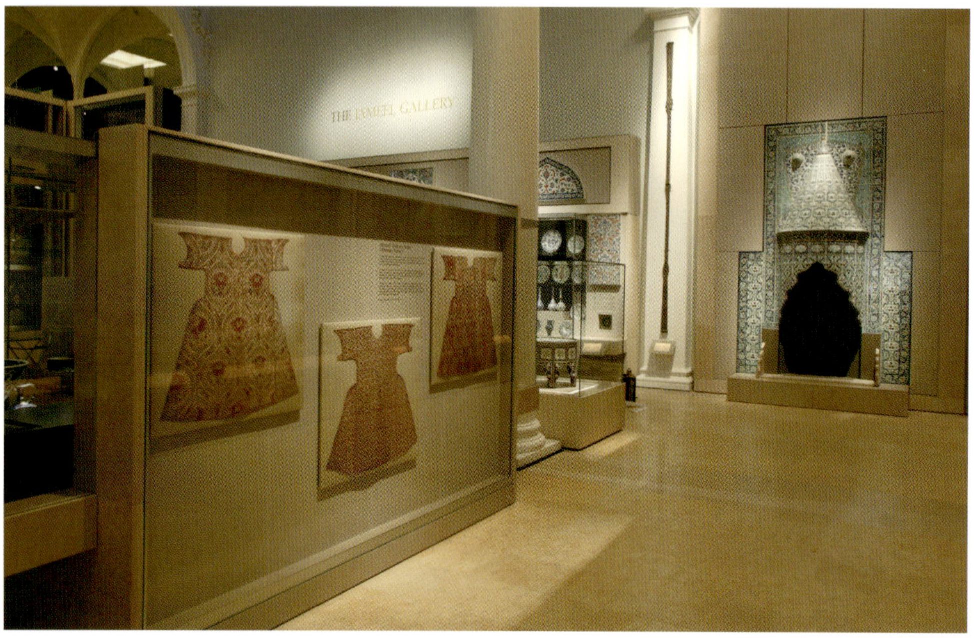

8.14 *(above)* A case illustrating artistic exchanges between the Islamic world and Europe

8.15 Part of the Ottoman section, showing three children's kaftans and the Ottoman fireplace

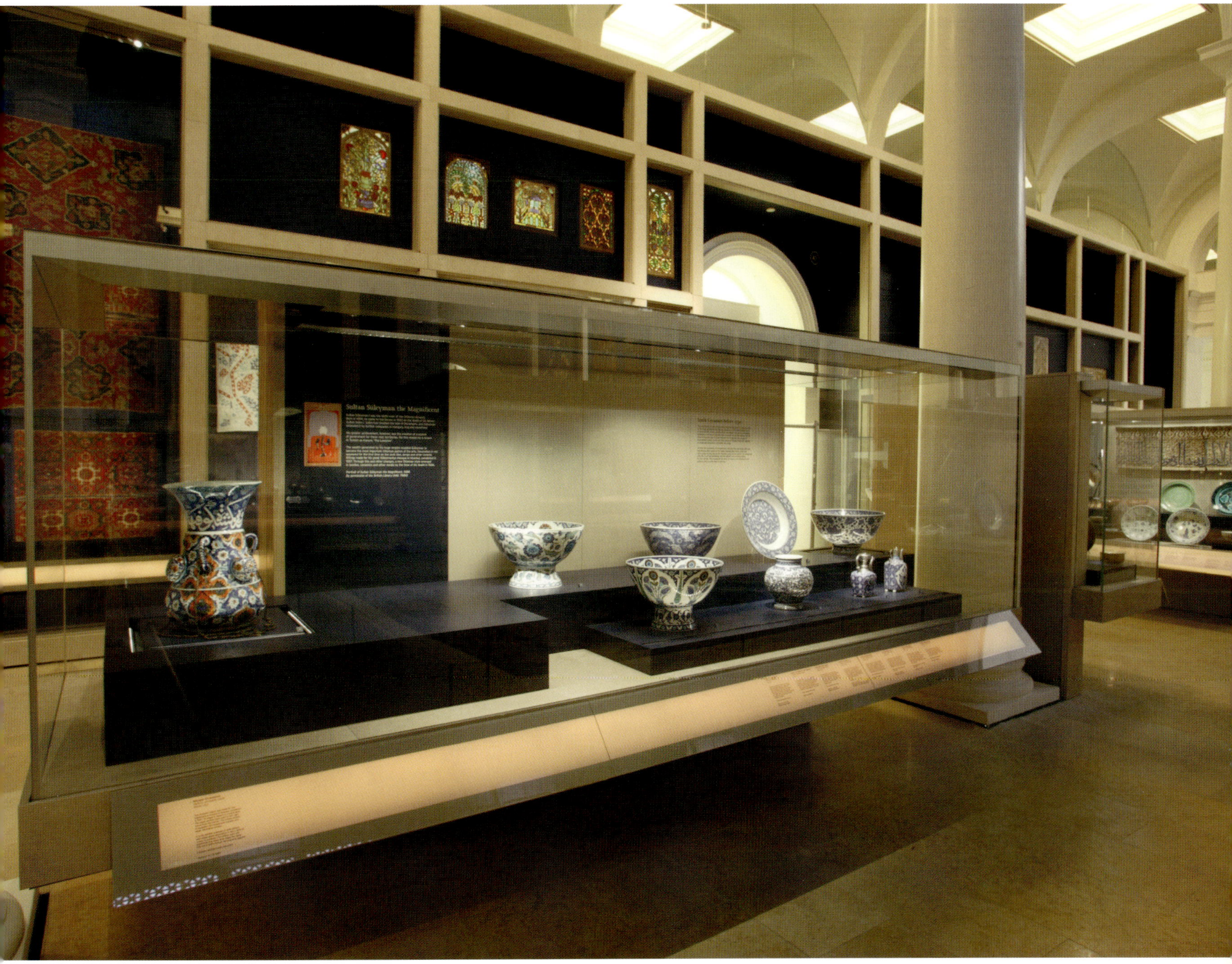

8.16 The early Iznik ceramics display, with 19th-century Egyptian coloured glass windows visible above

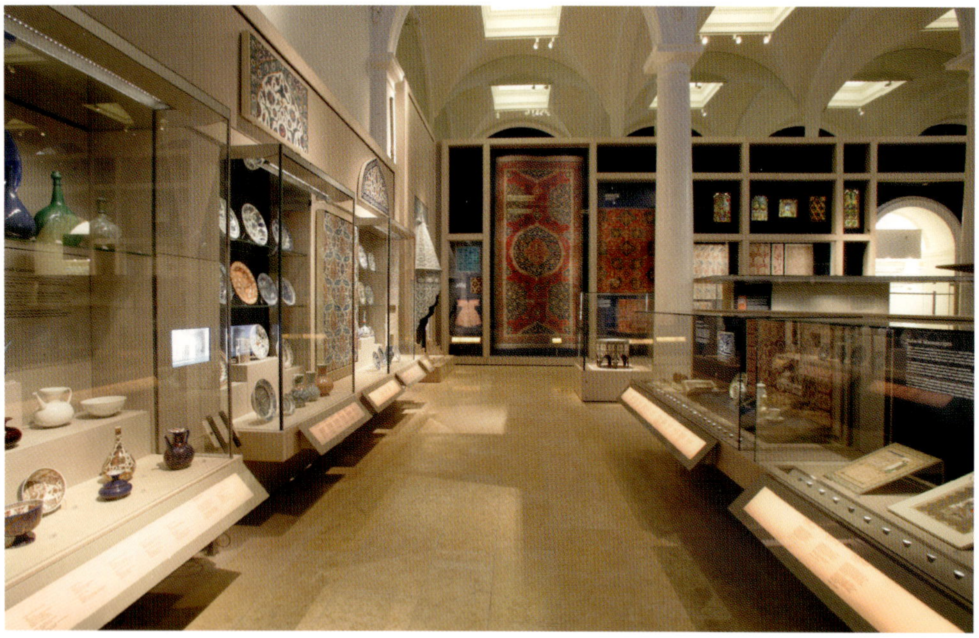

8.17 A view of the north-east corner of the Gallery, showing Turkish carpets, textiles and ceramics, and part of the Safavid ceramics display

8.18 (*below*) The display of ceramics from Safavid Iran, separated from the Ottoman Turkish ceramics by the video screen playing a short film entitled *Three Palaces*

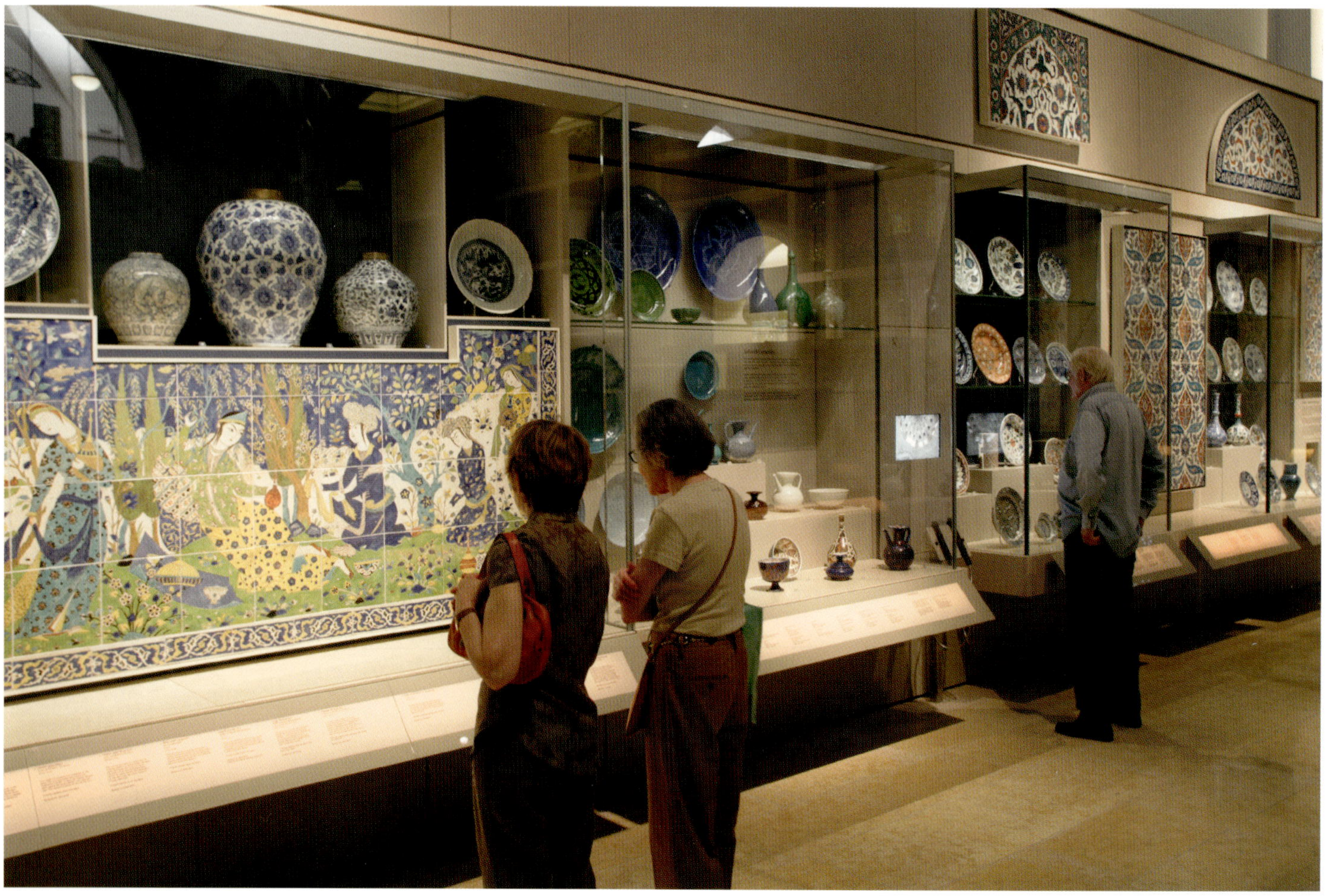

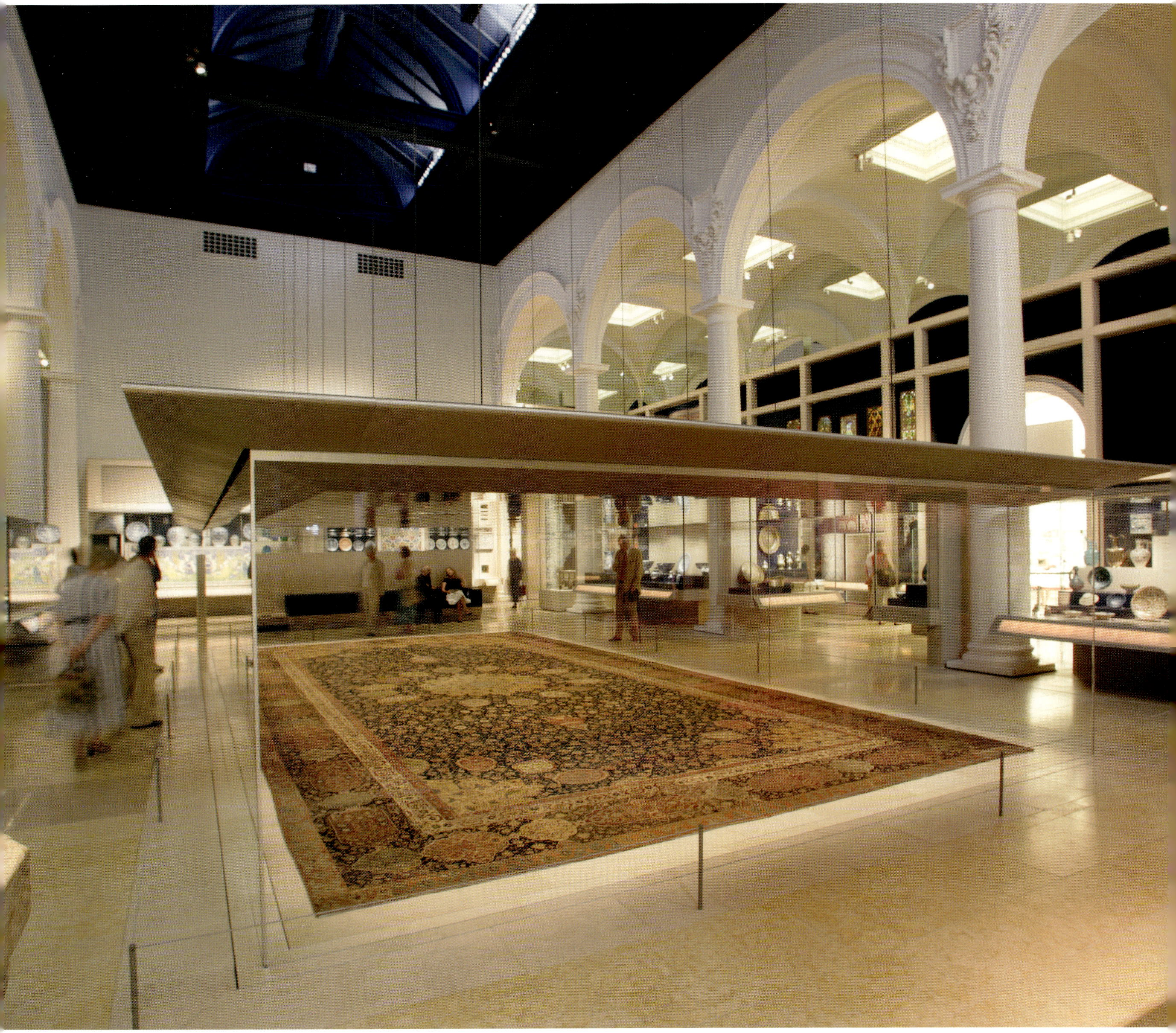

8.19 A view of the Ardabil carpet from the south-west corner

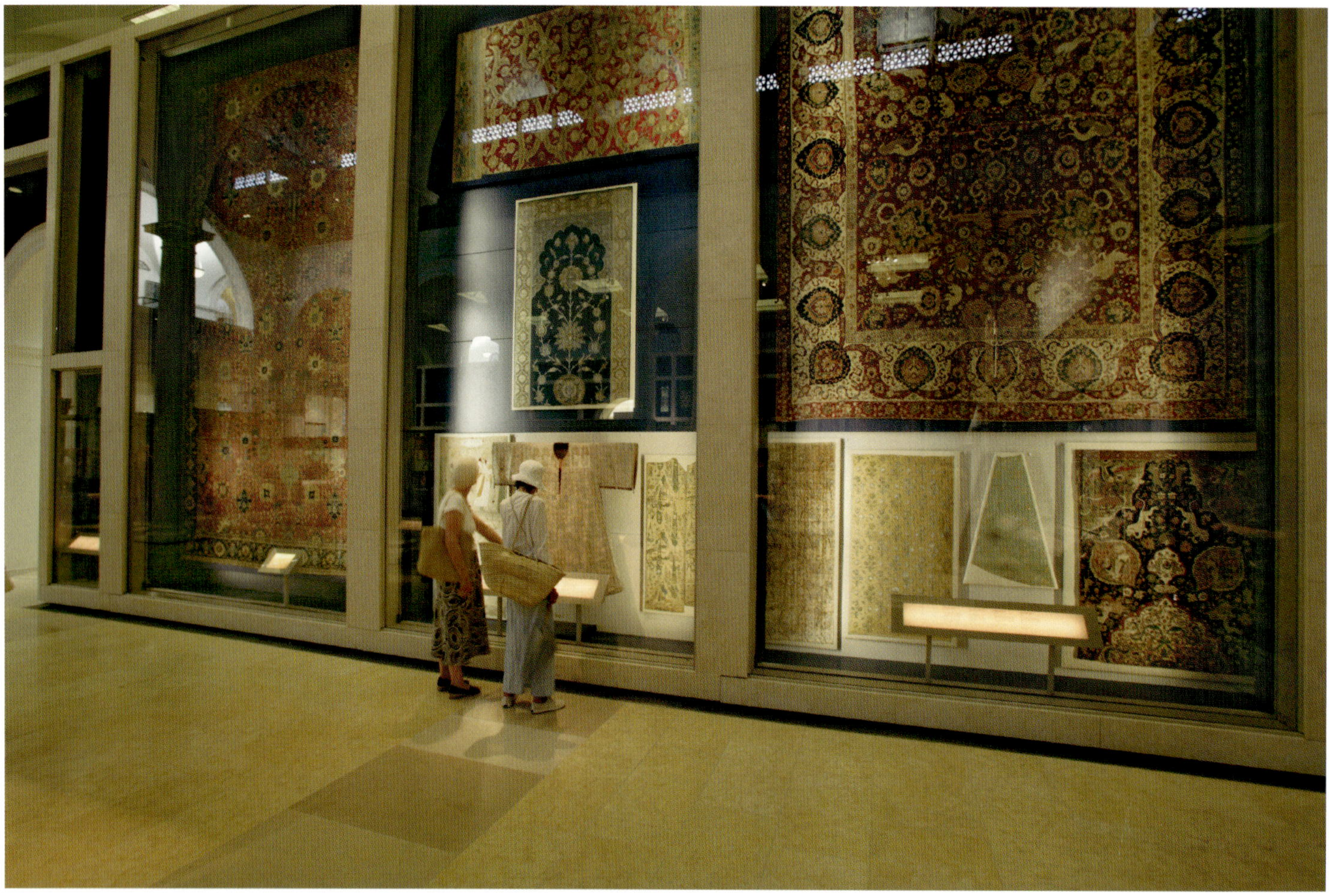

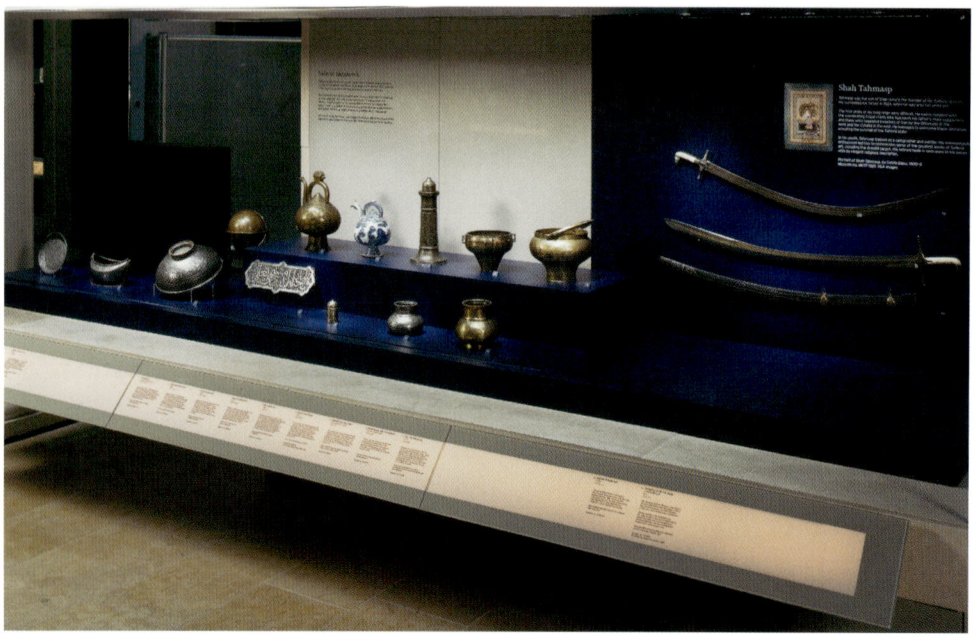

8.20 (*above*) The display of Safavid carpets and textiles

8.21 (*left*) The Safavid metalwork display

8.22 (*top right*) The Safavid cope and astronomical instruments

8.23 (*right*) A view of the Jameel Gallery taken from the Ironwork Gallery during the private view on 18 July 2006

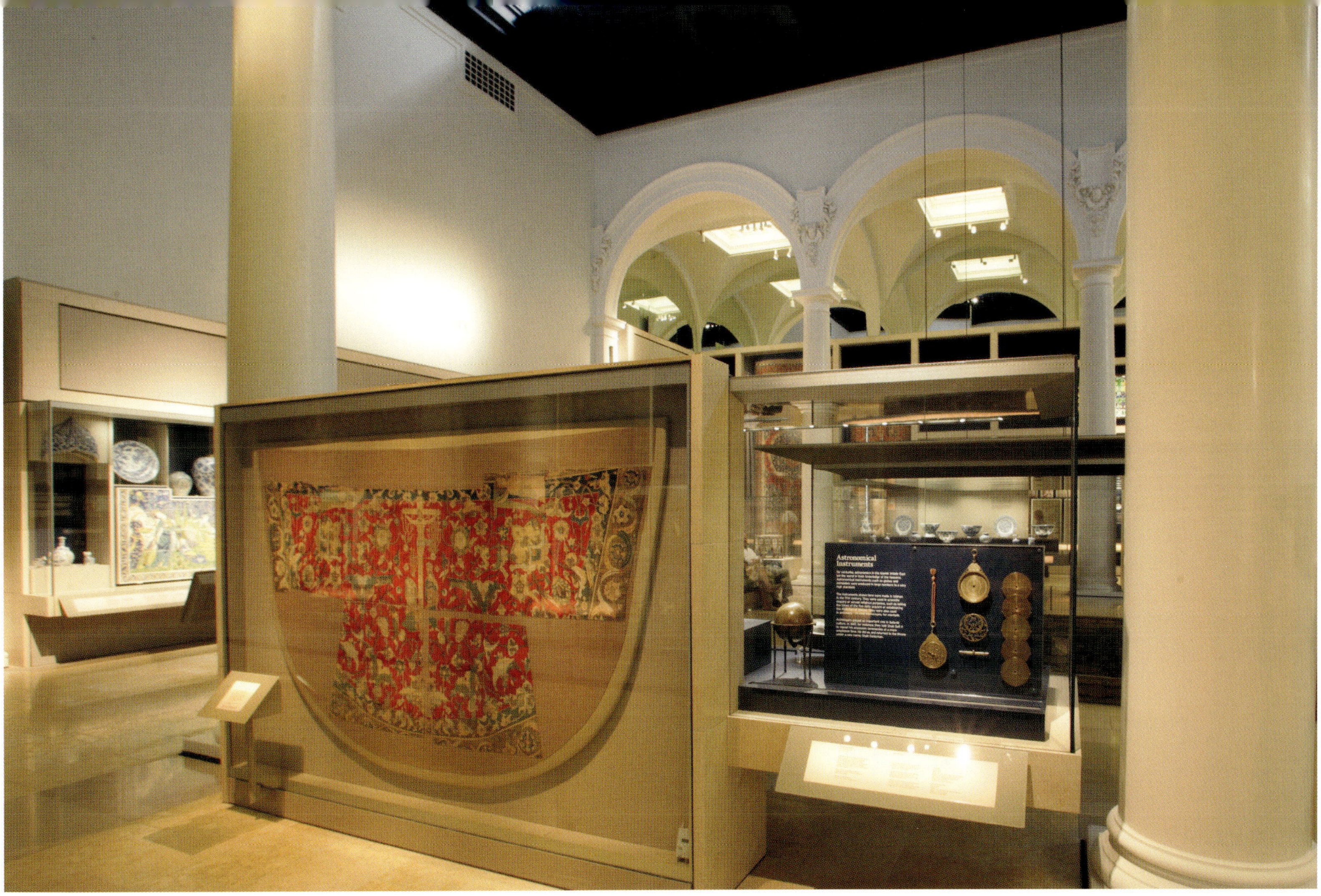
Astronomical Instruments

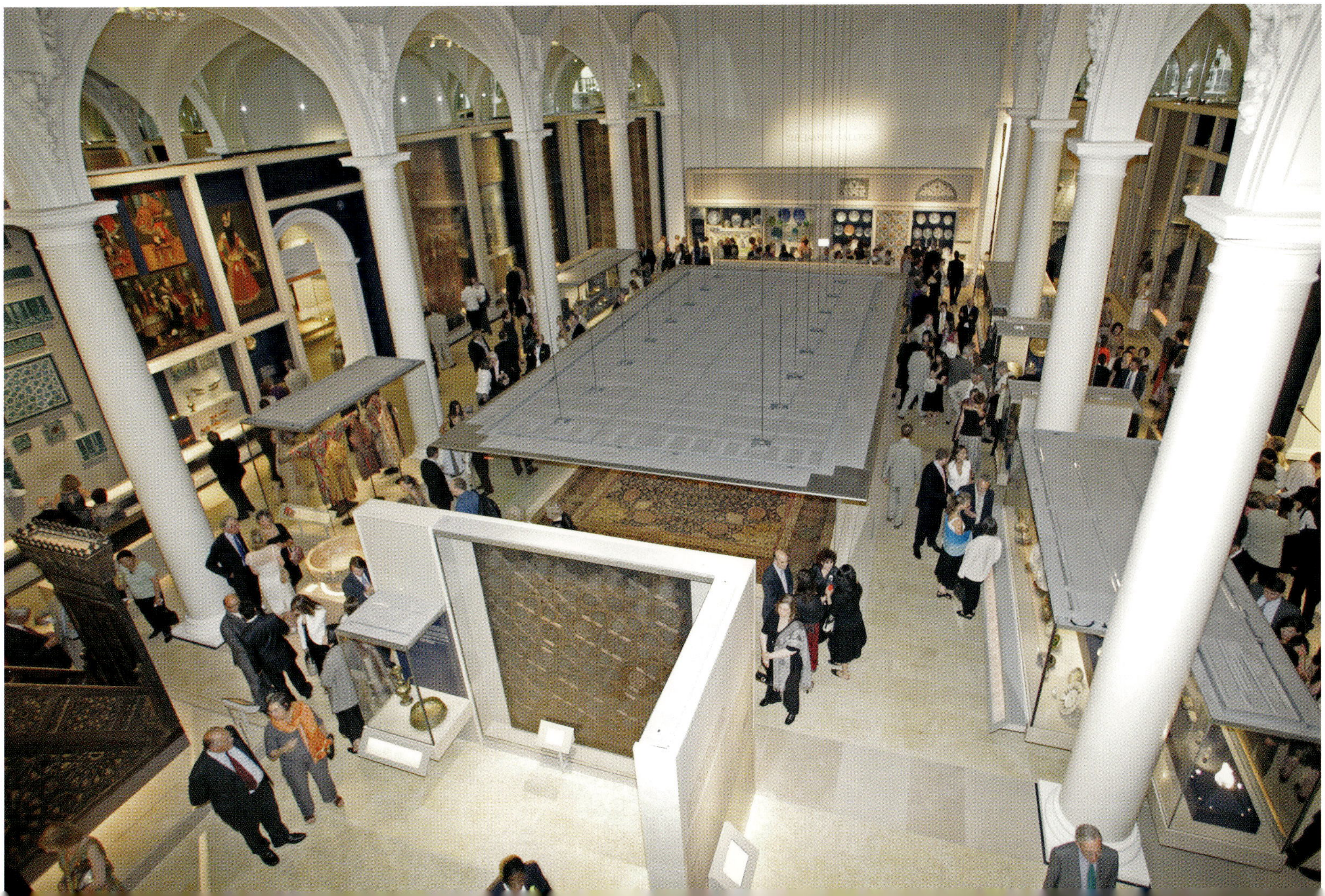

THE ISLAMIC DYNASTIES

The most important dynasties in terms of the artefacts discussed in this book are:

THE UNIVERSAL CALIPHATE

The Umayyads

The founder of the dynasty, Mu'awiyah ibn Abi Sufyan, was a distant cousin of the Prophet. He became Caliph in AD 662 and converted the caliphate into a hereditary office, which his successors held until AD 750. Their capital was Damascus in Syria. After their fall, a single survivor, 'Abd al-Rahman, made his way to Spain, where he established an emirate centred on the city of Córdoba. In the tenth century, after the Fatimids had set up a Shi'ite imamate in North Africa, the Umayyads again assumed the title of Caliph and held it until 1012, after which they reigned intermittently until 1031.

The Abbasids

The Abbasids were closer relatives of the Prophet than the Umayyads, being descended from his uncle, al-'Abbas. The first caliph of the dynasty overthrew the Umayyads in AD 750 and moved the capital of the Islamic empire to central Iraq, where the dynasty founded Baghdad, Samarra' and other cities. In the tenth century the Abbasids were challenged by counter-caliphs in Egypt and elsewhere, and lost their independence of action, first to lords of the Buyid dynasty and then, in the eleventh century, to the Seljuk sultans. After the fall of the Seljuks at the end of the twelfth century, the Abbasids regained their independence as rulers of Iraq, but in 1258 they were finally overthrown by Mongol invaders. Thereafter a titular caliph of the Abbasid dynasty resided in Cairo until the Ottoman conquest in 1517.

EGYPT AND SYRIA, TENTH TO FIFTEENTH CENTURIES

The Fatimids

Members of the Shi'ite movements regard the Sunni caliphs as usurpers: the leadership of the Muslim community rightfully belongs to the descendants of the Prophet Muhammad through his daughter Fatimah. In AD 909 one of these descendants became the focus of a successful Shi'ite political movement in North Africa, and a Fatimid state was established. In 969 the Fatimid army conquered Egypt, and the capital was moved to the newly founded city of Cairo. The Fatimid caliphate lasted until 1171, when it was overthrown by the Ayyubids.

The Ayyubids

The first Ayyubid, Salah al-Din (Saladin), was the Sunni chief minister of the last Fatimid caliph. In 1171 he overthrew his master and declared his allegiance to the Abbasid caliph in Baghdad, who eventually, in the 1240s, awarded a member of the dynasty the title of Sultan. In Egypt the dynasty was replaced by the rule of the Mamluks in 1250.

The Mamluks

Although *mamluk* means 'owned, possessed', the term indicates political privilege rather than social ignominy, and designates a political system rather than a single dynasty. During the Abbasid period it became normal for the ruler to recruit his household troops from outside the Islamic world, often from the Turkish lands of Central Asia, since they could be trained as soldiers from childhood and had allegiance only to the ruler. Nevertheless, their role as military strongmen gave these men access to power when their masters faltered, and in 1250, after the branch of the Ayyubid dynasty ruling Egypt had failed to supply a male heir, the sultanate passed to a royal *mamluk*. Mamluk sultans were succeeded either by their sons or by a *mamluk* who had proved his military prowess or political wiliness. This system continued to supply rulers until the Ottoman conquest in 1517, which it survived, providing administrators at a lower level until 1811.

Iraq and Iran, tenth to fifteenth centuries

The Samanids
As the Abbasid caliphate became less dynamic during the ninth century, provincial governors began to exercise greater autonomy, and many of them established local dynasties. Among the most important were the Samanids, one of whom was appointed Amir of Farghana in western Central Asia in AD 819. By 874 a member of the family was governor of the whole of western Central Asia and of parts of eastern Iran, and the Samanids held power continuously until 1005.

The Buyids
Buyid governors ruled Iraq and western Iran from the 930s until the mid-eleventh century. They were under the nominal suzerainty of the Abbasid caliphs, even though they were themselves Shi'ites. They were eventually overthrown by the Seljuks, who posed as the restorers of Sunnism in these regions.

The Seljuks
The Seljuk Turks invaded the Islamic world from the north-east in the early eleventh century and eventually established a great empire that stretched from Anatolia to Central Asia. After they had conquered Baghdad from the Buyids in 1055, they were acknowledged by the Abbasid caliph as his protector, with the title of Sultan. The Seljuks lost control of eastern Iran in the mid-twelfth century and were removed from power in Iraq in the 1190s, but a junior branch remained as rulers of Anatolia until the first decade of the fourteenth century.

The Ilkhanids
Devastating Mongol incursions into Muslim Central Asia and Iran in the early thirteenth century were followed by a full-scale invasion in the 1250s, culminating in the conquest of Baghdad in 1258. The Mongols' leader, Hulagu, became ruler of Iran and Iraq as vassal of the Great Khan in China, with the title of Ilkhan. The Ilkhanids fostered an economic and artistic revival of their territories, but their dynasty failed in the 1330s.

The Timurids
Amir Timur emerged as one of the contenders for power in western Central Asia after the collapse of the Ilkhanid empire, and he proved the most successful, destroying those who opposed him. From the 1370s he rapidly acquired a huge empire of his own, ranging from the Aegean coast of western Turkey to the northern plains of India. After his death in 1405, his successors ruled a more restricted domain, eventually comprising eastern Iran and western Central Asia, with capitals in Herat and Samarqand. They were overthrown by the Uzbeks in 1507, but a Timurid, Babur, was later able to establish the Mughal empire in India.

Spain and North Africa, eleventh to fifteenth centuries

The Almoravids
The Almoravids began as a militant religious movement among the Berbers living in modern Mauritania and adjacent regions. Their name, *al-Murabitun* in Arabic, conveys the idea of 'the frontier garrison of Islam'. In the early eleventh century the movement conquered much of the Sahara region. In the 1050s the Almoravid armies turned north to conquer Morocco and western Algeria, and Marrakesh was founded as their capital. From 1061 the northern, more developed part of the Almoravid empire was governed by Yusuf ibn Tashufin (d. 1107), who established a dynastic state. In 1086 Yusuf's armies crossed to Spain, where they consolidated the Muslim-held territories and halted the southward expansion of the peninsula's Christian rulers for a time. Yusuf was succeeded by his son and grandsons, but the last of these was killed in 1147, when Marrakesh fell to his Almohad enemies. Nevertheless, the Almoravid movement remained influential in its original Saharan home.

The Almohads
The Almohads' name derives from the Arabic *al-Muwahhidun*, 'believers in God's unity'. They originated as a moral reform movement among the Berbers of Morocco, and their leader was Muhammad ibn Tumart, who was active from 1123 until his death in 1130. Over the following 20 years his successor, the caliph 'Abd al-Mu'min (d. 1163), gained political control of Morocco and established a dynastic state. He also began to intervene in other parts of North Africa and in Muslim Spain, where he made Seville his capital in 1147. In 1212 the Christian rulers of northern and central Spain smashed the Almohad armies and began to occupy most of their territories in the south. In the 1230s the Almohad governors in Algeria and Tunisia threw off their allegiance to the Almohad caliph. Finally, in 1269, the Almohad capital, Marrakesh, was conquered by a new Berber dynasty, the Marinids.

The Nasrids
In the first half of the thirteenth century most of southern Spain was conquered by Christian kings. An exception was the mountainous south-east of the peninsula, where members of the Nasrid dynasty were able to establish the last Muslim state in Spain. The state's founder, Muhammad ibn Yusuf ibn Nasr, established a small domain of his own in 1232. In 1237 the population of Granada invited him to rule their city, and it remained the Nasrid capital until its fall to Christian armies in 1492. Although the Nasrids paid tribute to their Christian neighbours, they were able to develop their kingdom economically and to make it a notable centre of Muslim religious and secular culture.

Later dynasties

The Ottomans

Anatolia was settled by Muslim Turks from the end of the eleventh century. They soon gained political control of the central plateau, and after the Mongol invasion of the mid-thirteenth century, Turkish warlords began to move into the coastlands. One of the most successful was Osman, who established himself in Byzantine territory in north-west Anatolia. From here his descendants were able to invade south-east Europe, beginning in the 1360s. Having survived Timur's invasion of Anatolia in 1402, they established themselves as the leading power there and in the Balkans. In 1453 the Byzantine empire was extinguished when the Ottomans conquered Constantinople, which became their new capital, and in 1516–17 they made themselves masters of the Mamluk empire. Further expansion followed, so that the Ottomans were probably the world's most powerful state in the later sixteenth century. Although they subsequently lost ground, the dynasty proved immensely durable, remaining in power until 1922.

The Safavids

The leaders of the Turcoman tribes of eastern Anatolia, Iraq and western Iran gained political power in the region after Timur's death at the beginning of the fifteenth century. Some allied themselves with the Safavi Sufi brotherhood, which had its centre in Ardabil in north-west Iran. The brotherhood converted to a form of Shi'ism late in the century and, beginning in 1501, its leader, the future Shah Isma'il, began to seize political power for himself. He succeeded in uniting all of Iran under his rule, and he and his successors established a Shi'ite state that survived until 1722.

The Qajars

The collapse of the Safavid state in Iran was followed by a period of political instability, during which the leaders of the Qajar tribe began to play an important political role. Towards the end of the century its forceful leader, Agha Muhammad, was able to gain control of the whole country, with Tehran as his capital. He was assassinated soon afterwards, but was succeeded by his nephew Fath 'Ali Shah (ruled 1797–1834) and the dynasty ruled Iran until 1925.

Further reading

Baker, Malcolm and Richardson, Brenda, eds, *A Grand Design: The art of the Victoria and Albert Museum*, New York, Abrams, 1997

Burton, Anthony, *Vision & Accident: The story of the Victoria and Albert Museum*, London, V&A Publications, 1999

Physick, John, *The Victoria and Albert Museum: The history of its building*, London, V&A, 1982

Somers Cocks, Anna, *The Victoria and Albert Museum: The Making of the Collection*, Leicester, Windward, 1980

Stanley, Tim, *Palace and Mosque: Islamic art from the Middle East*, London, V&A Publications, 2004

Wilk, Christopher, ed., *The Making of the British Galleries at the V&A: A study in museology*, London, V&A Publications, 2004

Picture credits

All illustrations © V&A Images except for the following:

Jame L. Anderson, AIA, Architect, Design Coordinator, Design Department, National Gallery of Art, Washington, DC: 2.9, 2.10

Atacama Ltd: 6.9

Christopher Bagot: 4.13

Lucia Burgio: 5.10

Rosemary Crill: 3.12, 3.13, 3.14, 3.15, 3.17

Tyeth Gundry: 4.19

Heritage Tiles Conservation Ltd: 7.9, 7.10

Sean Hignett: 6.10

Martin Jacobs Art Design + Direction: 6.2, 6.3

Andrea Jemolo: 8.9, 8.13, 8.21

Kimbell Art Museum, Fort Worth: 2.1, 2.11, 2.12, 2.16, 2.17, 2.18, 2.19, 2.20

The Millennium Galleries, Sheffield: 2.22

National Gallery of Art, Washington, DC: 2.2, 2.3, 2.4, 2.5, 2.6, 2.7, 2.14, 2.15

Juanita Navarro: 5.3, 5.5

Nykris: 6.5, 6.6, 6.7, 6.8

Joseph Parsons, Liverpool Museums Conservation Centre: 6.13, 6.14

RIBA Library Drawings Collection: 1.3

Mariam Rosser-Owen: 3.27, 3.28, 3.29

Oliver Salway: 3.18, 3.22, 4.3, 4.6, 4.11, 4.18

Setagaya Art Museum, Tokyo: 2.21

Phil Sofer: 2.8, 2.13, 5.20, 5.21, 5.22

Softroom: frontispiece, front jacket, 3.2, 4.1, 4.2, 4.4, 4.5, 4.7, 4.8, 4.9, 4.10, 4.12, 4.14, 4.15, 4.16, 4.20

Tim Stanley: 3.25, 3.26

Mike Wheeler: 5.16

Sophy Wills: 5.18, 5.19

Index

Page numbers in *italics* refer to illustrations